The Journalist in the French Fin-de-siècle Novel
Enfants de la presse

LEGENDA

LEGENDA is the Modern Humanities Research Association's book imprint for new research in the Humanities. Founded in 1995 by Malcolm Bowie and others within the University of Oxford, Legenda has always been a collaborative publishing enterprise, directly governed by scholars. The Modern Humanities Research Association (MHRA) joined this collaboration in 1998, became half-owner in 2004, in partnership with Maney Publishing and then Routledge, and has since 2016 been sole owner. Titles range from medieval texts to contemporary cinema and form a widely comparative view of the modern humanities, including works on Arabic, Catalan, English, French, German, Greek, Italian, Portuguese, Russian, Spanish, and Yiddish literature. Editorial boards and committees of more than 60 leading academic specialists work in collaboration with bodies such as the Society for French Studies, the British Comparative Literature Association and the Association of Hispanists of Great Britain & Ireland.

The MHRA encourages and promotes advanced study and research in the field of the modern humanities, especially modern European languages and literature, including English, and also cinema. It aims to break down the barriers between scholars working in different disciplines and to maintain the unity of humanistic scholarship. The Association fulfils this purpose through the publication of journals, bibliographies, monographs, critical editions, and the MHRA Style Guide, and by making grants in support of research. Membership is open to all who work in the Humanities, whether independent or in a University post, and the participation of younger colleagues entering the field is especially welcomed.

ALSO PUBLISHED BY THE ASSOCIATION

Critical Texts
Tudor and Stuart Translations • *New Translations* • *European Translations*
MHRA Library of Medieval Welsh Literature

MHRA Bibliographies
Publications of the Modern Humanities Research Association

The Annual Bibliography of English Language & Literature
Austrian Studies
Modern Language Review
Portuguese Studies
The Slavonic and East European Review
Working Papers in the Humanities
The Yearbook of English Studies

www.mhra.org.uk
www.legendabooks.com

EDITORIAL BOARD

Chair: Professor Jonathan Long (University of Durham)
For *Germanic Literatures*: Ritchie Robertson (University of Oxford)
For *Italian Perspectives*: Simon Gilson (University of Warwick)
For *Moving Image*: Emma Wilson (University of Cambridge)
For *Research Monographs in French Studies*:
Diana Knight (University of Nottingham)
For *Selected Essays*: Susan Harrow (University of Bristol)
For *Studies in Comparative Literature*: Duncan Large
(British Centre for Literary Translation, University of East Anglia)
For *Studies in Hispanic and Lusophone Cultures*:
Trevor Dadson (Queen Mary, University of London)
For *Studies in Yiddish*: Gennady Estraikh (New York University)
For *Transcript*: Matthew Reynolds (University of Oxford)

Managing Editor
Dr Graham Nelson
41 Wellington Square, Oxford OX1 2JF, UK

www.legendabooks.com

The Journalist in the French Fin-de-siècle Novel

Enfants de la presse

KATE REES

LEGENDA
Modern Humanities Research Association
2018

Published by Legenda
an imprint of the Modern Humanities Research Association
Salisbury House, Station Road, Cambridge CB1 2LA

ISBN 978-1-78188-651-9 (HB)
ISBN 978-1-78188-652-6 (PB)

First published 2018

All rights reserved. No part of this publication may be reproduced or disseminated or transmitted in any form or by any means, electronic, mechanical, photocopying, recording or otherwise, or stored in any retrieval system, or otherwise used in any manner whatsoever without written permission of the copyright owner, except in accordance with the provisions of the Copyright, Designs and Patents Act 1988, or under the terms of a licence permitting restricted copying issued in the UK by the Copyright Licensing Agency Ltd, Saffron House, 6–10 Kirby Street, London EC1N 8TS, England, or in the USA by the Copyright Clearance Center, 222 Rosewood Drive, Danvers MA 01923. Application for the written permission of the copyright owner to reproduce any part of this publication must be made by email to legenda@mhra.org.uk.

Disclaimer: Statements of fact and opinion contained in this book are those of the author and not of the editors or the Modern Humanities Research Association. The publisher makes no representation, express or implied, in respect of the accuracy of the material in this book and cannot accept any legal responsibility or liability for any errors or omissions that may be made.

Trademark notice: Product or corporate names may be trademarks or registered trademarks, and are used only for identification and explanation without intent to infringe.

© Modern Humanities Research Association 2018

Copy-Editor: Charlotte Brown

CONTENTS

	Acknowledgements	ix
	Abbreviations	x
	Introduction	1
1	Maupassant: Illusions, Echoes, Anxieties	17
2	Zola: Ambiguities, Battles, Jolts	52
3	Verne: Foreign Correspondence, Mimesis, and the Senses	95
4	Newspaper-Detectives: Reality, Fantasy, Banality	131
5	The Woman Journalist: Reportage, Romance, *Écriture féminine*	169
	Conclusion	214
	Bibliography	219
	Index	230

For my family, and especially for Tom and Meg

ACKNOWLEDGEMENTS

I am very grateful to The Queen's College, Oxford, for the Career Development Fellowship in French which afforded me the time to complete this book, and for the support provided by the college throughout this period. Particular thanks go to Roger Pearson for his insight and warm encouragement, and to Patrick McGuinness for his advice. The many students I have taught at Queen's have provided continued inspiration and enthusiasm. I am also grateful to the anonymous readers at Legenda for their constructive criticism.

Part of Chapter One appeared in different form in my article, 'Scenes of Debris in Charles Fenestrier's *La Vie des frelons*' (*Dix-Neuf*, 17.3 (2013), 251–64). I thank the editors for their advice in the publication of that paper. Part of Chapter Three appeared in the article 'Sensory Reportage and the 'Steeplechase' between novels and newspaper in Verne's *Michel Strogoff*, *Dix Neuf*?, and I thank my co-editor, Edmund Birch, for his careful reading.

K.R., Oxford, July 2017

ABBREVIATIONS

References to texts by the authors central to this study are given in abbreviated form. The abbreviated form of the title of each novel, indicated in the key below, is followed by the page number from the original French text. All English translations are my own, unless otherwise stated.

Eugène Brieux

FS   *La Femme seule*, in *Théâtre complet*, 9 vols (Paris: Stock, 1924), VII, 1–149

Pierre Giffard

VP   *Le Sieur de Va-Partout: souvenirs d'un reporter* (Paris: Maurice Dreyfous, 1880)

Gaston Leroux

M   *Le Mystère de la chambre jaune*, in *Les Aventures extraordinaires de Rouletabille reporter*, 2 vols (Paris: Robert Laffont, 1988), I

Paul & Victor Margueritte

FN   *Femmes nouvelles* (Paris: Librairie Plon, 1899)

Guy de Maupassant

BA   *Bel-Ami*, ed. by Jean-Louis Bory (Paris: Gallimard, 1973)

Camille Pert

LE   *Leur égale* (Paris: Simonis Empis, 1899)

Pierre Souvestre and Marcel Allain

F   *Fantômas*, 8 vols (Paris: Robert Laffont, 2013), I

Marcelle Tinayre

LR   *La Rebelle* (Paris: Calmann-Lévy, 1906)

Jules Verne

MS   *Michel Strogoff* (Paris: Hachette, 1966)
CB   *Claudius Bombarnac: carnet d'un reporter*, ed. by Zoé Commère (Médias19, 2014), <http://www.medias19.org/index.php?id=17989> [acc. 13 January 2016]

Émile Zola

FR   *La Fortune des Rougon*, in *Les Rougon-Macquart*, ed. by Henri Mitterand, 5 vols (Paris: Gallimard-Pléiade, 1960–67), I

N   *Nana*, in *Les Rougon-Macquart*, ed. by Henri Mitterand, 5 vols (Paris: Gallimard-Pléiade, 1960–67), II

V   *Vérité*, in *Œuvres complètes*, 50 vols (Paris: Fasquelle, 1928–29), XXVI & XXVII

INTRODUCTION

In a fin-de-siècle novel which dedicates itself to the representation of late nineteenth-century French journalism, Paul Brulat's *Le Reporter* (1898), one of the characters is a jaded former hack who has moved away from active reporting, instead devoting himself to the practice of faking news:

> Il s'ingéniait à mystifier toute la presse, utilisant de la sorte sa connaissance du métier et son sens aigu de l'actualité. Contrefaisant toutes les écritures, il expédiait aux journaux les lettres signées des noms les plus illustres, et chacune de ses missives annonçait quelque grave évènement.[1]
>
> [He delighted in outfoxing the press, using his knowledge of the job and his acute sense of what made the news. By forging handwriting styles, he sent off letters to the newspapers signed by the most illustrious names, each missive announcing some dramatic event.]

This depiction acts as a reminder of the affinities between the increasingly media-saturated age of the dawn of the twentieth century and the perceived rise of 'fake news' in a post-Trump election era in the twenty-first century. In our day and age, newspaper circulation rates might be declining, but alternative online sources of news are the subject of much popular debate and critique. An article by Stephen Armstrong in the *Daily Telegraph*, 6 January 2017, 'Pizza, Politics and Pure Fiction: The Rise of Fake News', summarizes key examples of such purposefully erroneous news stories (mixing 'outright lie, partisan opinion and conspiracy theory') from the previous election year.[2] These included the rumour that Hillary Clinton and her campaign team were running a child sex trafficking network from the Comet Ping Pong pizza restaurant in Washington, DC, which prompted a vigilante with a rifle to 'self-investigate' such stories. The *Telegraph* piece itself reminds its readers that such bogus news stories are not new, citing a *New York Sun* feature in 1835 which declared that civilization had been found on the moon.

This book examines the relationship between the novel and the newspaper in late nineteenth- and early twentieth-century France. Taking inspiration from the title of Paul Brulat's novel *Le Reporter*, I focus here on the representation of the journalist in works of the period, by writers including Guy de Maupassant, Émile Zola, Jules Verne, Gaston Leroux, and Marcelle Tinayre. Through analysis of the plots, structures, mimetic techniques, and narrative voice at work in these texts, I evaluate the novel's response to the increasingly powerful domain of journalism at the fin de siècle and track the changing and ambiguous depiction of the figure of the reporter, variously perceived as scurrilous, opportunistic, dynamic, and heroic. In so doing, I offer an understanding of the developments at work in the world of the press; chapters chart the rise of the foreign correspondent's role and the growth of publications aimed at women. The twenty-first century furore surrounding fake news draws attention to aspects of news reporting — its source, its power, its potential proximity to fiction, as highlighted in the headline of the *Telegraph* story — which will recur in this book. And as the glimpse of the cynical journalist Lavertal in Brulat's novel indicates, discussion of media practices at the turn of the century, the heyday of the press, will reveal their ever-resonant topicality. Indeed, the representation of the figure of the journalist in these fin-de-siècle texts will be seen to anticipate postmodern theories of the media and its influence. In Chapter Four, for example, which explores the rise of a new literary hero, the reporter-detective in crime fiction, questions are raised about the banalization of crime as reported in the newspapers and echoed in often parodic excerpts in detective novels; such questions can be compared with Jean Baudrillard's critical evaluation of television news in the second half of the twentieth century which 'inculcates indifference, distance, unconditional apathy'.[3] Although these are novels which in many ways can be thought to champion journalism through their depiction of intrepid reporters who challenge criminal behaviour, often exposing the inadequacies of the police, they also interrogate the stylistic clichés of reportage, incorporating, as their contemporary writer Joseph Conrad puts it, 'the mystery of a human brain pulsating wrongfully to the rhythm of journalistic phrases'.[4]

In a letter of 22 September 1881, at the end of a year-long campaign of articles in *Le Figaro*, Émile Zola summarized attitudes to the press over the course of the century and affirmed his own belief in the role of the newspaper as a kind of school for aspiring novelists. Coining the phrase 'Nous sommes tous les enfants de la presse' [We are all children of the press], he aligns himself with fellow writers and insists on the dominant influence of the media on literature; recent commentators on Zola and the press have foregrounded this line in their analyses.[5] As the figure who best combines literary and journalistic output in the second half of the nineteenth century, Zola is well-placed to view the press critically, but also to assert its prominence and value; in his 'Adieux', he addresses the view commonly held of the press, that 'elle tuait la littérature, elle traînait la langue dans tous les ruisseaux, elle était l'agent démocratique de la bêtise universelle' [it was killing off literature, dragging language through the gutter, it was the democratic agent of human stupidity], but contradicts this in his metaphor of the newspaper as an *enclume*, an anvil, on which writers might shape their own burgeoning talents: 'c'est elle [la presse] qui a rompu notre style et qui nous a donné la plupart de nos documents' [it is the press which has changed our style dramatically and provided us with most of our documents].[6] The present study takes Zola's idea of late nineteenth-century writers as 'children of the press' as its motif. It assesses a range of writers, many of whom — Maupassant, Charles Fenestrier, Leroux, Tinayre — were prolific contributors to newspapers. It examines their literary output for thematic and stylistic reactions to the journalism in which they were engaged. In order to contain a potentially vast study of representations of the newspaper in the novel at this period in history, focus falls on the 'enfants de la presse' in the novels themselves, on novels which foreground a metacommentary on journalism by incorporating journalistic writers or practitioners within their plots. Christian Delporte describes journalists at the fin de siècle, the period of the hegemony of newspapers:

> 'L'âge d'or' de la presse, selon un cliché bien connu — où le mot journaliste rime avec presse écrite, où le journalisme radiophonique reste marginal et l'information télévisée un projet, est aussi celui où se dessinent puis s'enracinent les référents culturels d'une profession, où se forge une identité qui légitime le journalisme d'aujourd'hui. C'est également la période des grands enjeux et des grands utopies, où, au nom de leur mission sacrée, les journalistes croient possible de construire une information sans contraintes, ni politiques, ni financières.[7]

> [The 'golden age' of the press, according to well-known clichés, when the word 'journaliste' rhymed with 'presse écrite', when radio journalism was still in its infancy and television news still some years off, was also when the cultural basis of a profession was being established and then embedded, and the identity of our modern journalism was being forged. It was also the period of high stakes and utopian dreams when journalists believed it possible to devote themselves as if to a sacred mission, to develop a practice of newsgathering free from restraints, whether political or financial.]

As Zola's 'Adieux' would suggest, there is a shift in literary representations of journalism towards the end of the nineteenth century. Self-conscious and anxious depictions of the would-be writer, forced through financial pressures to begin his career in the corrupting field of journalism, give way to more celebratory portrayals of heroic reporters in the 'romans populaires' of turn-of-the-century crime-fiction; the reporter becomes a redemptive figure, rescuing the increasingly professionalized sphere of journalism from the indignities associated with the representation of the writer-journalist. Guillaume Pinson tracks such shifting perceptions: 'je serais tenté de voir ici à l'œuvre la force d'imprégnation de l'imaginaire médiatique ainsi qu'un transfert en provenance de la fiction vers ce discours qui témoignent d'une admiration unanime envers le nouveau journalisme' [I would be tempted to see at work here the influence of the 'media imaginary' becoming more rooted, as well as a shift, originating in fiction, towards a narrative of unanimous admiration for the new journalism].[8] Noting this development, discussion in this book also emphasizes ways in which the novels in the former category, so-called 'romans de journalisme', reflect negatively on the press yet incorporate its practices, while popular novels featuring intrepid foreign correspondents or newspaper-detectives problematize the questions of realism and representation they raise. The objective is to highlight the way in which the novels discussed reflect on their own practices of mimesis and teleology. In embedding the trajectories of journalist characters within their plots, they respond self-consciously not only to newspaper-writing, but to plotting and narrating in a broader sense.

This study focuses, in the main, on novels from the period described by press historian Claude Bellanger as 'l'apogée de la presse' [the heyday of the press] in France: the years 1880–1914, though two of the texts discussed predate this slice of time, notably the first novel in Zola's Rougon-Macquart series, *La Fortune des*

Rougon (1871) and Jules Verne's *Michel Strogoff* (1876), chosen for the significant insight they offer into representations of the reporter-figure and the burgeoning 'presse d'information'.[9] These halcyon days of the press were inaugurated, in part, thanks to the laws of July 1881, which reduced the legal formalities on publishing a paper. This move, which facilitated much greater freedom of the press following Second Empire censorship, was seen by those who voted for it as a consecration of republican principles which were to make the press the supreme instrument of progress and democracy. Bellanger cites Eugène Pelletan, whose report to the Senate in June 1881 argued for the change in law; it offers an idealistic glimpse of a press which could unify a nation:

> La presse et surtout la presse à bon marché, cette parole présente à la fois partout et à la même heure grâce à la vapeur et à l'électricité, peut seule tenir la France tout entière assemblée comme sur une place publique et la mettre, homme par homme, jour par jour, dans la confidence de tous les événements et au courant de toutes les questions.[10]

> [The press, especially the penny press, available everywhere at the same time thanks to steam power and electricity, is the only form of communication which can gather the whole of France together as if in a public square, and inform each man, each day, about all events and keep him abreast of all issues.]

In the wake of July 1881, circulation rates increased dramatically; Bellanger notes the growth in the readership of the popular *Le Petit Parisien*, from a figure of 583,000 copies daily, which in 1880 already dwarfed many contemporary publications, to sales of 1.4 million copies a day by 1910.[11] Christian Delporte observes that the number of publications also rose, from 1316 Parisian titles in 1880 to 2685 by 1899.[12] The 1880s in particular marked the accelerated growth of the mass press, and the expansion of the reading public; for Delporte this decade signifies the shift from an 'âge artisanal' to an 'âge industriel', and from 'le temps des élites' to 'l'ère des masses'. Lower prices, new advertising methods and new content — a focus on crime and everyday life — ensured the transformation of the newspaper into a mass cultural commodity. Ideas about the influence of the newspaper and its capacity to bring people together through concurrent modes of reading, thereby facilitating the public conception of nationhood, can be found in Benedict Anderson's *Imagined Communities*.[13] The appearance of newspapers changed over this period. Although in his study of Maupassant's novel of journalism, *Bel-Ami*, Christopher Lloyd notes how different a newspaper of the 1880s would have looked compared to today, in its layout and size and also in the function it serves ('"news", in the modern sense of the term, does not actually bulk very large') he also observes the radical transformation in a popular paper such as *Le Petit Parisien* over the thirty-year period from 1880 to 1910: 'in 1880, we still have the feuilleton at the bottom and a long chronique above; whereas in 1910, there are large headlines crossing the columns, photographs, and articles devoted to news items like the flooding of the Thames'.[14] The results of such changes lead Mary Louise Roberts to observe that 'with its sometimes unlikely juxtaposition of articles and its narrative disruptions and displacements, as well as its "snapshot style", the Parisian newspaper presented a distinctly modernist way of seeing — one that captured the movement and discontinuity of the large urban space it chronicled'.¹⁵

Such spectacular developments in the funding, readership, and design of newspapers heightened awareness of the political and cultural influence of the press. Bory remarks of the representation of journalism in *Bel-Ami* (1885) that it had become 'un état dans l'état, parce qu'elle se dresse au carrefour, vital en démocratie, où se rencontrent politique, finance et opinion publique' [a state within a state, taking up a position on that crossroads where politics, finance and public opinion intersect, which is so vital in a democracy].¹⁶ In such comments on the press as a 'state within a state', Bory recalls the description of journalism as a 'Fourth Estate', a label disparaged by Oscar Wilde in 1891, as he noted the ascendency of journalistic power in fin-de-siècle Britain:

> In old days men had the rack. Now they have the Press. That is an improvement certainly. But still it is very bad, and wrong, and demoralizing. Somebody — was it Burke? — called journalism the fourth estate. That was true at the time no doubt. But at the present moment it is the only estate. It has eaten up the other three. The Lords Temporal say nothing, the Lords Spiritual have nothing to say, and the House of Commons has nothing to say and says it. We are dominated by Journalism.¹⁷

As Wilde's comment suggests, the expansion of the press and celebration of its democratic potential were countered by fear and anxiety. In France, the late 1890s saw discussion of the so-called 'crise de la presse' in the pages of the weekly *Revue bleue*; different public figures were invited to publish their views across a series of issues. An article on 1 January 1898 by the theologian Louis Auguste Sabatier refers to the press as the 'quatrième pouvoir', echoing the English 'fourth estate', and while for the most part his piece mounts a defence of the press, it notes differences between French and British expectations of the newspaper. The English, according to Sabatier, are more likely to seek news in their papers: 'ils veulent être promptement et bien renseignés [...] ils traitent leur journal comme un bureau d'informations utiles' [they want to be swiftly and effectively informed [...] they treat their newspaper as an office of usual information]; the French seek amusement from their press and so the more nefarious aspects of journalism are accepted: 'on passe très facilement sur l'injustice des calomnies, sur la fausseté des informations, sur l'ignominie de ceux qui nous amusent' [we turn a blind eye to unjust slander, to fake news, to the disgrace of those who amuse us].¹⁸ The Abbé Augustin Lemann offers a hyperbolic vision of the perceived dirt, disease, and degeneracy of the mass press at the fin de siècle; he describes it as being more destructive than war, plague, or famine: 'Quand la peste sévit, les gouvernements, les villes, les municipalités, les services publics, prennent des précautions. On organise des quarantaines, on isole, on désinfecte. Aucune précaution de ce genre contre la mauvaise presse' [when the plague is raging, governments, towns, councils and public services take precautions. They organize isolation units and disinfection regimes. No such precaution is taken against the corrupt press].¹⁹ Roberts sees this 'crise de la presse' as 'a master narrative of fin-de-siècle anxiety, a rival of the depopulation crisis at century's end', noting connections between fears about the press and anxiety about greater understanding of unconscious forces in the mind. This in turn was linked with growing unease about the changing social roles of women at the time: 'anxiety about the moral corruption of the press was organized around [a] female image — the prostitute selling herself to the masses'. Fierce competition, the economic dependence of editors on financiers and advertisers, and political extortion all led to the newspaper being increasingly held responsible for perceived moral degeneracy.[20]

Although Sabatier, in his letter to the *Revue bleue*, approves of the English model of journalism, the growth of an increasingly information-driven reportage brought new concerns. The emphasis on the *chose vue* seemingly started to take precedence over the quality of the writing. The thirst for facts and *témoignage* was perceived as a threat to the literary journal which had been the cornerstone of the nineteenth-century press, and so to literature itself. In a piece in *Le Temps*, written to mark the opening of a new school of journalism in 1899, which itself denoted the new professionalization of journalism, Adolphe Brisson wrote scathingly of the new model of journalism to be taught: 'cet affreux reportage des feuilles anglo-saxonnes, ces relations froides, banales, impersonnelles, d'où l'émotion, la verve, la fantaisie sont exclues!' [that dreadful reportage found in Anglo-Saxon newspapers, those cold, banal, impersonal accounts which allow no room for feeling, verve or imagination!].[21] A sense of menace crystallized around the notion of reportage. In contrast to the perception of the press as a murky social scourge, a counter current arose which sought to capture something of the cleanliness and almost clinical precision of the newspaper. Newspaper editor and politician Yves Guyot wrote in 1901: 'Pendant longtemps la presse a été une chaire. Elle deviendra de plus en plus un bureau de renseignements et un laboratoire' [For a long time the press has been a pulpit. Increasingly, it is becoming an information bureau and a laboratory].[22] Journalism began to emphasize its own distance from the novel with its focus on new styles of journalism, on reportage rather than on literary articles and opinion pieces. Gaston Leroux's series of detective novels, which feature the journalist Rouletabille as super-sleuth, are narrated by Sainclair, whose name evokes cleanliness, rationality, and clear-sightedness. Sainclair is a lawyer, but he too writes for the press. Pierre Giffard, a pioneer of reportage and editor of the sports journal *Le Vélo*, becomes an early defendant of new forms of journalism, setting out, in his novel *Le Sieur de Va-Partout*, a model of the indefatigable near-heroism of the reporter figure who is ready to leap into the business of witnessing and reporting at a moment's notice. Félicien Champsaur writes favourably of new journalistic practices in the preface to his 1889 novel *Dinah Samuel*, arguing that the added emphasis on news has positive implications for novels which can be said to reflect 'le modernisme': 'En effet j'adore en ces besognes de journalisme l'anecdote documentaire qui dévoile et qui est aussi bien jugement, l'attitude qui résume un caractère ou un talent, les menus traits de synthèse qui peignent' [Indeed, I adore the documentary-style anecdote which reveals and also offers judgement, the approach which sums up a character or a talent, the little techniques of synthesis which paint a picture].[23] This book explores the impact of such conflicting attitudes to the growth of journalism in the literature of the period, as well as ways in which the fin-de-siècle novel endorses or recoils from the practices and visual heterogeneity of the developing newspaper.

Two images, taken from recent studies of journalism in the nineteenth-century novel, indicate something of the ubiquity of the newspaper in the literature and culture of the time, and also reflect recent critical interest in the study of the relationship between fiction and the press. Pinson's wide-ranging study of the 'imaginaire médiatique' examines the reflection of the press in nineteenth- and early twentieth-century French texts. He includes the detail that at the end of Maupassant's short story 'Boule de suif', the comtesse de Bréville, extracting food from a basket of provisions, pulls out a piece of cheese which, having been wrapped in newspaper, now bears the imprint of the type: '"faits divers" sur sa pâte onctueuse' ['News in brief' on its creamy surface].[24] Pinson observes: 'le récit réaliste est quelque chose comme cette pâte onctueuse marquée des mots, de l'imaginaire et des références au journal' [the realist narrative is a bit like this creamy surface imprinted with word and references taken from the newspaper].[25] Nicholas White also picks out an image of the newspaper as material object, this time in Zola's *La Débâcle* (1892). Here, the increasing degeneration in the text of the newspaper as a vehicle of information about developments in the military campaign is highlighted by a reference to the newspaper being used as a kind of lampshade: Mme Delaherche 'avait mis un journal devant la lampe, et tout ce coin de la chambre se trouvait à demi obscur' [had put a newspaper in front of the lamp, and the whole of that corner of the room was in semi-darkness].[26] Says White of this shift : 'The newspaper is no longer to be read, but to be used as a lampshade; to shade the light, not to enlighten; to be used as an ornament rather than to inform'.[27] However critically we view this 'shading' of the light with the newspaper, these images indicate something of the way in which everyday life is filtered and consumed through the print of the newspaper and its discourse by the end of the nineteenth century, an awareness which is reinforced by the title of the compendious study of the press in France, *La Civilisation du journal: histoire culturelle et littéraire de la presse française au XIXè siècle*. The many contributors to this volume, edited by Dominique Kalifa, Philippe Régnier, Marie-Ève Thérenty, and Alain Vaillant, indicate the wide-ranging interests in the relationships between literature and the media across the period. Indeed, one of the central questions in the study remains the interrogation of what 'literature' itself might mean: 'L'histoire littéraire de la presse, précisément parce qu'elle bouscule nos habitudes (et le privilège arbitraire accordé au livre imprimé), nous ramène-t-elle de façon opportune et salubre à la sempiternelle question: "Qu'est-ce que la littérature?"' [The literary history of the press brings us back, in timely fashion, to the eternal question, 'What is literature?', precisely because it shakes up our way of thinking (and the privilege accorded to the printed book)].[28]

This influence of *La Civilisation du journal* within nineteenth-century studies of French literature is highlighted by the references made both to it, and to the massive digitization of newspaper archives which has facilitated its findings, in the inaugural dialogical instalment of the journal *Nineteenth-Century French Studies*. In this 'conversation', David Bell and Catherine Witt reflect on the future of the field, and draw attention to the processes of research which have engendered greater understanding of the 'distinctive spatio-temporal complex of writing and reading that came to impose its relentless rhythm (la périodicité) on nineteenth-century society and its [...] representation of the world' as forged by the press.[29] The present book builds on the invaluable insight into the press provided by *La Civilisation du journal*, its contributors, and the website founded by Thérenty and Pinson, *Médias19*.[30] It also considers studies of the influence of the press on English literature. Matthew Rubery shows how nineteenth-century English novels, while seeming to reject the dominance of the press, nevertheless incorporate valuable and self-conscious commentary on its discourses.[31]

Rubery makes the argument, in his study of the nineteenth-century English novel's response to the newspaper, that 'the English novel during the era of the commercial press drew on news as a rival practice of realistic representation and as an authoritative form of public knowledge'.[32] The dialectical relationship he suggests is an interaction which evokes both rivalry and an admiration bordering on imitation. Such interactions are examined in relation to the French novel in the present study. The opening chapter evaluates the very idea of rivalry as a mode of behaviour which is evoked and satirized in Maupassant's *Bel-Ami*, the novel which acts as a lynchpin in a study of literary responses to the press. The idea of the relationship between literature and the press as one of a struggle for supremacy is suggested, already, through the hostile characterization of the fin-de-siècle media discussed above, and is foregrounded in Richard Terdiman's analysis of discourses at work in the French nineteenth century, *Discourse/Counter-Discourse*. Terdiman sees literature organizing its forces against the perceived hegemony of a newspaper culture increasingly seen as commodified; for 'the disenchanted intelligentsia, the alienated writers' — he cites Charles Baudelaire and Stéphane Mallarmé as examples[33] — the newspaper became 'the quintessential figure for the discourse of their middle-class enemy, the name for the writing against which they sought to counterpose their own'.[34] Hostility on the part of literary writers was the result, suggests Terdiman, of the perceived threat represented by the newspaper as the 'first culturally anti-organicist mode of modern discourse' which 'overturns the consecrated canons of text structure and coherence which had operated in the period preceding its inception'. In the present work, discussion of Zola's late novel, *Vérité*, his fictional modelling of the Dreyfus affair, sees it attempting an organicist, totalizing mode of discourse which would eradicate the contradictions of the press.

Bakhtin's theory of the novel suggests, too, an inharmonious relationship between literature and other genres, which would include the many forms of the press, though the model he describes offers a more dynamic and incorporative process than that set out by Terdiman: 'the novel parodies other genres [...] it exposes the conventionality of their forms and their language; it squeezes out some genres and incorporates others into its own peculiar structure, re-formulating and re-accentuating them'.[35] Parody is the trope adopted by the writers examined in later chapters of this book, in the works of popular novelists such as Jules Verne and the early practitioners of the detective novel genre. Pinson argues, in contradiction to Bakhtin, that it is the newspaper, rather than the novel, which is the most authentically incorporative and polyphonic form of the nineteenth century.[36] Certainly the porous relationship between literature and the press reaches a zenith in the period at the heart of this book. Bakhtin maintains that 'of particular interest are those eras when the novel becomes the dominant genre. All literature is then caught up in the process of "becoming"'.[37] The fin de siècle is an era of tension in the history of the novel. It is the continuation of the era when the novel reigns supreme; it is the period which sees the growth of new forms of popular literature, including the detective novel and fiction penned by women writers; yet it is also the moment when the novel reflects on its own surplus and decline, sometimes at the expense of the newspaper. Even Jules Verne, characterized by his prolific output, and by buoyant texts embracing new technologies of speed and science, expresses the view that the novel will be supplanted by the dynamism of journalism:

> Je ne pense pas que d'ici cinquante ou cent ans on publie encore des romans, du moins en volumes. Ils seront complètement supplantés par le journal quotidien, qui a déjà pris une telle emprise sur l'existence des nations qui progressent. [...] Les journalistes ont bien appris à donner des événements de tous les jours un récit coloré qu'en lisant ce qu'ils ont décrit, la postérité y trouvera un tableau plus exact qui celui que pourrait donner un roman historique ou descriptif.[38]
>
> [I do not think that novels will still be published fifty or a hundred years from now, at least not in volumes. They will be replaced by the daily newspaper, which has already established such a hold on the life of progressive nations. [...] Journalists have learned the skill of producing a colourful account of everyday events, such that in reading what they have written, posterity will find a more accurate depiction there than in a historical or descriptive novel.]

In Huysmans's *À rebours* — a text whose date (1884) makes it contemporaneous with the depiction of the newspaper in *Bel-Ami* — Des Esseintes's retreat from the world in the opening chapter is connected with the disgust he feels for both the press and commercialized literature: '[il] en arrivait à [...] souffrir des balivernes patriotiques et sociales débitées, chaque matin, dans les journaux, à s'exagérer la portée des succès qu'un tout-puissant public réserve toujours et quand même aux œuvres écrites sans idées et sans style' ('he was constantly [...] wincing at the patriotic or political twaddle served up in the papers every morning, and exaggerating the importance of the triumphs which an omnipotent public reserves at all times and in all circumstances for works written without thought or style').[39] His ultimate preferred form of literature, the prose poem, the 'osmazome' of aesthetic digestion, represents an idealized alternative to the late nineteenth-century novel: 'le roman, ainsi conçu, ainsi condensé en une page ou deux, deviendrait une communion de pensée entre un magique écrivain et un idéal lecteur' [the novel, thus conceived, thus condensed in a page or two, would become an intellectual communion between a hieratic writer and an ideal reader].[40] This is a concentrated literary 'huile'; it rejects the nefarious commercial influences which make Des Esseintes shudder in the opening chapter of Huysmans's novel, but is only fully realizable within the confines of the artificial retreat from society he has cultivated, and which he will be forced to abandon by the end of the text.

In his analysis of the impact of the press on the Victorian novel, Rubery claims that:

> Novelists used newspapers in a variety of ways: retelling events reported by the press; reproducing journalistic voices, styles, and features; the pastiche of news items through headlines and quotations; recording the process of news production; and, most dramatically, portraying the individual reader's reaction to the news.[41]

French writers at the end of the century incorporate the newspaper in similar ways. In novels which include journalist characters, questions will be raised about the degree of aesthetic distance placed between the narrative voice and the writings of the reporters represented in the texts and about the critique or celebration of new models of journalistic technique and style — such as the focus on *raconter* [telling the story] which comes to dominate newspaper articles throughout the nineteenth century, marking a shift from an age of polemical opinion pieces.[42] Such a focus on event-based reporting is found in particular in the rise of crime reporting, and is reflected in the turn-of-the-century detective novels. Rubery suggests that the techniques he examines are 'narrative conventions inherited from Victorian journalism' which 'have become [...] standard features of realism to this day'.[43] The impact of journalism on the realism of the French texts in question will be a particular consideration. Vaillant comments on the increasing attention paid to the real in journalism; he maintains that up to the advent of the 'presse moderne', literature in its widest sense — described as 'tout texte à destination d'un public' [all texts aimed at a public readership] — adopted a discursive, persuasive model, but that 'le journal inaugure le règne de la représentation généralisée, qui caractérise nos sociétés contemporaines. L'écriture — ou la littérature — est donc devenue un *art de la représentation*' [the newspaper ushers in the reign of generalized representation, which characterizes our modern societies. Writing — or literature — has thus become an art of representation].[44] A recurring theoretical focus of this book falls on practices of realism and mimesis. The central dichotomy at work within realism — the dialectical movement between categorization, knowability, and assertion on the one hand and the subversion of those tendencies on the other — is manifested through the incorporation of journalism as a theme and a mode of characterization.[45]

Through an emphasis on the publication of news and the practice of assembling and announcing it, the realist and naturalist novel signals its engagement with the contemporary world and with the cataloguing of the everyday. At the same time, the representation of journalism, often ironized, sets up not only the sense of rivalry between the novel and the newspaper but also highlights the novel's critical and self-reflexive evaluation of the processes of reporting and ordering information. Fredric Jameson's *The Antimonies of Realism* offers insight into the 'discursive opposition' which lies at the heart of realism itself: that realism is a massive, multitasking enterprise, the characteristic of which is that it is always juggling two time-frames, refusing to choose between temporal possibilities. In the past, these might have been described as 'récit' and 'roman', or 'telling versus showing'; Jameson articulates these contrasts as 'destiny versus the eternal present', or narrative versus affect. As Ben Parker clarifies:[46]

> Those two things are, roughly, the prodding eventfulness of storytelling, as found in pre-novelistic forms like the Gospels, the epic, the medieval Romance — and simultaneously, the technologies of experience and sensation that modernism would go on to sunder from the chains of plot and the naturalist illusions of the Victorian doorstops.[47]

For Yee, 'exoticism is one of Realism's antimonies, incorporated [...] as an antagonistic presence within the realist mode'.[48] The incorporation of the journalist and the newspaper in the realist text functions in an inverse direction to that of exoticism suggested by Yee. While the exotic is inserted into the realist text to query ideas of verisimilitude, the introduction of journalism acts, on one level, seemingly to embed and reinforce such verisimilitude, proffering a bridge between the fictional text and the real world via the reportage of journalist or article. Yet at the same time, the ways in which the novel treats such insertions playfully or ironically suggests that journalism is represented so as to contrast the *récit* or the 'destiny' of the newspaper's realism with the *roman* or the 'eternal present' of the novelistic discourse itself; the pastiche of the press becomes an oppositional antimony which contributes to the concept of realism as a dialectical mode. Jameson maintains:

> My experiment here claims to come at realism dialectically [...] above all by grasping realism as a historical and even evolutionary process in which the negative and the positive are inextricably combined, and whose emergence and development at one and the same time constitute its own inevitable undoing; its own decay and dissolution.[49]

Jameson's theories, and their impact on discussions of realism's incorporation of journalism, will be discussed further in Chapter Three, which examines the emphasis placed on the senses in the information-gathering processes of reportage. Jameson's dialectic of 'narrative' and 'affect' will be seen in Jules Verne's take on realism, which represents and undermines the sensory imperatives of the new journalism.

Théranty offers the image of the 'icône renversée' [overturned icon] as a way of discussing the reflection of the newspaper in the novel. The presence of a journalistic article — or, in my evaluation, the presence of the journalistic character — illustrates the negotiation of a theoretical space within the novel whereby the novel signals its intent to interrogate both its own procedures and those of the genre it incorporates.[50] In an analysis of acts of 'remediation', the representation of one medium within another, Bolter and Grusin suggest that there will always be an ongoing critique and reshaping of competing media. Such a dialogue can be found in the novel's 'remediation' of the newspaper.[51] These practices of interrogation and remediation are discussed in Chapter One, via analysis of *Bel-Ami*. Here, the very idea of an antagonistic relationship between literature and the press is examined and diffused through consideration of the journalistic duel in the novel.

In producing and undermining dualism, *Bel-Ami* is also examined as a text which generates echoes. Not only are the gossip columns, the 'échos' penned by Duroy, emblematic of the processes of reflection and illusion embedded in Maupassant's novel, but the representation of the world of journalism evoked here is itself echoed in later fin-de-siècle novels: in Brulat's *Le Reporter* (1898) and in Fenestrier's *La Vie des frelons* (1908). Analysis of these two little-discussed texts considers the 'anxiety of influence' — the influence both of the newspaper and of the newspaper-novel embodied by *Bel-Ami* — on turn-of-the-century novels intensely aware of their struggle for originality.

Chapter Two addresses the ambiguous response to changing models of journalism found in Zola's novels. It explores Zola's conflicted attitudes to the press through close analysis of two texts, chosen to represent the beginning and end of his career. Focus falls on the inaugural novel in the Rougon-Macquart cycle, *La Fortune des Rougon* (1871), and the third novel in the projected *Quatre Évangiles*, *Vérité* (1903), the text which acts as a deliberate echo of the Dreyfus Affair. Both texts centre around conflicts, and the newspaper plays a significant role in each of these pivotal moments in nineteenth-century French history. The lively and humorous depictions of the reporter-figure in Verne's adventure novels offer a contrast with the cynicism of Maupassant and the ambiguity of Zola.

Chapter Three focuses in particular on two novels by Verne in which the newly developing practice of reportage is brought to the fore: *Michel Strogoff* (1876) and *Claudius Bombarnac* (1892). These are texts which emphasize and ironize such reportage and offer ludic analysis of the interplay between newspaper discourse and that of the realist novel. Discussing the 'grand reporter' figure sent to document foreign news stories and wire back war reports, this chapter centres its attention on the rhetoric associated with the senses in contemporary representations of journalism: the imperative of the eyewitness account, or the emphasis placed on aural attentiveness; it compares the primacy placed on the visual in late nineteenth-century reportage with criticism of the reifying tendencies of sight.

The representation of the journalist as heroic, rather than as an ethical and aesthetic threat, reaches its zenith with the growing popularity of crime fiction at the turn of the century. Chapter Four discusses a range of early twentieth-century detective stories, in particular the Rouletabille series by former *Le Matin* reporter Gaston Leroux, and the Fantômas books by Pierre Souvestre and Marcel Allain, also journalists. It focuses on the role played by 'newspaper-detectives' in these texts, investigators employed by the press who aid or better the efforts of the police in uncovering criminal activity. Emphasis on the heroization of such characters is accompanied by the frequently ironic tone of the detective stories themselves; distinctions between reporters, detectives, and criminals are often blurred, as in Souvestre and Allain's texts, in which the name of the journalist Fandor echoes that of the arch-criminal Fantômas, and in which both characters are products of the *fantasmagorical nature of the tales themselves. The practice of narrative is held up to scrutiny and shown to be in opposition to the dynamism and drive of the energetic young investigators.

Chapter Five explores the creation of a new literary character, examining the representation of the female journalist in three novels in particular: Marcelle Tinayre's *La Rebelle* (1906), Camille Pert's *Leur égale* (1899), and Paul and Victor Margueritte's *Femmes nouvelles* (1899). Unlike earlier *romans de journalisme*, these novels which depict women writing for, editing, or establishing publications aimed at a female market are not necessarily preoccupied with the threat of the newspaper. Instead they reflect both the potential power and the limitations of such media outlets for engaging and motivating their women readers, for encouraging reflection on changing attitudes towards marriage and employment. Discussion of these texts focuses on plot, on the conflict between the social realism of the novels' backdrops, and on the idealized romantic fates they envisage for their would-be 'rebellious' protagonists, asking whether, in Rachel Blau DuPlessis's term, these writers and journalists can be considered to practise a form of 'writing beyond the ending'.[52]

A trajectory is mapped across the period under scrutiny. The predominantly negative representation of the press in novels which represent a battle between hallowed forms of literature and commercial journalism is modified. It becomes, by the end of the nineteenth century, a more optimistic vision which celebrates the opportunities afforded by a career in journalism, whether for women, or for Verne's adventurers, or for astute reporter-detectives. This is an arc reflected in the ordering of the chapters, which move from the satirical evaluation of journalism afforded by *Bel-Ami*, through the ambiguities of Zola, to the heroization of journalist and detective novel. Temporally, this path also parallels the shift from realism into modernism, anticipating the ambivalent response to the press found in modernist texts: Patrick Brantlinger discusses the role of the press in helping to catalyze the dialectical tension between 'mass culture and its apparent opposite, the artistic avant-garde [...] the symbiotic corollaries of advanced capitalism between the 1880s and 1914'.[53] The progression I suggest here, though, is also complicated by a counter-movement, which sees that the denigration of the press is coupled, in the earlier novels, by techniques within those novels themselves which reflect journalistic practices, and by the continuing sense of parody and critique levelled at the press by the popular novel of the turn of the century.

This book goes to press at a time when the role of news is under particular scrutiny. Following the election of Donald Trump, and his early anti-media interventions suggesting the threat to 'close down the elite press', journalists have responded with fury and an intensified commitment to interrogate the political world. An article in the American magazine *Politico*, published in the week of the inauguration of the new President, articulated a new challenge for reporters:

> Instead of relying exclusively on the traditional skills of political reporting, the carriers of press cards ought to start thinking of covering Trump's Washington like a war zone, where conflict follows conflict, where the fog prevents the collection of reliable information directly from the combatants, where the assignment is a matter of life and death.[54]

In the wake of the massacre of cartoonist and satirical journalists at the newspaper

Charlie Hebdo in 2015, the co-ordinators of *Médias-19* responded with a message of solidarity and with the comment that, 'Depuis plusieurs siècles, la presse est l'objet d'attaques, de toutes natures, lors même que son développement était indissolublement lié à la mise en place des grandes valeurs démocratiques' [For centuries, the press has been the object of attacks of all kinds, when we consider that its development is inextricably linked to the establishment of core democratic values].[55] At the time of the attacks Pinson and Thérenty published, too, an article in homage to the murdered cartoonists, on the role and subversive significance of the satirical press in the nineteenth century, again underlining the many echoes between the role and perception of the press at the time of its phenomenal growth and the present day.[56] As twenty-first-century readers apparently turn in their droves to dystopian fiction for insight into and understanding of current political movements and their efforts to control the distribution of information, so the current study turns to fiction for evaluation and critique of the processes of journalism and information gathering in the nineteenth century.[57] And it finds that representations of the press enable the novel to examine its own practices and discourses, holding both itself and the journalism it critiques to account.

Notes to the Introduction

1. Paul Brulat, *Le Reporter: roman contemporain* (Paris: Perrin, 1898), p. 84.
2. <http://www.telegraph.co.uk/men/thinking-man/pizza-politics-pure-fiction-rise-fake-news/> [accessed 27 January 2017]
3. Jean Baudrillard, *The Illusion of the End* (Cambridge: Polity, 1994), p. 61.
4. Joseph Conrad, *The Secret Agent* (London: David Campbell, 1992), p. 283.
5. Émile Zola, 'Adieux', *Le Figaro*, 22 September 1881, reprinted in *Zola journaliste*, ed. by Adeline Wrona (Paris: Garnier-Flammarion, 2011), pp. 309–19 (p. 318). Wrona's introduction to *Zola journaliste* cites the 'Enfants de la presse' quotation (p. 7); Nicholas White draws attention to it in his article on Zola and the press 'L'Enclume toujours chaude: Émile Zola's Newspaper Trilogy', in *Literature and the Press 1789–1914*, ed. by Edmund Birch and Kate Rees, special issue of *Dix-Neuf* (forthcoming); Corinne Saminadayar-Perrin's article in *Cahiers naturalistes* also employs the citation in its title ('Portrait d'Émile Zola en 'enfant de la presse', in *Dossier: Zola au pluriel*, ed. by Claire White and Nicholas White, *Cahiers naturalistes*, 91, (September 2017), 109–21).
6. Zola, 'Adieux', p. 318.
7. Christian Delporte, *Les Journalistes en France: naissance et construction d'une profession, 1880–1950* (Paris: Seuil, 2009), p. 15.
8. Guillaume Pinson, *L'Imaginaire médiatique: histoire et fiction du journal au XIXè siècle* (Paris: Classiques Garnier, 2012).
9. *Histoire générale de la presse française*, ed. by Claude Bellanger and others, 5 vols (Paris: Presses universitaires de France, 1969–76), III (1972).
10. Ibid., III, 241.
11. Ibid., III, 137.
12. Delporte, *Les Journalistes en France*, p. 43.
13. Benedict Anderson, *Imagined Communities: Reflections on the Origins and Spread of Nationalism* (London: Verso, 1991).
14. Christopher Lloyd, *Maupassant: Bel-Ami* (London: Grant & Cutler, 1988), p. 73.
15. Mary Louise Roberts, *Disruptive Acts: The New Woman in Fin de Siècle France* (Chicago, IL: University of Chicago Press, 2002), pp. 77–78.
16. *BA*, 13–14.
17. Oscar Wilde, 'The Soul of Man under Socialism', *Fortnightly Review*, 49 (February 1891), 292–319 (p. 290).

18. Auguste Sabatier, 'Les Responsabilités de la presse', *Revue bleue* (1 January 1898), 8–12 (p. 11).
19. Augustin Lemann, *Un fléau plus redoutable que la guerre, la peste, la famine* (Lyon: Librairie Catholique Emmanuel Vitte, [n.d.]), p. 14.
20. Roberts, *Disruptive Acts*, pp. 78–79. On the 'crise de la presse', see too René Mazedier, *Histoire de la presse parisienne* (Paris: Éditions de Pavois, 1945), René de Livois, *Histoire de la presse française*, 2 vols (Lausanne: Éditions Spes, 1965), and Thomas Ferenczi, *L'Invention du journalisme en France: naissance de la presse moderne à la fin du XIXè siècle* (Paris: Plon, 1993).
21. Adolphe Brisson, 'Promenades et visites: l'école de journalisme', *Le Temps*, 3 November 1899.
22. Cited in *Histoire générale de la presse française*, ed. by Bellanger and others, III, 270.
23. Félicien Champsaur, *Dinah Samuel* (Paris: Paul Ollendorff, 1889), p. xvi.
24. Guy de Maupassant, 'Boule de suif', in *Contes et nouvelles*, 2 vols (Paris: Gallimard-Pléaide, 1974–79), I, 119.
25. Pinson, *L'Imaginaire médiatique*, p. 98.
26. Émile Zola, *La Débâcle*, in *Les Rougon-Macquart*, ed. by Henri Mitterand, 5 vols (Paris: Gallimard-Pléaide, 1960–67), V, 720.
27. White, 'L'Enclume toujours chaude'.
28. 'Introduction', in *La Civilisation du journal: histoire culturelle et littéraire de la presse française au XIXè siècle*, ed. by Dominique Kalifa and others (Paris: Nouveau Monde, 2011), pp. 7–21 (p. 20).
29. David Bell and Catherine Witt, '*Incipit*: On the Present and Future of the Field', *Nineteenth-Century French Studies*, 44.3–4 (2016), 145–82 (p. 154).
30. *Médias19* offers a platform for researchers working on the nineteenth-century press, both in France and worldwide; it incorporates a database listing journalists of the period and selected literary publications featuring reporters: <http://www.medias19.org/index.php?id=165> [accessed 31 January 2017]. Separate studies by the editors of *La Civilisation du journal* offer important resources for studies of the nineteenth-century French press. See Marie-Ève Thérenty's *La Littérature au quotidien: poétiques journalistiques au XIXème siècle* (Paris: Seuil, 2007) for analysis of the ways in which newspapers reflect and anticipate literary strategies; also the collection of essays edited by Thérenty and Alain Vaillant, *Presse et plumes: journalisme et littérature au XIXè siècle* (Paris: Nouveau Monde, 2004), and Anne-Marie Thiesse, *Le Roman du quotidien: lecteurs et lectures populaires à la Belle Époque* (Paris: Chemin Vert, 1984). Dominique Kalifa's *L'Encre et le sang: récits de crimes et société à la Belle Époque* (Paris: Fayard, 1995) offers insight into the rise of *faits-diversiers* and crime-reporting at the end of the century. Pinson's *L'Imaginaire médiatique* takes particular inspiration from Marc Angenot's wide-ranging study, *1889: un état de discours social*, an investigation into social discourses circulating in that year; focus in Angenot's work falls on the detail of the everyday, aided by an understanding of the daily press. Angenot's book is one of the publications accessible via *Médias19*, <http://www.medias19.org/index.php?id=11003> [accessed 14 June 2017].
31. Matthew Rubery, *The Novelty of Newspapers: Victorian Fiction after the Invention of the News* (Oxford: Oxford University Press, 2009). See too Dallas Liddle, *The Dynamics of Genre: Journalism and the Practice of Literature in mid-Victorian Britain* (Charlottesville: University of Virginia Press, 2009), and Laurel Brake and Julie Codell, *Encounters in the Victorian Press: Editors, Authors, Readers* (Basingstoke: Macmillan, 2005).
32. Rubery, *The Novelty of Newspapers*, p. 1.
33. In Baudelaire's 'Mon cœur mis à nu', for instance, the pure hand recoils from touching a newspaper (in *Œuvres complètes*, 2 vols (Paris: Gallimard-Pléaide, 1975–76), II, 676–708. On Mallarmé's complex response to the press see Max McGuinness, 'Literature and "Universal Reportage" in Mallarmé's "Livre"', in *Literature and the Press 1789–1914*, ed. by Birch and Rees.
34. Richard Terdiman, *Discourse/Counter-Discourse: The Theory and Practice of Symbolic Resistance in Nineteenth-Century France* (Ithaca, NY: Cornell University Press, 1985), pp. 120–21.
35. Mikhail Bakhtin, *The Dialogic Imagination: Four Essays*, ed. by Michael Holquist, trans. by Caryl Emerson and Michael Holquist (Austin: University of Texas Press, 1987), p. 5
36. Pinson, *L'Imaginaire médiatique*, p. 101.
37. Bakhtin, *The Dialogic Imagination*, p. 5.
38. Jules Verne, 'Jules Verne Says The Novel Will Soon Be Dead', *Pittsburgh Gazette*, 13 July 1902,

translated in *Entretiens avec Jules Verne*, ed. by Daniel Compère and Jean-Michel Margot (Geneva: Slatkine, 1998), pp. 177–80 (p. 178).
39. Joris-Karl Huysmans, *À rebours* (Paris: Garnier-Flammarion, 1978), p. 65. The English translations of *À rebours* are taken from *À Rebours*, trans. by Robert Baldick (Harmondsworth: Penguin, 2003)
40. Ibid., p. 222.
41. Rubery, *The Novelty of Newspapers*, p. 11.
42. See, for example, Alain Vaillant, 'Écrire pour raconter', in *La Civilisation du journal*, ed. by Kalifa and others, pp. 773–92.
43. Rubery, *The Novelty of Newspapers*, p. 11.
44. Vaillant, 'Écrire pour raconter', p. 787.
45. Jennifer's Yee's discussion of imperialism in the French realist novel summarizes the dialectical movement within realism itself, citing Christopher Prendergast's *The Order of Mimesis*: 'Many writers using the realist mode, who give high priority to mimesis, *also* incorporate anxieties about the possibility of semantic stability, foregrounding the referential or poetic functions and thus, as Christopher Prendergast puts it, encountering the experience of the "limit" (of representation)' (Yee, *The Colonial Comedy: Imperialism in the French Realist Novel* (Oxford: Oxford University Press, 2016), pp. 10–11; Prendergast, *The Order of Mimesis: Balzac, Stendhal, Nerval, Flaubert* (Cambridge: Cambridge University Press, 1986), p. 15).
46. Fredric Jameson, *The Antinomies of Realism* (London: Verso, 2013), p. 26.
47. Ben Parker, 'The Moments of Realism', in *Los Angeles Review of Books*, 28 July 2015, <https://lareviewofbooks.org/article/the-antinomies-of-realism/> [accessed 16 January 2017].
48. Yee, *The Colonial Comedy*, p. 13.
49. Jameson, *The Antinomies of Realism*, p. 6.
50. Marie-Ève Thérenty, 'Le Journal dans le roman du XIXè siècle ou l'icône renversée', in *Le Roman du signe: fiction et herméneutique au XIXè siècle*, ed. by Andrea del Lungo and Boris Lyon-Caen (Saint-Denis: Presses universitaires de Vincennes, 2007), pp. 25–38.
51. Jay Bolter and Richard Grusin, *Remediation* (Cambridge, MA: MIT Press, 2000).
52. Rachel Blau DuPlessis, *Writing Beyond the Ending* (Bloomington: Indiana University Press, 1985).
53. Patrick Brantlinger, 'Mass Media and Culture in fin de siècle Europe', in *Fin de Siècle and its Legacy*, ed. by Miculàs Teich and Roy Porter (Cambridge: Cambridge University Press, 1990), pp. 98–114 (p. 100). See too Andreas Huyssen, *After the Great Divide: Modernism, Mass Culture, Postmodernism* (Bloomington: Indiana University Press, 1986).
54. See Jack Schafer, 'Trump is Making Journalism Great Again', *Politico*, 16 January 2017, <http://www.politico.com/magazine/story/2017/01/trump-is-making-journalism-great-again-214638> [accessed 30 January 2017].
55. Anon., 'Soutien à Charlie Hebdo', *Médias-19*, 7 January 2015, <http://www.medias19.org/index.php?id=21506> [accessed 30 January 2017].
56. Guillaume Pinson and Marie-Ève Thérenty, 'D'où viens-tu, Charlie?', *Médiapart*, 31 January 2015, <https://blogs.mediapart.fr/edition/bookclub/article/140115/d-ou-viens-tu-charlie> [accessed 30 January 2017].
57. Brian Wheeler, 'The Trump Era's Top-Selling Dystopian Novels', BBC News, 29 January 2017, <http://www.bbc.co.uk/news/magazine-38764041> [accessed 30 January 2017].

CHAPTER 1

Maupassant:
Illusions, Echoes, Anxieties

Mid-way through Maupassant's seminal novel representing the nineteenth-century newspaper office, *Bel-Ami*, the upcoming journalist Duroy is encouraged to fight a duel with a reporter from a rival publication. The resulting combat is a farce. Although Duroy spends the night before the duel agonizing over his own mortality, the encounter itself sees the two men fire once, miss, and retreat. The contest is then written up in the pages of the newspaper, and recounted by Duroy, as a more dramatic episode than the non-event that Maupassant depicts it as being. It is a moment which helps to cement Duroy's career as a celebrated writer of 'Les Échos', the gossip column he pens for the paper *Vie française*:

> Son duel avait fait passer Duroy au nombre des chroniqueurs de tête de *la Vie Française*; mais, comme il éprouvait une peine infinie à découvrir des idées, il prit la spécialité des déclamations sur la décadence des mœurs, sur l'abaissement des caractères, l'affaissement du patriotisme et l'anémie de l'honneur français (il avait trouvé le mot 'anémie' dont il était fier). (*BA*, 201)
>
> [His duel had established Duroy as one of the principal staff writers on *La Vie française*; however, as he found it extremely difficult to come up with ideas, he made it his speciality to rail against moral decline, a new weakness of character, the demise of patriotism, and the anaemia affecting the French sense of honour. (He himself had discovered the word 'anaemia,' and was very proud of it).][1]

As this quotation makes clear, Duroy's renown is achieved despite his frequently-documented inability to come up with ideas; his pride in the employment of the noun 'anaemia', parenthetically inserted here as a summation of his linguistic inadequacy, is emblematic of his wishy-washy character, his writing, and the farcical duel which enables him to turn these attributes into social success. The duel itself takes place against an anaemic background, an icy landscape leeched of colour. This chapter will begin by considering the duel, discussed by Maupassant as characteristic of the charlatantism endemic in journalism of the period, which saw reporters turn to the ritual of the swordfight as a means of garnering publicity they failed to achieve through the merits of their writing alone. The duel and its increasingly anaemic representation in fiction will be seen as allegorical of the combat taking place in the nineteenth century between literature and journalism, an antagonism which is represented as being increasingly ritualistic. Maupassant says of the duel that it has descended into a conflict which is 'de plus en plus une chose coquette et mondaine' [more and more of a stylish and fashionable thing].² The swords drawn between the newspaper and the novel, much discussed in nineteenth-century literature and in critical comment on that period, end up, by the time of *Bel-Ami*, in a combat almost as empty as the puffs of smoke which characterize Duroy's brief flirtation with danger.

This chapter will focus on *Bel-Ami*, one of the best-known literary representations of journalism, and particularly resonant in the wake of the 1881 press reforms. It argues that Maupassant's novel does not evoke the idea of lost illusions, and a golden age of literature under threat from the monetary compulsions of journalism, as does Balzac's *Illusions perdues*. Instead it depicts a world composed almost entirely of illusions, in which the newspaper office plays a fundamental role in generating such trickeries, as seen in the fraudulent write-up of Duroy's duel. Anticipating postmodern theories of the 'hyper-real', *Bel-Ami* is composed of mirror images, repetition, and echoes, key among them being the increasing sense of the reflection between narrator and character, as the narrator who recounts the vacuity of Georges Duroy, the soon-to-be eminent reporter in the text, becomes increasingly difficult to disentangle from that journalist. The chapter also considers *Bel-Ami* as a text which generates echoes. Not only are the gossip columns, the 'échos' penned by Duroy, emblematic of the processes of reflection and illusion embedded in Maupassant's novel, but the representation of the world of journalism evoked here is itself echoed in later fin-de-siècle novels: in Brulat's *Le Reporter* (1898) and in Fenestrier's *La Vie des frelons* (1908). Analysis of these two little-discussed texts considers the 'anxiety of influence' — the influence both of the newspaper and of the newspaper-novel embodied by *Bel-Ami* — on turn-of-the-century novels intensely aware of their struggle for originality, as they simultaneously critique and incorporate techniques associated with the press. The term is taken from Harold Bloom's influential study of poetry, although Bloom's analysis is of the way that 'strong poets' 'wrestle with their strong precursors, even to the death', and maps out clear stages of the life-cycle of poets, involving a swerving away from their predecessors, before retaining and developing their influence, and ultimately stationing their own poems in a solitary relationship to the 'parent-poems'. My use of the phrase is much less positive, arguing that the late-nineteenth century novelists whose work I discuss in this chapter are overwhelmed by the 'anxieties of indebtedness' they owe both to earlier novelists and to models of the press, and so become insecure about the status and genre of their works.³

Duroy's Duel

The 'Échos' written and generated by Duroy illustrate the much-discussed themes of repetition, copying, and duplicity which pervade Maupassant's text.⁴ A sequence of gradually fading reverberations of an original sound, the weakening power of the echo is counteracted in its journalistic definition, a column in the newspaper which reflects society gossip generates public interest, and can cause a stir. Edmund Birch's article on the way that *Bel-Ami* interrogates the nature and values of 1880s *actualité* draws connections between the act of being 'découvert' — uncovered as a news item, as well as undressed — between the various liaisons at work in Maupassant's novel and the practices of social discourse, including journalism. Birch's argument acts as a reminder that 'les échos [...] come to resemble precisely the kind of duplicitous language evident during the scene at the Café Riche'.[5] This restaurant scene, which sees Duroy dine with the Forestiers and Clotilde, connects linguistic play with suggestive flirting, 'ce fut le moment des sous-entendus adroits, des voiles levés par des mots, comme on lève les jupes, le moment des ruses de langage' (*BA*, 113) ('they had now reached the stage of artful suggestiveness, of words lifting veils like a hand lifting a skirt, the stage of plays on meaning'). Trevor Harris sees that:

> Maupassant's choice of a newspaper as the setting for much of his novel is especially suitable in that *La Vie française* is appropriate as a vehicle for Maupassant's satire on dishonest big business and as a context to accommodate a sustained reflection on language and its Protean properties', and that 'Les Echos' illustrate such commentary on language: 'expression is achieved by means of allusion rather than direct statement [...] In short, the language does not mean what it says'.[6]

The description of the role of the reporter in charge of the 'échos' ironically pre-empts the scene of Duroy's duel in its military terminology:

> L'homme qui les dirige et qui commande au bataillon des reporters doit être toujours en éveil, et toujours en garde, méfiant, prévoyant, rusé, alerte et souple, armé de toutes les astuces et doué d'un flair infaillible pour découvrir la nouvelle fausse du premier coup d'œil, pour juger ce qui est bon à dire et bon à celer, pour deviner ce qui portera sur le public, et il doit savoir le présenter de telle façon que l'effet en soit multiplié. (*BA*, 155)
>
> [The man in control of the column and in command of the legion of reporters must always be on the alert, always on his guard, distrustful, far-sighted, cunning, vigilant, and flexible, capable of every kind of guile and endowed with an infallible gift for uncovering a bogus news item at a glance, for judging what should be communicated and what should be kept quiet, for guessing what will make an impression on the public; and he must know how to present it in such a manner that its effect will be intensified.]

Although Duroy is considered to possess the 'rouerie native' [native cunning] necessary for such a key brief at the newspaper, his demeanour on the morning of the duel is hardly that of the vigilant and clear-sighted commander.

As these ironic repetitions would suggest, the duel scene which will cement Duroy's position as master of the 'Échos' is itself composed of echoes and copies. Unable to sleep through fear on the night before his planned combat, he examines his face in the mirror and fails to recognize himself — an echo of the earlier scene which saw him pause on the stairwell when visiting the Forestiers for the first time in his new clothes, momentarily stunned by his own alien reflection. Thoughts of morbidity cannot be shaken off: 'il avait ce visage creux qu'ont les morts et cette blancheur des mains qui ne remueront plus' (*BA*, 189) ('he had the sunken face of a corpse, and those white hands that will never move again'). Both the lack of colour and the reference to Duroy's hands (reinforced just a couple of lines later with a depiction of his trembling hands) are part of a network of echoing images throughout this text. The whiteness, which will be reflected in the frosty landscape through which Duroy will travel en route to his duel and in his pride in 'anaemic' vocabulary, is a recurring suggestion, associated with Duroy's status as something of a void. His struggles to put anything down on paper are given resonance by the text's repetition of whiteness as an emblem for blank pages, and Duroy's empty thoughts: his actions are sometimes reported alongside the inserted clause 'sans penser' [without thinking]. When commissioned to write his first article, on his time in Algeria, one of the only sentences he can bring himself to write is 'Alger est une ville toute blanche' (*BA*, 65) ('The town of Algiers is completely white'). Such anaemia is emphasized several paragraphs later when Duroy casts his mind around his room for inspiration and his gaze falls on 'la note de sa blanchisseuse' (*BA*, 66) ('his laundry bill'); this is a glimpse which suggests the vacuity associated with journalistic productions in the text. As will be discussed later in this chapter, there is the repeated implication, in texts of the period which offer commentary on journalism, that the late nineteenth century is an 'âge de papier', in which papers of all kinds — banknotes, newsprint, discarded scraps — are seen to blur; the blank page of Duroy's article is juxtaposed with his laundry bill as if the two were almost interchangeable. The note from the *blanchisseuse* is also a reminder of Duroy's debts, of the financial impetus to write, and of the superficiality of the demand to scrub up properly in order to progress in society.

The focus on Duroy's trembling, white hands also embeds the duel episode in a sequence of textual interconnections; Birch notes the prevalence of references to hands in the novel, suggesting that hands, as in Maupassant's short story 'La Main d'écorché', 'figure in his depiction of the paranoia of copy, an anxiety of influence which [...] refuses to leave the protagonist alone'.[7] The significance of such echoes is further reinforced through the symbolic references to 'glace' and 'miroirs' in the description of the icy landscape of the duel-scene: 'les arbres, vêtus de givre, semblent avoir sué de la glace' [the trees, decked out in frost, seemed to have sweated ice]; 'le ciel bleu paraît brillant à la façon des miroirs' (*BA*, 193) ('the blue sky is as bright as a mirror'). And indeed, the duel scene also highlights something of the anxiety of influence at work throughout Maupassant's novel, since the episode reads as a copy, both of duels which take place in Maupassant's own texts (notably the two short stories which feature duels, 'Un duel' and 'Un lâche'), and of those in other nineteenth-century novels. The farcical nature of the duel fought by Duroy is, in particular, an echo of the similar clash entered into by Flaubert's Frédéric, in *L'Éducation sentimentale*, which is also something of a damp squib; it ends with Frédéric's opponent, Cisy, collapsing in a faint and grazing his thumb in the process, with the result that the two men give up on their combat and 'se serrèrent la main, mollement' [shook hands, limply].[8]

The fact that Flaubert's *Dictionnaire des idées reçues* includes an entry under 'duel' is indicative of its formulaic status in nineteenth-century culture: 'DUEL. Tonner contre. — N'est pas une preuve de courage. — Prestige de l'homme qui a eu un duel' ('Thunder against it. It is no proof of a man's courage. Prestige of the man who has fought a duel').⁹ Flaubert's definition is an indication of the incongruity between the fact that the duel appears not to require courage, yet is able to elevate the prestige of the combatant. John Leigh's recent study of the duel in literature makes clear both the intertextual way in which literary representations of such combat are informed by earlier such models and the resulting understanding that these representations will come with fixed expectations; both the tortuous night before the duel experienced by the protagonists of both Flaubert and Maupassant, and the beauty of the morning on which the duel takes place, have their place in a codified pattern.¹⁰ The duel scene is composed of an echo-chamber of resonances, given comedic emphasis through the instruction that Duroy mutters to himself on no fewer than six occasions throughout the episode: 'quand on commandera feu, j'élèverai le bras' (BA, 194–95) ('when I hear the order to fire, I'll raise my arm').

Leigh discusses the duels which feature in Maupassant's two short stories, both of which were published at the time when he was also writing Bel-Ami. He contrasts the antagonism which takes prominence in 'Un duel' (1883), which sees the bourgeois Monsieur Dubois compelled to challenge a Prussian soldier who insults him on a train journey, with the rather different tone and outcome found in 'Un lâche' (1884), in which the protagonist is dismally unable to fight a duel he has engineered and opts for suicide instead. The opposition between two individuals in 'Un duel' becomes allegorical for the conflict between nations, albeit discussed by Leigh as necessarily unheroic.¹¹ The duel which never takes place in 'Un lâche', on the other hand, bears certain resemblances to the farcical duel scene in Bel-Ami. It becomes a study in narcissism, precipitated by an absurd encounter in an ice-cream parlour which leads Leigh to comment on the effects of mirroring caused by the references to 'une glace' [an ice-cream/mirror]. Leigh focuses on the reflexive verb 'se battre' in the tale:

> Ainsi, il allait se battre! Il ne pouvait plus éviter cela. Que se passait-il donc en lui? Il voulait se battre, il avait cette intention et cette résolution fermement arrêtées; et il sentait bien, malgré tout l'effort de son esprit et toute la tension de sa volonté, qu'il ne pourrait même conserver la force nécessaire pour aller jusqu'au lieu de la rencontre.¹²

> [And so he was going to fight! He could no longer avoid it. What then was happening to him? He wanted to fight, his intent and resolution were firmly decided and he felt certain that despite all the efforts of his spirit and the tension of his will, that he could scarcely even keep up the necessary strength to head out to the meeting-place.]

For the vicomte in 'Un lâche', the idea of 'se battre' becomes increasingly reflexive; instead of opposition with another, he turns on himself: 'and he does kill his man, in killing himself. Suicide would seem to be at once a product of cowardice and courage, which weep into each other, like two scoops of ice cream'.¹³

The ideas at work in this discussion of duels in Maupassant can be used to show that the duel in Bel-Ami is allegorical of a broader sense of conflict or opposition evoked by the text: the antagonism, or the illusory antagonism, between forms of writing, in particular between literature and the press. Leigh analyzes a short story which illustrates the duel as conflict, however 'grotesque', between Dubuis and the Prussian soldier. By the following year, 1884, when Maupassant was also writing *Bel-Ami*, this version of events has been countered by an inverted tale which sees the would-be dueller turn on himself in fear. This particular account has ramifications for the representation of the duel in the novel of the same period, and for the conflict I focus on, between the novel and the newspaper. Increasingly, the focus is on the sense of a lack of differentiation between the rival forces in the duel and — as in 'Un lâche' — of the idea of 'se battre', of the self turning on the self.

The mechanistic nature of the duel is illustrated in the preparations for Duroy's encounter with his antagonist. As his seconds count the steps between the two combatants and ready themselves for the firing of shots, 'il firent les mouvements du jeu de pile ou face, comme des enfants qui s'amusent' (*BA*, 195) ('they went through the motions of tossing for heads or tails, like children at play'). The risk to Duroy is rendered banal by these references to childish play, or to the ritual of a game, just as the world of the newspaper office itself is associated with the reporters' enjoyment of the game of cup and ball; or Duroy later suggests he can learn from Madeleine Forestier's sexual prowess by imitating the stance of a child learning a lesson. The reality of the news, or sexual relationships, or the moral threat of the duel are all reduced to programmed patterns of behaviour, with frivolous associations of play, and all three of these realms are interconnected through the imagery of childishness. The late nineteenth-century duel has been described as particularly formulaic: 'what had been a secret ceremony was turning into a theatrical stunt to attract notice'.[14]

The symbolic duel depicted in *Bel-Ami* employs repetition and structural echoes to reinforce the idea that Duroy and his adversary are as good as one and the same. Here is Duroy first noticing his opponent: 'Alors il aperçut un homme debout, en face de lui, tout près, un petit homme ventru, chauve, qui portait des lunettes. C'était son adversaire' (*BA*, 195) ('he saw a man standing opposite him, very close, a bald, pot-bellied little man wearing glasses. It was his adversary'). The order to fire comes — in an echoing voice, again underlining the notion of reverberation in this scene — and Duroy finds that 'il n'écouta rien de plus, il ne s'aperçut de rien, il ne se rendit compte de rien, il sentit seulement qu'il levait le bras en appuyant de toute sa force sur la gâchette. Et il n'entendit rien' (*BA*, 195–96) ('he listened to nothing more, he was aware of nothing more, he felt only that he was raising his arm and pressing as hard as he could on the trigger. And he heard nothing'). The emphasis on the nothingness perceived by Duroy here is reflective again of the blankness with which he is associated throughout the novel, and renders the duel itself particularly 'anaemic'. And then, once the shots are fired: 'il vit aussitôt un peu de fumée au bout du canon de son pistolet; et comme l'homme en face de lui demeurait toujours debout, dans la même posture également, il aperçut aussi un autre petit nuage blanc qui s'envolait au-dessus de la tête de son adversaire' (*BA*, 196) ('instantly he saw a small amount of smoke at the end of the barrel of his pistol; and, seeing that the man opposite was still standing upright, he noticed another little white cloud flying up over the head of his adversary'). The echoes and positioning of the 'homme [...] debout [...] en face de lui [...] adversaire' indicate that the passage sets a before-and-after glimpse of the shooting side by side, set apart almost as the duelling pair are set a fixed number of paces away from one another, but fundamentally paralleled in their construction. The replica puffs of smoke illustrate the nebulous quality of the encounter, and are resonant too of the earlier description of journalistic output as a series of puffs of smoke produced by the pen/cigarette of Madeleine Forestier as she dictates Duroy's article for him, a scene to which the final chapter of this book will return. Although the two men in the duel scene are presented as 'adversaires', the repetitive structures make them seem non-individualized, while the combat becomes little more than a puff of smoke.

As, in the earlier scene in which Madeleine turns Duroy's blank page into a sequence of smoke curlicues, creating something tenuous out of nothing, so Jacques Rival — his name evocative of the arbitrariness of tension and opposition in the text — writes up the duel by inflating the number of puffs of smoke involved. Duroy is surprised, on reading the account of his combat before it is inserted among 'les Échos', to see that he is described as having exchanged two bullets with his rival. Interrogating Rival about the claim, he is assured that 'Oui, une balle... une balle chacun... ça fait deux balles' (*BA*, 197) ('Yes, one shot... one each... that makes two shots'). The amplification of the 'deux balles' is itself echoed in the references to pairs which follow the publication of the gossip snippet about the duel. On touring the large newspaper offices and cafés the evening after the conflict in order to attract further publicity, the pair of duellers, Duroy and Langrement, meet 'deux fois', though refuse to shake hands, as they might have done had one of them been injured; Duroy then couples the inflated write-up of the event which his own account of it to Clotilde; 'il fit un récit dramatique' (*BA*, 197) ('he made a dramatic story of it'). There is the sense of a doubling which — as with the erroneous detail about the number of bullets fired by each man — is in fact substance-less. Ironically, the duel itself is a product of Langremont's barbed comments about Duroy's own journalistic hyperbole:

> Quand au reporter dont il s'agit, il ferait mieux de nous donner quelqu'une de ces bonnes nouvelles à sensation dont il a le secret: nouvelles de morts démenties le lendemain, nouvelles de batailles qui n'ont pas eu lieu, annonce de paroles graves prononcées par des souverains qui n'ont rien dit. (*BA*, 180)

> [As for the reporter concerned, he would do better to give us one of those sensational news flashes he alone can provide: reports of deaths denied the following day, news of battles that never took place, reports of momentous statements by sovereigns who have said nothing.]

The duel which becomes such a puffed-up non-event is occasioned by a critique of the nothings penned by Duroy; nothing engenders further nothingness.

The duel in *Bel-Ami* is clearly a representation of exactly the kind of industrial combat scorned by Maupassant in his article on the tradition. Writing critically and mockingly of the modern French version of the duel, he describes the kind of encounter entered into by Duroy:

> Et vraiment on ne sait quand prendra fin cette grotesque habitude d'aller se faire des piqûres à la main dans les environs de Paris, avec des baguettes d'acier

pointues qu'on agite éperdument au bout du bras, tandis que, la face pâle, les yeux agrandis, les lèvres pincées, on fait involontairement à son adversaire d'épouvantables grimaces.¹⁵

[And truly I do not know when that grotesque practice of going to prick one another in the hand on the outskirts of Paris will cease; it entails waving pointed steel rods around wildly around at arm's length, and making appalling faces at your opponent, all the while pale, wide-eyed and with pinched lips].

Although the sword-fight might have seemed logical and necessary in earlier ages, it has become, suggests Maupassant, little more than 'élégance', and he reserves his particular satire for the journalistic encounter: 'le duel pour la réclame, le duel entre journalistes' [the duel for publicity, the duel between journalists]. Often encouraged when the circulation rates of a newspaper are in decline, the duel is a way of boosting interest in a publication, and is carried out by reporters who might be better suited to gain renown through their ability to carry weapons than through any linguistic skill: 'il est infiniment drôle de voir ces spadassins de la phrase s'injurier comme des portefaix, jeter leur encrier, et dégainer des flamberges à la façon des soudards sans orthographe' [it is hugely amusing to see these swordsmen of the sentence insult one another like porters, hurl their inkpots and unsheathe their blades like drunkards who cannot spell].¹⁶ Maupassant's claim that the armed fight between journalists is thus encouraged as a way for newspaper men to 'se passer de talent' [do without talent] is reflected in the ridiculousness of the quarrel which leads Duroy into combat in the first place; it is related to his denial of a story published in *La Plume*, the paper which will be referenced in the closing stages of the text with the suggestion that Madeleine Forestier is now ghost-writing articles for one of its contributors, Jean Le Dol. *La Plume* has written up a story about an old woman's encounter with the vice squad; on looking into it, Duroy finds that it is yet another non-event, a squabble instead between the woman and her butcher over the weighing of 'deux livres de côtelette' [two pounds of cutlets] which turn out to be composed of scrap bones — another comical reference to a pair which is barely a pair at all. It is this banal encounter over scraggy meat which provokes the duel. Henri Mitterand notes that other novels of the period depict mortal combat, with the character Henri Mauperin killed in the Goncourts' *Renée Mauperin*; Zola's *Les Mystères de Marseille* also features a fatal duel.¹⁷ The textual version in *Bel-Ami*, though, is much more banal.

The textual nature of the duel is brought out in the description of the night that Duroy spends before the duel, when he reads the name of his opponent, Langremont, in the paper and stabs it with a pair of scissors: 'C'était stupide cette histoire-là! Il prit une paire de ciseaux à ongles qui traînaient et il les piqua au milieu du nom imprimé comme s'il eût poignardé quelqu'un' (*BA*, 188) ('This business was so stupid! He picked up a pair of nail scissors that lay there and dug them into the middle of the printed name, as if he were stabbing someone'). The banality of the eventual duel is juxtaposed with the viciousness of this attack on a 'morceau de papier' and a 'nom imprimé', an attack via the medium of paper. This duel scene echoes the antagonism established between forms of paper or writing in the text.

It is a facsimile of the moment in 'Un lâche' when the vicomte, contemplating the prospect of his duel, takes up a penknife and pricks the name of his would-be opponent, printed on a name-card ('comme s'il eût poignardé quelqu'un' [as if he were stabbing someone]). The attack on paper is emblematic of the non-event of the conflict and of the role played by textuality in the manufacture and dissemination of such conflict in *Bel-Ami*.

This discussion of the farcical, non-combative nature of the duel in *Bel-Ami* suggests that, as in 'Un lâche', it can be seen as narcissistic, an attack on the self. As Leigh summarizes, 'Fear divides the self in two, leaving it prey to an internalized battle'.[18] This fundamental focus on the self is evoked in tongue-in-cheek form in the very title of the article in *La Plume* which acts as the provocation for the duel in the first place. Entitled 'Duroy s'amuse', it has been suggested that this is a reference to Paul Bonnetain's 1883 novel about masturbation, *Charlot s'amuse*;[19] the duel is thus the product of an implicit reference to self-pleasuring rather than a coupling.[20] The evocation of this contemporary novel is indicative of *Bel-Ami*'s intertextual mirrors. It not only focuses its plot on the newspaper but incorporates reference to a number of publications of the period, as in the opening pages, when Duroy is described as resembling the 'mauvais sujet des romans populaires' [the ne'er-do-well of popular novels], suggested by Lethbridge as exemplified by the work of Georges Ohnet (*Le Maître des forges*, 1882) and Xavier de Montépin (*La Porteuse de pain*, 1884), in whose sentimental fictions the villain likely to seduce the innocent daughter of the house is characterised by a roguish charm.[21] Such intertextual resonances can be used to show how Maupassant's text acts as a reflection on the medium of the novel itself, considering its literary stance via a meditation on journalism and frequent references to alternative forms of the novel, and to predecessors such as Flaubert and Balzac. Ultimately, the gradations evoked between contemporary publications, whether novels or newspapers, can be seen to fade; as is the case with the duel, the rivalry between them is increasingly narcissistic. Rather than being separate entities, oppositions — such as that between novel and newspaper — bleed into one another in *Bel-Ami*, as in the image of the 'glaces' (ice creams and mirrors) in Leigh's discussion of 'Un lâche'.

Newspaper versus Novel: A Duel?

In literary representations and critical discussions of the relationship between novels and newspapers earlier in the nineteenth century, the dialogue between the two forms of discourse is often depicted as antagonistic. Birch notes the ways in which Maupassant's own journalism was critical of media hypocrisy, suggesting antagonism between his *chroniques* and a model of press-reporting which lacked epistemological confidence, particularly in relation to colonial knowledge: 'the novelist thus fights journalism with journalism'. *Bel-Ami*, serialized in the *Gil-Blas*, could be considered part of this fight.[22] In Balzac's *Illusions perdues*, the members of the artistic Cénacle are scathing in their contempt for the nefarious world of journalism as a form of trafficking in ideas and intellect; the would-be poet Lucien de Rubempré is faced with the choice between abiding by an aesthetic ideal or writing for the papers:

> Il ne se savait pas placé entre deux voies distinctes, entre deux systèmes représentés par le Cénacle et par le Journalisme, dont l'un était long, honorable, sûr; l'autre semé d'éceuils et périlleux, plein de ruisseaux fangeux où devait se crotter sa conscience.
>
> [He did not know where to position himself between two distinct paths, the two systems represented by the Cenacle and by Journalism: one of them was long, honourable and certain; the other perilous and strewn with pitfalls, running with murky streams in which his conscience could sully itself.][23]

Laurel Brake suggests that in Britain the nineteenth century saw, in a sense, the birth of 'literature' as a separate and seemingly sanctified notion. The creation of literature as a subject for study at university in the later years of the century was part of a move to establish it as an erudite entity with links to Classics. This was all a concerted effort to create a 'clear-cut dichotomy between literature and journalism', despite the fact that 'attempts to stress the divide [...] belied the involvement of almost all Victorian writers with the periodical press'.[24] As referenced in the introduction to this book, Terdiman envizages literature in nineteenth-century France as increasingly counter-discursive, encouraged to embody an oppositional stance faced with the growing ubiquity and banality of the newspaper industry, emblematic of 'dominant discourse self-confidently bodied forth'.[25] There is a necessary power struggle between literature and the press, each seeking to carve out a distinctive place within nineteenth-century culture. However, by the end of the century, this conflict had itself become so codified, so expected, that it had — like the duel — become formulaic, an 'élégance', as Marieke Dubbelboer notes in an examination of writers, the press, and income at the fin de siècle. She observes that 'the *Paris-Parisien* guide to Paris in 1899 [...] has a chapter entitled "Parisianismes", a list of useful phrases to use in polite society. One of the first listed is: "le journalisme écrase la littérature et la littérature s'en ressent"' [Journalism crushes literature and literature feels the effects of it].[26] The supposed crushing of literature by the dominant venality of the press had become a cliché, a rivalry as contrived and anaemic as Duroy's duel.

In an 1884 article, composed at the same time as *Bel-Ami* was being written, Maupassant suggested key differences between literary writers and journalists:

> L'observation du chroniqueur doit porter sur les faits bien plus que sur les hommes, le fait étant la nourriture même du journal [...]. Les qualités maîtresses du romancier qui sont l'haleine, la tenue littéraire, l'art du développement méthodique des transitions et de la mise en scène, et surtout la science difficile et délicate de créer l'atmosphère où vivront les personnages deviennent inutiles et même nuisibles dans la chronique qui doit être courte et hachée, fantaisiste, sautant d'une chose à une autre et d'une idée à la suivante sans la moindre transition.[27]
>
> [The journalist's observations must be based on facts rather more than on men, since facts provide the sustenance for the newspaper [...]. The main qualities of the novelist — suspense, literary standards, the art of crafting careful transitions between scenes, the care paid to setting and in particular that difficult business

of creating a background for characters — all of that becomes useless, even harmful, in the *chronique*, which must be short and pithy, gimmicky, leaping from one subject to another without worrying about the connections.]

Anne de Vaucher-Gravili describes Maupassant's ambiguous relationship with the press, arguing that he sees it as 'à la fois un produit industriel soumis au lois économiques du marché et une création intellectuelle qui doit répondre aux exigences du lecteur' [at one and the same time an industrial product at the mercy of market forces, and an intellectual creation which must meet the reader's demands].[28]

Critics, though, discuss his own innovations in writing for the newspapers, such as his increased embrace of reportage in the articles he sent back from Algeria.[29] Maupassant responded to colleagues who rejected his pessimistic representation of journalism in *Bel-Ami* with the article 'Aux critiques de "Bel-Ami"', claiming that Duroy is not a proper journalist and that *Vie française* was 'une de ce feuilles interlopes, sorte d'agence d'une bande de tripoteurs politiques et d'écumeurs de bourses, comme il en existe quelques-uns, malheureusement' [one of those dubious publications, put together by a gang of shady political dealers and pirate brokers, of the sort that exist nowadays, unfortunately]; claims have been made, though, that the portrait offers a depiction of *Gil Blas*, in which the novel was serialized.[30]

In contrast, discussions of literature draw attention to an aesthetic ideal, as in the preface Maupassant wrote for an edition of Flaubert's *Lettres à George Sand*, in which he praises Flaubert for being 'par-dessus tout, un artiste [...] De très grands écrivains n'ont pas été des artistes' [an artist above all else [...] There are great writers who have not been artists].[31] Despite evoking this ideal in such pieces, however, Maupassant tends to represent writers pessimistically in his works. This is the case with the 'vieux raté' in *Bel-Ami* itself, Norbert de Varenne. Daniel Sangsue asks: 'pourquoi faut-ils que les écrivains apparaissent, de plus, comme des petits gros, laids et sales?' [why must writers be depicted, for the most part, as short, fat, ugly and dirty?],[32] and concludes of the portrait of the writer across Maupassant's *œuvre*: 'les récits de Maupassant présentent donc une vision non seulement démythifiante, mais aussi démystificatrice de l'écrivain' [Maupassant's narratives thus not only serve to demythologize but also to demystify the figure of the writer].[33] Maupassant himself therefore helps to establish the notion of a divide between literature and journalism, but blurs it in his own literary works.

Gerald Prince's article on the literary self-consciousness at work in Maupassant's novel sees a clash of discourses characterize the text. Not only does the novel pit its own aesthetic endeavour against that of the newspapers; it forges a sense of conflict between the mundanities of a 'narrative' mode of writing and an artistic ideal, which may or may not be realizable in the novel itself. The title of Prince's piece, '*Bel-Ami* and Narrative as Antagonist', makes clear that this self-reflexive encounter is perceived as an opposition.[34] I would argue that, persuasive though Prince's argument is, the way in which *Bel-Ami* draws attention to the very act of opposition through the pivotal scene of the duel, yet also renders such opposition banal and pallid, would suggest that the antagonism evoked between discourses can ultimately be seen as further commentary on 'la vie française', the broad and satirical social comment evoked by the title of the newspaper in the text. Prince argues that 'in its affinity for repetition, its dependence on formula, fiction and falsehood, its manipulative concerns, its scantiness, its commercial nature, journalistic writing constitutes an important manifestation of the novelist's ultimate enemy: narrative (and the novel based on narrative)'.[35] He notes that Maupassant frequently and explicitly refers to narrative in *Bel-Ami*, via a number of instances of the verb *raconter* and associated nouns such as *conte* and *conteur*.

Vaillant's article on the shift towards narration in nineteenth-century journalism emphasizes the ways in which *raconter* as narration rather than argumentation came to dominate the press, and was seen 'comme une régression' [as a regression]; 'la culture de l'écrit serait phagocyté par un récit omniprésent et polymorphe, construit par la modèle journalistique du récit de reportage' [written culture would be swallowed up by an omnipresent and polymorphous narrative, built on the journalistic model of reportage].[36] He suggests:

> Ainsi voit-on [...] de la part d'intellectuels et d'écrivains attachés à la tradition lettrée [...] des stratégies de défense visant à disqualifier à la fois la vacuité du jeu médiatique, la fausseté de toute entreprise narrative et le triomphe des passions et des pulsions au detriment de la raison critique.[37]
>
> [And so we see strategies of defence on the part of intellectuals and writers attached to the literary tradition, aimed at discrediting the vacuity of the media world, the false nature of all narrative, and the triumph of passion and instincts at the expense of critical reason].

The strategies of defence evoked by Vaillant could include the subversion of conventional plot, as discussed by Prince in relation to *Bel-Ami*. In Maupassant's discussion of Flaubert's work, he distinguishes between artists and writers who are preoccupied by 'la chose racontée':

> Quand un homme, quelque doué qu'il soit, ne se préoccupe que de la chose racontée, quand il ne se rend pas compte que le véritable pouvoir littéraire n'est pas dans un fait, mais bien dans la manière de le préparer, de le présenter et de l'exprimer, il n'a pas le sens de l'art.[38]
>
> [When a man becomes preoccupied with the narrated event, when he does not realize that the true power of literature lies not in facts but in the manner of crafting, presenting and expressing them, then he has no artistic sense, no matter how talented he may be.]

The idea of plot is espoused by Duroy himself, suggests Prince — he is obsessed with endings and intrigues — and the association between this 'reptilian' character and the practice of plot indicates the vacuity with which such narrative teleology can be viewed in Maupassant's novel.[39] Instead, *Bel-Ami* itself incorporates features which could be argued to transcend conventional narrative and its chronology: 'By undermining closure, avoiding repetition, eschewing explanation, maintaining an impassive stance, and criticising the conventional orderings and developments of narrative, Maupassant's text aspires to equal these two works and defines itself as NOVEL'.[40] The two works Prince refers to in this quotation are the two moments in *Bel-Ami* which can, arguably, be seen as attempts to represent the idealized 'real' work of art which the novel itself hopes to emulate: the display of fencing attended by Duroy in Part Two of the text, and the Marcowitch painting of 'Christ marchant sur les flots' [Christ walking on water] displayed by editor Walter; both these render spectators silent, and thus seem to represent a resistance to banal interpretation.

Prince's argument is compelling in its suggestion that Maupassant challenges conventional narrative patterns as exemplified by journalistic writing and so attempts a move beyond *raconter*. Yet he acknowledges that such an attempt is, perhaps, impossible, that the text still adheres to a story of conventional ascent (symbolically represented by Duroy's stance on the steps of the Madeleine church in the closing sequence of the text), and that the text 'has the episodic quality of an adventure novel'.[41] The two scenes picked out by Prince as potentially representative of Maupassant's incorporation of an alternative aesthetic to that of telling a story, the painting and the fencing display, are themselves ambiguous. Both are envizaged against the characteristic backdrop of *Bel-Ami*, the faked natural landscape; the audience cram into a cavern decked with foliage for the occasion to watch the fencing, while Mme Walter faints in the heat of the conservatory in which the painting is kept.[42] The impressive performance put on by the two swordsmen is, before long, imitated by the hot and bothered spectators: 'ceux qui n'avaient jamais tenu un fleuret en leur main esquissaient avec leurs cannes des attaques et des parades' (*BA*, 287–88) ('people who had never handled a foil sketched lunges and parries with their walking sticks'). The idealized aesthetic is quickly copied, in a text which, as White notes, offers a 'cynical vision of recycled narratives'.[43] So even if offering a glimpse of aesthetic transcendence in a text bogged down in *raconter*, these two scenes are characterized by the fake, the copy, and pseudo-opposition in the theatricality of the display of swordsmanship.

To read *Bel-Ami* as a sequence of recycled narratives, as when Duroy regurgitates his own earlier article on Africa when *Vie française* is engaged in manipulating government policy on Morocco, is to become aware of the text's self-consciousness of its own status as an echo,[44] and as a particular echo of Balzac's *Illusions perdues*.[45] *Illusions perdues*, though, suggests — as in the idea of conflict noted above — the sense of a world in which values are shifting and ideals are being prostituted, as Lucien opts for writing for money rather than writing for aesthetic perfection. Yet it is still a world in which the ideal, represented by the members of the Cénacle, is juxtaposed with the fakes and copies which threaten to tarnish that ideal. In Maupassant's novel, the ideal itself has disappeared, reinforced by the acknowledgement in the text that Duroy 'n'avait pas lu Balzac' (*BA*, 92) ('had never read any Balzac'). Although characters around him recognize themselves and their acquaintances as seemingly Balzacian models ('est-il à la Balzac, celui-là?' (*BA*, 92) ('straight out of Balzac, isn't he?'); 'il a des mots à la Balzac, ce grigou' (*BA*, 91) ('the old skinflint says things straight out of Balzac')), Duroy's own mind is, again, blank when it comes to any perception of himself as having literary predecessors. In this way, he suggests the third stage of Baudrillard's procession of simulacra.[46] If *Illusions perdues* evokes the second stage, in which the sign is an unfaithful copy which 'masks and denatures' reality, but also harks back to the 'sacramental order' of the first stage, evoking nostalgia for the idea of the sign as a reflection of a profound reality, then *Bel-Ami* suggests the absence of that reality; Duroy's ignorance of Balzac is emblematic of his status as a copy with no original. Lethbridge evokes this connection between Maupassant and Balzac, arguing that 'Maupassant's art of illusion generates a fiction not about the loss of illusions — that clichéd nineteenth-century theme — but about their construction and their reality'.[47] Maupassant's 'vie française', emblematized by the newspaper, substitutes illusoriness itself for a world of lost illusions. Any sense of literature being different from other forms of writing is, itself, an illusion. Lloyd draws a connection between the illusory success associated with literature in the novel, and Maupassant's own essay on 'Le Roman', which defined gifted Realist writers as being 'illusionistes', capable of blurring the dividing line between the imaginary worlds of fiction and the reality outside that fiction; 'perhaps, like the illusionism of fiction which Maupassant defined [...], all literature and the success it brings is a mirage'.[48]

This idea is reinforced by Pinson's observation on *Bel-Ami*, that it represents a development in the depiction of the *écrivain-journaliste* in the nineteenth-century novel: the evolution being a diminution of the role of writing itself. As a reporter, Duroy is far less concerned with the practice of writing than with the idea of social advancement. Pinson asks:

> Est-ce dire que la fiction de la fin de siècle enregistre la perte d'influence de la littérature dans le monde médiatisé, qu'elle témoigne d'une forme de 'délittérisation' de l'imaginaire médiatique [...]. Je serais porté à penser qu'il s'agit là de l'un des savoirs essentiels de ces romans du journalisme.[49]

> [Does this suggest that fin-de-siècle fiction reflects the loss of the influence of literature in the journalistic world, that it is testament to a kind of 'delitter-arization' of the media imaginary [...]. I would be inclined to think that here lies one of the essential truths of these novels about journalism.]

He suggests that the political and financial concerns of the press are foregrounded instead of the act of writing, and that *Bel-Ami* anticipates the advent of the mass press and so of new methods of reportage. I would argue that such 'délittérisation' of the novel of journalism relates not only to the depiction of the press in such texts, but to fears, emphasized by Maupassant, of the debunking of literary value in a broader sense. The loss of illusions is associated with a loss of literature.

The Echoes of Duroy's Duel

Advertising the Newspaper Office

Duroy's role in *Bel-Ami* is to produce and edit the 'echoes', in a text which itself is composed of reverberating echoes of lost illusions, foregrounding its central protagonist as an echo ignorant of his own source. The remainder of this chapter will examine two further novels which, in echoing *Bel-Ami*, show how reverberations of the representation of journalism continue to sound, with the demarcation between literature and the press becoming ever more of an opposition-less duel at the turn of the century. Brulat's *Le Reporter* (1898) and Fenestrier's *La*

Vie des frelons (1908) both follow on from the depiction of the reporter figure found in earlier nineteenth-century texts; both evoke the *Bildungsroman* tradition in their focus on young aspiring male writers, obliged to turn hack for financial reasons.[50] Pinson's evaluation of the 'imaginaire médiatique' in fiction of the period sees the trajectory of such reluctant journalist characters divided into familiar stages. They are often 'déracinés' [rootless] (as in Maurice Barrès's novel of the same title, 1897):[51] 'l'apprenti journaliste traverse les mondes, les groupes, les journaux, sans se fixer nulle part, pratiquant parfois même "la vie du reporter errant"' [the apprentice journalist crosses worlds, groups, newspapers, without becoming fixed anywhere, sometimes even leading the life of a 'roving reporter'].[52] Their encounters with the press act as a form of social induction; they often end up witnessing or becoming embroiled in scandal, and their experiences frequently lead them to renounce journalism, or abandon their literary hopes: 'dans tous ces romans, la fin des illusions peut être considérée comme une forme de critique formulée à l'égard de la culture médiatique' [in each of these novels, the death of illusions can be considered a kind of criticism levelled at media culture].[53] Such characteristics can certainly be found in both the texts under discussion. As in *Bel-Ami*, both Fenestrier's novel and that of Brulat evoke opposition between the domains of press and literature, but eventually reflect the collapse of such dualities.

Le Reporter and *La Vie des frelons* contain prefaces which highlight the novels' positioning within a literary heritage, while focusing attention on their commitment to a representation of journalistic practices. Fenestrier's text both announces its debt to Flaubert's *L'Éducation sentimentale* and ironically celebrates the satirical representation of the game played by the journalists in the newspaper office in *Bel-Ami*:

> Depuis *L'Éducation sentimentale*, les jeunes provinciaux ont trouvé des moyens d'exercer leurs âmes et de conquérir Paris. Depuis *Bel-Ami*, époque heureuse du bilboquet, les journalistes ont marché: puissé-je contribuer modestement à montrer les progrès de ceux-ci, à signaler les raisons de ceux-là.[54]
>
> [Since the publication of *L'Éducation sentimentale*, young provincials have found ways of stirring their souls and conquering Paris. Since *Bel-Ami*, and the happy age of the *bilboquet*, journalists have been playing along; I aim to contribute in my modest way to depicting the progress of these figures and indicating their motives.]

Brulat's preface is dedicated to Zola, and insists on its debt to naturalism in its projected focus on truth; noting that numerous other professions have been subjected to the naturalist gaze, Brulat asks: 'pourquoi la presse échapperait-elle à l'enquête moderne?' [why should the press escape such current enquiry?].[55] He suggests that the press may consider itself above criticism, but defends the right of the 'écrivain libre' to subject it to scrutiny, arguing that 'elle (la presse) [...] a bec et ongle pour se défendre, tandis que ses victimes n'ont contre elle que des recours illusoires' [the press can defend itself tooth and nail, whereas its victims can only appeal against it but weakly] (p. 55). Here, then, he evokes right from the outset the battle between modern journalism and the naturalist literature which will be able to expose it.

Brulat's protagonist, Pierre Marzans, has just completed military service, and is first seen on a train heading towards Paris. This classic opening of a nineteenth-century *Bildungsroman* is enhanced by the intertextual references; Marzans has attempted to make his military service more bearable by reading passages of Flaubert and Balzac aloud to himself under his covers.

In *Bel-Ami*, Duroy first sees the offices of *Vie française* in the opening chapter. Columns of newsprint are spread out on the open panels of a glass door; the initial impression of the newspaper is acquired via an image of glass and light:

> Au-dessus de la porte s'étalait, comme un appel, en grandes lettres de feu dessinées par des flammes de gaz: La Vie Française. Et les promeneurs passant brusquement dans la clarté que jetaient ces trois mots éclatants, apparaissaient tout à coup en pleine lumière, visibles, clairs et nets comme au milieu du jour, puis rentraient aussitôt dans l'ombre. (*BA*, 37)

> [The words *La Vie française* were blazoned over the door like a challenge, spelt out in huge fiery letters by gas flares. The passers-by, moving abruptly into the brightness cast by these three dazzling words, would suddenly be bathed in light, as visible, clear and distinct as if it were the middle of the day, before quickly passing back into the shadows.]

This depiction reinforces the emphasis on mirrors and illusions in the text; the title of newspaper and the French society it evokes are composed of blazing gas flares, which alternately cause things to be seen illuminated or in shadow, evocative of the vagaries of news and its substance in the novel. The image also emphasizes the role of the office frontage, and the way it invites the reader to encounter the news by seeing it displayed in the glass of the window; it is an ambiguous evocation which suggests the transparency of the journalism at work, but also acts as a reminder that the façade is a prominent advertising tool for the paper, presenting its pages as spectacle first and foremost. Hannah Scott's focus on the representation of glass in French culture post-1870 draws attention to the ways in which writers, including Zola and Maupassant, associate this increasingly ubiquitous material with particular resonance; in Zola's retrospective depictions of the Second Empire, 'glass gains a doubly symbolic presence; first, as a symbol of the fantasmagoric commodity culture of Louis-Napoleon's new Paris [...]; and second, as a symbol evoking the terrible crises which befell that culture'.[56] Citing Baudrillard, Scott also highlights the ambiguities of the inside/outside dichotomy produced by the glass window display: 'la verre offre des possibilités de communication accélérée entre l'intérieur et l'extérieur, mais simultanément il institute une césure invisible et matériau, qui empêche que cette communication devienne une ouverture réelle sur le monde' ('glass offers faster communication between inside and outside, yet at the same time it creates an invisible caesura which prevents such communication from becoming a real opening onto the outside world at all').[57] The glass frontage of the newspaper offices in these *romans de journalisme* is characterized by these latent tensions of communicability and incommunicability, and fantasmagoria and threat.

This glimpse of the newspaper office in *Bel-Ami* is, in turn, reflected in Fenestrier's novel, when the protagonist Paul Toussaint, a relative newcomer to

Paris, passes the editorial bureau of the publication *Le Quotidien* and, along with an enraptured crowd, sees the front page of the paper emblazoned on the windows, admiring the view within:

> Ils contemplaient les machines à composer, ces admirables linotypes qui paraissent douées d'une pensée, et dont les bras prodigieux, sous la volonté d'un seul ouvrier, fondent, frappent et placent les caractères d'imprimerie. Ils admiraient les appareils télégraphiques où, sur de longs serpents, de papier bleu, se gravaient, avec un crépitement monotone, les vibrations des 'fils spéciaux'. (*La Vie des frelons*, p. 49)

> [They gazed at the composing machines, those admirable Linotype presses which almost seemed to have a mind of their own, with their prodigious arms, controlled by a single employee, placing and setting the printed letters. They were impressed by the telegraphic equipment, and the long rolls of blue paper unspooling, printing out the news from the wires with a monotonous rattle.]

The seeming organization and interconnectedness of the office induces a sense of Parisian pride: 'ils sentaient se composer à côté d'eux, et sous leurs pieds, la feuille qui leur donnait les "nouvelles du monde entier", la chère feuille, leur journal' [they sensed the sheet which would provide them with the 'news from around the world', their precious newspaper, being put together beside them, and beneath their feet] (pp. 49–50).

A similar scene is found in *Le Reporter*, when Pierre Marzans takes a night-time walk around Paris, and is struck by the frenzied activity of the printing presses in a newspaper office. Through the 'vitrage', he sees:

> La mise sous presse des journaux qui, à l'aube, devaient pleuvoir par milliers d'exemplaires sur Paris. L'atelier, dans le flamboiement du gaz, projetait une lueur fauve sur la chaussée et les maisons voisines. D'un carreau brisé s'échappait, par bouffées tièdes, cette odeur âcre de papier et d'encre d'imprimerie, portant en elle comme l'effervescence d'une production fiévreuse, la fermentation de cerveaux surchauffés. (*Le Reporter*, p. 91)

> [The newspapers going to press, which, at dawn, would flood Paris with their copies. In the light of the gas flares, the printing shop cast a tawny light over the pavement and the neighbouring houses. Through a crack in a broken pane of glass there wafted, in lukewarm gusts, that bitter odour of paper and printers' ink, carrying with it the frenzy of feverish production, the fermentation of overheated brains.]

Echoing the flickering gas flames and shadows of the offices in *Bel-Ami* (and reminiscent, too, of the 'odeur étrange, particulière, inexprimable, l'odeur des salles de rédaction' (*BA*, 37) ('strange, unique, indescribable smell, the smell of a newsroom') detected when Duroy enters the building), this scene strikes Marzans not as indicative of the mechanization of newspaper-copy production, but instead as an illustration of the power associated with the impressive reach of the massed piles of paper. This can be contrasted with the scene in George Gissing's *New Grub Street* (1891), in which Marian Yule sits in the reading room at the British Museum, making notes for her father's research, oppressed by the volumes of books and evidence of literary output around her.[58] She compares herself to a machine — 'a machine has no business to refuse its duty' — and idealizes a pre-industrial age when she might have been encouraged to go out and labour with her hands. Marzans instead senses 'cette puissance de la lettre imprimée, puissance terrible, maîtresse de l'opinion' [that power of the printed word, a dreadful power, governing opinion] and feels renewed within himself the urge to write, 'de prendre la plume, de noircir des feuillets, d'entasser des volumes' [to pick up his pen, scribble on sheets of paper, to pile up volumes] (p. 92). For both Marzans and Toussaint, the initial impressive view of the newspaper office will eventually seem but an illusion, once they are inducted into the banalities of writing up copy. These three scenes — from *Bel-Ami*, *Le Reporter*, and *La Vie des frelons* — suggest the intertextual echoes between the novels, reinforced by the fact that the editor of one of the papers featured in *Le Reporter*, the *Appel du matin*, is called Saint-Potin, as if in homage to the reporter of the same name in *Bel-Ami*.

These interconnected scenes also draw attention to the image of the newspaper as spectacle, using gas and glass as a means of self-promotion, and inducing an illusory sense of transparency. Guy Debord's comments in *Society of the Spectacle* can be applied to the depictions of the newspaper in the window in these texts. He observes that 'the spectacle presents itself simultaneously as society itself, as a part of society and as a *means of unification*. As a part of society, it is the focal point of all vision and all consciousness'. Debord argues that 'in societies dominated by modern conditions of production, life is presented as an immense accumulation of spectacles. Everything that was directly lived has receded into a representation'.[59] *Le Reporter* offers a particularly vivid depiction of this degenerative trend, in the attention paid by Marzans to the windows offering a view onto the printing presses, witnessing the 'modern conditions of production' as spectacle. The attempts to promote the newspaper by positioning it in the glass windows of the newspaper offices, or to showcase the production of copy in *Le Reporter* are efforts to simulate social interaction and to foreground the role of the press in uniting the public around a conception of shared common knowledge, as noted in Anderson's *Imagined Communities*, cited in the Introduction. Yet in the scenes in question, the would-be journalist is positioned outside the window, looking in, and Debord's analysis of the 'culmination of separation' announced by the advent of the spectacle is again of relevance: 'due to the very fact that this sector is separate, it is in reality the domain of delusion and false consciousness: the unification it achieves is nothing but an official language of universal separation'.[60] Even once the spectator in these *romans du journalisme* enters the office and becomes part of the production of the spectacle itself, the newspaper, the resultant impression is one of disillusionment at the idealized notion of 'unification'; the offices are instead 'domains of delusion'. Reinforcing the role of the newspaper in the advertising industry, and anticipating these texts' postmodern concerns, *Le Reporter* features a vignette of a newspaper mogul called Goguel, who aims to 'couvrir la France d'affiches, étourdir les gens de réclame, faire les choses en grand' [cover France in posters, to stun the public with advertising, to do things on a grand scale] (p. 132). As will be discussed later in this chapter, Goguel will eventually produce and advertise a publication called the *Universel* — an ironically named journal which incarnates the sense of social cohesion named as fallacious by Debord. Instead, Goguel's production is arguably evocative of the 'universal separation' announced in *Society of the Spectacle*.

Journalism and the Death of the Author

At the outset of both *Le Reporter* and *La Vie des frelons*, the protagonists consider literature as their ideal goal. The opposition between literature and journalism is, initially, palpable. In Brulat's text there is the echo of the duel scene in *Bel-Ami*, when Pierre Marzans challenges another journalist to combat over their shared interest in the young muse Méryem — although the futility of the conflict is also acknowledged here, 'entre journalistes, on ne se fait jamais grand mal' [journalists never really hurt one another when they duel] (p. 182). The antagonism between the press and a more ideal aesthetic is at its height when Marzans is introduced to the former journalist-turned-painter Lavertal, whose eclectic home even evokes the concept of battle; decorated with portraits of famous literary figures including Rabelais and Montaigne, it is also 'un véritable arsenal', adorned with firearms and swords. Lavertal has become jaded after ten years of the 'lutte' that is an attempt at social advancement through journalism, and so has — as illustrated in the opening lines of this book — retaliated by devoting himself to faking news.

A conversation early in *Le Reporter* sets out the threat represented by the newspaper. Marzans elaborates on his own optimistic theory of the novel, arguing not only that it still has a place, but that, after adventure novels which appeal to the masses, and naturalist novels offering an 'étude de mœurs' [study in morals], there is still scope for innovation in the novel-form; he has an ideal of a 'roman d'idées, s'élevant aux vues générales, synthétisant, mettant en action la morale et la philosophie' [novel of ideas, being taken up as popular views, bringing together philosophy and morals and putting them into action] (p. 20). His views are rebutted by his new journalist acquaintances, Passeriot and Cabestan, who maintain that there is already a surplus of books and that newspapers are suffocating novels: 'c'est ce papier-là qui tuera le livre. Il n'y a plus aujourd-hui, pour lire des romans, que les concierges, les femmes qui s'ennuient et les voyageurs qui ne peuvent dormir en chemin de fer' [it is that paper which will kill off the book. These days only caretakers, bored housewives and travellers who cannot sleep on train journeys read novels] (p. 21). Cabestan also comes out with the *Illusions-perdues*-esque mantra that 'le journalisme [...] c'est la mort de l'écrivain' [journalism [...] is the death of the writer]. In *La Vie des frelons*, Paul Toussaint's early aspirations of a career in Letters see him associating literature with cleanliness and purity, albeit in rather woolly terminology: 'Ce mot de "littérature" n'avait dans sa bouche qu'une signification très vague. Il paraissait embrasser, préserver de la boue tout ce qui n'était pas affaires, industrie ou commerce' [That word 'literature' only meant something very vague to him. It seemed to bring together all that was not business, industry or commerce, and keep it from being sullied] (p. 10). Yet when Toussaint heads off to Paris where he finds accommodation in a Montmartre apartment with an old classmate, the literary scene he finds is distinctly murky: the apartment is squalid, full of dirt, greasy saucepans, and pornographic artworks. And unlike the journalists, whose language, as will be seen, is envizaged as crisp and clear, Toussaint's Montmartre acquaintances indulge in conversation which he finds difficult to follow — a fact which acts as a comment both on the pretentiousness of the literary set and Toussaint's own naïve incomprehension. The would-be writers are hypocritical too, scathing of journalism while muddying the waters by dabbling in its practices: the aesthete Ravesenne submits a weekly article to an international review.

The rivalry between literature and the press in these novels is emphasized by an old schoolfriend of Toussaint in *La Vie des frelons*, who stresses the gap between the two professions or domains, privileging the order and accuracy of the new journalism at the expense of a literature which is made to seem dated. This former classmate, Jehu, who has already risen through the ranks of the popular daily paper, *Le Quotidien*, makes clear that journalism and literature are no longer to be seen as intersecting dimensions of a writing career: 'Le journalisme, mon ami, le journalisme tel que notre époque l'a fait, n'a rien de commun avec la littérature. Depuis moins de dix ans, il s'est produit, dans les mœurs parisiennes, une révolution' [Journalism, my friend, the journalism as produced by our generation, has nothing in common with literature. For ten years now, there has been a revolution in Parisian customs] (p. 74). The newspaper is no longer 'une école des belles-lettres' [a literary school]. Jehu is referring to the new model of journalism, described in the Introduction, which has become more and more commercial, producing increasing pages of print and incorporating a very different emphasis, a shift from the literary journal of the nineteenth century to an era of reportage. For Dupont, Head of News at *Le Quotidien*, reportage is the superior form of writing: 'Le journalisme, pour lui, se résume en des formules intangibles hors desquelles il n'est point de salut. Il méprise la littérature, journalisme des impuissants et des ratés, et n'admet pas d'autre style que le sien' [For him, journalism comes down to a set of words and phrases beyond which there lies no salvation. He despises literature, that journalism produced by the weak and the unsuccessful, and allows no other style than his own] (p. 100). Dupont made his name as a reporter by slipping into the house of a girl drowned in the Seine and taking notes by her coffin, then chastising the girl's father for making a noise so close to the dead when he angrily objected to the intrusion of the journalist.

The initial impression of journalism in Fenestrier's novel is one of order, precision, and a cleanliness which contrasts with the grease of literary Montmartre. In the scene referenced above, when Toussaint passes the offices of *Le Quotidien*, he is overwhelmed by its relationship with pride, efficiency, and professionalism:

> Toussaint avec les autres avait suivi d'un œil envieux les allées et venues des reporters qui, graves, pleins d'importance, l'orbite vitrée d'un monocle, la boutonnière fleurie d'un ruban, traversaient le hall et passaient vite, fendant la foule de gestes autoritaires. Être de ceux-là! Dicter sa pensée à tout Paris! Avoir chaque jour un contingent certain de cinq cent mille lecteurs! Quel rêve! Le journalisme n'était-il pas le vestibule de la gloire, l'antichambre de l'Académie, la serre chaude des grandes relations et des utiles influences? Mais comment y parvenir? De quel pontife se recommander pour être admis dans ce tabernacle? (*La Vie des frelons*, p. 50)

[Along with the others, Toussaint had watched the comings and goings of the reporters enviously, as they crossed the vestibule and passed by quickly, cleaving through the crowd authoritatively, serious, important-looking, one eye screened by a monocle, buttonholes decorated with ribbons. To be one of those! Announcing your thoughts to the whole of Paris! To have a certain readership of some five hundred thousand every day! What a dream! Journalism was the pathway to glory, a means of admission to the Academy, a hothouse of important relationships and key influences, was it not? But how to access it? What priest should he approach in order to be admitted into this temple?]

The images of glass in this description — the monocles of the well-dressed journalists and the 'serre chaude' — reflect the gleam and polish associated with the newspaper world, and indicate the sense of clarity with which the reporters seek to comment on events. Yet such images also evoke ambiguity, as will be suggested in Chapter Three; the presence of the monocles suggests an imperfect, and at best one-eyed, view of the world, while the 'serre chaude' echoes the artificiality of the conservatories in *Bel-Ami*. The impact that such a popular daily newspaper can have on the wider world is revealed through Toussaint's initial impressions, which are gained the day before a military parade and competitive cycle race is due to take place, organized and sponsored by *Le Quotidien*. The newspaper is placed in a position of authority which apparently transcends that of the army: 'voici qu'un journal prétendait faire marcher l'armée' [here is a newspaper which claims to run the army]. Almost military in its organization and regulation, and quasi-religious, as suggested in the metaphor above which connects the newspaper offices with a 'tabernacle', the impression of the press offered by Fenestrier's novel is initially one of polished glass, order, and power. Such ideas are anticipated, too, in Pierre Marzans's glimpse of the printing presses and the spread of the written word they engender in *Le Reporter*.

'Le plus effroyable désordre de papiers': Journalism and Literature Blurred

As Toussaint is inducted into the life of a journalist, the conflict between the well-oiled machine of the press and a seemingly outdated literature becomes less clear-cut. From the moment of Toussaint's initiation into the realm of the paper, there emerges an insight into the working patterns of a reporter which indicates that the realities of employment at such a paper are far removed from clarity and organization. A murkier world of journalism is revealed, while the realms of literature and reportage become blurred. This blurring effect can be seen not only overtly and thematically but, as will be shown, in examples of style and structure, with the narrative voice itself becoming muddied. In *Le Reporter*, too, the intersections between literature and the press become particularly prevalent via the emphasis in the text on the relatively new journalistic practice of the interview. Although difficult to say exactly when it appeared in the French press, the term 'interview' itself was used from 1884 onwards. Jean-Marie Seillan notes that although there were misgivings about the perceived Americanization of the practice of the interview, which retained its English label, it could also be seen as a move towards the democritization of the newspaper.⁶¹ In Brulat's text, Marzans is sent to interview a stalwart of the literary scene, Robur, an echo of Zola. The representation of this interview illustrates the hybridity of the novel itself, which draws on intertextual resonances of Zola's novels, and on his frequent role as interviewee in the late nineteenth-century press. Jules Huret's memoirs of his life as a journalist feature interviews with Zola, one of which is a discussion of Zola's failures at the *baccalauréat*; Huret's technique is to introduce the interview briefly before handing over 'parole' to Zola himself.⁶²

Robur is described as a novelist who has had a particular impact on Marzans; a writer both feted and reviled, who has had to battle for some fifteen years before achieving literary success, his career trajectory is an echo of that of Zola. The implicit connection between Brulat's fictional character and the real-life writer is brought out through Marzans's reminiscence about going to see a play based on one of Robur's novels, and then wandering the streets of Paris in awe at what he has seen: he wanders towards the 'quartier de la Goutte d'Or', the setting for Zola's *L'Assommoir*. Advised by the young painter's model, Méryem, to go and interview Robur since 'on débute maintenant dans le journalisme par un interview de Robur' [these days you launch yourself into journalism by going to interview Robur] (p. 58), when he gets to Robur's apartment block, Marzans is overcome with nerves. The result is that Robur senses his fear, and that although he normally speaks almost without interruption when being interviewed, he takes pity on Marzans and 'se décida à l'interroger, renversant les rôles, interviewant l'interviewer' [decided to question him, reversing the role, interviewing the interviewer] (p. 66). This decision to 'renverser les rôles' produces an inversion in the novel itself, which devotes space to a dialogue in which Robur interrogates Marzans about his origins and his literary ambitions. The interview — already discussed disparagingly in the text by jaded journalist characters — is therefore incorporated into the novel, albeit in a form which amalgamates novel and newspaper by having the fictional writer ask questions of the would-be reporter. In itself, the interview is a hybrid form: 'l'interview est un énoncé paradoxal. Forme hybride, à double voix et double signature (l'interviewé dans le titre, l'interviewer au bas de l'article), elle ne sauvegarde la voix qu'elle recueille qu'en la brouillant' [the interview is a paradoxical expression. It is a hybrid form, dual-voiced and signed by two names (the interviewee in the title, the interviewer at the end), it only saves the voice it records by blurring it].⁶³

This blurring is made particularly evident in Brulat's text. A snippet of interviewing practice is inserted amidst the echoes of Zola's own novels, as in the reference to *L'Assommoir*, and the subsequent advice as how best to succeed as a literary writer: 'le travail est le remède, l'unique salut' [work is the remedy, the only salvation] (p. 68). The critique of journalism voiced earlier in *Le Reporter* is that it is 'un sale métier' [a grubby profession] because:

> Ils ne prennent plus maintenant que des interviews. La plus grosse sottise, placée dans la bouche d'autrui, captive le public. Quant à nous, nous ne sommes que des enregisteurs, nous n'avons pas le droit d'avoir un opinion. Le reporter gagne sa vie bien plus avec ses jambes qu'avec sa plume. (*Le Reporter*, p. 18)

[These days they only carry out interviews. The public are captivated by the most facile nonsense when voiced by other people. For our part, we do little more than record, we do not have the right to an opinion. A reporter earns his living far more with his legs than he does with his pen.]

This is given ironic representation in the novel via this inverted form of the interview, which makes Zola/Robur himself an 'enregisteur', and Marzans a feeble interviewee.[64] The eventual interview, written up enthusiastically by Marzans, is printed on the front page of the *Appel au peuple*, but has been subjected to considerable editing: 'toutes les fioritures de son style avaient été impitoyablement biffées; c'était sec et aride' [all his stylistic embellishments had been mercilessly expunged; it was now as dry as dust] (p. 71).

Matthew Rubery discusses Henry James's scornful attitude to journalism, and to the practice of interviewing as an intrusion of privacy in particular.[65] His analysis of James's *The Reverberator* sees it as a novel which lays the blame for such new exposure of private life less at the door of journalism than with those who willingly seek publicity, and with a public keen to read the revelation of secrets. Rubery examines the ways in which James draws attention to parallels between the act of interviewing and the act of reading fiction, in that both expose for an implied reader a set of statements, as well as hints as to what is not being said:

> We are asked to approach the interview with the same hermeneutic sophistication with which we would analyze dialogue in a novel — particularly a Jamesian novel in which character emerges gradually through what is said as well as what is *not* said. This careful distinction reflects James's awareness of how close his own role as author could be at times to that of the journalist writing about other people's private conversations.[66]

The scene of the journalistic interview in Brulat's novel also gives rise to comment on ironic parallels between the novel and the press. Robur's scrutiny of Marzans, although presented as benign and even benevolent, sees him assign Marzans a place among the host of literary wannabes of the sort he encounters frequently. On hearing Marzans's answers to his interviewer's questions:

> Robur avait tout deviné, avant même que Pierre eût réédité cette commune histoire de l'adolescent pauvre, épris de gloire et fraîchement débarqué à Paris, avec la fièvre de la conquérir [...] il en avait tant vu de ces jeunes, tourmentés d'ambition littéraire, ne doutant de rien! La plupart étaient des simples bêtes, quelques-uns promettaient du talent et tous, presque tous, au bout de quelques années, grossissaient la classe lamentable des dévoyés, dont fourmillait le pavé de Paris. (*Le Reporter*, p. 67)

> [Robur had guessed everything, even before Pierre had repeated that familiar story of the poor adolescent, infatuated with glory and newly arrived in Paris, with the burning desire to conquer the city [...] he had seen so many of these youngsters, tormented by literary ambition, doubting nothing! The majority of them were simply fools, some showed signs of talent and all, almost all of them, would swell the ranks of those who had been led astray; Paris was swarming with them.]

Robur's playacting as journalist unpicks any individuality of the central protagonist of the novel, predicting his future and proleptically writing the ending of Brulat's own text (Marzans will, partly due to the recommendation and support of Robur, publish a novel, but he will be quickly disillusioned by the pressures of the literary marketplace). By having interviewer turn interviewee, then, the resultant irony of this scene is that it emphasizes the text's awareness of its own status as derivation, as it 'réédit cette commune histoire'.

In his novel, Fenestrier shows that the gap between literature and journalism is much narrower than either faction will appear to admit. The newspaper relies on practices established by the novel. Fiction is central to the business of reporting the facts, a point highlighted by Thérenty, who observes that the boundaries on the printed page between, for example, the news report about crime and the serialized fiction on the same page were often not clearly demarcated:

> Les distinctions pratiques entre fiction (récit d'un fait imaginaire), témoignage (narration d'un fait observé) et les différents régistres de la fictionalisation (récit d'un fait vrai comme s'il s'agissait d'un fait fictive ou récit d'un fait vrai illustré par un fiction) se révèlent difficiles.[67]
>
> [The distinctions to be made between fiction (the telling of an imagined fact), testimony (telling of an observed fact) and the different levels of fictionalization (telling a true fact as if it were fictional, or telling a true fact illustrated by fictional qualities) becomes difficult.]

This is indicated by a scene in which the *faits-diversiers* employed by *Le Quotidien* in *La Vie des frelons* relay their findings: ' "Empoisonné par des champignons? C'est usé, archi-usé! Remplacez les champignons par le canard à la rouennaise; voilà de l'actualité!" ' [Poisoned by mushrooms? That's hackneyed, more than hackneyed! Replace mushrooms with pressed duck; there's news for you!] (p. 96). Skilled reporters are able to compose articles referred to as 'ces petits romans de vingt lignes qui savent émouvoir la fibre sentimentale du lecteur' [those little twenty-line novels capable of stirring the sentiments of the reader]. The text suggests a muddying of distinctions between all forms of writing. The narrative voice makes clear the connections between two apparently different sets, the bohemian writers and the hack journalists:

> Comme les bohêmes de Montmartre, les reporters du boulevard sont des révolutionnaires de la pensée, des conquérants de la littérature et des arts: et comme eux, frelons pilleurs, ils enveloppent les ruches de leurs essaims turbulents et tuent les abeilles, souillent le miel, salissent le travail. (*La Vie des frelons*, p. 118)
>
> [Like the bohemians of Montmartre, the reporters of the boulevards revolutionize thought, conquer literature and the arts: and like them, like plundering hornets, they surround the hives in their rowdy swarms and kill the bees, spoil the honey, sully the profession.]

La Vie des frelons showcases the growing gap between the newspaper and the novel, yet also suggests that despite these developments, reporters and literary writers are fundamentally alike in their pillaging, in their pollution of an idealized artistic 'miel' or 'travail'. References are fleetingly made to famous literary names, inserted into the text to show the way that they are under attack from the writer-reporting 'frelons'; one journalist manages to sustain himself financially and pay for the maintenance of a mistress by writing pornography and plagiarizing Rabelais and Voltaire.

What *La Vie des frelons* offers is a glimpse of the intersecting worlds of newspapers and novels at the turn of the century, suggesting that the two spheres converge chaotically, producing a wealth of printed matter. In a letter in the novel, the experienced journalist Rogeot makes clear the shift from literary dignity to dilution: 'Nous ne faisons pas, comme nos prédécesseurs, des articles, mais des "papiers", et l'usage courant de ce terme indique assez en quelle estime on tient le fruit de notre travail' [We do not produce articles, like our predecessors, but 'papers', and the fashionable use of this term is sufficient indication of the extent to which the fruits of our labour are valued] (p. 126). Articles and novels have given way to 'paper'. This reductive analysis of all literary or journalistic output as mere 'paper' is also made in the title of Charles Legrand's *L'Âge de papier* of 1889, in which parallels are drawn between newspapers and banknotes: the journalist character muses on the article he has been commissioned to write as he enters the Bourse where he finds 'que de petits papiers griffonnés, brandis, échangés, jetés dans la corbeille!' [so many scraps of paper, scrawled on, swapped, thrown in the wastepaper basket].[68] In several scenes, *La Vie des frelons* gives visual impetus to this sense of textual debris. In the Montmartre apartment of the literary devotee, Ravesenne, a newspaper lies amid the grease and clutter; when Toussaint penetrates the inner offices of *Le Quotidien* he finds scenes which contrast with the newspaper's pristine appearance on the boulevard. There are desks overflowing with printed matter, whether it be in Jehu's domain, ('des documents, des dossiers, des piles de brochures jonchaient le sol) [documents, folders, piles of pamphlets were strewn over the floor] (p. 56); or in the office of the Head of Information, Dupont, there is 'le plus effroyable désordre de papiers blancs et verts, de revues et de journaux' [the most incredible mess of white and green paper, of periodicals and newspapers] (p. 81). In *Le Reporter*, too, there are piles of *paperasses*, the previous day's papers, crowding the floor. This confusion of papers, reviews, and newspapers reflects the nature of Fenestrier's novel itself. *La Vie des frelons* is encumbered with different manifestations of printed matter, incorporating snippets of *faits divers*, letters from Toussaint's colleagues, and pages from Toussaint's diary.

Toussaint's diary entries are included in the novel from the point at which he is taken on by the *Le Quotidien* and begins to understand what it is to be a journalist in the first decade of the twentieth century. While the first half of the novel views him from the detached stance of the third person narrator, the second half — which indicates the way the newspapers borrow from fiction, and which makes clear that journalism is not the glossy new profession Jehu claims it to be — adopts a more heterogeneous flavour, interspersing Toussaint's own observations with the narrator's comments. Not only, then, does *La Vie des frelons* provide a first-hand account of journalistic life; as the novel gets closer to opening up the world of the newspaper, so it starts to borrow journalistic traits. Toussaint's daily diary entries reflect the desire to record the material of the everyday heralded by the title of *Le Quotidien*. The introduction of the first-person voice which accompanies the observations of the previously anonymous narrator suggests the properties of polyphony and the increasing preference for the first-hand account which characterize the newspaper. These properties are discussed by Thérenty, who refers to the emphasis on the *je* in nineteenth-century journalism: 'malgré ses ambitions collectives, le journal dit *je* tout au long du XIXè siècle' [despite its ambitions towards collectivity, the newspaper uses 'I' throughout the 19th century].[69] She also comments on the newspaper as a collective of voices: 'Le journal constitue également une entreprise collective où s'expérimente la création du sens par fusion de voix plurielles et quelquefois discordantes. Bien plus que le roman, il est conçu comme un lieu authentique de la polyphonie' [the newspaper also offers a model of a collective enterprise, trialing the creation of meaning as put together by multiple and at times discordant voices. The newspaper is the authentic space of polyphony, much more so than the novel].[70] The heterogeneity of voice in both newspaper and novel intrinsically connects these Bakhtinian polyglossic enterprises.[71]

Increasingly both polyphonic and personal, the structure of *La Vie des frelons* begins to imitate the patterns of the newspaper at the point when the novel begins to suggest more overtly that literature and journalism have much in common. The text is divided into two halves. The first details Toussaint's attempts to fix on a career, his arrival in Paris, his stay in Montmartre, and his first glimpses of the newspaper offices. The second part takes up the account of his time at the paper. This divide is marked by a shift in voice. As soon as Toussaint begins working at the paper, a new chapter begins, with the sub-heading, 'Le Journal d'un journaliste', playing on the etymological connections between the intimate act of diary-writing and the public display of the newspaper. From this point onwards in the novel, the voices become more heterogeneous; the text fluctuates between third person omniscience, free indirect style, and Toussaint's diary entries. Letters too are introduced in this second half; one short chapter is entirely taken up by a letter written by the cynical journalist Rogeot. The voice changes in almost every chapter from the middle of the novel onwards, as if the reader is confronted with a different 'article', penned by a different reporter. At one point Toussaint gives up on his diary as he can no longer bear to confess his guilt at the sordidness of his chosen career; almost immediately afterwards the reader is once again immersed in the pages of his journal, so compulsive is Toussaint's writing habit, so imperative the need to confess, and so changeable the narrative voice by this point in the text.

Alongside the changes in voice are inserted examples of journalistic style and even layout. One reporter comes up with a jokey 'Manuel du parfait journaliste' [Manual for the perfect journalist]; a set of formulae covering the different sorts of *faits-divers* and satirizing the ubiquitous style of reportage:

> A la rubrique SUICIDE AU REVOLVER:
> Un suicide, dont les causes paraissaient encore mal définies... Au bruit de la détonation, les voisins accourent: on enfonce la porte; un horrible, affreux, ou navrant spectacle s'offre à leurs yeux. — Gisant dans une mare de sang... — L'arme dont s'était servi le malheureux pour exécuter son sinistre projet fumait encore... — Une lettre laissée en évidence, sur la table [...] On se perd en conjectures sur... etc. (*La Vie des frelons*, p. 106)

[Under the heading: Suicide with a revolver... A suicide, the causes of which are still unclear. At the sound of the gunshot, the neighbours come rushing, they break open the door: a horrible, dreadful or distressing sight meets their eyes. Lying in a pool of blood... the weapon used by the victim to carry out his macabre plan still smoking... A letter left as evidence on the table [...] There is much speculation about... etc..]

The ellipses here reflect both the abruptness of the *fait-divers* tone and the spacing of a newspaper page. The second half of Fenestrier's novel imitates devices at work in the newspaper: the patchwork effect of different reportorial voices set side-by-side, the up-to-dateness of the diary entry reflecting the demand for immediacy, the fragmented typographical appearance of the *faits-divers*. The effect created is one of both diversity and uniformity, as in the above example of Tuquet's 'manual' with its implications of repeated formulae. This dual effect is a further reflection of the newspapers of the time, which attempted to unite both polyphony and uniformity, to gather together the different voices of their reporters under an umbrella title offering a particular political or social slant on the world.

Polyphonic diversity in the novel is accompanied by the increasing awareness of similarity between the voices. Toussaint's diary indicates a blurring of the boundaries between different forms of writing. The voice of the character and the voice of the narrator become difficult to differentiate. Toussaint emerges throughout the text as a vague and vacuous character who yearns alternately for a career in the press and a career in Letters, attempting and failing ultimately to move beyond writing altogether to make his name as a commercial agent working for the newspaper. His diary entries record his disillusion, and the narrative voice offers frequent critical judgment of him: 'pour lui, plus que pour tout autre, "admirer c'est imiter" et jusqu'aux épaules, à la suite de ses camarades, il s'enfonça dans la boue mouvante, suivit le courant' [for him, more than for others, 'imitation was a form of admiration' and, following the example of his comrades, he plunged himself into the quagmire up to his neck, and let the current take him] (p. 116). Increasingly, as the novel nears its end, the gap between narrator and character becomes blurred. The judgemental narrator who offers aesthetic and moral commentary on his character's fate is implicated too in the 'boue mouvante' of the written word into which Toussaint is sucked, drawn to imitate and echo as the text itself imitates and echoes and despairs of originality. The text ends with the meditation of the narrative voice on Toussaint's ejection from the paper and back into the world of the Montmartre literary set: 'qu'il bourdonne sur le boulevard ou sur la Butte, peu importe! Il vivra du labeur et de l'esprit des autres, et toute nourriture lui sera bonne' [it hardly matters whether he buzzes on the boulevard or the hill. He will live off the hard work and wit of others, and all sustenance will suit him well] (p. 179). Yet the metaphor of the bee and the hornet has already been taken up by Toussaint himself, in a farewell letter to a colleague: 'Adieu, frelons, qui pillez les ruches saintes de la pensée et du travail, qui volez le miel sur les lèvres qui l'ont produit, qui tuez le talent, l'espérance, la vertu, la gloire' [Farewell, hornets, who plunder the sacred hives of thought and labour, who steal the honey from the mouths of those who have produced it, those who snuff out talent, hope, virtue, and glory] (p. 170).

This is an image already called up by the unsentimental Head of News, who describes the editorial office: 'voici la ruche au travail!' [witness the hive at work!] (p. 85). The metaphor of the hive, with its implications for both productivity and potential pillaging, is employed in the text to connect journalism and literature, merging the voice of the insipid character, who can never create but only imitate, the words of the satirical Head of News, and the voice of the narrator.

The blurring of voices between narrator and journalist-character is a feature, too, of *Bel-Ami*, noted by Harris, who maintains that the distinction Maupassant sets up between narrator and character diminishes as the novel progresses: 'the classic disjunctive 'il' is dropped in favour of narrative viewpoint which implicitly condones or lends credence to Duroy's meteoric rise'. White observes the opposite effect, though, that there is an ironic 'gap between the narrator's fluency and Duroy's stumbling compositions, initially staged as a gap between script and speech'.[72] As in the duels, in which the opponents appear almost interchangeable and the conflict little more than a puff of smoke, so in these texts which ironize both the processes of journalism and the act of literary composition, narrator and character can seem indistinguishable duellers. This further echo of one of Maupassant's strategies in his representation of journalism is another example of the reverberations of *Bel-Ami* as felt by these later texts. Structurally, *La Vie des frelons* borrows from newspapers and their demands. But the printed debris out of which it is constructed reveals its debt, too, to nineteenth-century novelistic heritage. Toussaint's quest to make his name as a literary writer is reinforced by the text's own quest through different literary *Bildungsroman* models. Toussaint perceives himself as Rastignac: 'En route donc! rugit le poète, et montrant Paris qui grouillait avec des scintillements d'étoiles dans le brouillard et dans la nuit, il eut le geste de Rastignac' [Off I go then, cried the poet, and, gesturing towards Paris, which was glowing with the twinkle of stars in the mist and the darkness, his manner was that of Rastignac] (p. 30), so echoing Deslauriers's advice to Frédéric Moreau in *L'Education Sentimentale* that he should become a Rastignac and conquer the city. Fenestrier evacuates meaning from both Balzac's novel and that of Flaubert. His Toussaint is a more vacuous character even than Flaubert's Frédéric; his yearnings are still vaguer and still more clichéd. Peter Brooks observes of the scene in Flaubert's novel when Frédéric wanders along the Champs-Elysées contemplating the traffic that it is a deliberate dissipation of the desire experienced by Balzac's Lucien de Rubempré at the same location in *Illusions perdues*.[73] In *La Vie des frelons*, Toussaint also finds himself at the Champs-Elysées evoking similar longings, but in even more desperate terms: the mystical 'Œuvre' of which he dreams seems even more distant here than in Flaubert's text. Even the ability to desire is lacking in *La Vie des frelons*: 'Oh! Pouvoir vouloir! Pouvoir entreprendre l'œuvre, l'œuvre certaine, définitive, à quoi tendent tous les efforts, à quoi l'on dévoue toute sa vie' [oh, to be able to desire! To be able to undertake a task, a certain task, and to devote all effort to it, to dedicate your whole life to it] (p. 43). The echoing vowels in 'pouvoir vouloir' indicate the emptiness or inadequacy of the desire.

In its echoes of novels and newspapers alike, Fenestrier's text borrows another tendency associated with the fin-de-siècle newspaper, that of cutting and pasting. In *Le Reporter*, Marzans is taken aback when he first gets a glimpse of the editorial secretary cutting a story out of another paper, inscribing 'nous recevons de notre correspondent particulier' [we hear from our special correspondent] at the top, and pasting it onto a sheet in preparation for the next day's paper: 'Un rédacteur agitait, comme un lambeau, le journal *Le Temps*, si découpé qu'on ne voyait plus que les quatre bandes blanches, formant un carré; et lui-même passa sa tête au travers, en criant: "Voici *l'Appel du peuple* de demain!"' [an editor was waving a scrap of the newspaper *Le Temps*, cut into so many pieces that all that could be seen were four white strips in a square; he put his head through the hole shouting 'Behold tomorrow's *Appel du peuple!*'] (p. 101). *Bel-Ami* also suggests that newspapers are composed of recycled material. Asked to compose an article on the opinions of India and China on England's activities in the Far East, Saint Potin maintains that 'Je n'ai qu'à reprendre mon article sur le dernier venu et à le copier mot pour mot' (*BA*, 64) ('I simply have to take the article I wrote most recently and copy it word for word'). Ghost-writing is also a regular practice. Toussaint finds his first article, a laudatory account of a meeting at an insurance agency, rewritten in order to blacken the name of the agency's treasurer, editor of a rival paper. Cutting and pasting, pillaging and plagiarizing: such practices are featured across a range of novels depicting the production of the fin-de-siècle newspaper. *La Vie des frelons* enacts these processes, consciously or unconsciously, as part of its commentary on the literature and journalism of the era. The way in which writers and reporters overlap in their pillaging tendencies is reinforced through the character of Rosine in Fenestrier's novel. First introduced to Toussaint as the lover of the writer Ravesenne, it emerges that she has also been in a relationship with the journalist Jehu. The closing scene of the text sees her offering herself to Toussaint. Representing the muse who attracts writers of all kinds, and connecting the worlds of Montmartre and the mass-produced press, Rosine is 'pillaged' in more ways than one, in that she also provides an echo of Flaubert's Rosanette, the woman who links the dreamy literary wannabe Frédéric with the world of Jacques Arnoux and industrial art. Toussaint's very name reflects something of his everyman status; it evokes and dilutes the idea of art as sacred. It is evocative of Walter Benjamin's discussion of the aura of a work of art, and its dissolution in an age of mechanical reproduction; Toussaint suggests the copying and tarnishing of the aura.[74]

The reductiveness of Toussaint's name reflects the ideas of sameness found earlier in the discussion of the duel in this chapter, and the equation of all written production with the dismissive term 'papier'. The closing chapter of *Le Reporter* offers a fitting synopsis to this discussion of the convergence of literature and journalism in these novels; the novel ends with the production of a flurry of paper, a battle between publications, and a capitulation. Goguel, the character introduced earlier in the text, and who has a fascination with the possibilities of advertising, has launched a new large-scale literary periodical and called it the *Universel* — the very name evoking the union of literature and the press under a new umbrella title. This is in deliberate competition with an existing journal run by some of Pierre

Marzans's acquaintances. Goguel and the *Universel* bid to cover Paris in paper, and to suffocate their rivals with the force of their advertising campaign. The result of this *lutte*, which entertains Paris for a month, is an image of a city drowning in identical sheets of paper, a memorable emphasis on the power of advertising (which transcends any content of the proposed publication itself) in a text published on the cusp of the twentieth century:

> Des affiches de toutes les couleurs et de toutes les dimensions, répandant jusque dans les moindres communes, les noms et les portraits des redacteurs. Quelques-unes, gigantesques, couvraient des murs de dix mètres de haut. Mais ce n'était là qu'un commencement. Goguel s'affirma comme le génie incarné de la réclame. Des régiments d'hommes-sandwichs envahirent Paris, traînèrent en défilés interminables dans tous les quartiers. Des ballons partirent, laissons tomber sur les villes une pluie de prospectus. (*Le Reporter*, p. 288)
>
> [Posters in all colours and sizes, spreading the name and pictures of the editorial board throughout even the poorest districts. Some of them were enormous, covering walls ten metres tall. But that was only the beginning. Goguel was making a name for himself as a veritable genius of advertising. Regiments of sandwich-board men invaded Paris, dragging themselves in never-ending parades around the city. Hot air balloons took off, dropping showers of pamphlets over the towns.]

This saturation of paper comes after Marzans's disillusionment with his own book, which has been published to relative success following an influential critical review and subsequent advertising, but has led him to doubt his own talent, and to feel that 'le journalisme, même littéraire, loin de développer le talent, ne fait le plus souvent que de brillants pasticheurs de ceux qui y réussissent' [More often than not, journalism, even literary journalism, just makes brilliant imitators out of those who can succeed in it. It scarcely fosters talent] (p. 288). These scenes are placed before the closing image of the book, the recognition of a figure whom Marzans had encountered earlier in the text, a renowned author whose 'silhouette timide et silencieuse s'effaçait dans l'ombre' [timid and silent shadow disappeared into the gloom] (p. 297), reflecting the dissolution of literature in the novel. As the *Universel* journal crushes its rival, so now the universal press has stamped out literature, in favour of 'une pluie de prospectus' proclaiming the conjoining of the two realms.

In a discussion of *New Grub Street* (1892), the British text of this period which best reflects the rivalry between a hallowed form of earlier literature and a new age of commercial print, Patrick Brantlinger sees Gissing's novel as the product of a dialectical tension which has a particular effect on works of art which fail to incarnate either one opposing force or another. He discusses the connections and conflict between the artistic avant-garde and mass culture at the turn of the century, and finds that the opposition between them is both 'contestatory and symbiotic'. Neither a product of mass culture nor the result of a modernizing avant-garde art, *New Grub Street*, suggests Brantlinger, is:

> Instructive in its failure to be one or the other. [...] [Gissing's] novelist characters yearn for a popularity they despise while also yearning for a literary originality they cannot achieve. The novels they imagine and write [...] merely reproduce

the exhaustion of *New Grub Street* itself, marking the slide of realism from critical form to mass cultural formula. For Gissing, every conceivable form of writing falls under the sign of journalism, another name for the commercial prostitution of art.[75]

This statement on *New Grub Street* and its status as neither one thing nor another can also be attributed to the representations of journalism under discussion here — to the echoes of Maupassant's echoing text, and even to *Bel-Ami* itself, uncertain of whether it can be considered a text which transcends the banalities of the *récit*. Reflecting the anxiety of influence associated both with the ubiquity of journalism and with a tradition of nineteenth-century realism, these novels posit conflict and tension as faded models of historical etiquette, like the duel.

That said, these texts — even as they dissipate the sense of opposition — evoke a form of social Darwinism which places emphasis on a struggle for survival. In *New Grub Street*, Jasper Milvain, the character who embodies the future, in contrast to the outdated ideals of the novelist Reardon, incarnates the embrace of a newly commercialized art which will also see him triumph socially; Rachel Bowlby cites critic John Goode on the Darwinism of Jasper Milvain: 'Realism and adaptability define an area of freedom in a highly determined world — it is crucial to our understanding of the novel that we shouldn't just think of Milvain as an appalling cynic'.[76] *Le Reporter* persistently defines life as a journalist as a form of Darwinian struggle. Journalism is referred to in Brulat's preface as 'cette terrible lutte pour vie qu'est le journalisme contemporain' [modern journalism, that terrible struggle for life]; journalist characters in the text even use English terminology evoking Darwinian theory: 'nous sommes d'une génération de struggles-for-life féroces' [we are part of a generation of those who desperately struggle for life] (pp. IV & 14). Even while self-consciously and disparagingly reducing the value of their own production as that of mere paper, these texts can be said, in their reflections of journalism and its practices, to embody a Bakhtinian response to influence:

> No new artistic genre ever nullifies or replaces old ones. But at the same time each fundamentally and significantly new genre, once it arrives, exerts influence on the entire circle of old genres: the new genre makes the old ones, so to speak, more conscious: it forces them to better perceive their own possibilities and boundaries.[77]

Bakhtin's discussion here, in his *Problems of Dostoevsky's Poetics*, which postdates *The Dialogic Imagination* cited in the Introduction, offers a less antagonistic model than is evoked in the earlier texts, and one which suggests the potential for reinvigoration of the novel form through its assimilation of journalistic discourse. And indeed, the texts examined in this chapter reflect, implicitly and explicitly, on their own boundaries and, in their incorporation of illusions, echoes, and interviews, explore the possibilities of containing practices increasingly associated with journalism. As they are reduced to paper, so they meld together to create papier mâché.

As will be seen in the following chapter on Zola, that papier mâché can become a viscous form, a mud from which literature can be thought to generate. As David Trotter's *Cooking With Mud* suggests, the very imagery of mud — frequently employed in the fin de siècle, as seen in quotations in the Introduction, to suggest the contamination of literature by journalism — is taken up by writers who use the very terminology of waste, and its dialectics, including contamination/ decontamination, contingency/purpose to literary effect. Trotter sees novels reflecting on mess by way of pattern.[78] Even in reducing all printed matter, whether literary, artistic, journalistic, to mess and clutter, the texts evaluated in this chapter arguably salvage the 'papers' they denigrate by turning them to self-conscious literary analysis. Chapter Two will examine the representation of journalism, and the journalist figure of Saccard in particular, in the first of Zola's Rougon-Macquart novels. In *L'Argent*, though, the text which has been most discussed recently by commentators on Zola's attitudes to journalism, there is (as in the novels seen here) a focus on the equivalence of forms of paper, which coalesce, in one memorable chapter, in an oozing slime of rubbish formed of printed matter.[79] The bank in that novel, itself promoted by the newspaper funded by Saccard, is the Banque Universelle. Brulat's closing images of the trumpeting of the *Universel* journal can be read as a final intertextual nod to the novel of Zola's which comes closest to being a *roman de journalisme*. As in *L'Argent*, paper comes raining down, but whereas that paper represents the cataclysmic plunge of shares in the bank, in Brulat's novel the paper celebrates the successful enterprise of the new literary journal. The advertising marks the death of literary idealism, and the embrace of the convergence of literature and the press, an ambivalent celebration of modernity.

Notes to Chapter 1

1. The English translations of *Bel-Ami* are taken from *Bel-Ami*, trans. by Margaret Mauldon (Oxford: Oxford University Press, 2008).
2. Guy de Maupassant, 'Le Duel', in *Chroniques*, 3 vols (Paris: Union générale d'éditions, 1980), I, 349–54 (p. 350). Originally published in *Gil Blas*, 8 December 1881.
3. Harold Bloom, *The Anxiety of Influence* (Oxford: Oxford University Press, 1973), p. 5.
4. See Trevor Harris, *Maupassant in the Hall of Mirrors: Ironies and Repetition in the work of Guy de Maupassant* (Basingstoke: Macmillan, 1990); Stirling Haig, 'The Mirror of Artifice: Maupassant's *Bel-Ami*', in *The Madame Bovary Blues: The Pursuit of Illusion in Nineteenth-Century French Fiction* (Baton Rouge: Louisiana State University Press, 1987), pp. 152–62; Lloyd, *Maupassant*; Robert Lethbridge, 'Introduction', in *Bel-Ami*, trans. by Margaret Mauldon (Oxford: Oxford University Press, 2001), pp. vii–xlvii.
5. Edmund Birch, 'Maupassant's *Bel-Ami* and the Secrets of Actualité', *Modern Language Review*, 109.4 (2014), 996–1012 (p. 1002). See too Gérard Delaisement's introduction to *Bel-Ami*, which notes that in the novel, Maupassant denounces a 'presse à renseignements de laquelle on ne peut vraiment pas se fier' [a press based on information, which does not induce pride] (Delaisement, *Maupassant, Bel-Ami* (Paris: Hatier, 1972), p. XIV).
6. Harris, *Maupassant in the Hall of Mirrors*, pp. 161–62.
7. Birch, 'Maupassant's *Bel-Ami* and the Secrets of Actualité', p. 1007.
8. Gustave Flaubert, *L'Éducation sentimentale* (Paris: Garnier-Flammarion, 1985), p. 295.
9. Gustave Flaubert, 'Dictionnaire des idées reçues', in *Bouvard et Pécuchet*, ed. by Claudine Gothot-Mersch (Paris: Gallimard-Pléiade, 1979), p. 509. Translation from *Bouvard and Pécuchet*, trans. by A. J. Krailsheimer (London: Penguin, 1976), p. 303.
10. John Leigh, *Touché: The Duel in Literature* (Cambridge, MA: Harvard University Press, 2015), p. 3.
11. Ibid., pp. 210–11.

12. Guy de Maupassant, 'Un lâche', in *Contes et nouvelles*, 2 vols (Paris: Gallimard-Pléaide, 1974), I, 1159–66 (p. 1165).
13. Leigh, *Touché*, p. 216.
14. V. G. Kiernan, *The Duel in European History* (Oxford: Oxford University Press, 1986), p. 269.
15. Maupassant, 'Le Duel', p. 350.
16. Ibid., p. 353.
17. Henri Mitterand, in Maupassant, *Chroniques*, pp. 406–07.
18. Leigh, *Touché*, p. 219.
19. This is noted in Robert Lethbridge, 'Notes', in *Bel-Ami* trans. by Mauldon, p. 299.
20. *Charlot s'amuse*, which features a foreword by Henry Céard praising its attention to clinical detail, asserts its association to Zola's naturalism via an epigraph from *Thérèse Raquin*; rather than being a celebration of onanism, it depicts the physical suffering undergone by the protagonist Charlot, which culminates in suicide; like the duel in 'Un lâche', then, it ends in self-destruction. Paul Bonnetain, *Charlot s'amuse* (Brussels: Henri Kristemaeckers, 1883).
21. Lethbridge, 'Notes', in *Bel-Ami*, trans. by Mauldon, p. 291.
22. Birch, 'Maupassant's *Bel-Ami* and the Secrets of Actualité', pp. 1003–04.
23. Honoré de Balzac, *Illusions perdues* (Paris: Gallimard, 1961), p. 264.
24. Laurel Brake, *Subjugated Knowledges: Journalism, Gender and Literature in the Nineteenth Century* (Basingstoke: Macmillan, 1994), p. xii.
25. Terdiman, *Discourse/Counter-Discourse*, p. 117.
26. Marieke Dubbelboer, 'Il faut vivre: Writers, Journalists and Income 1890–1914', in *Literature and the Press*, ed. by Birch and Rees.
27. Guy de Maupassant, 'Messieurs de la chronique', in *Chroniques*, III, 40–46 (pp. 40–41). First published in *Gil Blas*, 11 November 1884.
28. Anne de Vaucher-Gravili, 'Maupassant et le journalisme', in *Maupassant et l'écriture: actes du colloque de Fécamp 21–22–23 mai 1993*, ed. by Louis Forestier (Paris: Nathan, 1993), pp. 29–39 (p. 31).
29. See Gérard Delaisement, *Maupassant journaliste et chroniqueur* (Paris: Albin Michel, 1956); Marie-Claire Banquart, 'Maupassant journaliste', in *Flaubert et Maupassant, écrivains normands* (Paris: PUF, 1981), p. 156.
30. Guy de Maupassant, 'Aux critiques de "Bel-Ami"', in *Chroniques*, III, 164–68 (p. 166). See Lloyd, *Maupassant*, p. 71: 'for a novel which supposedly denounces the corruption of journalism, *Bel-Ami* is itself strangely embedded in journalism'.
31. Guy de Maupassant, 'Gustave Flaubert', in *Chroniques*, III, 77–124 (p. 109).
32. Daniel Sangsue, 'De quelques écrivains fictifs dans les récits de Maupassant', in *Maupassant et l'écriture*, ed. by Forestier, pp. 229–39 (p. 233).
33. Ibid., pp. 238–39.
34. Gerald Prince, '*Bel-Ami* and Narrative as Antagonist', *French Forum*, 11 (1986), 217–26.
35. Ibid., p. 220.
36. Vaillant, 'Écrire pour raconter', p. 774.
37. Ibid., p. 776.
38. Maupassant, 'Gustave Flaubert', p. 109.
39. The adjective 'reptilian' is used by Lloyd: 'morally, Duroy must be one of the most reptilian characters in French literature' (*Maupassant*, p. 15).
40. Prince, '*Bel-Ami* and Narrative as Antagonist', p. 224.
41. Ibid., pp. 225–26.
42. Stirling Haig notes the artificiality of the milieus found in *Bel-Ami*, emblematized by the conservatory setting of the Forestiers' dinner in the second chapter of the novel (*The Madame Bovary Blues*, p. 160).
43. Nicholas White, *The Family in Crisis in Late Nineteenth-Century French Fiction* (Cambridge: Cambridge University Press, 1999), p. 91.
44. For discussion of the 'présence de Flaubert' in Maupassant's works, see Yvan Leclerc, 'Maupassant: le texte hanté', in *Maupassant et l'écriture*, ed. by Forestier, pp. 259–70 (p. 261).
45. The connection with Balzac has been noted, among others, by André Vial, *Guy de Maupassant*

et l'art du roman (Paris: Nizet, 1954), p. 358, and Delaisement, *Maupassant, Bel-Ami*, p. 46. Birch notes the comparison between Maupassant's text and *Illusions perdues*, seeing Duroy and Lucien de Rubempré connected in their change of names, epitomizing their lack of fixed value; he concludes that 'the difference between such questions of value for the respective protagonists [...] lies in the degree of success [...] put simply, duplicity works for Duroy' ('Maupassant's *Bel-Ami* and the Secrets of Actualité', p. 1006).

46. Jean Baudrillard, 'Simulacra and Simulations', in *Selected Writings*, ed. by Mark Poster (Stanford, CA: Stanford University Press, 1988), pp. 166–84 (p. 173).
47. Lethbridge, 'Introduction', in *Bel-Ami*, trans. by Mauldon, p. xlvii; see too Haig: '*Bel-Ami* does not claim to set before the reader's glance a window-pane like language gesturing towards pure, uncoded reality; rather, it intercepts that glance by means of a tain, and, mirrorlike, reverses its referential quest upon itself. What it sets before the reader is a nothingness [...] Illusion has now become substance' (*The Madame Bovary Blues*, p. 162).
48. Lloyd, *Maupassant*, p. 15.
49. Pinson, *L'Imaginaire médiatique*, p. 97.
50. Brulat (1866–1940) was a novelist and journalist who wrote two novels about journalism; *La Faiseuse de gloire* (1900) is the sequel to *Le Reporter*, analyzed here. He wrote articles for a range of publications including the *Revue socialiste* and the *Revue indépendante*; Fenestrier was a journalist for *Le Matin*.
51. Maurice Barrès, *Les Déracinés* (Paris: Gallimard-Folio, 1988).
52. Pinson, *L'Imaginaire médiatique*, p. 73. The embedded quotation is taken from Brulat, *Le Reporter*, p. 274.
53. Pinson, *L'Imaginaire médiatique*, p. 91.
54. Charles Fenestrier, *La Vie des frelons: histoire d'un journaliste* (Paris: Éditions de la Société nouvelle, 1908), p. 6. All subsequent quotations from this text are referenced in the main text.
55. Brulat, *Le Reporter*, p. v. All subsequent quotations from this text are referenced in the main text.
56. Hannah Scott, *Broken Glass, Broken World: Glass in French Culture in the Aftermath of 1870* (Oxford: Legenda, 2016), pp. 47–48.
57. Jean Baudrillard, *Le Système des objets* (Paris: Gallimard, 1968), cited and translated by Scott, *Broken Glass, Broken World*, p. 51.
58. George Gissing, *New Grub Street* (Oxford: Oxford University Press, 2008), p. 107; Marzans's wonder at the printing press initially suggests more of an embrace of mechanized processes of journalistic and literary production.
59. Guy Debord, *Society of the Spectacle* (London: Rebel Press, [n.d.]), p. 7.
60. Ibid., *Society of the Spectacle*, p. 7.
61. Jean-Marie Seillan, 'L'Interview', in *La Civilisation du journal*, ed. by Kalifa and others, pp. 1025–40 (pp. 1026–27).
62. Jules Huret, 'Le Bachot', in *Tout yeux, tout oreilles* (Paris: Charpentier, 1901), pp. 28–35. See Dorothy Spiers and Dolores Signori, *Entretiens avec Zola* (Ottawa: Presses de l'Université d'Ottawa, 1990); also Elizabeth Emery, *Photojournalism and the Origins of the French Writer House Museum* (Farnham: Ashgate, 2012).
63. Seillan, 'L'Interview', p. 1028.
64. Thérenty discusses the rise of the interview in the French press in *La Littérature au quotidien*, noting that it arose in the 1870s and, although ostensibly factual, was in fact infiltrated by fictional techniques, employing narrative modes found in realist novels such as free indirect style and description: 'l'interview est une forme plus romanesque que journalistique' [the interview is a form which has more in common with the novel than with journalism] (p. 144).
65. 'When Henry James complained about the age of 'newspaperism' he was really complaining about the 'age of interviewing' (Rubery, *The Novelty of Newspapers*, p. 109).
66. Ibid., p. 128.
67. Thérenty, *La Littérature au quotidien*, p. 126.
68. Charles Legrand, *L'Âge de papier, roman social* (Paris: Ernest Kolb, 1889), p. 126.
69. Thérenty, *La Littérature au quotidien*, p.184.

70. Ibid., pp. 60–61.
71. Mikhail Bakhtin, 'Discourse in the Novel', in *The Dialogic Imagination*, pp. 259–422.
72. Harris, *Maupassant in the Hall of Mirrors*, p. 103; White, *The Family in Crisis in Late Nineteenth-Century French Fiction*, p. 86.
73. Peter Brooks, *Reading for the Plot: Design and Intention in Narrative* (Oxford: Clarendon Press, 1984), p. 185.
74. Walter Benjamin, *The Work of Art in an Age of Mechanical Reproduction*, trans. by J. A. Underwood (London: Penguin, 2008).
75. Brantlinger, 'Mass Media and Culture in Fin de Siècle Europe', p. 104.
76. Rachel Bowlby, *Just Looking: Consumer Culture in Dreiser, Gissing and Zola* (New York: Methuen, 1985), p. 103.
77. Mikhail Bakhtin, *Problems of Dostoevsky's Poetics* (Manchester: Manchester University Press, 1999), p. 323.
78. David Trotter, *Cooking With Mud: The Idea of Mess in Nineteenth-Century Art and Fiction* (Oxford: Oxford University Press, 2000).
79. See, for example, Nicholas White's discussion of the role of the press in *L'Argent*: 'Le papier mâché dans *L'Argent*: fiction, journalisme et paperasse', *Cahiers naturalistes*, 87 (2013), 151–68, and Adeline Wrona, 'Mots à crédit: *L'Argent*, de Zola, ou la presse au cœur du marché de la confiance', *Romantisme*, 151 (2011), 67–79. Both discuss the accumulation of paper in the novel — whether banknotes, promissory notes, or journalistic articles.

CHAPTER 2

Zola:
Ambiguities, Battles, Jolts

'Faux-chéri': Zola's Ambiguous Journalists

The mirrors which collapse the boundaries between narrator and character in *Bel-Ami* are mirrored in Zola's *Nana* (1880), the story of a prostitute observed, in part, by a society journalist, and so reinforcing conventional nineteenth-century observations about the practice of journalism as prostitution. A cartoon sketch of a newsroom published in the satirical paper *Le Grelot* in 1880, the year *Nana* was published, depicts the journalists gathered around the editorial desk as pigs. On a table strewn with newspapers there also sits a pile of novels: *Nana* lies at the bottom, while Sade's tale of sexual depravity, *Justine*, is on the top, the implication being that the production of newsprint and the publication of novels representing prostitution are analogous.[1] At the centre of Zola's novel lies a scene characterized by reflections, in which the shadow of the journalist Fauchery looms both as an image within the text, and as an influence on the plot. The seventh of the fourteen chapters ends with Nana's lover Count Muffat standing in the street watching Fauchery's shadow as he takes a woman with an outline like that of his wife to bed. It is also in Chapter Seven that Nana and Muffat together read Fauchery's article in *Le Figaro*, the article which acts as a key document for the interpretation of Nana's character — and, indeed, incorporates many phrases from Zola's preliminary sketch of her in his drafts.[2] This central chapter full of mirrors offers a glimpse into Zola's representation of the figure of the journalist, flitting like a shadow across his works. Éléonore Reverzy describes how *Nana* was the subject of a publicity battle between newspapers, as Zola opted to advertise his forthcoming serialization of the text in *Le Voltaire* by including an excerpt in that publication: none other than the fictionalized piece of journalism penned by Fauchery, the 'Golden Fly' article printed, in the novel, in the pages of *Le Figaro*. In response, *Le Figaro* itself published a lengthy plot summary of *Nana*, in an attempt to trump *Le Voltaire*.[3]

Fauchery's article depicts Nana as a 'mouche d'or' [golden fly], an agent of rot and destruction, although 'de chair superbe' (N, 1269) ('with superb flesh').[4] And if Nana is the fly, spreading her deadly germs amongst those with whom she sleeps, then Fauchery, who spreads the word of her contaminating capacity, can also be described as fly-like, dipping his pen into the muck of the dung-heap from which

Nana springs so as to forecast her end and disseminating his predictions across Paris. The chapter which features the laughing Nana kissing herself in the mirror encourages reflections between the prostitute and the hack-writer, and, in turn, between the journalist and Zola himself, all drawing sustenance from the 'dungheap' to fuel their activities. As the 'mouche d'or' article suggests, and as numerous commentators on the novel have discussed, the presentation of Nana is characterized by ambiguity.[5] So too is the presentation of the journalist who views and frames the dichotomies surrounding the prostitute, seen as both a cheerful, healthy 'bonne fille' and a degenerate, corrupting force. Fauchery's very name conjures such ambiguity; *chéri* suggesting the indulgent affection with which is he embraced in the different spheres of society to which he has access, *faux* implying that such emotion is necessarily fake. He is always out for what he can get, but at the end of the novel, on hearing of Nana's death, he is 'réellement touché dans sa blague de petit journaliste' ('for all his cheap journalist's flippancy, Fauchery was genuinely moved') as he 'mâchait nerveusement son cigare' (*N*, 1475) ('was chewing nervously away on his cigar'); the only man among those hanging around outside the Grand Hotel to be depicted as touched by the news. Nana refers to him in various terms across the novel as a nice chap or a dirty swine. The name also echoes Nana's own superficiality, giving off an illusion of wealth, *cher*, which is ultimately but a façade. Reverzy describes the intentional parallels set up between journalist and prostitute: 'La prostituée et le journaliste sont soumis au même régime: se vendre. C'est aussi sur leur dépendance réciproque qu'insiste le romancier. Ils sont au service l'un de l'autre' [Both prostitute and journalist are subject to the same order: selling themselves. The novelist emphasizes their mutual dependency].[6]

The blurring of boundaries between writer and journalistic character encouraged by the 'mouche d'or' article is reinforced by the awareness that narrative perspective is attributed to Fauchery at key points in the novel. Fauchery acts as a guiding voice in the pivotal opening scene at the theatre. He is also there in Chapter Three at the opulent home of the Muffats, and it is he who is obsessed with the connections between Nana, the girl from the slums, and the wealthy Sabine Muffat. He therefore provides commentary on the infiltration of Nana's all-consuming sexuality across all levels of society and acts as the mouthpiece for the persistent parallels and echoes embedded in the text. These echoes include interconnections between the triad Nana-Fauchery-Zola. In Chapter Five, Fauchery leads Count Muffat up the stairs backstage at the theatre, the journalist unveiling the grime of the world behind the stage just as Zola exhibits the underbelly of Second Empire glitz to the reader. Embodying journalistic instincts in his efforts, both as moralizing author of the 'mouche d'or' piece and as protean guide to the middle-class drawing-rooms and the seamy world of the theatre alike, Fauchery is also depicted in the text as a failed writer. The play he puts on is a fiasco; by the end of the novel his printing presses are eventually washed away by Nana's desire for a water garden.

The ambiguous role played by Fauchery in *Nana* is emblematic of Zola's oscillating views of journalism across his career. More than any other writer of the period, even Maupassant, Zola's career is intimately bound up with journalism and its developments in the later decades of the nineteenth century. His work offers a vista onto the profession, and his own comment pieces summarize, evaluate, and criticize changing practices, as documented by Henri Mitterand and, more recently, Adeline Wrona and the collection of essays edited by Corinne Saminadayar-Perrin for *Cahiers naturalistes*.[7] Wrona evaluates Zola's wide-ranging contribution to a plethora of publications over the course of his career, and notes the simultaneity of Zola's literary output alongside that of his journalism; his serialized novels sharing space in the newspapers with his pieces of criticism and his political discussions: 'Zola romancier voisine couramment, dans le journal, avec Zola chroniqueur, ou critique'.[8] Zola's career is forged within the pages of the newspaper and develops against the backdrop of radical changes in press practice, including the increasing professionalization of the reporter and the phenomenal growth of the daily paper; he wavers between enthusiasm for the virtues of journalism and apprehension about its expansion. Frederick Brown suggests ways in which journalism was influential in enabling Zola's fiction to flourish, and not just because it provided him with financial stability: 'In the language of a canal builder or a man afflicted with urinary problems, Zola explained to [Edmond de Goncourt] how journalism helped his creative work'; quoting Goncourt, Brown describes how 'previously he'd get so choked with ideas and phrases tumbling upon him that he'd sometimes let his pen drop. Now he produces a controlled gush, a stream less copious but flowing without impediment'.[9] Wrona summarizes Zola's fluctuating responses to the press, claiming that his writings see him 'oscille[r] entre enthousiasme et inquiétude' [fluctuate between enthusiasm and concern].[10] Such equivalence can be seen, for instance, in his so-called 'adieux' to journalism, published at the end of a year of polemical articles in *Le Figaro* in 1880–81, and already cited in the Introduction, in which Zola sets out the conventional wisdom on literary reaction to journalism, that the press 'tuait la littérature, elle traînait la langue dans tous les ruisseaux, elle était l'agent démocratique de la bêtise humaine' but also defends journalism as a training ground for writers of talent; arguing that though 'les paresseux' [the idle] and those of limited ambition will be contented to remain writing articles for the papers rather than exercising their literary muscle, 'les forts, [...] ceux qui travaillent et qui veulent' [the strong, those who work and desire], will make the most of their journalistic opportunities: 'qu'ils entrent sans peur dans les journaux: ils en reviendront comme nos soldats reviennent d'une campagne, aguerris, couverts de blessures, maîtres de leur métier et des hommes' [let them enter into newspapers without fear: they will return as our soldiers return from a campaign, battle-hardened, covered in wounds, masters of their trade and of men].[11]

Such contradiction reaches a peak at the time of the Dreyfus Affair, when the press is both antagonist — fuelling anti-Semitic feeling and projecting Zola as scapegoat — and champion of Zola's vision of an educated and emancipated society. This chapter examines Zola's conflicted attitudes to the press via close analysis of two texts, chosen to represent the beginning and end of his career, *La Fortune des Rougon* and *Vérité*.

Despite the influence exerted by the press on Zola's development as a writer, and, in turn, his own impact on key social and political debates and events via his interventions in the press, it has been pointed out that Zola does not substantially devote any one of his novels to depicting the figure of the journalist or the setting of the newsroom. Auguste Dezalay maintains that Zola had, according to the preparatory notes for the Rougon-Macquart cycle, contemplated a novel which would substantially reflect the world of the newspaper in the closing years of the Second Empire. Yet that novel never materialized, and so, despite the detailed studies of politicians, artists, and workers across the texts, not one of them features 'en pleine lumière' the man of the press or the *chroniqueur*. Dezalay suggests several possible reasons for this apparent absence within Zola's *œuvre*. He argues that Zola may, in the wake of the publication of *Bel-Ami*, have been reluctant to compose a novel about journalism which would seem to be echoing or competing with that of Maupassant. Alternatively, he may have wished to place such a distance between his role as a reporter and that of documentary researcher for his naturalist novels that he felt he could not introduce a similar reporter into his works. He may have perceived the two roles — journalist and novelist — as being fundamentally in competition with one another: 'Ou bien encore y avait-il eu, au moins jusqu'à sa "campagne" de 1880, concurrence entre ses deux activités, de "témoin engagé" des journaux de son époque et de créateur de fictions?' [Or indeed was there competition between these two roles, the 'committed observer' of the newspapers of the age, and creator of fiction, at least up until the time of his 'campaign' of 1880?] [12]

There are indeed journalist characters who make appearances throughout the Rougon-Macquart series in particular — not only Fauchery, but the art critics Vernier and Jory in *L'Œuvre* and the aspiring writer Jordan in *L'Argent*.[13] The later novel, in its representation of the expansion and collapse of the Banque Universelle, set up by the youngest of the Rougon brothers, Aristide Saccard, comes closest to a portrayal of the iniquities of journalism, as Saccard also takes on a selection of newspapers whose role is to extol the strength of the bank and maintain its illusion of legitimacy. White notes that in *L'Argent*, Saccard at one point walks 'parmi les urinoirs et les kiosques à journaux' [between the public urinals and the newspaper stands], and that this sets up an equivalence between forms of street furniture that dictates the way in which the press is viewed throughout the novel.[14] It is through recurring glimpses of the character of Saccard across the novels that Zola invites a commentary on the enduring possibilities and pollution of the newspaper industry. The intertwining of the press with the careers of Second Empire wheeler-dealers is illustrated through Saccard's own alternating roles as property speculator (as seen in *La Curée*), banker, and media mogul.[15] Following the downfall of the bank and the prosecution of its owners at the end of *L'Argent*, Saccard's later fate is documented in *Le Docteur Pascal*, as his brother notes that he has become the editor of the republican newspaper *L'Époque* in the wake of the Franco-Prussian war, a position which Félicité Rougon boasts is really equivalent to that of a minister. The title of his new publication itself suggests Saccard's role as representative of the changing times across the span of the Rougon-Macquart cycle.[16]

This chapter will argue that although no one Zola novel focuses its attention on the minutiae of the newsroom or centres on the fate of one single journalist character, the elasticity of the figure of Saccard, who makes his first appearance in the cycle in the inaugural novel, *La Fortune des Rougon*, is illustrative of Zola's observation that journalism can be seen as 'une gymnastique excellente'.[17] Journalism offers not only a training ground, a set of muscle-developing exercises for the would-be writer, but also, for Saccard, a springboard for the leaps and landings of a career which will be characterized, as his adopted name suggests, by jolts and jerky movements, the 'saccades' of a newspaper-writer under the Second Empire. Dezalay comments on the words of Saccard's brother Eugène, who understands that Aristide will always land on his feet; he recognizes that 'un journaliste est un acrobate' [a journalist is an acrobat].[18] Not only is the figure of the journalist, emblematized by Saccard, a recurring and significant one in Zola's novels, but the representation of such a figure indicates tension within Zola's own narrative practices. There is antagonism between a Naturalism which has much in common with the increasingly dominant nineteenth-century 'presse d'information' commented on by Zola himself, and alternative aesthetic forms. The affinity between contemporary forms of reportage and the naturalist novel is examined in Ferdinand Brunetière's critical evaluation of the genre, *Le Roman naturaliste*. In this text, which offers a negative discussion of Zola's own novels, Brunetière laments the rise of those novelists who, unlike others who have come to prose writing having had experience of the theatre or of poetry, have begun their careers in journalism: 'et vous les reconnaissez justement à cette préoccupation qu'ils ont de construire leurs romans sur les choses du jour, et d'imaginer, si je puis ainsi dire, dans la direction de la curiosité publique' [you will recognize them by that tendency they have to construct their novels based on current affairs, and to imagine what will stir the public curiosity].[19] He writes disapprovingly of writers such as Jules Claretie who incorporate techniques of reportage in their novels: unlike earlier realist writers, who might use news events as the inspiration for their plots, Brunetière sees the naturalists:

> Prendre enfin à ce qu'il y a de plus superficiel dans le spectacle de la vie courante et, chose bizarre! sous prétexte d'exactitude dans l'observation, c'est précisément aboutir à ne représenter des choses que ce qu'elles ont de moins réel.[20]
>
> [Picking up on what is most superficial in the spectacle of everyday life and, citing the need for observational accuracy, bizarrely depicting those things for their least realistic aspect.]

In Zola's work, naturalist practices are set against the romanticism or idealism he criticizes in *Le Roman expérimental*: 'Notre querelle est là, avec les écrivains idéalistes. Ils partent toujours d'une source irrationnelle quelconque [...] Nous, écrivains naturalistes, nous soumettons chaque fait à l'observation et à l'expérience' [That is where our quarrel lies, with idealistic writers. They always start from some kind of irrational source. We naturalist writers subject each fact to observation and experiment].[21] These earlier genres are incorporated in the opening chapter of *La Fortune des Rougon* through glimpses of the stories and legends engendered by the seminal depiction of the cemetery in the novel. Tension is prevalent, too, in the shift from Naturalism to the utopian and moralizing discourses of the later novel *Vérité*.

Telling Stories and Engendering Journalism in *La Fortune des Rougon*

A journalistic springboard is provided, in *La Fortune des Rougon*, by the provincial paper for which Aristide's mother encourages him to write, *L'Indépendant*. This title is of course ironic. The novel depicts the opposing factions in the provincial town of Plassans in the immediate wake of Louis-Napoleon's *coup d'état* in December 1851 — not only the conflict between the insurgents who rise up against the *coup* and the bourgeoisie of the town who seek to defeat them, but also the petty squabbles among the middle-class conservatives who frequent the soirées at the yellow drawing room owned by the Rougon branch of the family, Pierre and Félicité. Conflict dominates this first novel in the Rougon-Macquart cycle, which announces the initial split in the family tree in the clash between the legitimate and illegitimate sides. The very idea that in such a split society there could be a voice of 'independence' seems impossible, and the publication to which Aristide eventually ends up sending his contributions is anything but. The first half of this chapter will argue that the representation of the press in *La Fortune des Rougon* gives satirical insight into the way in which information is gathered and disseminated at this moment of crucial historical significance. It will also suggest that the patterns of opposition which characterize the text are enhanced through an antagonism which is described not only explicitly, between competing publications in the town of Plassans, but also implicitly, between forms of reportage — both newspaper discourse and naturalist style — and more traditional forms of storytelling. Mitterand flags up the dominance of conflict as a theme and practice within Zola's theoretical writing, noting that in *Le Roman expérimental*, he pits different forms of literature against each other. In the same article, Mitterand describes the three criteria seen as essential to Naturalism: 'le refus du romanesque, celui du héros, et celui de l'engagement personnel du narrateur dans son récit' [the rejection of the romantic, the heroic, and the personal].[22] In *La Fortune des Rougon* the 'refus du romanesque' is manifested through the increasing need for a journalistic interpretation of events, however ambivalently this is presented. The practice of Naturalism is affirmed in this novel through a rejection of traditional, romantic forms of literature which is set alongside a preference for a model of narrating history — however imperfect or subjective — such as that provided by the press. This reading is reinforced by the fact that Zola's own journalistic articles, written on the theme of the *coup d'état* and published in the years immediately before the collapse of the Empire itself, when he was writing *La Fortune des Rougon*, are embedded in the commentary of the plot. So too can be found in this novel a representation of the developments in journalism he was tracking at the time of writing the opening text in his monumental cycle. The shift marked in this first Rougon-Macquart novel, from an age of storytelling to an alternative model of narrative emblematized by the press, anticipates Walter Benjamin's lament in his essay 'The Storyteller' about the increasing distance of 'the storyteller in his living immediacy' from modern society. That 'the art of storytelling is coming to an end' is, for Benjamin, illustrated by the rise of the press: 'experience has fallen in value [...] Every glance at a newspaper demonstrates that it has reached a new low'.[23]

This inaugural novel, and its opening chapter in particular, have often been discussed by critics as instrumental not only in charting the origins of the Rougon-Macquart family, but in illustrating a concern with the processes of writing such a history. The initial description of the Aire Saint Mittre in Plassans, burial ground turned lumberyard, has been seen as emblematic of the production of Zola's writing processes. Marie-Sophie Armstrong argues that the phonetic account of the machines at work in the sawmill — the 'régularité et sécheresse de la machine' [machine-like regularity] — echoes sounds within the Rougon-Macquart names, and that there is a 'symbolic equivalence between the "aire Saint Mittre" and the space of Zolian writing'. Armstrong's discussion of the connections between the Aire Saint Mittre and Zola's wider narrative strategies links Zola's conception of his own project with his intertextual inflexions of works by Balzac and Zola.[24] Susan Harrow uses the image of the Aire Saint Mittre to illustrate her argument that Zola combines modernist tendencies with more traditional realist description; it is 'a space of representation that combines a Realist's concern for detail with a modernist's concern for de-realisation and simultaneity'.[25] This opening scene of the novel offers a particular parallel with the first chapter of Balzac's *Illusions perdues*. The description of the Stanhope press and the reference to the Angoulême paper mills in the introductory lines of that novel set the scene for a text which will recount the increasing industrialization of literature as a result of increased capacities for paper production, and the concomitant rise of the press. Zola's sawmills suggest an intertextual echo of Balzac's seminal account of the competition between literature and journalism; *La Fortune des Rougon*, too, will stage battles between antagonistic genres. Ziegler's discussion of the significance of the Aire Saint Mittre also sees it as a 'chantier' for the wider Rougon-Macquart project, and suggests the contradictions embedded in this former cemetery: 'beginning with the disintegration of the corpses, Zola's novel is structured on the opposition of randomness and determination, damning and spillage, walls and anarchy, the exuberant ineffability of the organic and the disciplined linearity of the narrative'.[26] For Ziegler, the Aire witnesses 'the generational progression of its changing functions'. Those changing functions reflect, too, the increasing emphasis placed on journalism, both in the text and wider society. Journalism is a practice of narrative little examined as one of the 'scriptural enterprises' seen by critics as so self-reflexively analyzed in this opening chapter of the Rougon-Macquart cycle.

The ancient cemetery of the Aire Saint Mittre is a site of storytelling. When the two young lovers, Silvère and Miette, hold their regular rendez-vous there, they try to recreate the stories of lives memorialized in the differently-shaped bones lying around: 'ils se questionnaient sur les ossements qu'ils découvraient [...] A chaque nouvelle trouvaille, c'étaient des suppositions sans fin. Si l'os était petit, elle parlait d'une belle jeune fille poitrinaire' (*FR*, 207) ('they often questioned each other about the remains they discovered [...] At each new discovery, she launched into endless suppositions. If the bone was small she spoke of some girl who had been carried off by consumption').[27] The tombstone with its mutilated inscription to the unknown dead Marie not only incarnates past legend but also anticipates the plot of Zola's novel; Miette is terrified by the echo of her own name on the grave and imagines it portends a bleak future for her, a premonition which will be endorsed with the description of her death at the hands of the soldiers who fight to put down the insurgents. Naomi Schor sees the presence of the tombstone as primordial among the mythoi which, for her, structure Zola's thought and works; it is 'the true centre of the novel' and its fragmented inscription is emblematic of the disjointed textual fabric of La Fortune des Rougon itself, 'shot through with holes'. For Schor, the founding myth in Zola's work is the slaying of the scapegoat, and the unknown dead Marie represents the first sacrificial victim in the subsequent family cycle.[28]

These seminal scenes of storytelling are reflected in the representation of journalism in the text in two ways. Firstly, the process of constructing tales seen in these examples is found, too, in the business of assembling newspaper stories described later in the novel. From the decomposing bodies in the cemetery comes the fabrication of legends, whether they be the anecdotes invented by Silvère and Miette using the bones found in the fertile soil, or the wider symbolic image of Zola's family saga which grows from the pear trees which flourish in that same earth. The narrative about journalism in the novel also sees decomposition result, eventually, in the production of flowering print. Aristide Rougon has established a newspaper in his home town, initially to give voice to the republicanism he sees as the dominant political ideology following 1848, and also to forge a deliberate rivalry with the existing publication in Plassans, La Gazette, edited by the bookseller Vuillet and championing the Church and conservatism. With the *coup d'état*, though, Aristide's self-interested instincts, which are to ride with the prevailing mood, are unsettled. Having penned an article condemning the *coup*, he gets cold feet, wondering whether he should not, instead, be encouraging support for Louis-Napoléon. He runs to the offices of L'Indépendant and demands that his explosive article be torn apart: 'L'article était déjà mis en page. Il fit desserrer la forme, et ne se calma qu'après avoir décomposé lui même l'article, en mêlant furieusement les lettres comme un jeu de dominos' (FR, 105) ('the article had already been typeset. He had the forme unlocked and would not rest until he had destroyed the setting with his own hands, furiously mixing up the type, like a set of dominoes'). Through this act, the page of journalism is subject to 'decomposition' — like the corpses in the Aire Saint Mittre — and the letters are jumbled and rendered fragmentary like the lettering on the tombstone. When, later in the novel, Aristide receives proof that he was right to destroy his original opinionated piece as the *coup d'état* is proved a success, he writes an alternative article extolling the defeat of the insurgents in Plassans and celebrating 'l'aurore de la liberté dans l'ordre et de l'ordre dans la liberté' (FR, 292) ('the dawn of liberty in order and of order in liberty'). This edition of L'Indépendant will be sent to Aristide's brother Eugène in Paris, and Eugène will use his influence and the proof of patriotism provided by Aristide's pro-Napoleonic rhetoric to procure the Legion of Honour for their father: such will be the 'fruits' of the original decomposed article.

Schor's image of a 'text shot through with holes' is echoed, too, in the patchiness of the journalistic output assembled in the text. Aristide's disassembling of his republican text leads to an issue of *L'Indépendant* composed only of bits and pieces — 'presque entièrement composé de faits divers' (*FR*, 106) ('composed almost entirely of miscellaneous items of news') — including a note declaring that Aristide has injured his hand and so will be unable to contribute to the paper for an unspecified period of time (he binds his arm in a sling while the uncertainty over the political outcome continues, so as to avoid having to commit written support to either one side or the other). And when he finally does switch sides and come out in favour of the *coup d'état*, it is suggested that his articles will only be based on partial evidence, as will be seen later.

The second way in which the inaugural scene of the novel is significant in charting journalistic development in the text is that the processes of change discussed by critics suggest the move from an age of legend to a more modern age of narrative. Schor remarks on this in her comments on the opening pages of *La Fortune des Rougon*: 'There is a curious and marked progression from an obscure point in the past — a pre-text — to a clearly specified moment in the present; we seem to emerge slowly from the realm of legend ("anciennement" [in the past]) into an era of clocks and calendars ("un dimanche soir, vers sept heures"... [on a Sunday evening, around seven o' clock])'.[29] This sense of a shift into the modern age and into the rhythms of measurable time has been described elsewhere as having been catalyzed, in the nineteenth century, by the expansion of the press. It is encapsulated in the title of Thérenty's work on journalism of the period, *La Littérature au quotidien*: the new Parisian dailies gave rise to a new form of journalistic writing which defined modernity by its rhythms. In the city, the cries of newspaper sellers punctuated the day. Like railway timetables, the increasingly regular publication and distribution of papers served to unite a nation in an understanding of temporality; Thérenty refers to it as the 'mise en place d'une temporalité nationale' [establishment of a national understanding of time].[30] The shift in the recording of time in the first chapter of *La Fortune des Rougon* is emblematic of a shift, too, towards a practice of Naturalism which incorporates an increasingly journalistic mode of recording events. Thérenty also notes the connections between new developments in later nineteenth-century journalism, such as the rise of the *fait-divers*, and Naturalism; while the naturalist novel 'est voisin dans l'esprit du grand reportage' [is related in spirit to news-gathering], it is more closely aligned with the narrative model of the *fait-divers*: 'roman naturaliste et fait-divers partagent le rêve d'une écriture scientifique dont la forme même garantirait l'effectivité' [both naturalist novel and fait-divers share the ideal of a scientific mode of writing whose very form will be the guarantee of its success]; although certain narrative techniques such as free indirect style 'éloignent l'écriture naturaliste du protocole informatif artificiel inventé dans le journal et réinvesti largement dans le roman' [distance naturalist writing from the artificial procedures of information created by the newspaper and reinserted into the novel].[31]

Prefiguring the 'presse d'information' in *La Fortune des Rougon*

A detailed commentary on the changes in the mass press, written by Zola in the 1870s, is enlightening in that it not only provides a summary of Parisian-based publications of the period, but also highlights the writer's ambiguous response towards the journalism of his day. Wrona summarizes:

> Zola journaliste se révèle être un penseur du journalisme: grand praticien de la presse, il est un observateur passionnée et contradictoire. La richesse et l'ambivalence de ses analyses témoignent de sa situation historique bien particulière: l'écrivain vit en effet au plus près une mutation décisive du paysage journalistique, qui conduit à la professionalisation du métier de journaliste, et à la massification du journal.[32]

> [Zola the journalist revels in the role of reflecting on journalism: himself a frequent contributor to the press, he is a passionate and contrary observer. The depth and ambiguity of his analyses are testament to this very particular historical period: the writer witnesses at close hand a decisive shift in the journalistic landscape, leading to the professionalization of the trade of journalism and the phenomenal growth of the newspaper.]

Although published several years after the appearance of the first Rougon-Macquart novel, the account of a burgeoning 'presse d'information' set out in Zola's columns in the Russian paper *Messager de l'Europe* and intended to explain French journalism to his foreign readers, describes, too, a shift in journalism and narration at work in *La Fortune des Rougon*. Zola's explanation of developments in the press refers to the increased speed with which news could travel, chiming with Thérenty's depiction of an progressively more temporal, 'quotidien' society and its expectations of regular news: 'au fur et à mesure que chemins de fer et fils télégraphiques faisaient disparaître la distance, le lecteurs devenaient de plus en plus exigeants' [as steam trains and telegraphic wires made distances disappear, readers became ever more demanding].[33] His article sets out the contrast between what he calls the 'véritable siècle d'or' [veritable golden age] of journalism under the July Monarchy, and the 'crise sérieuse' [serious crisis] of the 1870s. Zola's depiction of a pre-1848 provincial newspaper culture in the same article has echoes of his novel:

> Il fallait une semaine pour la confirmation d'un évènement important. Dans certains villages, le journal du lundi gardait tout son intérêt pendant la semaine entière [...] La presse vivant uniquement de nouvelles n'était pas encore née; chaque journal n'existait donc que grâce aux opinions dont il était le porte-parole [...]. On ne saurait s'imaginer la solidité que lui donnait cette communauté de convictions.[34]

> [It took a week for confirmation of an important event to be received. In some villages, Monday's newspaper remained a source of interest for the whole week. The press based wholly on news had not yet arrived; each publication survived only thanks to the opinions it voiced [...]. It is difficult to imagine the strength that such a community of convictions provided.]

In *La Fortune des Rougon*, the *Gazette de Plassans*, founded by Vuillet before 1848, is hardly illustrative of a golden age of journalism: the almost illiterate bookseller 'rédigeait lui-même les articles [...] avec une humilité et un fiel qui lui tenaient lieu de talent' (*FR*, 79) ('he wrote all the articles himself [...] with a humility and venom that compensated for his lack of talent'). Yet in other respects, it fits the description provided by Zola in his later article on the press; the *Gazette* is based not on news but on opinion, and acts to bind together the sense of community in the yellow drawing room of Plassans.

When, in the wake of the 1848 revolution, Aristide Rougon establishes *L'Indépendant*, he finds the lack of news inhibiting; cut off from Paris in an age which just precedes that depicted by Zola in the *Messager de l'Europe*, he flounders, committing himself to republican support but doubting his own convictions. In this pre-*presse d'information* era, Aristide craves information; without it, he cannot satisfy his own ferret-like desire for self-interest and advancement. Lacking confirmation of what the mood in Paris might be, he is near-blind: 'il marchait en aveugle; il se sentait perdu, au fond de sa province, sans boussole, sans indications précises' (*FR*, 83) ('he was groping in the dark, shut away in the provinces, without a guide, without any precise information'). The more blinkered he is, the more he is driven to opinionated diatribes: 'il tomba sur les conservateurs avec plus de rage, pour se venger de son aveuglement' (*FR*, 83) ('he attacked the conservatives with even greater ferocity, as if to avenge his own blindness'). The theme of Aristide's blindness, as a journalist, is echoed later in the novel when the *coup d'état* breaks out: 'Aristide écoutait d'ordinaire aux portes de la sous-prefecture, pour avoir des renseignements précis; il sentait qu'il marchait en aveugle, et il se raccrochait aux nouvelles qu'il volait à l'administration' (*FR*, 104) ('Aristide was in the habit of listening behind the doors of the sub-prefecture in an attempt to get precise information, for he felt he was groping in the dark, and clutched hold of every shred of information he could glean from official sources').

Zola is disparaging, in his account of the modern French press, of the practice of news-gathering, and of the substitution of a rage for facts and information at the expense of longer literary and political pieces:

> La presse ne tarda pas à pénétrer partout. Actuellement, l'indiscrétion est devenue sa règle; il n'y a pas de domaine où elle ne se soit glissée; elle est là pour tout savoir et tout dire [...]. Le journalisme y perdit sa dignité. Il est trop commode de ne plus devoir penser pour écrire, et de tout remplacer par la grossière nudité des faits.[35]
>
> [The press will soon penetrate everywhere. These days, indiscretion has become its rule of thumb; there is no field it has not infiltrated; it is there, listening to everything and reporting it [...]. Journalism has lost its dignity. It is too easy to avoid thinking when writing, and to substitute raw, unrefined facts for everything else.]

He also comments on the *faits-divers*:

> Le journal nouveau tend à mettre à la porte la littérature. Les faits-divers, sous plusieurs appellations différentes, ont envahi les quatre pages. La presse à information est née. Il ne s'agit plus d'analyser un livre [...]. Il faut leur raconter le crime de la nuit en trois cents lignes, avec le portrait de l'assassin, ce qu'il

mangeait, ce qu'il buvait; il faut tout réduire en petits faits précis, brutaux, sans ornements aucuns.[36]

[The newspaper these days tends to eject literature. The *faits-divers*, under various different headings, have taken over all four pages. The press based on information has been born. Books are not discussed any more [...] you must narrate the crime of the night before in three hundred lines, with a description of the assassin, what he ate and drank; everything must be reduced to hard, cold facts, with no embellishment.]

This craving for news described by Zola in his summary of the French press is manifested in *La Fortune des Rougon*. Not only does Aristide desire the facts behind the *coup d'état* in Paris, refusing to pen any more articles until he has access to proper information, but the people of Plassans, too, orchestrated by Aristide's mother Félicité, require the endorsement of the newspaper's response to the political crisis in order to calm their fears or solidify their prejudices. When Pierre Rougon, Aristide's father, achieves his first successes in his attempts to do battle with the insurgents, capturing his own brother Macquart and taking up watch in the mayor's armchair, the resulting story of his heroics becomes increasingly inflated as it is retold. Félicité and her husband encourage Vuillet to publish a 'bel article pour rassurer la population' (*FR*, 239) ('a well-wrought article to reassure the townspeople'). Vuillet, still unconvinced that the insurgents have been fully defeated, defers such a mission; Aristide, too, is reluctant to commit himself to taking sides in the conflict until he can be convinced of victory. Without the write-up in any newspaper, Pierre's antics remain but oral legend, the townspeople remain unsettled, and further action against the insurgents is required and planned. The lack of 'information' provided by the press means that the plots — both the schemes hatched by Félicité and Pierre Rougon, and Zola's own narrative — are furthered by the refusal of the journalist characters to set down any facts or proffer any opinions.

Two subsequent scenes in the text illustrate the processes of garnering such information for the newspapers. The first offers an example of the impact of news arriving in the provinces from Paris, particularly at this crucial moment in French history. Having originally refused to provide an account against the republicans, Vuillet changes his mind and writes, in the *Gazette*, a sweeping diatribe condemning the insurgents. Suspecting the reason for his change of heart, Félicité realizes that he must have received some form of news from Paris confirming the outcome of the *coup d'état*. He has been infiltrating the box of mail at the post office, and has used information supplied by Eugène Rougon's account of Louis-Napoléon's victory to fuel his journalistic invective, an example of 'la lourdeur du journalisme de province' ('the heavy-handedness of French provincial journalism') in which 'il enfilait des périphrases ordurières' (*FR*, 260) ('periphrastic abuse was piled up'). Vuillet's theft of letters which are not addressed to him offers another example of the ways in which stories are uncovered in this novel, which is rich in unveiling the processes of creating or discovering narratives. Dezalay comments on the significance of information-gathering in the text:

La lutte pour le pouvoir devient ainsi une bataille pour s'assurer le contrôle des

> sources d'information, où la presse finit par jouer un rôle essentiel, puisque c'est Vuillet qui, en interceptant la lettre décisive d'Eugène à Félicité et en se déclarant ouvertement contre les insurgés, donne le signal du dénouement et conduit les Rougon à déclencher le massacre des républicains, qui doit leur assurer la victoire.[37]

> [The battle for power thus becomes a battle to control the sources of information, in which the press ends up playing an essential role, since it is Vuillet who, in intercepting the decisive letter from Eugène to Félicité, with its open condemnation of the insurgents, signals the denouement and leads the Rougon to carry out the massacre of the republicans, and make sure of their victory.]

The second scene which sees news being proven cements Aristide's occupation as a journalist. When the insurgents fall into the trap laid by Rougon and four are shot, Aristide finally emerges to examine the corpses. The resulting description is pivotal in showing how he overcomes his previous *aveuglement* and adopts the penetrating vision of the reporter in search of facts:

> Comme on enlevait les cadavres, Aristide vint les flairer. Il les regarda sur tous les sens, humant l'air, interrogeant les visages. Il avait la mine sèche, les yeux clairs. De sa main, la veille emmaillotée, libre à cette heure, il souleva la blouse d'un des morts, pour mieux voir sa blessure. Cet examen parut le convaincre, lui ôter un doute. Il serra les lèvres, resta là un moment sans dire un mot, puis se retira pour aller presser la distribution de *l'Indépendant*, dans lequel il avait mis un grand article. Le long des maisons, il se rappelait ce mot de sa mère: 'Tu verras demain!' Il avait vu, c'était très fort. (FR, 290).

> [When the corpses were being removed, Aristide came to look at them. He examined them from all angles, sniffing and studying their faces. His eyes shone, and he had a hard expression. In order to see a wound more clearly he even lifted up the smock of one of the corpses, with the hand which on the previous day had been hanging in a sling. This examination seemed to convince him and remove any lingering doubt from his mind. He pursed his lips, stood there for a moment in silence, and then went off to hasten the distribution of *L'Indépendant*, which was carrying a long article of his. As he hurried past the houses he remembered his mother's words: 'Tomorrow you'll see!' He had indeed seen; it was all very clever.]

The following chapter will evaluate the emphasis placed on sensory perception, and on vision in particular, associated with the growth in reportage in the fin-de-siècle years. This scene, which sees Aristide lifting the shirts of the dead in order to investigate and verify the nature of the incident, unveiling the truth and leaving behind his blinkered insight, enacts a shift in the very nature of the journalism produced in *La Fortune des Rougon*. The youngest of the Rougon sons here indicates something of the mania for 'tout savoir', for the 'grossière nudité des faits' which Zola describes in relation to the journalism of the 1870s. The *presse d'information*, driven by the crisis of the *coup d'état*, is illustrated as coming into being in the pages of *La Fortune des Rougon*.

With this glimpse of the outcome of the insurgency in Plassans, Aristide is able to remove his sling, symbol of his incapacity to act until he is sure he can commit to the winning side, and he writes his article announcing that victory lies with Louis-Napoléon. His early republican instincts are suppressed, and he hints, in his piece in *L'Indépendant*, that such leanings were youthful folly: 'il avait fait aussi une délicate allusion au salon jaune, reconnaissant ses torts, disant que "la jeunesse est présomptueuse"' (*FR*, 293) ('He had also made a delicate allusion to the yellow drawing-room, acknowledging his errors, declaring that "youth is presumptuous"'). The revelation gleaned by Aristide as he leans over the bodies, sniffing and sensing, 'les yeux clairs', is mirrored in the fabric of the novel itself, which postpones its own revelations and insight so as to maximize them. As Aristide uncovers the truth, so in turn the truth is uncovered about Aristide, with Zola's text including the detail, in its closing pages, of the truth of the death of the republican Silvère: that he was shot by the one-eyed gendarme seeking revenge for his own earlier injury, but that the scene was witnessed by the newly observant Aristide, who admits to his parents, 'J'étais là quand le gendarme lui a cassé la tête d'un coup de pistolet' (*FR*, 306) ('I was there when the gendarme blew his brains out with a pistol'). As he utters this confession, he starts to rock backwards and forwards on his chair, suggesting the jerky action of the 'saccades' which will become embedded in his new name. In the opening chapter of *La Curée*, it is noted that Saccard bartered his name of Rougon for his new designation; his wife Renée associates the sound of it with the collection of wealth: 'ce nom de Saccard, dont les deux syllabes sèches avaient sonné à ses oreilles, les premières fois, avec la brutalité de deux râteaux ramassant de l'or' ('that name Saccard, the two dry syllables of which, when she first heard them, had reverberated in her ears like two rakes gathering up gold').[38] Brian Nelson suggests, in his comments on Zola's second Rougon-Macquart novel, *La Curée*, in which Aristide has become the property speculator Saccard, that he is 'a hyperbolic projection of Haussmannization in its most ruthless and spectacular forms [...] (he) personifies the energy, the life-force of Zola's vision of modern life'.[39] That transition to embodying the energy of modern life is inaugurated in these closing sequences of *La Fortune des Rougon*, when Aristide steps forward to become the witness and scribe to destruction, to the ravaging of the republic, darting here and there to check the facts, peering beneath surfaces to seek evidence.

Saccard and Saccades: Journalistic and Narrative Parallels

The delayed revelation as to Aristide's culpability in the death of Silvère evokes parallels between the transmission of news via the provincial papers and the patterns of the narrative itself. As there are gaps in journalistic output caused by the slow arrival of news from Paris, so Zola's novel, too, reflects temporal ruptures in its chronology. *La Fortune des Rougon* opens in the distant past, and then shuttles backwards and forwards in time, first introducing the reader to Silvère and Miette in the opening chapter but then deferring the account of their relationship for several chapters. And in the closing sequences, the reader receives detail of Tante Dide's shock and collapse before being told what has caused such a reaction, namely the fact that she, too, has been witness to the shooting of Silvère. This novel, then, which narrates the coming-to-knowledge of the journalist Saccard, is itself composed of saccades. Susan Harrow's account of Zola's modernity refers to such manipulation of temporality; she maintains that:

> Saccades and jolts are a generalised feature of the Rougon-Macquart novels. They involve elision, a sudden acceleration of tempo, the contraction of duration, and the rushing of narrative action [...]. Related to elision and saccadic style in its disruption of linearity is splicing, the interruption of one discursive moment by another as rival discourses inscribe the simultaneous rhythms of modernity.[40]

These 'rhythms of modernity' are found in the inaugural novel of the cycle, and given prominence by the disruptions and momentum applied to the production of newspaper articles in the text. As the Second Empire is brought into being in the pages of the novel, so Zola's narrative gives insight into 'rival discourses' — between the *Gazette de Plassans* and Aristide's *L'Indépendant* — and into the alternating cadences of the dissemination of news, enacting both the 'somnolence' and the 'vie [...] fiévreusement agitée' [feverishly agitated life] of the shift towards the *presse d'information* set out in his article for the *Messager de l'Europe*.

Harrow suggests too that Zola is often considered an antimodernist because his work aims too comprehensively for objectivity, for a panoptic vision; she argues that he purposefully undermines such objectivity even as his naturalist ambition seems to encourage it.[41] Again, such a contradiction between a panoptic gaze and ambiguity can be found in *La Fortune des Rougon*, and exemplified in the representations of journalistic output. Aristide's climactic moment of seeing, the 'il avait vu' which summarizes his sensory comprehension of the outcome of the battle in Plassans, is not only a glimpse into the drive towards the *presse d'information* but also into the practices of Naturalism itself. It evokes, for example, Zola's description of the experimental practice of the novel in *Le Roman expérimental*, in which he sets out his evaluation of Claude Bernard's practices, distinguishing between observation and experiment and announcing the key claim that 'le romancier est fait d'un observateur et d'un expérimentateur' [the novelist is made up of both observer and scientist].[42] The experimental method enables the novelist to exercise 'toute son intelligence de penseur et [...] tout son génie de créateur. Il lui faudra voir, comprendre, inventer' [all his capacity for thought and all his creative genius. He must see, comprehend and invent].[43] This, in essence, is the process set in motion by Aristide's awakening in the aftermath of the battle in Plassans: he sees clearly for the first time as he peeks under the clothing of the wounded insurgents, comprehends what the victory means for the political future of France, and sets about inventing the lyrical phrases of his article for *L'Indépendant*. In *Le Roman expérimental*, Zola cites Claude Bernard's description of the journey towards clarity offered by the observational demands of science:

> S'il fallait donner une comparaison qui exprimât mon sentiment sur la science de la vie, je dirais que c'est un salon superbe, tout resplendissant de lumière, dans lequel on ne peut parvenir qu'en passant par une longue et affreuse cuisine.[44]
>
> [If I had to give a comparison which would sum up my feelings on science and

life, I would say that it is a superb drawing-room, flooded with light, which you can only get to by passing through a long and disgusting kitchen.]

La Fortune des Rougon charts Aristide's journey from the obscurity of his hesitant response to the *coup d'état*, towards being feted in the 'salon jaune' of bourgeois triumph, following the enlightenment provided by his understanding of the insurgency.

At the same time, though, the narrative's own gaze onto the scene investigated by Aristide suggests that his observational acuity is flawed. The text recounts the ways in which the citizens of Plassans inflate, in their imaginations, what they think has happened, and what they think they have witnessed. Although the victors are heard 'grossissant le chiffre de leurs adversaires' ('exaggerating the number of their adversaries') and 'des bourgeois prétendirent s'être mis à la fenêtre et avoir vu passer [...] le flot épais des fuyards' ('some of the good townsfolk asserted that when they had looked out of their window they had seen a great stream of insurgents fleeing past'), Zola's description also claims that 'jamais l'histoire vraie de cette fusillade ne fut connue' (*FR*, 288) ('the true story of the shooting was never known'). He fractures the panoptic view of the insurgency even as Aristide seems to affirm it, creating instead the sense of a narrative full of gaps, of stories untold, in keeping with the seminal image of the tombstone in the opening chapter with its obliterated phrases.

Aristide, through his failure to intervene and save his cousin Silvère, has blood on his hands, 'avait son cadavre' by the end of the novel. Silvère has been seen, notably by Mitterand, as representative of Zola himself in this novel, the first such incarnation in the Rougon-Macquart series:

> Ne dirait-on pas que le narrateur vient se confondre lui-même avec son personnage? En tête des Rougon-Macquart, l'homme qui erre parmi les monuments d'une société disparue, qui la tire du sommeil pour lui rendre son identité et lui révéler le sens de son histoire, n'est-ce pas une figure du romancier? Comme si l'auteur des Rougon-Macquart, à l'orée de cette histoire, se mettait lui-même en abîme dans son récit, avec son pouvoir tout neuf, juvénile et encore fragile, de résurrection du passé.[45]

> [Could it not be said that the narrator himself ends up becoming confused with this character? Is this not the figure of the novelist, the man who, at the opening of the Rougon-Macquart, wanders between the monuments of a vanished society, and who awakens it in order to restore its identity and reveal the meaning of its history? It is as if the author of the Rougon-Macquart self-consciously inserts himself into the narrative, with all his fresh, youthful, and still fragile power, to bring back the past.]

Silvère, then, this 'fragile' character, who conjures stories from the inscriptions and bones in the former cemetery, and who stands as the representative martyr of the republican cause in the text, is killed by a one-eyed gendarme and his death witnessed by the now clear-sighted Aristide. Naomi Schor points out, using Zola's pre-texts, that in his work 'murder and artistic creation are somehow linked'.[46] In *La Fortune des Rougon*, the murder of Silvère engenders both the plot of the novel and the material for Aristide's article. If Zola, the novelist and naturalist, is variously embodied in the opening novel by both Silvère and Pascal, the doctor and genealogist, he is also, surely, paralleled in the figure of Aristide, who learns, in the text, how to construct a story by getting up close to the scene of the crime and seeking out information. No matter how disparagingly the journalist is represented in the text, he represents a hybrid, half spinner of tales, writing, as he does, of the 'aurore' represented by the *coup d'état*, half observer of evidence. He is an amalgamation of the insightful doctor and the imaginative Silvère, a former republican who chooses instead to profit from the *coup d'état* through his writing. Indeed, later comments by Zola on the *presse d'information* suggests a more favourable, and literary, view of the practice than his comments on 'La Presse française' of 1877, suggesting the novelist's increasing embrace of journalistic methods. In his replies to an interviewer for *Le Gaulois* some ten years later, he remarked that: 'J'aime la presse d'information; elle est la coupe de la vie; on y puise les extases passagères, les impressions fugitives, toutes choses qui me paraissent bonnes, parce qu'elles sont courtes' [I love the information-based press, it is the heartbeat of life; it extracts fleeting ectasy, ephemeral impressions, all those things which seem good to me, because they are short-lived].[47]

Brian Nelson notes 'the caustic nature of Zola's satire' in the text, which includes first-person references to detail such as the 'ridiculous' fortifications which surround the town of Plassans, and suggests that 'it is as if Zola, whether consciously or not, has not yet found his voice as a Naturalist novelist, and reverts to the vigorous personal style of the polemical articles he published in *La Tribune* throughout 1868 and 1869'.[48] These articles saw Zola condemning the *coup d'état*, in the years when he was compiling the preparatory material for the Rougon-Macquart cycle and for *La Fortune des Rougons* in particular; he was particularly stirred by the publication of Noël Blache's *Histoire de l'insurrection du Var en décembre 1851*, an account of the brutal repression of republican insurrection in the provinces. He wrote, in *La Tribune*, of details emerging almost twenty years after the *coup d'état*, 'Que la vérité historique est lente parfois à se faire! Il semble que les faits contemporains devraient être connus de tout le monde, dans leurs moindres détails' [How historical truth is sometimes slow to be put together! It seems that the facts of the time in all their detail must be known by all].[49] Thus Zola's journalism makes its presence felt in the pages of his novel, as he endeavours to bring out, in *La Fortune des Rougons*, the 'vérité historique', in the sometimes polemical style which Nelson sees as characteristic of Zola's own political articles. At the same time he, like Aristide, turns the fodder of the *coup d'état* into material for profit, both in his fiction and his 'Causeries' for *La Tribune*. This is arguably why he depicts his journalist with symbolically blood-stained hands, bearing responsibility for the death of idealism, republicanism, and an oral tradition of storytelling. He sees himself in the Aristide who confesses culpability for his vision.

La Fortune des Rougon is a seminal text in the development of Zola's Naturalism, as seen through critical discussion of the description of the Aire Saint Mittre and its role in symbolizing key naturalistic patterns of germination, decay, and cylicity. Yet it suggests, through its incorporation of a narrative about the generation of newspaper copy, parallels between journalism and naturalism and, in turn, an underlying discomfort with the business of recounting history based on the key term of 'observation' which recurs throughout *Le Roman experimental*. Aristide Saccard is a figure who, arguably, represents a Zola coming to terms with his own stance as a naturalist writer, positioning himself in opposition to 'idealistic' literature such as that represented by Silvère, while retaining a nostalgia for such a tradition. Discussions of the role played by Saccard in the later novel *L'Argent*, suggest he incarnates the figure of the novelist in that text too.[50] David Baguley notes the paradoxes associated with Zola's theory of Naturalism, commenting on Zola's tendency, in *Le Roman expérimental*, to equate the writer's genius and subjectivity with the processes of observation and experiment: 'we therefore arrive at the somewhat paradoxical view that Zola's theory was not merely an attempt to arrive at a more scientific type of realism, but also, on the contrary, a way of vindicating scientifically his deep-seated Romantic belief in individual genius'.[51] Ann Jefferson's work on the idea of 'genius' in France suggests that Zola explores the term both positively and negatively, as in *L'Œuvre*:

> Genius may be a largely positive term for Zola the art critic who regards disruption as a virtue, but for Zola the novelist these 'disruptions' are an ambivalent quality that allows him to explore it *both* positively as central to the artistic enterprise *and* negatively as a sterile or destructive pathology.[52]

These ambiguities and tensions are brought out, in *La Fortune des Rougon*, in the critical glance cast at the character of Saccard-the-reporter, who embodies observation and, by the end, a form of genius for inventing both self and style which will facilitate his later successes and failures across the Rougon-Macquart cycle. Gillian Beer comments on the double sense of 'experience' and 'experiment' in Zola's conception of the experimental practice of the novel, as 'a procedure quite in accord with current intellectual endeavour in the sciences which were preoccupied with the demonstration of hidden relations and analogies'.[53] The illuminating moment of Aristide's observational insight when he examines the bodies in the wake of the attack on the insurgents is pivotal in his subsequent experiment — the newspaper article he writes evaluating the *coup d'état* — and in his experience, enabling his move to Paris and his future financial and journalistic ventures. Discussion of Zola's last completed novel, in the second half of this chapter, will also explore the paradoxes in Zola's conception of Naturalism, this time in a text, *Vérité*, which might be thought to reflect a conclusive move beyond the ideas of literature set out in *Le Roman expérimental*.

Later Battles: Journalism, the Dreyfus Affair, and *Vérité*

Zola's own prolific journalistic output, critically and self-reflexively echoed in the first of his Rougon-Macquart novels, reaches a zenith with his role in the Dreyfus affair. The celebratory note proclaimed by Aristide Rougon in his article in praise of the *coup d'état*, which sees 'l'aurore de la liberté dans l'ordre', reads ironically when it is considered that this hyperbolic and profiteering slogan prefigures the title of the publication, *L'Aurore*, which would feature Zola's most famous contribution to journalism, the 'J'Accuse' letter of January 1898.[54] This chapter has so far argued that Zola's representation of journalism is more deeply embedded than commentators on his novels, such as Dezalay, have so far suggested. It will now focus on a post-Rougon-Macquart novel, the third of the *Quatre Évangiles*, *Vérité*. While *La Fortune des Rougon* centres on the conflict surrounding the 1851 *coup d'état*, *Vérité* takes as its subject an allegory of the Dreyfus Affair and the vicious conflicts articulated in the newspapers of the time between Dreyfusards and anti-Dreyfusards, stoked by Zola's own press contributions of the time. Whereas the earlier novel represents the coming-into-being of modern reportage via the developing perception and understanding of news incarnated by Aristide Rougon, the last of Zola's completed novels envisages a complete remodelling of the press in the aftermath of the Dreyfus affair.

This change in the desired output of the newspapers is matched by a change, in the *Quatre Évangiles*, to a novelistic model which breaks away from Zola's own Naturalism. On the one hand, then, this discussion of *Vérité* will suggest the differences between the early Zola novel and his later representations of journalism and narrative strategies. On the other, the connections explored in the first half of this chapter between the processes of news-gathering and Zola's text, such as the impact of delays in reporting stories, can also be traced in his last novel. Although *Vérité* castigates journalistic practice and heroizes those characters who stand up to the anti-Semitic diatribes in the press, as a novel it also borrows from the newspaper-discourse it features and critiques. The following analysis of Zola's fictional retelling of the Dreyfus affair will explore developments and similarities in his ongoing attempts to represent and report on a tradition of nineteenth-century journalism.

A reworking of the vehement campaigns on both sides of the Dreyfus affair is focalized in *Vérité* through the rape and murder of the schoolboy Zéphirin and the miscarriage of justice which sees the conviction and exile of his Jewish uncle Simon. The anti-Dreyfusard press is clearly represented in the novel through the repeated vitriolic articles published by the local newspaper, the *Petit Beaumontais*, the title of which reflects the role played by the anti-Semitic *Petit Journal* in the Affair itself, the paper with the highest circulation during the Third Republic. The publication also epitomizes the petty-mindedness of the average citizen of Beaumont, only too keen to believe what he reads about the Simon case. Yet Zola's late novel, often considered a *roman à thèse* [thesis novel] in its attempts to put forward a clear moralizing and utopian message, reveals ambiguities which raise questions about the caricature of journalism evoked by the text, but also about the status of the novel itself: its relationship to Naturalism, its own sense of purpose, and the opposition between speech and writing suggested in it.

Although the anti-Dreyfusard press is represented in *Vérité* through the 'feuille immonde', *Petit Beaumontais*, and the religious publication *Croix de Beaumont*, there is a lacuna in the text when it comes to the representation of any opposing journalistic discourse. Instead, the character and voice of the secular schoolteacher Marc, and the mantra put forward by the novel itself, which heroizes Marc and borrows his pedagogical attributes, stand in for press opposition to the *Petit Beaumontais*. Zola the public figure, writer, and journalist who pens 'J'accuse' is both absent and present in his novel — absent insofar as there is not, in Beaumont, an *Aurore* which allows Marc to articulate his support for Simon. The text itself, and the educational practices it promotes, become the 'Aurore', reflected in the persistence of the imagery of light which characterizes the text and seen, for instance, in the antithesis between the darkness of the home of the strict Catholic grandmother, Mme Duparque, and the intellectual illumination provided by the secular schools. For much of the text, a battle is staged between the novel, with its evocation of a utopia based on pedagogy, and the press, which publicizes the vision of the Church. The clear metaphoric opposition of light and dark gives resonance throughout to the meticulously systematized, and frequently reiterated, nature of this divide. The closing lines of the novel, when Marc stands with his family around him, many of whom are schoolteachers themselves, emphasize the conflict that has taken place in the text: 'Rome avait perdu la bataille, la France était sauvée du grand danger de mort, la poussière de ruine où disparaissent les unes après les autres les nations catholiques' [Rome had lost the battle, France was saved from the threat of death and the dust of ruin which saw Catholic nations disappearing one by one] (*V*, XXVII: 667).[55] As Catholicism is vanquished, so too is the scurrilous press overturned.

The celebration of Simon's return from exile, and Beaumont's gift of a house to him by way of reparation, are marked by the publication of a 'compte rendu enthousiaste' [an enthusiastic account] of the ceremony in the pages of the *Petit Beaumontais*. The purification of the newspaper is described in the following terms:

> Depuis longtemps, l'immonde journal s'était transformé sous le souffle nouveau qui haussait le niveau moral et intellectuel de ses lecteurs. Il avait fallu en balayer, en désinfecter les bureaux comme des sentines, engorgées de tant de poisons depuis des années. La presse doit devenir le plus admirable instrument d'instruction, lorsqu'elle ne sera plus aux mains des bandits politiques et financiers, abêtissant et détroussant leur clientèle. Et le *Petit Beaumontais*, renouvelé, rajeuni, commençait à rendre de grands services, aidait chaque jour à faire plus de lumière, plus de raison et de bonté. (*V*, XXVII: 633–34)

> [That once filthy print had been quite transformed by the new spirit, which had raised its readers both morally and intellectually. Its offices, so long infected by poison, had been swept and purged. The Press will, indeed, become a most admirable instrument of education when it is no longer, as now, in the hand of political and financial bandits, bent on debasing and plundering their readers. And thus *Le Petit Beaumontais*, cleansed and rejuvenated, was beginning to render great services, contributing day by day to the increase of enlightenment, reason and brotherliness.]

The narrative voice here, with its futuristic predictions as to the potential of the press, is an example of the novel's own vision. Freed from the affiliation to character, such discourse makes clear Zola's own denunciation of contemporary press corruption and his conception of its necessary role. *Vérité* sets out, more clearly than any of Zola's Rougon-Macquart novels, the classic battle so often articulated in the *romans de journalisme*, between the polluting force of the press and the business of the novel itself, whose role here is to make sense of the original crime, reveal and publicize the truth, and pave the way for the 'truth and justice' so frequently reiterated as ideals within the *Quatre Évangiles*. The transformation of the newspaper illustrates that the novel is in the process of completing its work of change, and has moulded the press in its own image as an instrument of education and enlightenment. However, the clarity of the opposition so frequently insisted on, between light and dark, church and state, cleansing pedagogy and poisonous press, tends to break down. The separation between the discourses is increasingly blurred. The negative depiction of journalism will be discussed, before an analysis of the ways in which *Vérité* disturbs its own pretensions to truth.

The Press as 'l'exécrable poison': *Petit Beaumontais*

The iniquitous role played by the newspaper, *Petit Beaumontais*, in *Vérité* is vehemently denigrated by the local educational officer, Salvan, in a tirade to the schoolteacher Marc. The paper has just announced that Simon, the Dreyfus figure in the text, is to be sent for trial; Salvan launches into his castigation of the publication, scathingly critical of its strategies. Its scapegoating of Simon is more insidious than the overt dogma of the religious paper, the *Croix de Beaumont*, because it has set itself up as having mass crowd appeal. Salvan makes references to the paper's back story — that it began as a neutral publication printing serialized fiction, 'de faits divers, d'articles de vulgarisation aimables, à la portée des moindres intelligences' [matter of fact accounts of current events and pleasant articles popularizing general knowledge] but has gradually forged connections with political and financial backers keen to exploit it as a mouthpiece. His rhetoric draws on the persistent metaphor, articulated throughout *Vérité*, of the paper's 'poison': 'cette feuille immonde, elle est l'exécrable poison qui corrompt et détruit tout un peuple' [the filthy rag! If iniquity becomes possible it is because that paper poisons the poor and lowly with its lies]:

> Que *Le Petit Beaumontais* ait publié les ignobles et lâches articles que vous savez, ces délations, ces calomnies ramassées tous les impudents, toutes les louches dans la boue, il y a là un crime, l'empoisonnement sournois d'un peuple. S'être introduit chez les simples d'un air de bonhomie, et mêler ensuite de l'arsenic à chaque plat, les faire délirer, les pousser aux actions monstrueuses, dans l'intérêt du tirage, je ne sais pas de crime plus grand. (*V*, XXVI: 100–01)

> [When *Le Petit Beaumontais* publishes the ignoble and cowardly articles with which you are acquainted, those charges and slanders picked up in the gutter, it is a crime. To penetrate among the simple by affecting bluff good nature and then to mingle arsenic with every dish, to drive the masses to delirium and to the most monstrous actions in order to increase one's sales, I know of no greater crime!]

The impact of the paper on the public consciousness is brought out clearly in a number of scenes, as on the occasion of Simon's arrest and Zéphirin's funeral, when the crowd is stirred to violence and angry shouting, the free indirect style of the passage indicating the way in which the paper's rhetoric has moulded the fiction of popular opinion:

> Cette foule, nourrie des contes du *Petit Beaumontais*, encore secouée par l'horreur du crime, poussa-t-elle des cris, dès qu'elle aperçut l'instituteur, le juif maudit, le tueur de petits enfants, qui avait besoin pour ses maléfices de leur sang vierge, encore sanctifié par l'hostie. C'était la légende désormais indestructible, volant de bouche en bouche, affolant la cohue grondante et menaçante. (*V*, XXVI: 83)

> [This crowd, which had gorged itself with the tales of *Le Petit Beaumontais*, and which was still stirred by the horror of the crime, raised angry shouts as soon as it perceived the schoolmaster, that accursed Jew, that slayer of little children, who for his abominable witchery needed their virgin blood, whilst it was yet sanctified by the presence of the Host. That was the legend, never to be destroyed, which sped from mouth to mouth, maddening the tumultuous and menacing crowd.]

During the trial, the press manipulation of the case is illustrated through the naming of the jurors so as to pressurize them into delivering the verdict which will meet with the approval of the crowd; subsequently, a further press campaign is launched against Marc himself, echoing the vilification of Zola in the anti-Dreyfusard newspapers. The strength and colour of the rhetoric employed to depict the *Petit Beaumontais*, which rivals the vitriol described as printed in the pages of the paper itself (Marc is accused of 'des crimes les plus noirs' [the blackest of crimes]; 'des abominations se passaient dans une petite ville voisine' [abominable things were happening in a little neighbouring town], *V*, XXVI: 241–42), indicates the battleground opening up between the factions at work in the text, between the discourse of the novel and the discourse of the newspaper it represents, as between the religious and the secular in the Affair. The press is intimately bound up with the dogma of the Church in the text. Even during Simon's trial, the journalists reporting on the case are described as scribbling their notes by the light of church candles, as if the illumination they shed on the affair itself is necessarily provided by the Church.

Salvan's condemnation of the gossip-mongering of the *Petit Beaumontais* as a 'crime' evidently draws connections between the damaging tendencies of the popular press and the crime which initiates the drama of the novel, the rape and murder of Zéphirin. This hyperbolic association between the words of the newspaper and the original crime are indicated and reiterated right from the early descriptions of the murder scene. The arrival of the newspaper at the Duparque household in the opening pages also brings news of the murder, since it is the delivery boy who informs the maid Pélagie of the crime. More significantly, the piece of writing which acts as the crucial clue in the narrative — and represents Zola's incorporation of the 'bordereau' [slip of paper] incriminating Dreyfus in the real-life affair — the torn-off copy-slip found in Zéphirin's bedroom, is wrapped in crumpled newspaper: 'le tampon était fait d'un journal, et [...] il y avait, avec ce journal, une étroite feuille blanche, froissée, maculée [...] c'est un numéro du *Petit Beaumontais*, daté d'hier 2 août' [the ball had been formed of a newspaper, in the midst of which a narrow, crumpled and stained slip of white paper appeared [...] a number of *Le Petit Beaumontais* dated yesterday, August 2] (*V*, XXVI: 20). Throughout the pages which narrate the description of the crime scene, the conjunction of the two pieces of paper, the copy-slip, which will be proven to have originated from the religious Brothers' school, and the previous day's copy of the *Petit Beaumontais*, is frequently re-asserted, the novel's rhetoric kneading together these two scraps of evidence through repetitive clauses as the papers themselves are melded, 'froissé, comme pétri' [crumpled, almost kneaded] (*V*, XXVI: 22): the 'crimes' of Church and press could not be more closely intermingled.

Orality connects the original rape and murder with the articles appearing in the newspaper throughout the rest of the novel. As the stories published by the *Petit Beaumontais* are swallowed by the public in metaphors consistently associating such gullibility with a form of poison, an 'abominable breuvage qui corrompt et fait délirer' [the hateful beverage which corrupts and brings delirium] (*V*, XXVI: 158), or a method of 'nourrir' [feeding] (*V*, XXVI: 83), so the assumption on the part of the investigating magistrate who examines Zéphirin's body is that the crumpled, soggy ball of paper, the copy-slip rolled up in the newspaper, has been used to gag the child while the attack took place. In this way, as the newspaper contributes to the concealing of the crime in the original rape, so later the rhetoric of the publication will be employed to mask the unveiling of the real perpetrator and to accuse Simon falsely. There is a distinction between the two pieces of paper — the 'modèle d'écriture' which might serve to identify the criminal and the generic newspaper cutting which might belong to anyone ('un numéro du *Petit Beaumontais* du jour, cela se comprenait, pouvait être dans n'importe quelle poche' [it was clear that a copy of the day's *Petit Beaumontais* could be found in anyone's pocket], *V*, XXVI: 22). Yet, implicitly, while an individual is responsible for the murder of Zéphirin, so too the readers of the newspaper, 'n'importe quelle poche', share culpability in swallowing the beverage distributed by the press. Zéphirin and Simon are the final scapegoats in Zola's œuvre, the later echoes of the idealistic Silvère in *La Fortune des Rougon*.

Novel and Newspaper, 'froissé, comme pétri'?

Yet while *Vérité* sets up a clear distinction between its own pedagogical discourse and the 'fictions' broadcast by the press, making the mystery of the origins of the 'modèle d'écriture' the narrative that the truthful text will seek to uncover, so at the same time the melding together of the scraps of newspaper and copy-slip represents, in a wider sense, the intermingling of those apparently oppositional factions, *Vérité* and the *Petit Beaumontais*. The novel's rhetorical techniques echo those of both the fictional world of journalism, and of Zola's own opinion pieces published in the press at the time of the Affair. The enmeshing of the novel with the newspaper is reflected even in the juxtaposition of the 'modèle d'écriture' and the 'numéro du *Petit Beaumontais*': the inscription on the copy-slip, which acts as the ultimate giveaway as to its provenance, 'Aimez-vous les uns les autres' [Love one another], will become part of the mantra of the overarching novel. The 'bonté' which the newly cleansed press will epitomize, referenced in the quotation above, will be the novel's solution to the corruption represented by Catholicism; and the inter-marriages between Marc's family and that of Simon will reflect such concerns with 'loving one another' emblazoned on the original incriminating slip. It is also the message brought about by Zola's own journalistic campaign in *Le Figaro* and epitomized by his article, 'Pour les juifs', published in response to the increasingly virulent anti-Semitism of Drumont's *Libre Parole*, in which Zola concludes with an invocation to 'cette unité humaine' [this human kinship]: 'désarmons nos haines, aimons-nous dans nos villes, aimons-nous par-dessus les frontières' [let us lay aside our hatred, find love in our communities, love beyond boundaries].[56]

In part, such enmeshing is deliberate, and is bound up with the overall mission of Zola's *Quatre Évangiles* — to borrow the discourse of the Church so as to reappropriate it for secular ends, as represented, of course, in the naming of Marc and his brothers, Luc, Jean, and Mathieu, the central protagonists of the Gospels. Marc is meant to figure as one of the 'bataillon sacré des instituteurs primaires' [sacred battalion of elementary schoolteachers] (*V*, XXVI: 153), whose rhetoric of enlightenment will supplant the light of the church. Yet such borrowings muddy the waters of the light-dark antitheses set up by the text, to such an extent that it becomes, in fact, difficult to distinguish the language of the crime, articulated by the newspaper, from the language of the novel which sets itself in opposition to the paper. Such symmetries are noted by Jeffrey Mehlman, who points out the similarity between the name 'Simon', Zola's fictionalized Dreyfus, and the crime, 'simony', of the Catholic brothers who are pitted against him, and who promote the hawking of fraudulent religious favours: for Mehlman, 'the very language of the novel' is 'intent on underscoring, against the author's own argument, a perilous symmetry'.[57] Andrew Counter, too, finds that the apparent boundaries which the novel aims to set up between discourses prove unstable in his discussion of the role of sentiment in *Vérité*. The adjective *délicieux*, which is applied to evoke both the angelic innocence of the child and the sexualized desire for Marc's wife Geneviève, indicates the insidious blurring of sex and sentiment in the text.[58]

Oppositional languages are, I would argue, like the scraps of paper found at the crime scene, 'comme pétri'. Zola suggests an understanding of this in his description of the geography of Beaumont, and in the significant positioning of the stationer's shop in the town. The secular and religious dimensions of the town are represented by street names, the place de la République, where the state primary schools for girls and boys are to be found, and the place des Capucins. These squares are connected by the 'rue Courte', on which the *papeterie* run by the Milhomme sisters is situated: a significant landmark in the text, given that the origins of the copy-slip will first be denied, and then affirmed, in the stationery shop, by Sebastien Milhomme. The heterogeneity of the papers sold in the shop reflects both the divisions at work within the town, and the intermingling of those factions. When Marc steps into the shop to show the 'modèle d'écriture' to the Milhomme boys, he is met by an abundance of paper: 'il regarda un instant cette papeterie, avec sa vitrine où les images de sainteté se mêlaient à des tableaux scolaires, exaltant la République, tandis que des journaux illustrés, pendus à des ficelles, barraient presque la porte' [he examined the windows of the stationery shop, in which religious prints were mingled with school pictures glorifying the Republic, whilst illustrated newspapers, hanging from strings, almost barred the doorway] (*V*, XXVI: 74). These newspapers, which almost block Marc's entry, as the articles in the *Petit Beaumontais* will block Simon's access to a fair trial, give further illustration of the processes of *pétrir* seen in the enmeshing of the copy-slip and the previous day's paper.

As in Zola's earlier novel about the impact of the press, *L'Argent*, this text offers a sense of the equivalence of all papers, all forms of writing. In *L'Argent*, the interdependency of press and finance in Second Empire France is brought out through the frequent glimpses of paper in the novel; the sense of uniformity of banknotes and newsprint visualized through the scraps of torn order slips which rain down on the trading room floor of the Bourse on the day of the bank crash, and represented also in the papers crammed into the bag of the debt-collector's aide, Mme Méchain, who tyrannizes the journalist Jordan, recognizing the name he publicizes via his signed articles as that on the handwritten credit-notes stuffed into her bulging sack. Wrona, who describes the 'puissance de circulation de papier' [powerful circulation of paper] in *L'Argent*, draws attention to the role played by the stationer's wife, Mme Conin, 'un personnage [qui] focalise [...] les désirs secrets des spéculateurs' [a character who acts as the focus for the secret desires of the speculators], sleeping with a range of investors associated with Saccard's bank, while acting too as a 'symbole de ce caractère stratégique du support papier' [symbol of this key characteristic of paper].[59] White's article on *L'Argent* as a text of papier mâché makes the point that the emphasis on paper in the novel is reflected clearly in the 1928 Lherbier film of the text, which sees scraps of paper raining down on the floor of the bourse.[60] As Mme Conin draws together threads of plot and textual symbols in Zola's banking novel, so too the stationery shop in *Vérité*, which stands, along with the presbytery, on the rue Courte, acts as a locus of interconnections between Church, press, and narrative, supplying the 'papers' from which the text itself is forged. In *L'Argent*, as Minogue points out, the papers pinned to the walls of the engineer Hamelin's workroom remind the reader of Zola's metafictional awareness of his own project, 'repeatedly foregrounding the act of writing'.[61] These plans and maps document the narrative's trajectory, shaping the overseas railways and constructions which require the speculation at the heart of the plot; a portfolio is pinned up early in the text, and taken down following the bank's collapse, reflecting the novel's consciousness of its arcs and endings. These papers setting out the plan of the text rank alongside the order slips and banknotes and debtors' bills which multiply throughout the infrastructure of the novel. In *Vérité*, the only other Zola novel to give quite such emphasis to the nefarious role of the press, such textual self-consciousness is also reflected in the stress placed on paper and the imprints of writing.

The intertwining of the novelistic enterprise with the concerns of the press and the 'crime' it reports on and helps to perpetrate is also suggested by the role of Marc. Marc clearly incarnates the role of the novelist as he goes about unravelling the story of the crime and expresses, as schoolteacher, the values so consistently evoked by the text. He also reflects Zola's own role in the Dreyfus affair. Yet just as the slogan imprinted on the incriminating copy-slip, 'Aimez-vous les uns les autres', becomes the novel's own message, so there are connections between Marc's role and this piece of paper. Before becoming a schoolteacher, he trains as a 'dessinateur lithographe' [lithographic draughtsman]: it is indeed his capacity for clearly delineated pictures that facilitates his career move:

> Chargé de l'exécution de tableaux scolaires, il s'était ingénié à les simplifier encore, il avait créé de véritables chefs d'œuvres de clarté et de précision, qui lui avaient indiqué sa voie, son bonheur à instruire les petits de ce monde. (*V*, XXVI: 46)
>
> [Entrusted with the execution of many school diagrams, he had exercised his ingenuity in simplifying them, creating perfect masterpieces of clearness and precision, which had revealed to him his true vocation, the happiness that he found in teaching the young.]

His background connects him with the image of the lithographed print, all the more so when, in the process of investigating the source of the slogan and questioning his pupils, he copies out the phrase on the copy-slip. The recurrence of the mantra 'Aimez-vous les uns les autres', like the recurrence of the image of the copy-slip itself and the repetition which reminds the reader of its provenance in the crumpled page of newsprint, binds Marc together with the incriminating scraps of paper even as he stands in opposition to the press and the Church in his attempts to seek the source of the crime. He is a detective whose investigation necessarily embeds him in the world of the crime he aims to expose.

In addition to the entanglement of Marc in the discourses against which he is simultaneously pitted, there are broader connections to be drawn between the representation of the press in the novel and the function of the novel itself. Ostensibly, the novel incarnates the title with which it emblazons itself, a truth value which is employed to combat the fictionalized versions of the crime bandied about by the press. Iterations in *Vérité* frequently describe the poison served up by the *Petit Beaumontais* as a form of 'legend'. When the paper first publishes its condemnation of Simon, Marc reflects on it as 'un tel mélodrame, aux mystérieuses complications, aux invraisemblances extraordinaires de conte bleu, allait être, il le sentit bien, la légende devenue réalité, la vérité certaine dont les gens ne voudraient plus démordre' [That newspaper melodrama with its mysterious intricacies, its extraordinary fairy-tale improbabilities, would prove, Marc felt it, a legend changing into truth, positive truth, from which people would henceforth refuse to depart] (*V*, XXVI: 79). The legends seen in the storytelling of the past in *La Fortune des Rougon* have become embedded in fin-de-siècle journalism. Despite the way that Zola castigates modern journalism for its obsession with facts as in his critique of the 'presse d'information' discussed above, in *Vérité* it is the fictions of the press which are perceived as threatening. The verb 'démordre' in the previous citation, which encapsulates the public's expected response to the fictions of the newspaper, connects once again the crime perpetrated and the myth perpetuated by the *Petit Beaumontais* with the ball of paper constituted of the copy-slip and page of newsprint; as Zéphirin will be unable to spit out the gagging mush, so will the public be unable to release the entailing fictions from their jaws. Later, Simon's lawyer, Delbos, will make similar claims of fictionality about the case to be put forward by the prosecution and supported by the newspaper:

> Ce conte effroyable se tient suffisamment debout pour s'emparer de l'imagination de la foule et devenir une de ces fables légendaires, qui prennent la force des vérités inattaquables... Et notre faiblesse est de ne pas avoir une histoire, une vraie, que nous puissions opposer à la légende en train de se former. (*V*, XXVI: 116)
>
> [This frightful tale is sufficiently well-constructed to seize hold of the masses and to become one of those legendary fables which acquire the force of truth. Our weakness proceeds from the fact that, not knowing the real story, we cannot set it up in opposition to the legend now being forged.]

These reflections as to the melodramatic and novelized nature of the case against Simon are echoes of Zola's 'J'Accuse' article, in which he expresses and repeats an impression of Commandant du Paty de Clam, who oversaw the initial framing of Dreyfus, as an inventor of serialized fiction: 'Il apparaît comme l'esprit le plus fumeux, le plus compliqué, hanté d'intrigues romanesques, se complaisant aux moyens des romans-feuilletons' [he appeared to be complicated and woolly-minded, preoccupied with fairy-tale intrigues, delighting in the practices of serialized fiction].[62] Zola's own article is an unveiling of the truth, in stark opposition to the damaging fictions invented by the anti-Dreyfusards. Such is the battle he then re-enacts in the pages of *Vérité*.

The difference is that in *Vérité* he is setting fiction against fiction. His own re-created and invented vision of the Dreyfus affair, set in the symbolically imaginative town of Beaumont, is pitted against the 'invraisemblance extraordinaire du conte bleu' [extraordinary fairy-tale improbabilities] articulated by the newspaper. Counter sees in *Vérité* an attempt to distance this later novel from a Naturalism which Zola himself may have come to see as 'extravagant' and 'hanté' — the adjectives employed to describe du Paty du Clam, and echoed in scathing criticisms of Zola's writing as in Nordau's *Degeneration*: 'in figuring the architect of Dreyfus's ordeal not as a novelistic villain but as a novelist, these passages seem to announce a new suspicion of the literary imagination, which now emerges as a kind of psychological disturbance in itself'.[63] Yet for all its intentions, *Vérité* still highlights its own status as fiction: Zola turns the Dreyfus affair into legend in his work. Susan Suleiman reminds the reader of this fictionality when, in her book on the structures of the *roman à thèse*, she notes that *Vérité* 'is nevertheless not the story of the Dreyfus Affair; it is a fictional story, which its readers in 1903 could recognize as an obvious transposition of the historical event'.[64] The embedding of the real-life Affair in the text engenders a paradoxical awareness of the distance between the novel's own structures and the events it reflects; the reflection of the Affair and its accompanying journalistic debates serves as a reminder of the novel's own fictions.

To reinforce such an awareness of fictionality, *Vérité* is also composed of rhetorical constructions which align it with the press whose fairy tales it seeks to expose. Descriptions of the modes of expression employed by the *Petit Beaumontais* in the novel can also be used to refer to the patterns at work in the text itself, with the result that, as with the collapse of opposition seen by Mehlman between the 'Simonists' and the practice of simony, Zola establishes something of a phoney war in his clash between thesis novel and popular press. The press articles frequently characterized as 'contes' or 'légendes' by the narrative are echoed in the novel's own presentation of Brother Gorgias, who will later confess to the crime in dramatic fashion. Gorgias is singled out in descriptions early on in the text as a likely suspect thanks to his caricatured criminal features which make of him a fairy-tale villain; he is first depicted as 'un homme maigre et noueux au front bas et dur sous des cheveux noirs crépus, au nez en bec d'aigle entre des pommettes saillantes, à la bouche épaisse laissant voir des dents de loup' [a thin and knotty man with a low stern forehead below black frizzy hair, a nose shaped like an eagle's beak between projecting cheek bones, his thick lips allowing a glimpse of wolf's teeth] (*V*, XXVI: 40). This big bad wolf figure is defined in almost identical terms when he stands to give evidence at the trial: 'maigre et noueux, au front bas et dur, aux pommettes saillantes, la bouche épaisse, sous le grand nez en bec d'aigle' [thin, dark and knotty man, with a low stern forehead, projecting cheek-bones, and thick lips under a big nose shaped like an eagle's beak] (*V*, XXVI: 130).

Not only does this exaggerated sense of characterization give a sense of melodrama to the 'truth' of Zola's narrative, the use of repetition acts as a further link between the practices of the *Petit Beaumontais* and the novel's own devices. The press is referred to in the novel as waging a campaign based on repeated refrains: 'on avait empoisonné ce peuple, des journaux [...] lui versaient *chaque matin* l'abominable breuvage' [the people had been poisoned by the newspapers, which poured them this abominable brew every morning] (*V*, XXVI: 158, my emphasis); the paper attacks Marc by 'ouvrant une rubrique quotidienne' [starting a daily campaign] (*V*, XXVI: 242). As the *Petit Beaumontais* hammers home its mantra through regular reiteration, so too the novel exploits such exhaustive tendencies, linguistically and structurally. As already seen in the quotations above, the metaphor connecting the journalistic output with poison recurs on a number of occasions, as does the insistence on the *clarté* of the secular school system versus the darkness of the Catholic church. Repetition is a necessary product of the text's insistence on the imperative of education; as Marc drills his students so the text drills its readers, enacting the pedagogical practices it promotes — as it will represent the utopian newspaper doing by the end of the novel. Repetition is intended to engender clarity. Hence the usefulness of Marc's original work as a lithographer: he brings a pictorial lucidity to the lessons he teaches. The text, too, strives for such symbolic and lithographic intelligibility. Yet these features evoke further comparisons between the practices of the novel and those of the newspapers, an illustrative dimension which acts as a reminder of the force of the visual images and caricatures of the Dreyfus affair so frequently included in newspapers such as the *Petit Journal*. One of the more ludicrous articles incorporated in the *Petit Beaumontais* sees a defence of père

Philibin, at the time when Simon appears to be exonerated and the blame falls on the actions of the Church:

> Le même journal inventa la canonisation du vol et du mensonge, saint Philibin, héros et martyr. Des portraits furent publiés, avec une auréole et des palmes. Une légende se créa, le père dans un couvent ignoré des Apennins, au milieu de forêts sauvages, portant un cilice [...] et de petites images pieuses circulèrent, le représentant à genoux, avec une prière au verso, qui gagnait des indulgences. (*V*, XXVI: 323)
>
> [The very same newspaper proceeded to canonise theft and falsehood. St Philibin, hero and martyr, was portrayed amidst a setting of palms, and with a halo about his head. A legend likewise arose, showing the reverend Father in a remote convent of the Appennines, surrounded by wild forests, [...] wearing a hair-cloth next to his skin [...] And on the back of the pious little pictures which circulated, showing him on his knees, there was a prayer by repeating which the faithful might gain indulgences.]

Yet Zola's text works to create its own legend around Marc and Simon's brother David. The text uses its strategies of hyperbole and repetition to 'crown' the characters of Marc and David with halo-like or superhuman capacities, positioning Marc in patriarchal stance at the end of the novel. David, for instance, is described in his quest to exonerate his brother as having taken on 'la tâche surhumaine de sauver et de réhabiliter son frère' [the superhuman task of saving and exonerating his brother] (*V*, XXVI: 147). As the newspaper prints a prayer for its credible readers to recite, so too Zola's novel seeks to become a secular catechism, its mantra of truth and justice to be learned by heart by his readers.

Through such identification of the novel's own language and strategies with those of the oppositional journalism it seeks to discredit, the clarity evoked by the would-be lithographic style of the text becomes, instead, something blurred and darker. Mehlman argues, 'the novel's onslaught against Catholicism [...] is so unrelenting as to figure as no more than the flip side of his adversaries' antisemitism';[65] the discourse of the novel, pitted against that of the press which binds the voices of Marc's adversaries, matches its vehemence and one eyed-ness. Chaitin too suggests that 'it is remarkable to what extent Zola's conception of Marc's endeavour mimics the system he is trying to oust' and notes that in this, Marc 'is merely following the lead of the anticlerical campaign undertaken by the journalists of *L'Aurore*, who accused the Church, especially the Jesuits, of exactly the same misdeeds as the latter did the Jews'.[66] Repetition is of course a mainstay of Zola's rhetoric in the 'J'Accuse' article, manifested in the accusatory list of names which closes the article and also in the refrain of the exclamatory 'ah!' and the echoing claim that 'la vérité est en marche' [truth is advancing].[67] The passionate defence of Dreyfus in Zola's newspaper campaign becomes challenging to read, though, when repeated at length in the six-hundred page novel. Claire White argues of Zola's previous *Évangile*, *Travail*, that the very frenzied overworking of its style and structure induces a 'passive state of contemplation, an almost alienating leisure', an indolence towards reading which runs counter to the emphasis on labour reiterated by the text.[68] A similar claim could be made of *Vérité*, which encourages the reader to become something of a rebellious schoolchild, reading against its pedagogical mantras and the clarity of its ambitions. There is irony in the fact that such reaction is inspired by the novel's own instruction. Marc's mission, in educating the children of the Beaumont farmers and workers, is to encourage them first to read, and then to read with discernment, and finally to move beyond reading to practical action. *Vérité* is a novel which argues against itself, a piece of writing which seeks to transcend writing. This paradox is illustrated by the structural repetitions of the text.

The text's very fabric is composed of structural echoes. Not only is the entire novel a transfigured reprise of the Dreyfus affair — itself composed of re-enactments, the second trial and conviction of Dreyfus re-enacted in *Vérité* — the action of the plot unfolds in sequential repetitions, as, for example, in Marc's recurring encounters with the parents of the schoolchildren he teaches, who represent the social strata found in Beaumont, Bongard the farmer, Doloir the mason, and Savin the clerk, who variously epitomize the public acceptance of the stories spun by the local newspaper. Recurrence is intended to promote an understanding of difference: each time Marc comes across these three families and their offspring, repetition prompts an awareness of the slow progress taking place in Beaumont. This progress involves a rejection of the discourse of the *Petit Beaumontais* and its fictions but, increasingly, a rejection more broadly of textuality itself in favour of speech and action. On Marc's first visit to the poorer districts of Maillebois, this trio sees Bongard represent illiteracy, the masons reflect anti-Semitic and anti-Simonist public opinion but claim not to bother reading the newspapers as they give them a headache, and the clerk Savin incarnates blind faith in the power of the printed word of the press; he is first seen reading the paper and hoping that the *Petit Beaumontais* will start a campaign waged against allowing Jews to become schoolteachers. Subsequent visits to the children of these original workers see increased rates of literacy and even of a certain discernment regarding what they read, but still little regard for Simon's fate; although Doloir's son Auguste dismisses the fairy-tale rumours spread by the newspaper of a plot involving Simon commissioned to have a Catholic priest guillotined in exchange for a heap of treasure which he will dig up on his return from exile, he still finds that 'J'ai beau lire souvent ce qu'on imprime, ça se brouille de plus en plus dans ma tête' [though I often read what is printed, my mind only gets the more fogged by it] (*V*, XXVII: 393). By the end of the text, however, the idea of 'lire ce qu'on imprime' is itself presented as an outmoded form of knowledge.

The rejection of writing is symbolized by the closure of the stationery shop which previously acted as the locus for the amalgamation of 'papers' in the town and text. This end of 'paper' — a move, too, beyond the floods of financial and journalistic paper produced within the pages of *L'Argent* — is brought about in part by Marc's pedagogical practices, which emphasize oral instruction and practical application rather than written work; he takes his pupils into the fields to learn. In keeping with his grounding in the pictorial art of communication, he increasingly distrusts language:

> S'il redoutait les phrases, les mots dont le sens échappait à ses petits paysans, et s'il efforçait de les traduire en paroles simples et claires, il craignait davantage

> les légendes dangereuses, les erreurs devenues des articles de foi, les leçons abominables données au nom d'une religion menteuse et d'un faux patriotisme. (*V*, XXVII: 529)
>
> [If he distrusted phrases and words, the sense of which seemed likely to escape little peasants, and endeavoured to interpret them in clear and simple language, he feared yet more the dangerous legends, the errors of articles of faith, the abominable notions set forth in the name of mendacious religion and a false patriotism.]

The papers which poisoned and gagged are rejected in favour of a prominence given to an alternative orality, the clear and concise spoken word. Marc is described as retaining the book, teaching 'sans exclure le livre,' [without excluding books] yet giving 'le plus grand développement à l'explication orale, à la leçon vécue et vivante' [greater emphasis to oral explanation, to lived and living lessons] (*V*, XXVII: 527). This preference for the oral over the written once again raises questions about the status of Zola's own novel and its dense textuality. Its written composition, although putting forward its vision repetitively as if striving for the 'paroles simples et claires' favoured by Marc, also reads as something of a 'copybook', the kind of material no longer really required by the schoolchildren of Beaumont. It is a copybook which 'copies' the Dreyfus affair, persistently copies out its own phrases, and copies the slogan found in the original copybook clue left at the scene of the crime, 'aimez-vous les uns les autres'. In depicting the growing literacy rates of the workers, *Vérité* paradoxically argues at the same time for an abandonment of written language, a regurgitation of the papers woven together in the mouth of the child Zéphirin and the forms of textuality — journalistic, religious, novelistic — that they represent.

Chaitin sees the novel as a 'Manichean battle between two diametrically opposed forces that is played out in the novel's three plots' (the Simon case, the growing divide between Marc and his wife Geneviève, the competition between the secular and parochial school systems), a battle that I would extend to the opposition between the novel and the newspaper it represents.[69] The result of such opposition is elimination:

> The goal in these plots is not simply to outdo the competition, but, as in many a political contest, to eliminate the rival at any price. This murderous urge becomes all the more imperative the more the two competing forces resemble each other.[70]

The more the novel adopts the practices of the journalistic discourses it echoes and rebels against, the more the effect is to suggest similitude. And the more similar the practices of writing become, the more the destructive tendencies of the text are self-directed. In combating the rhetoric of the *Petit Beaumontais*, *Vérité* argues against itself as a mode of written communication. Yet the plot of the novel, which ends by privileging speech and action, develops such oppositional destruction/ elimination in its depiction of oral discourse too. The battle between Church and state, secular and Catholic schools, poisonous press and purifying pedagogy, is represented, increasingly, by the diametric figures of Marc and Brother Gorgias, who eventually confesses to the crime against Zéphirin. In contrast to the wolf-like figure of Gorgias, Marc is described as 'un esprit logique et de lumière' [a logical and luminous mind] (*V*, XXVI: 45). Both, though, initially rely on the newspaper as a source of truth. To Marc's relief, the first issue of the *Petit Beaumontais* produced after Zéphirin's death, the day after the prize-giving at the Brothers' School, proves favourable to Simon: it is only in the days to come that the paper becomes prey to the fabrications of the Church; the truth is twisted and fictionalized by the unknown powers (suspected as being Fathers Crabot and Philibin) who manipulate the paper's policies. And later Gorgias turns to the written word, to the newspaper, to try and put forward his side of the story, and comes much closer to the truth than his superiors would like: in his 'confidential chats' with the writers of the *Petit Beaumontais*, he says too much, and 'il avait donc laisser percer sa version à lui, plus raisonnable, avouant une partie de la vérité' [he gave some inkling of a version of his own, one which was more reasonable that that of his superiors, one in which a part of the truth appeared] (*V*, XXVI: 309). Yet 'cette version, indiquée le premier jour dans le journal, comme sortant d'une source sûre, fut énergiquement démentie le lendemain, et par le frère Gorgias en personne, qui prit la peine de protester lui-même aux bureaux de la rédaction' [although this version of the affair was at the first moment given by the newspaper, which declared that it emanated from a most reliable source, it was on the morrow contradicted energetically, even by Brother Gorgias himself, who repaired to the newspaper office to express his protest] (*V*, XXVI: 309).

When the 'truth' of the written word fails, both Marc and Gorgias end up declaiming their truths orally, Marc in the classroom and in his verbal attempts to persuade Geneviève and the Beaumont inhabitants of Simon's innocence, and Gorgias in the pivotal scene in the closing sequences of the novel when he returns to the scene of the original crime and finally narrates his actions. Even though Gorgias remains convinced that acknowledging his sins will gain him access to heaven, still prey to the delusions instilled in him by his religion, his confession sees him stripping away layer after layer of fiction in an attempt to get closer to the truth. Having once suggested that 'Satan m'emportait, m'aveuglait' [Satan was driving me, blinding me], he realizes the artifice of what he is saying, 'ce n'est pas là encore, c'est arrangé et embelli' [that's not it either, it has been made up and embellished], and strives for greater veracity: 'Je veux tout dire, je veux tout dire' [I will tell you the truth, the whole truth] (*V*, XXVII: 626). And so follows his confession, the narrative employing the anaphoric 'il dit' to emphasize the scope of his totalizing speech: 'il dit tout, en termes crus, abominables, avec des gestes qui évoquaient l'ignominie de l'atroce scène [...] Il dit l'acte, sans taire aucun détail, [...] il dit sa terreur lâche [...] Et il dit enfin le meutre, l'étranglement' [he recited it all, in crude, abominable terms, using gestures which illustrated the appalling nature of the horrific scene [...] He narrated the act, leaving out no detail, [...] he told of his cowardly terror [...], and finally he narrated the murder, the strangling] (*V*, XXVII: 626–27). The 'termes crus', accompanied by illustrative gestures, evoke the stripped down, plain discourse advocated by Marc as the most effective form of instruction. For both men, despite their oppositional differences, the implication is that the oral — whether instructive or revelatory — comes closer to the 'vérité' of the novel than the fabrications spun in the pages of the press.

The shift thus evoked in *Vérité*, from the suspicious written word to the preferred oral forms of explanation, can be seen as the inverse of the pattern described in *La Fortune des Rougon* which, in its symbolic representation of the production of narrative, suggested the journey from oral folklore to written forms. Ziegler's discussion of the earlier novel sees gossip as inaugural in the creation of Zola's text; as Tante Dide becomes the subject of public interest in Plassans, so Ziegler sees the narrative itself set in motion: 'following the move from the fullness of the cemetery to the emptiness of Plassans' incomprehension, Zola's narrative is born with the beginning of public discourse'; and he argues that the 'speculative, ill-informed and calumnious speech of his characters becomes the basis for the author's own story'.[71] The shift from the oral to the written can be detected, too, in the desperation of the Rougons to see their support for the *coup d'état* represented in print. Pierre Rougon tries to persuade the editor of the *Gazette de Plassans*, Vuillet, to record his initial victory against the insurgents. This scuffle, which has resulted in the shattering of the mayor's glass mirror and has been orally disseminated throughout the town, loses credence until cemented in the newspaper; Rougon reassures Vuillet: 'C'était justement parce que des bruits faux et inquiétants couraient, que l'article en question aurait rendu un grand service à la bonne cause' (*FR*, 247) ('It was precisely because disturbing false rumours were circulating that the article in question would have been of great service to their cause'). Where *La Fortune des Rougon*, then, privileges textuality in announcing the processes of narrative which will result in the founding of Zola's naturalist cycle, the quest for truth in *Vérité* sees the unravelling of texts and the questioning of Naturalism itself.

The passage cited above, narrating Gorgias's confession, ironically reveals the inadequacies of the fictional text and the written word. It shifts from the direct speech of Gorgias which immediately precedes the core of his account, into the indirect discourse which is employed, ostensibly to record the practice of *tout dire*, which in fact obscures the actual words of the crime itself. Gorgias's oral account also suggests the negation of practices at work in Zola's novel. Before he gets to the crux of his confession, finally announcing himself as the author of the crime, and recounting the details of his actions, the crowd grows weary of his prefatory speeches. The audience's rhetorical questions, narrated in free indirect style, subvert not only the length and diversionary nature of Gorgias's excuses, couched in religious language, but also something of the length and practices of *Vérité* itself, which aims to crush the Catholic sentiments of Gorgias's tirade in its own expansive prose. The crowd asks: 'Que voulait-il dire? pourquoi ne contait-il pas simplement les choses? a quoi bon tant de préparations, puisque dix mots auraient suffi?' [What was he trying to say? Why didn't he give a simpler account? What good were all these preliminaries, when ten words would have been sufficient?] (*V*, XXVII: 623). The crowd has, in the course of the text, learned to 'read', and what they want are the facts, in as condensed a form as possible. In their rejection of Gorgias's verbose rhetoric, they also, however, reject the length and circumvention of the narrative itself, preferring the 'dix mots' of the crime's revelation to the otiose detail which furnishes the prior explanations of the text.

Counter argues that Gorgias's eventual speech, in its coarseness and graphic violence, is emblematic of the practices of Zola's own Naturalism, and therefore that the defeat of Gorgias in the text represents a farewell to earlier strategies of literary representation, and 'abominable language.' Suggesting that Zola has come to perceive corrosive affiliations between his own naturalist novels and the decadent fiction which initially appeared as its rival, and that 'the Dreyfus Affair had made Zola believe, as George Sand before him, in the enhanced political purchase of an idealizing, prescriptive fictional aesthetics', Counter sees the destruction of the figure of Gorgias in the wake of his naturalist monologue as the burning of a form of literature he had himself once adored.[72] What Zola creates in *Vérité* is a novel which tries, in its repetitive practices, to boil down the 'dozen words' of truth and justice. Indeed, its closing and moralizing penultimate sentence, 'il n'est de justice que dans la vérité, il n'est de bonheur que dans la justice' [justice resides in truth alone, and there is no happiness apart from justice] (*V*, XXVII: 686), comes close to the desired brevity of the crowd's ideal summation. And yet in the very desire to render literature down to such conclusivity, Zola's novel argues for its own suppression.

Despite the apparent divide between the naturalistic character, who is wiped out from the text, and the new moralizing literature Zola embraces and incarnates in the person of Marc, the connections between Marc and Gorgias, and so between Naturalism and the 'new' literature, persist. Marc, the character who fulfils the role of Zola himself in the Dreyfus Affair, articulating and working to clarify the meaning of the text, is paralleled by Gorgias who, in his confession scene, orally unravels the truth of the crime. Echoes of the original crime scene, viewed through the perspective of Marc, recur in the language and imagery of Gorgias's monologue. While the opening scene stresses the angelic appearance of Zéphirin ('cette tête [...] gardait son charme délicieux, une tête d'ange blond et frisée [his face retained much of its charm; it was the face of a fair curly-haired angel], *V*, XXVI: 18), so too does Gorgias emphasize the cherubic nature of his victim: 'vous aviez fait l'enfant si délicieux, avec sa tête blonde et frisée de petit ange' [you made the child so charming, with his face of a fair curly-haired angel] (*V*, XXVII: 626). As Marc has sought to uncover the truth in patterns which suggest something of the model of the detective story, so here Gorgias effects the final unravelling in the starkness of his confession. In fact, one of the ironies of the novel is that its mystery never really is a mystery. Marc's perspective as he goes about seeking evidence for the truth behind the crime suggests that there are forces working in the dark, in the original crime and in the attempts to cover up its discovery, and yet the narrative, in the way it has provided overt clues as to the persona of the culprit through the lithographed and fairy-tale like depiction of Gorgias, has never really bought into its own ostensible veiling of the crime. It is a text which evokes the structures of the detective novel only to offer a parody of mystery, thanks to its mission to render clarity at all times.

Homogeny versus Deleuzian 'fêlure'

As the exaggerated differences between Marc and Gorgias tend towards collapse, with both seeking to abandon textual codes and newspaper discourse in favour of oral declamation, and with both endeavouring to announce the truth of the crime in *Vérité*, so the homogenizing tendencies of the text are announced. A drive towards uniformity is evoked, evidenced by the idealized voice of the newspaper celebrated in the closing section, which will replicate the clarity of Zola's novel as an 'admirable instrument d'instruction'. As earlier the novel borrowed from the newspaper without necessarily intending to, in its fairy-tale imagery and reiterative practices, so by the end of the novel the purged, purified novel and newspaper are to be alike. The marital divide between Marc and Geneviève is overcome, and as they work side by side in the girls' and boys' schools respectively, 'ils en eurent une joie nouvelle, comme s'ils s'étaient senti désormais un même cœur et un même cerveau' [fresh joy came to them; it was as if they now had but one heart and one brain] (*V*, XXVII: 517). Such homogeny is in many respects already the guiding principle of the narrative, and is exemplified, in fact, in the way that *Vérité* deviates from the Rougon-Macquart titles in terms of its borrowing from newspapers. In their polyphony, fragmentation, and in the parody of their own sense-making structures via the representation of journalist characters, Zola's naturalist novels replicate certain practices of the press.

As referenced earlier, Vaillant discusses the ways in which Zola's incorporation of a Bakhtinian dialogism, borrowing the voices of such a range of characters, offers an empathetic mimesis, and has affinities with the new practices of interviewing found in newspapers, with detail given in such lifestyle pieces to the minutiae of decor and physical appearance, as in naturalist description. The result, suggests Vaillant, is that 'la poétique zolienne résulte ainsi d'une intrication de plus en plus grande entre la fiction narrative et l'écriture journalistique' [Zola's prose is thus the result of increasing interconnections between narrative fiction and journalistic writing].[73] In *Nana*, the inclusion of Fauchery results in the self-conscious querying of strategies of representation in the newspaper and the novel alike. In *Vérité*, these modernist aspects of the newspaper appear to have been silenced, as the novel opts to borrow instead from the opinion piece, contributing narrative form and characterization to Zola's 'J'Accuse'. It is a novel which abandons the polyphony found in the newspaper in favour of a mainly monologic account, filtered through Marc's perspective: the 'undifferentiated and insistent voice of didacticism', according to David Meakin.[74] Henri Mitterand notes that in the *Quatre Évangiles*, 'le langage du héros et celui du romancier' [the language of the hero and that of the novelist] merge.[75] The murk of the naturalist novel has given way to the cleanliness of a *roman à thèse* which seeks to purge itself of the fragmentation of newspaper discourse in favour of the monologizing rhetoric of the opinion piece. Its narrative sees the destruction of Gorgias and the naturalist vision he represents; he is found, his skull split and his body filthy, 'devant la maison louche, où l'on avait déjà ramassé Victor Milhomme' [outside the same suspicious house before which, some time previously, a passer-by had already found the body of Victor Milhomme] (*V*, XXVII: 635), a déjà vu in the text which reads as a déjà vu of the 'maison louche' of the naturalist novel. The churches, too, are subject to fatalistic forces; the Capuchin chapel at Maillebois is ravaged by fire and destroyed, and the church of St Anthony of Padua, the place of worship which was earlier in the text seen encouraging its parishioners to purchase relics, is struck by lightning when the guilty Father Crabot is within preaching a sermon, and burned to the ground. The plot which steers itself towards 'truth' acts as an incendiary, burning and purging the symbols of religion, fakery, and, in the figure of Gorgias, Naturalism itself.

Yet these very plot devices, introduced as mysterious natural events imitating the punishments of a vengeful God, once again see Zola's novel enacting the forces it simultaneously critiques. The veracious text becomes anti-real, constructing its material from the stuff of fairy tales. As it endeavours to eradicate Naturalism and religious discourse alike, so the text borrows from biblical patterning and from the fabric of the naturalist novel, dumping Gorgias's begrimed body in the same spot as that of the older Milhomme boy, hinting at the intrigue of a work of crime fiction. As suggested above, the text has set itself up as a detective novel only to resist the systems of uncovering promoted by the genre. Yet in these closing sections, *Vérité* hints at a murky drama which it refuses to uncover: the crime it purports to reveal is never really veiled, while the bodies of Milhomme and Gorgias are left suggestively as clues of a crime the text ostensibly has no interest in unravelling. What they do suggest though is the cumbersome material presence of a body of work — Zola's Naturalism — which cannot be fully abandoned in his evangelical quest for a different form of expression and writing. Gorgias's soiled body hints at the problematic death of the author of Naturalism; it reminds the reader that the birth of a new Zolian discourse is not without the dead weight of its past.

Such conflict in the presentation of the newly homogeneous *Vérité* is reflected in the fact that the structure of the text also refuses such purification. The erosion of difference, reflected in the newly-shared goals of newspaper and novel, proves illusory. Chaitin comments on the addition of the fourth part of the text, which enables the narrative to spiral onwards after the apparent resolution at the end of Book Three, and comments in particular on the 'fourth antiutopian chapter' of this part itself, which follows on from the attempt to tie up loose threads in the third chapter, with the death of Gorgias and the razing of the churches. For Chaitin:

> The three parts plus one composition of the fourth book of the novel is thus itself a repetition in miniature of the structure of the entire text, as though no matter how much the novel displays, there will always be something that lies beyond its capacity for representation.[76]

In the final chapter of the fourth part of the novel, there is a re-enactment of the original crime, in the attack on Marc's great-granddaughter Rose. The patterns of this crime, which echo so meticulously the events of the original, force Marc into a reliving of the text: 'comme en un fulgurant éclair, à cette minute horrible, il vit se dérouler sa vie, il revécut toutes ses luttes et toutes ses souffrances'[as if by the glow of a great lightning flash, Marc, at the horrible moment, saw all his past life spread out, and lived all his battles and all his sufferings anew] (*V*, XXVII: 649). Rose herself is described in terminology which evokes the girlish beauty of Zéphirin, 'délicieuse' and with 'un envolement de fins cheveux blonds' [a mass of fair and wavy tresses] (*V*, XXVII: 645); again, there is the clue left at the scene of the crime. This time, though, the difference between the handkerchief left in the bedroom in which the attack has taken place, and the original scraps of paper, suggests, too, something of the contrast Zola strives to establish between the scenes. The density of textuality reflected in the copyslip from the Brothers' school, wrapped in its layering of newspaper, is replaced by the single initial on a piece of fabric, a scrap of material whose function is to wipe away grime and bodily fluid; the *mouchoir* epitomizes the gradual erasing of writing which has been written into the progress of the text. The incriminating letter 'F' which points to Rose's father François, Marc's grandson, as responsible for the attack, indicates, on the one hand, the entwining once more of the Froment family with the culpability for the crime. On the other hand, the fact that François is eventually cleared through the willingness of the townspeople to speak up and provide evidence testifies to the newly ingrained desire for truth; of particular note is the fact that although gossip is spread and the story is embellished, the newspapers will not print word of the suspicion that falls on François, or of the story that he has committed the crime as a Freemason seeking ritualistic blood: 'les inventeurs de ce conte inepte ne trouvèrent pas un journal pour l'imprimer, et ils durent le répandre eux-mêmes parmi le petit peuple' [the inventors of that idiotic fable could not find a single newspaper to print it, and thus they had to spread it by word of mouth among the poorer folk] (*V*, XXVII: 653).

Yet still this closing chapter, which insists on the values of the text, and on the purification of the newspaper industry, cannot, despite its reassuring mantras of pedagogy and progress, erase suspicion, or discontent, or the persistent imagery associated with cracking and fragmentation which it has sought to eradicate in its drive for homogeny and harmony. Marc remains disturbed by the potential of human passion to interfere in his quest for satisfaction. Despite the attempts to stifle desire in the town — for example in the razing of the land of the former aristocratic estate named 'La Désirade' and the renewal of it as a public park — nevertheless, it is Marc's grandson François's lust for Colette which contributes to the ruptures of the final chapter. Although one of the other crucial differences between the original crime and its later echo is that is does not involve rape, and that Rose's virginity remains intact, the chapter does bring about the breach in the union of Marc's descendants, François and Thérèse. The imagery associated with this rift is of a prickling and piercing thorniness which will threaten the otherwise utopian harmony of the closing reiterations of the text. Such a lexicon is set alongside the blossoming of the 'Rose' who represents the flowering of future generations, yet who is, too, broken in this concluding chapter, characterized by vocabulary associated with 'brusque séparation' and 'brouilles' [quarrels]. 'Rose avait bien le bras droit cassé' [Rose's right arm was indeed broken]; the doctor is sufficiently concerned about her to stay by her bedside, 'après avoir fait la réduction de la fracture' [when he had reduced the fracture] (*V*, XXVII: 650). Here Zola draws attention to the fractures still at work in his would-be homogenized text, despite his attempts to mend and reduce them. As the body of Gorgias dumped outside the brothel acts as a reminder of the weight of Naturalism, so the threat of desire ruptures, naturalist-style, the harmony of the closing sequences of the text, which see Marc's family assembled in the schoolroom, symbolic of the marriage between education and family which act as hallmarks of Zola's utopian vision. Fleshiness is, in Marc's mind, left torn on the thorniness of the path to the 'Cité heureuse', emblematic of the remnants of Naturalism at work in this evangelizing text: 'il n'en était pas moins profondément triste de voir cette dolente humanité laisser volontairement de sa chair à toutes les ronces du chemin' [he felt very sad as he saw mankind voluntarily leaving some of its flesh on all the briars of the path] (*V*, XXVII: 644). The discord which clouds the final paragraphs of the novel, which sees Thérèse and François resolve to live apart, each in separate schoolhouses, also indicates, at the apparently most dogmatically optimistic moment of the text, a move beyond the persistent monologism which has characterized *Vérité*. Thérèse is granted a dissenting voice, which punctures the emphatically pronounced vision of her grandfather Marc. In answer to his insistence that 'la force du meilleur avenir est dans l'entente absolue du couple' [the strength of the future will lie in the absolute agreement of man and wife] (*V*, XXVII: 664), Thérèse responds that 'toujours nos pauvres cœurs saigneront, toujours nous les déchirerons dans les heures de passion exaspérée [...] et cela est peut-être l'aiguillon nécessaire du bonheur' [our poor hearts will always bleed, we shall always rend them in hours of exasperated passion [...] and perhaps, that is the necessary good for happiness] (*V*, XXVII: 666). The ambiguous 'aiguillon' [prickle] she evokes here suggests irreconcilability; the tiny but rupturing crack at work despite the text's eradication of difference; the reminder of a naturalist discourse which recurs and a fleeting move beyond the monologic voice of the text, which promotes Marc's vision but sees him silenced at the same time.

The image of the *aiguillon* acts as an echo of the crack, or the *fêlure*, analyzed by Deleuze in his study of *La Bête humaine*. Deleuze's distinction between 'la petite hérédité des instincts' and 'la grande hérédité' leads to the identification of 'la fêlure' with the death drive, which underpins all other instincts or hereditary transmissions:

> L'essentiel de l'epopée, c'est un double registre où les dieux, activement, jouent à leur manière et sur un autre plan l'aventure des hommes et de leurs instincts. Le *drame*, alors, se réfléchit dans un *epos*, la petite généalogie dans une grande généalogie, la petite hérédité dans une grande hérédité, la *petite manœuvre* dans une *grande manœuvre*.

> [What is essential in the epic is a double register in which the gods actively play out, in their own way and on another plane, the adventure of men and of their instincts. The *drama* in this case is reflected in an *epos* — the small genealogy is reflected in a grand genealogy, the small heredity in a big heredity, and a *small maneuver* in a *large maneuver*.][77]

Counter relates Deleuze's terms to ideas of patrilinearity and rupture in *La Bête humaine*, arguing that the 'very structure of patrilinearity can [...] be said to rest on a series of ruptures', and that Zola's text about a steam train is characterized by a 'chronic dearth of connectivity', visualized through the image of the knife which makes its appearance in the opening chapter.[78] *Vérité* seeks to seal up such ruptures, marrying the discourses of novel and newspaper and ending with a celebration of patrilineariy, with Marc and his three descendent generations united in the schoolroom. The *Quatre Évangiles* see their central protagonists reaching grand old ages as if to transcend the necessary rupture implied in Counter's evaluation of patrilinearity — a transmission from father to son which rests only on the death of the former.

The division between Thérèse and François in the final chapter of *Vérité* not only insists on the presence of a rupturing discord even in this would-be *fêlure*-free finale, but is itself something of a legacy of Marc's own generation, in the way it echoes the split between himself and Geneviève earlier in the text, when his passionate espousal of Simon's cause and her commitment to the church drove them apart. When separated, they seemed to speak different languages: 'nous ne donnons plus aux mots les mêmes sens' [we no longer speak the same language] (*V*, XXVI: 281). The echoes of such differently understood signifiers linger in the concluding rift between Marc and Geneviève's descendants, contributing the sense of there being competing dialogues at work in Zola's text despite all attempts to silence them. In the conclusion to his study of *la fêlure*, Deleuze himself suggests such a possibility in relation to Zola's later, 'rose-coloured' novels:

> On les interprète très mal (les romans roses) en invoquant une alternance: en fait, la littérature optimiste de Zola n'est pas autre chose que sa littérature putride. C'est dans un même movement, qui est celui de l'épique, que les plus bas instincts se réfléchissent dans le terrible Instinct de mort, mais aussi que l'Instinct de mort se réfléchit dans une espace ouverte, et peut-être contre lui-même.
>
> [It would be a mistake to interpret (his rose-coloured novels) by invoking some sort of alteration; in fact, Zola's optimistic literature is not anything other than his putrid literature. It is in one and the same movement — the movement of the epic — that the basest instincts are reflected in the terrible death Instinct, but also that death Instinct is reflected inside an open space, perhaps even against itself.]

He goes on to argue that:

> Comme si la fêlure ne traversait et n'aliénait la pensée que pour être aussi la possibilité de la pensée, ce à partir de quoi la pensée se développe et se recouvre. Elle est l'obstacle à la pensée mais aussi la demeure et la puissance de la pensée, le lieu et l'agent.
>
> [It is as if the crack runs through and alienates thought in order to be also the possibility of thought. In other words, from the vantage point of which thought is developed and recovered. It is the obstacle to thought, but also the abode and power of thought — its field and agent.][79]

Vérité appears to shut down 'thought' as it closes down writing and division, but it may, too, represent the 'ce à partir de quoi' from which thought recuperates.

Vérité strives for homogeny, then, for a vision of a literature and a press unified, as in the idealized image of the pedagogical press created in the closing sections of the text — and indeed, for a world beyond textuality altogether, for a secular state in which ideas and messages unfold with lithographic clarity, aided by the animation of speech. The resulting schematized and dogmatic text would appear to exclude it from the recent critical attempts to re-evaluate Zola as a modernist, as in Susan Harrow's monograph, *Zola and the Body Modern*. Counter points out the paradox in that it is precisely Zola's most blatantly forward-looking texts, the *Quatre Évangiles*, which cannot seem to be redeemed as modernist, and are omitted from Harrow's analysis.[80] The text suppresses the newspaper, in its persistent denigration of the press, in its depiction of a watered-down journalism, and in its own stylistic monologism; it eradicates the modernist aspects of fragmentation and self-ironization associated with the representation of the press and evident in Zola's naturalist novels. As a result, the truth of *Vérité* would appear to be its datedness. And yet, as Suleiman argues, the *roman à thèse* is necessarily a manifestation of modernity. The very term suggests a split between the words *roman* and *thèse*, between the complexity of an attempt to render the complexity and density of everyday life, and the necessity of simplifying and schematizing in order to get a message across, between ideology and a fiction which combats the possibility of such an ideological mission. Says Suleiman of the *roman à thèse*: 'An impure, unstable genre, rent by contradictory desires, inevitably inscribed in a position of lack, of guilty conscience — could we not say that the *roman à thèse* is one of the emblems, if not one of the manifestations, of our modernity?'[81] For all its drive towards purity, emblematized by light and truth, *Vérité* proves itself, as in the questions raised in its concluding section, to be the classic 'impure, unstable' example of modernity epitomized by the *roman à thèse* as evaluated by Suleiman.

It is precisely the drive to homogeny, advocated so vociferously in the novel and yet paradoxically achieved subconsciously, in the parallels between Marc and Gorgias, and in the novel's appropriation of the tactics of the *Petit Beaumontais* so derided, that the text muddies its own lithography. It is the very process of striving for sameness which in fact reveals difference and a cracking fragmentation. Harrow draws connections between Barthes's pictorial summary of Zola's intermingling of discourse as a kind of collage with the practices of Cubism, 'putting science into the picture as if it were a papier collé'.[82] The 'papier collé' image, with its connotations of Cubism, and, indeed, of Cubist pictures which incorporate the typography and image of the newspaper, is particularly vividly figured in the gummed-together bits of paper which stand at the heart of *Vérité*, the chewed, regurgitated, interpenetrating pieces of paper that are the 'modèle d'écriture' and the page of newsprint which can barely be disentangled from it.[83] These scraps of paper intertwine the *bordereau* in the Dreyfus case with the newspapers which will scream Jewish guilt, but also, in Zola's novel, make a collage out of these fragments of the Dreyfus case and the fictional text, crumpling together scraps so as to make a whole which reveals the drive for homogenization and an inevitable fragmentation at one and the same time. Harrow defines literary modernism as being associated with writers who 'question their own relations to mastery and to a desire for totalization, which is never fully renounced yet always deflected and displaced as it is reiterated'. In *Vérité*, the desire for totalization resonates more deafeningly than in many, if not all, of his other works; and yet in this text, in which reiteration is also written into the *papier collé* of the narrative to an even greater extent than in the naturalist novels, that desire for totalization is always 'deflected and displaced'. In setting up its battle between discourses, Zola's novel defeats itself. The newspaper industry as seen in *Vérité* ultimately enhances the modernism of the text when initially it seemed to reinforce the novel's desired homogeny.

Notes to Chapter 2

1. Caricatural sketch by Alfred Le Petit in *Le Grelot*, 22 August 1880, reprinted in *Zola journaliste*, ed. by Wrona, p. 223.
2. See Charles Bernheimer, *Figures of Ill-Repute: Representing Prostitution in Nineteenth-Century France* (Cambridge, MA: Harvard University Press, 1993).
3. See Éléonore Reverzy, 'Littérature publique: l'exemple de Nana', *Revue d'histoire littéraire de la France*, 109.3 (2009), 87–604. See also Kate Rees, 'Plague, Sewer, Cesspool: Fin de Siècle Mirrors of the Mass Press. Zola, Maupassant and *The Hornets' Life*', *Bulletin of the Émile Zola Society*, 49–50 (October 2014), 16–23.
4. The English translations of *Nana* are taken from *Nana*, trans. by Douglas Parmée (Oxford: Oxford University Press, 2009).
5. See, for example, Bernice Chitnis, *Reflecting on 'Nana'* (London: Routledge, 1991).
6. Reverzy, 'Littérature publique', p. 597.
7. See Henri Mitterand, *Zola journaliste: de l'affaire Manet à l'affaire Dreyfus* (Paris: A. Colin, 1962); also essays on Zola's role as journalist in *Dossier: Zola journaliste: histoire, politique, fiction*, ed. by Corinne Saminadayar-Perrin, *Cahiers naturalistes*, 87 (2013), 3–207.
8. *Zola journaliste*, ed. by Wrona, p. 14.
9. Frederick Brown, *Zola: A Life* (London: Macmillan, 1996), p. 243. Brown describes, in his biography of Zola, the interweaving of his career as a literary writer and his diverse employment as a journalist. Even when he achieved real success as a novelist, for instance, with the publication of *L'Assommoir* in 1877, he was still prolific in his journalistic output.
10. *Zola journaliste*, ed. by Wrona, p. 33.
11. Zola, 'Adieux', in *Zola journaliste*, ed. by Wrona, p. 318.
12. Auguste Dezalay, 'Le Personnage du journaliste chez Zola', *Travaux de linguistique et de littérature*, 22.2 (1985), 93–103 (pp. 96–97).
13. Despite the claim that no one novel is devoted to the backdrop of the press, or focuses primarily on a journalist character, there are studies which discuss the impact of the newspaper on Zola's work. See, for example, Alain Vaillant, 'Portrait du romancier réaliste en reporter-interviewer du peuple', in *Les Voix du peuple XIX et XXè siècles*, ed. by Corinne Grenouillet and Éléonore Reverzy (Strasbourg: Presses universitaires de Strasbourg, 2006), pp. 101–12.
14. White, 'Le Papier mâché dans *L'Argent*', p. 155.
15. See Dezalay, 'Le Personnage du journaliste chez Zola', p. 103.
16. Émile Zola, *Le Docteur Pascal*, in *Les Rougon-Macquart*, ed. by Henri Mitterand, 5 vols (Paris: Gallimard-Pléiade, 1960–67), v, 928.
17. Émile Zola, 'Alexis et Maupassant', *Le Figaro*, 11 July 1881.
18. Dezalay, 'Le Personnage du journaliste chez Zola', p. 99.
19. Ferdinand Brunetière, *Le Roman naturaliste* (Paris: Calmann Lévy, 1883), p. 225.
20. Ibid., p. 231.
21. Émile Zola, *Le Roman expérimental* (Paris: Flammarion, 2006), p. 75.
22. Henri Mitterand, 'Une archéologie mentale: *Le roman expérimental* et *La fortune des Rougon*', in *Le Discours du roman* (Paris: Presses universitaires de France, 1980), pp. 164–85 (pp. 169–70).
23. Walter Benjamin, 'The Storyteller: Reflections on the Works of Nikolai Leskov', in *Illuminations*, trans. by Harry Zohn, ed. by Hannah Arendt (New York: Schocken Books, 1969), pp. 83–109 (p. 85).

24. Marie-Sophie Armstrong, 'The Opening Chapter of *La Fortune des Rougon*, or the Darker Side of Zolian Writing', *Dalhousie French Studies*, 44 (Fall 1998), 39–53 (p. 40). Armstrong sees Zola staging questions of literary ethics, suggesting that Miette's father's trial is emblematic of Zola's own self-questioning of the way he plagiarizes from other authors (p. 52).
25. Susan Harrow, *Zola, the Body Modern: Pressures and Prospects of Representation* (Oxford: Legenda, 2010), p. 152.
26. Robert Ziegler, 'Blood and Soil: The Stuff of Creation in *La Fortune des Rougon*', *Studia Neophilologica*, 69 (1998), 235–41 (p. 236).
27. The English translations of *La Fortune des Rougon* are taken from *The Fortune of the Rougons*, trans. by Brian Nelson (Oxford: Oxford University Press, 2012).
28. Naomi Schor, *Zola's Crowds* (Baltimore, MD: Johns Hopkins Press, 1978), p. 19.
29. Schor, *Zola's Crowds*, p. 9
30. Thérenty, *La Littérature au quotidien*, p. 49.
31. Ibid., p. 24.
32. Wrona, 'Introduction', in *Zola journaliste*, ed. by Wrona, p. 22.
33. Émile Zola, 'La Presse française', *Messager de l'Europe*, August 1877, reprinted in *Zola journaliste*, ed. by Wrona, pp. 224–55 (p. 226).
34. Ibid., p. 225.
35. Ibid., p. 227.
36. Émile Zola, 'Documents littéraires', in *Œuvres complètes*, ed. by Henri Mitterand, 15 vols (Paris: Cercle du livre précieux, 1966–70), XII, 468–69.
37. Dezalay, 'Le Personnage du journaliste chez Zola', p. 100.
38. Émile Zola, *La Curée* (Paris: Gallimard, 1981), p. 70; *The Kill*, trans. by Brian Nelson, Oxford World's Classics (Oxford: Oxford University Press, 2004), p. 19. Jennifer Yee notes alternative possible symbolism in the name of Saccard; she suggests that the figure of Sabatini, who aids Saccard in his insider trading, can be seen as Aristide's 'alter-ego': 'The name Zola chose for his character links him by sibilance with Saccard, and both names are heavily suggestive: Saccard = "mettre à sac"; Sabatani = "saboter"; but perhaps still more, "sabbat", with its connotations of Judaism or devilry' (Yee, *The Colonial Comedy*, p.102, n. 60).
39. Brian Nelson, 'Introduction', in Zola, *The Kill*, pp. vii–xxxix (p. xxix).
40. Harrow, *Zola, the Body Modern*, pp. 106–07.
41. Ibid., p. 15.
42. Zola, *Le Roman expérimental*, p. 52.
43. Ibid., p. 56.
44. Ibid., p. 68.
45. Mitterand, 'Une archéologie mentale', p. 181. Armstrong also makes this observation, that Silvère 'acts indeed, as suggested by Mitterand, as the first representative of Zola in the series' ('The Opening Chapter of *La Fortune des Rougon*, or the Darker Side of Zolian Writing', p. 42).
46. Schor, *Zola's Crowds*, p. 20.
47. Émile Zola in *Le Gaulois*, 22 August 1888, cited in Spiers and Signori, *Entretiens avec Zola*, p. 32
48. Brian Nelson, 'Introduction', in *The Fortune of the Rougons*, pp. vii–xxx (p. xix).
49. Émile Zola, 'Causeries', *La Tribune*, 29 August 1869, reprinted in *Zola journaliste*, ed. by Wrona, pp. 154–60 (p. 157).
50. See Corinne Saminadayar-Perrin, 'Fictions de la bourse', *Cahiers naturalistes*, 78 (2004), 41–62; also Christophe Reffait, *La Bourse dans le roman du second XIXe siècle: discours romanesque et imaginaire social de la spéculation* (Paris: Champion, 2007).
51. David Baguley, *Naturalist Fiction: The Entropic Vision* (Cambridge: Cambridge University Press, 1990), p. 57.
52. Ann Jefferson, *Genius in France: An Idea and its Uses* (Princeton, NJ: Princeton University Press, 2015), p. 148.
53. Gillian Beer, 'Plot and the Analogy with Science in Later Nineteenth-Century Novelists', in *Comparative Criticism: A Yearbook*, 2, ed. by Elinor Shaffer (Cambridge: Cambridge University Press, 1980), p. 134.

54. Included in *Zola journaliste*, ed. by Wrona, pp. 341–56.
55. The English translations of *Vérité* are adapted from *Truth*, trans. by Ernest Alfred Vizetelly (Stroud: Sutton, 1994).
56. Émile Zola, 'Pour les juifs', *Le Figaro*, 16 May 1896, reprinted in *Zola journaliste*, ed. by Wrona, pp. 331–38 (p. 338).
57. Jeffrey Mehlman, 'Zola's Novel of the Dreyfus affair — Between Mystique and Politique', in *Jews, Catholics, and the Burden of History*, ed. by Eli Lederhendler (Cary, NC: Oxford University Press, 2006), pp. 243–51 (p. 246).
58. Andrew Counter, 'A Sentimental Affair: *Vérité*', *Romanic Review*, special issue on Zola, 102.3 (2011), 391–409.
59. Wrona, 'Mots à crédit', p. 74.
60. White, 'Le Papier mâché dans *L'Argent*', p. 151.
61. Valerie Minogue, 'Introduction', in Émile Zola, *Money* (Oxford: Oxford University Press, 2014), pp. vii–xxv (p. xxv).
62. Zola, 'J'Accuse', p. 342. Such claims are repeated throughout the article: 'c'est lui qui a inventé Dreyfus', p. 343; 'il n'y a eu, derrière, que les imaginations romanesques et démentes du commandant du Paty du Clam', p. 345; 'c'était l'écroulement du roman-feuilleton si extravagant, si tragique', p. 349.
63. Counter, 'A Sentimental Affair', pp. 404–05.
64. Susan Suleiman, *Authoritarian Fictions: The Ideological Novel as a Literary Genre* (New York: Columbia University Press, 1983), p. 275.
65. Mehlman, 'Zola's Novel of the Dreyfus Affair — Between Mystique and Politique', p. 246.
66. Gilbert D. Chaitin, *The Enemy Within: Culture Wars and Political Identity in Novels of the French Third Republic* (Columbus: Ohio State University Press, 2008), p. 211.
67. Zola, 'J'Accuse', p. 354.
68. Claire White, 'Rewriting Work and Leisure in Émile Zola's *Travail*', *Dix-Neuf*, 13.1 (2009), 55–70 (p. 60).
69. Chaitin, *The Enemy Within*, p. 210.
70. Ibid., p. 211.
71. Ziegler, 'Blood and Soil', p. 237.
72. Counter, 'A Sentimental Affair', (p. 406).
73. Vaillant, 'Portrait du romancier réaliste en reporter-interviewer du peuple', p. 112.
74. David Meakin, 'Zola's Utopian Fall: From Ironic Novel to Totalitarian Romance', *Romance Studies*, 26 (1995), 99–107 (p. 102).
75. Henri Mitterand, 'L'Evangile sociale de Travail: un anti-Germinal', *Mosaic: A Journal for the Interdisciplinary Study of Literature*, 5.3 (1972), 179–87 (p. 184).
76. Chaitin, *The Enemy Within*, p. 238.
77. Gilles Deleuze, *Logique du sens* (Paris, Minuit, 1969), p. 384; Deleuze, *The Logic of Sense*, trans. by Mark Lester with Charles Stivale (London: Athlone Press, 1990).
78. Andrew Counter, 'The Legacy of the Beast: Patrilinearity and Rupture in Zola's *La Bête humaine* and Freud's *Totem and Taboo*', *French Studies*, 61.1 (2008), 26–38 (pp. 36 & 33).
79. Deleuze, *Logique du sens*, pp. 385–86; *The Logic of Sense*, p. 370.
80. Counter, 'The Legacy of the Beast', p. 97.
81. Suleiman, *Authoritarian Fictions*, pp. 22–23.
82. Harrow, *Zola, The Body Modern*, p. 64.
83. Other *papier collé* impressions might include the image of the voluminous scraps of paper assembled by Pascal in *Le Docteur Pascal* which together offer the history of the Rougon and Macquart families; the opening chapter of the novel sees the doctor, for example, cutting out the article from *Le Temps* which announces the promotion of Saccard to the position of editor of *L'Époque*.

CHAPTER 3

❖

Verne: Foreign Correspondence, Mimesis, and the Senses

Gaston Leroux, reporter, foreign correspondent, and later writer of the crime series featuring the intrepid journalist-detective Rouletabille, described the necessary skills of a reporter as follows: 'Un journaliste peut commettre tous les péchés, mais il se doit de posséder sept qualités principaux: voir, entendre, savoir, retenir, deviner, choisir, écrire et être lu' [A journalist can commit all the sins, but must possess seven key qualities: sight, hearing, knowledge, retention, guesswork, selection, writing and being read].[1] As suggested by the privileging of 'voir' and 'entendre' here, journalists at the turn of the twentieth century defined themselves by the quality of their senses, and by sight and hearing in particular. This is indicated too in the title of journalistic memoirs such as that of Jules Huret, *Tout yeux, tout oreilles*.[2] The reporter was an eyewitness whose copy was, it was claimed, an undistorted picture of the real world. 'Ils retraceront ce qu'ils auront vu, rien de plus, rien de moins' [they will record what they have seen, nothing more, nothing less], was how a spokesperson for the new 'École de journalisme' described the job of the reporter in 1899.[3] Novels of the fin-de-siècle period which depict the world of the newspaper reinforce this image of the reporter as a character for whom the visual is all-important: Pierre Giffard's text, *Le Sieur de Va-Partout: souvenirs d'un reporter*, a fictionalized memoir of a dynamic and indefatigable reporter, mounts a vigorous defence of the practice of reportage in its early days; its opening chapter is given the subheading 'Comme quoi Va-Partout a tout vu' [How Va-Partout saw everything] (*VP*, 1). And in Verne's *Michel Strogoff*, which features two competing journalists, aurality is also established as a key skill of the new roving reporter; the English reporter Blount is described as 'spécialement organisé pour écouter et pour entendre' (*MS*, 8) ('especially well-adapted for listening and hearing').[4] His excellent ears are capable of recognizing the distinctive soundscapes which evoke a comprehension of the world, and of understanding the discourses around him in order to piece together a newspaper story. This chapter will examine the representation of reporters as observers and listeners in literary texts of the period, and the ways in which visual and aural senses are celebrated, ironized, and criticized, at a time when such capacities are highlighted as paramount in an increasingly mobile field of reportage, and yet are beginning to be subject to scepticism in contemporary phenomenological thought.

Reporters as 'témoins oculaires'

Reportage takes off in the French press in the 1870s and 1880s, facilitated thanks to improved communication and transport systems.[5] Christian Delporte describes the growth in public preference for information over opinion in the burgeoning newspaper industry as favouring a new mode of journalism. This new practice of news necessarily emphasizes the real world; Delporte refers to the reporter figure as one who, 'rompant avec le sédentarisme traditionnel du monde des journaux, [...] est celui qui va sur les lieux d'un événement pour y puiser des informations afin de rendre compte d'une réalité humaine' [breaking with the traditionally sedentary practices of the newspaper [...] becomes the one who goes directly to the scene of an event so as to gather the information needed to give an account of human reality].[6] This is a practice dominated by the need to convey the sensory vividness of the world being recorded, a practice in which the visual is paramount. The reporter — and in particular the 'grand reporter' sent to document foreign news stories and wire back war reports — relies on eyewitness accounts and precise information in order to inform his reader. The journalist Édouard Helsey, looking back on a career in reportage which began in 1912, insists on the unblinkered vision of his profession. Primarily a *spectateur*, Helsey observes that: 'Les verres de ses jumelles sont nets. Il observe et note de sang-froid' [the lenses of his binoculars are clear, He observes and records with composure].[7] Reactions to the new genre of reportage vary from those who decry the apparent banality of the factual style of writing to the increasing perception of reporters as heroes: 'le journaliste risque sa vie et se transforme en héros' [the journalist risks his life and becomes a hero] notes Delporte, citing the example of the reporter for *Le Journal*, Naudeau, arrested in 1905 by the Japanese when reporting on the war between Russia and Japan, and again in 1918, when taken prisoner by the Bolsheviks.[8]

Pinson argues that nineteenth-century representations of journalism tend to fall into two key categories. On the one hand there are texts, following *Illusions perdues*, which depict the *écrivain-journaliste* as an anxious type, forever striving towards the goal of authentic artistic creation while forced to dabble in the money-making opportunities afforded by the corrupting medium of the press. On the other, there are the texts dating from the end of the nineteenth century, when reportage was developing, which focus on the reporter's dynamism and heroism: 'Avec la figure du reporter, un profound renversement se produit dans l'imaginaire médiatique, bouleversement dont les répercussions s'avèrent capitales sur les reconfigurations du discours sur la presse autour de 1900' [The figure of the reporter brought about a complete reversal of the 'media imaginary', an upheaval which was to have important repercussions on the discourse surrounding the press at the turn of the century].[9] Beginning with the work of Jules Verne, such representations of the reporter-hero are associated with the popular novel and lead to the super-sleuth creations of Leroux, Souvestre and Allain, and Maurice Leblanc. In this chapter, through examination of one of the first texts to present the roving reporter as a hero, Giffard's *Le Sieur de Va-Partout*, and through discussion of the two novels by Verne which most clearly foreground the role of the reporter, focus will fall on this new representation of literary heroism. In assessing the emphasis placed on these characters' sensory acuity, the argument will turn to the ways in which these writers who in many ways admire the developing techniques of journalistic reportage also offer, in their works, self-conscious critique of ocularcentrism and aural expertise. In so doing, they contribute to phenomenological discussion about the dominance of certain sensory modes of recording the world, and provide often playful and amusing examples of generic hybridity, pitting journalism and literature against each other — in Verne's case, as a kind of race, or sport.

The emphasis on the visual and eyewitness accounts, found in journalism and the journalistic memoirs at the end of the nineteenth century, reflects an intensification of the move away from the *presse d'opinion* in the first half of the century — in which a paper argued in favour of a particular party — and towards the more neutral *presse d'information* discussed by Zola in the previous chapter. Thérenty notes that this development gathered speed from the late 1860s: 'Le journaliste devient donc la conscience observante du siècle en charge de l'examen du monde, responsable de la constitution des protocoles du témoignage oculaire. Cette fonction [...] participe à la promotion du journaliste au sein de la société' [The journalist thus became the watchful consciousness of the century, in charge of the examination of the world, responsible for the establishment of eyewitness protocol. This role [...] helped to elevate the position of the journalist within society].[10] She also emphasizes the shift in the nature of journalism, from the practice of *raconter* — perceived in Maupassant, as seen in Chapter One, as illustrative of the banalization of literature — to the increasing need for mobility, for the immediacy of presence demanded by *témoignage*. Hugues Le Roux attempts to define 'le reporter' in a piece in *Le Temps* in 1888, concluding that reportage is overtaking the *chronique* as the privileged style of newspaper writing, and declaring that the reporter is 'obscur, anonyme, à peine autorisé à signer d'une initiale ses articles, sans prétention littéraire, uniquement préoccupé d'exactitude' [obscure, anonymous, scarcely authorized to sign his articles even with a single initial, with no literary ambitions, preoccupied with accuracy alone].[11] The result is a focus on the imperative for visual acuity. As an example of this, an article in *Le Matin* in 1888 recounts the injuries sustained by Général Boulanger in a duel; alongside the paper's own report of the duel there is a separate account, 'récit d'un témoin oculaire' [eyewitness report] originally published in the *Gazette de France*, noting that 'd'une fenêtre je puis suivre toute la scène' [I can survey the whole scene from a window].[12]

The emphasis on the *choses vues* develops in part thanks to changes in the law and improvements in technology, enabling reporters to travel ever further in order to wire back their eyewitness accounts. It is also part of a rhetorical move: the increased prominence given to information over opinion encouraged journalists to promote the truth value of their copy in an attempt to combat criticism levelled at newspapers in the years following their liberalization, such as the suggestion that journalism was a polluting and polluted force, associated with a burgeoning commodity culture and likened to prostitution. Hugues Le Roux, commenting on journalism in 1889, claimed that *littérateurs* were attracted to reportage as 'la source essentielle de son renouveau' [the essential source of its renewal].[13] Roberts maintains that 'by defining reportage as a choice of reality over fantasy, the reporter buttressed the authority of journalism as a source of knowledge'; she evaluates the critique levelled at journalism in the 1880s and 1890s, and discusses its attempts at redeeming itself by emphasizing its factuality and its distinction from literature.[14] Although the focus on the visual echoes concerns of literature — and Naturalism in particular — there is at the same time an effort on the part of those practising the new reportage to try and distinguish it from the novel as part of the defence of such truth-value. A new sense of purpose and professionalization characterizes the journalism of the late nineteenth century; a new cadre of trained journalists was replacing a more bohemian literary elite, a move crystallized by the establishment of the American-style *école* for journalists in 1899, referred to above. At the same time it was in part the apparent obsession with the *chose vue* — with facts and the eyewitness report — which was associated with the sense of crisis surrounding journalism of the time, castigated for threatening the stylistic values of literature and literary journalism. See, for example, Brunetière's chapter 'Le Reportage dans le roman' in his *Roman naturaliste* (discussed in Chapter Two), in which he is particularly disparaging of writers such as Jules Claretie, for his novels *La Maîtresse* and *Les Amours d'un interne*, and Edmond Texier and Camille Le Senne for their *La Dame du lac*: 'Leur domaine, c'est *l'actualité*. Servons-nous du mot que les poètes, ayant licence de tout oser, et puisque aussi bien nous sommes en veine de barbarisme, n'ont pas craint de mettre à la mode. La *modernité*, c'est leur domaine' [Their domain is that of news. Let us employ the word that the poets, with their licence to risk all, and since too we are dealing with barbarism, are not afraid to make fashionable. Modernity is their domain].[15] Zola, for all the ambiguity associated with his reactions to journalism, as discussed in the previous chapter, suggests in the 1890s that reportage is the death of journalism: 'la presse est en train de tuer la littérature' [the press is in the process of killing off literature].[16]

Delporte stresses the emergence of a particularly French brand of reportage. He points out the tendency to see French reportage as an echo of the Anglo-American model, dating back to Gordon Bennett's reports on murder cases in the 1830s, when witnesses in murder cases were interviewed for the *New York Herald*. Indeed, claims Delporte, Bennett is a source for the material in the futuristic *La Journée d'un journaliste américain en 2889* by Verne, a text examined in the afterword to this book.[17] The French version of this new form of journalism, though, maintains its links with the literary and with the older practice of the *chronique*. Fernand Xau, founder of the paper *Le Journal*, analyzes the reasons why the French public prefer something other than the American model of reportage, even though the *journal d'information* is increasingly popular:

> Nous sommes trop raffinés pour nous contenter d'un reportage tout sec, et puis, le commerçant, le politicien, ne sont pas les seuls à lire le journal. Il y a l'écrivain, l'artiste, il y a les femmes aussi qui s'intéressent médiocrement à l'information banale et brutale. De là, deux nécessités: relever le reportage, en le confiant à des écrivains de talent, et en second lieu, faire une large place à la partie purement littéraire.[18]

[We are too sophisticated to be content with such a bland form of reportage, and besides, businessmen and politicians are not the only ones who read the newspaper. There are writers, artists, and women too who are only averagely interested in banal, blunt news. Two things, then, are necessary: elevate the practice of reportage by handing it to talented writers, and, secondly, make space for a purely literary element.]

It is not simply a case of printing a balance of news pieces alongside more traditional examples of literature and comment. Delporte goes on to suggest that even when practising 'grand reportage' and sending back accounts of the battlefield, there is a tendency for the French reports to privilege the position of the reporter and his personality; to see the eyewitness accounts coloured by subjectivity to a greater extent than that found in British and American newspapers: 'le grand reportage français se distingue nettement du modèle anglo-saxon où en général le fait prime le commentaire, où l'homme qui a vu s'efface devant ce qu'il a vu' [international reporting as carried out by the French is clearly distinguished from the Anglophone model in which facts tend to dominate over commentary, in which the eyewitness gives way to what he has seen].[19] French reportage maintains connections with literature.

This Gallic insistence on the subjectivity of the reporter characterizes the eyewitness accounts found in many newspapers and journals of the fin-de-siècle years, even in reports which seem most preoccupied with the emphasis on the immediacy and objectivity associated with on-the-spot journalism. References to the blunt facts of the seen are accompanied by dramatization, stylization, and the amplification of the reporter's own heroic role. As Thérenty observes, journalism during the Third Republic engages in paradox: 'sans céder à la tentation et à l'illusion d'une écriture objective, le journaliste assume le fait que l'événement est perçu par une conscience' [without relinquishing the temptations and the illusions of objectivity, the journalist assumes that an event has been witnessed by a particular perspective].[20] This 'conscience' frequently becomes manifest even while downplaying its own presence. The race to get to the telegraph which sees reporters pitting themselves against their competitors at times leads to a twofold sense of reportage: the bald facts of the event narrated alongside the acknowledgement that the reporter has beaten his rivals; a sense of both the story and the margins of the story, in which the journalist is heroized. The title of Huret's memoirs, *Tout yeux, tout oreilles*, also evokes this duality — it implies that these receptive ocular and aural senses are all-important, and it simultaneously reminds the reader of the acuity and sensitivity of the journalist who is so adept at watching and listening while downplaying these skills. The notion of the *chose vue* is in essence a rhetorical construction rather than an authentic attempt to grasp the real.

The Denigration of Vision

Even as reportage is developing its insistence on the primacy of the visual, literary texts are already satirizing and questioning such a preoccupation. Roberts cites a dramatic sketch of a reporter seeking employment in an editor's office, published in Chambure's history of journalism, À travers la presse, in 1913. Here, there is an acknowledgement of the importance of ocular perception, which transcends any capacity for literary flair; a would-be employee confesses that 'je ne me suis jamais connu aucune espèce d'imagination' [I have never thought of myself as having any imagination], but instead 'j'ai [...] des yeux qui voient à quinze cents mètres' [my eyes can see things up to 1500 metres away]. Yet once taken on by the newspaper, this aspiring journalist has cards made up which read 'homme de lettres' [man of Letters]; a humorous nod to the juxtaposition of literature and a reportage responsive to visual imperatives at work in French journalism.[21] This amalgamation is explored in one of the first texts to make a case for the new reportage, Pierre Giffard's *Le Sieur de Va-Partout*, which will be discussed shortly. In *La Vie des frelons*, discussed in Chapter One, Paul Toussaint is impressed by the stylish reporters arriving for their day of work at the offices of the newspaper, *Le Quotidien*, adorned with their monocles. Yet the sartorial code which requires the monocle as part of its superficial emphasis on appearance indicates both that these reporters have eyes which are not perfect and so necessitate the improving vision of the monocle, and also that their resultant vision is one-eyed, imbalanced, an impression also writ large in Verne's representation of intrepid reporters in *Michel Strogoff*. Toussaint's conclusion that 'Entendre, voir, écrire sont peu de chose en journalisme: il faut sentir et faire sentir' [Listening, seeing, writing: these things matter little in journalism. You have to feel and make other feel] debunks the supposed focus on objective impressions, as does a scene in which the newspaper in the text, having organized a large-scale cycle race as a way of garnering publicity, sees several of its competitors injured and one killed.[22] Reporters rush with doctors to one such competitor during the race, demanding ' "Vos impressions?" ', only to be met with the dismissive response: ' "Eh bien quoi? Mon impression? ... J'aurai une montre en or" ' [What? My impressions? ... I will have won a gold watch].[23] The scene in Fenestrier is a satire of sporting events organized by the newspapers; Delporte notes that there was a cycle race held in 1893 and organized by Pierre Giffard himself.[24]

These texts which challenge the emphasis on vision as the dominant new skill of the reporter chime with the increasing sense in philosophical thought in the second half of the nineteenth century and throughout the twentieth century that there is a need for a powerful critique of the 'hegemony of vision'. David Levin's volume of essays, *Modernity and the Hegemony of Vision*, incorporates a range of philosophical discussions critiquing the authority of sight. Levin discusses Heidegger's reading of ocularcentrism, arguing that while Heidegger was not against the hegemony of vision as such, he rejected modes of seeing in the modern world. According to Levin, Heidegger formulated a powerful double critique: a critique of our everyday way of seeing, a typically inauthentic mode which he regarded as calculative, narrowly instrumental, reifying, aggressive, and ontologically degenerate. Instead, Levin perceives that Heidegger was drawn to a radically different way of seeing, hoping for a 'redeeming moment of vision'.[25] Martin Jay's wide-ranging study also argues that 'a great deal of recent French thought in a wide variety of fields is in one way or another imbued with a profound suspicion of vision and its hegemonic role in the modern era', and situates the increased 'denigration of vision' in phenomenological study around the second half of the nineteenth century.[26] In a chapter on late nineteenth- and early twentieth-century thought and art, which evaluates, for example, the 'anti-retinal' art of Marcel Duchamp, Jay suggests that the status of visual primacy was questioned in three ways in particular in philosophical thought: 'The first concerns what can be termed the detranscendentalization of perspective; the second, the recorporealization of the cognitive subject; and the third, the revalorization of time over space'.[27] Citing Crary's *Techniques of the Observer*, Jay emphasizes the 'return of the body' and its fallibility in conceptualizing sight; the visible 'escapes from the timeless incorporeal order of the camera obscura' and becomes embedded instead 'within the unstable physiology and temporality of the human body'.[28] In discussion of the emphasis placed on journalistic vision in Verne's works later in this chapter, focus will fall on the way in which the physiological apparatus is accentuated to comic effect in descriptions, for example of the reporters in *Michel Strogoff*, but is proved to be unstable.

The late-nineteenth century is a period when vision is increasingly called into question and held to be dubious in its reifying tendencies; Andrea Goulet also situates the shift in conceptualizations of sight at this historical period, towards the end of the century, in her work on the eyeball and the retina as troubled sights of human epistemology in texts such as those by Villiers de l'Isle Adam and Gaston Leroux. She suggests that 'the nineteenth century in Western European thought has come to be seen as a transitional period between the idealist abstraction of a Cartesian age and the embodied contingency of early twentieth-century phenomenology', and argues that 'in France in particular, the literary history of visuality reflects the complex intersections of objective (Cartesian, transcendental, visionary) and subjective (bodily, phenomenal, naturalistic) vision, with neither effacing the other in any particular text'.[29] This is also the period when journalism develops and celebrates the visual acuity of its reporters, insisting on the immediacy of visual impressions and the need for foreign trips in order to wire back eye-witness accounts of events. David Howes notes that the business of wiring back itself impacted on the hegemony of the visual. The invention of the telegraph 'altered the balance of the senses [...] by rupturing the silence which had been imposed by print, and making communication instantaneous again. The new media [...] sensitized people to the auditory and tactile dimensions of experience'.[30] The best-known scene in Verne's *Michel Strogoff* sees Blount and Jolivet grappling for control of the telegraph booth, competing to see who can be first to send news of the battle between Russian and Tartar troops. The result is a pastiche of new-fangled journalism, communication, and forms of textuality. What the scene also demonstrates is Verne's embrace of both the auditory and the visual dimensions associated with reportage, and the ways in which his representation of sensory experience acts as a humorous riposte to practices of information-gathering associated with the new media, and to techniques of realist literature. Thérenty says that in 'cette scène bouffonne, Verne conteste et parodie le modèle du reportage' [this farcical scene, Verne is contesting and parodying the practice of reportage].[31] While reportage is indeed parodied in

Michel Strogoff, and in this scene in particular, it is the communicative endeavour more broadly which is questioned in this text. Anthropological studies of the senses suggest that:

> Different communications media 'distort' our experience of the world in the very process of making such experience possible, because of the differential way they call the senses into action. Thus, the newspaper extends the range and sensitivity of the eye, but suppresses other sensory functions; the African talking drum extends the normal range of functioning of the ear [...] but at the expense of sight.[32]

Jay suggests that the aural was investigated as a rival to the visual imperative: 'alternative traditions such as a hearing-centered hermeneutics can be discerned during the heyday of ocularcentrism, at least at the margins of philosophical discourse'.[33] *Michel Strogoff* acts as a key text in discussing the interplay between literature and reportage in the nineteenth century and argues for a multi-sensorial approach to the real.

The incorporation of the journalist figure in Verne's texts serves a mimetic purpose: Verne's inclusion of several reporters amongst his casts of characters acknowledges the increased presence of the journalist and the foreign correspondent in modern public life. The role of the reporter in Verne's texts such as *Michel Strogoff* and *Claudius Bombarnac* is to document the real, to give an impression of the immediacy of war in the former text, and the visual account of the train journey across Russia in the latter. The undermining of these characters can be read as a parodic take on realism itself. As Peter Brooks stresses in his survey of a range of key nineteenth-century realist novels, the visual is a dominant feature of the texts' mimetic aspirations.[34] The representation of reportage in Verne's work extols and subverts not only the paramount presence of sight in the realist novel, but couples it with an evaluation of the aural, in comedic and mimetically challenging ways. Paul Rodaway considers 'auditory geography' an alternative sensual way of comprehending our environment, suggesting that 'auditory phenomena penetrate us from all directions at all times. The auditory perspective is not linear but multidirectional'.[35] Hannah Scott argues for the triumph of aurality over the visual attractions of the modern department store in Zola's *Au Bonheur des dames*.[36] An appreciation of the aural dimensions of experience can provide a complement or an antithesis to the reifying tendencies of visual dominance. Yet in his representation of modern reporters, Verne problematizes the hegemony of both sight and sound.

Le Sieur de Va-Partout: Fiction and Reportage

Verne's novels are fictional texts which exaggerate their realist dimensions in part through reflections on the business of reportage. Before looking at Verne, though, consideration will turn to a text which begins as a celebration of reportage but increasingly demonstrates its literary ambitions. One of the earliest works to depict the new roving reporter figure is, as mentioned above, Giffard's 1880 text, *Le Sieur de Va-Partout*, which mounts a vigorous defence of the practice of reportage. Delporte refers to *Le Sieur de Va-Partout* as being instrumental in helping to define the varied role of the reporter; it was published just as the Larousse and Littré dictionaries were including the term 'reporter' in their 1879 editions, and illustrated the blurring of distinctions between 'petit' and 'grand' reportage. The 'petits reporters' tended to be based in Paris or in other towns, and were responsible for gathering urban news, such as reporting on crime. They were distinguished from the 'grand reporters' who were increasingly dispatched abroad to cover foreign affairs. Written by a seasoned journalist (Giffard wrote for a range of papers in the years following the Franco-Prussian war, edited the *Petit Journal* and was the founder of the sports journal *Le Vélo*), the text sees its narrator initiated into the dizzying life of a roving reporter as he attempts to piece together the biography of the inexorable Va-Partout, a correspondent who sleeps with his suitcase as a pillow, so prepared is he to leap off at any moment in search of copy for the papers. The narrator stresses the dynamism that characterizes this all-seeing reporter: 'Je le vis plus d'une fois traverser notre territoire comme une flèche, affamé, assoiffé, rompu de fatigue' [More than once I have seen him cross the landscape like an arrow, starving, parched, worn out with fatigue] (*VP*, 2). In the opening pages of the novel, sight is privileged. Yet this is a text which also indicates that the visual — even for Va-Partout, a character who epitomizes the immediacy and vibrancy of the eyewitness report — is necessarily accompanied by a demand for relating, and so selecting and presenting the 'choses vues': 'Lui, infatigable, allait voir et racontait' [tireless, he would see and relate] (*VP*, 2). The status of the observer is doubled with that of the storyteller, exemplifying the particular French brand of reportage discussed by Delporte.

Myriam Boucharenc analyzes *Le Sieur de Va-Partout* as a defence and an illustration of reportage, which also deliberately acts to blur the boundaries between literary genres: 'le reportage s'affirme comme fabrique narrative et comme nouveau genre littéraire' [reportage is thus affirmed as a method of producing narrative and as a new literary genre].[37] The framing and writing of the gaze is a particularly self-conscious act for Giffard; the closing pages of *Le Sieur de Va-Partout* consist of notes apparently collated by the narrator from papers left behind by the reporter Va-Partout on his departure for an investigative mission in Russia. These provide concise historical details about the life of a reporter. Va-Partout acknowledges that reportage originates from an Anglo-American tradition, but is then disparaging about the relative banality of American newspaper reporters:

> Ils n'ont aucun sens artistiques. Ce sont des machines à noter. Ils ne sont d'ailleurs ni écrivains, ni artistes, ni critiques. Il faut que nous autres, en France, nous soyons tout cela. Le lecteur français ne supporterait pas l'inventaire banal qui fait le fond du bagage des reporters Yankees. Il faut lui présenter le côté topique du personnage, ou ne rien lui présenter du tout.
>
> Il y a dans l'article de reportage comme au théâtre, la scène à faire. (*VP*, 330–31)
>
> [They have no artistic sense. They are but notation machines. They are neither writers, nor artists, nor critics. But in France, we must be all these things. French readers will not put up with the banal style of inventory which

is such a staple ingredient of Yankee reporters' equipment. You must show them the topical nature of the character, or nothing at all.

In a piece of reportage there is a scene to be laid out, as in the theatre.]

In contrast to the image of the American reporter as a 'machine à noter', Va-Partout creates a much more colourful image of himself in the opening chapter — in keeping with the theatricality apparently necessitated by the newspaper article suggested in his closing notes — when describing his past to the narrator:

> J'ai couru Paris entier comme le héros de cette pièce viennoise, par plaisir et par métier, regardant curieusement, soulevant discrètement les voiles et mettant au besoin l'œil droit, mon meilleur, au trou d'aiguille des murs capitonnés où les indiscrets sont admis dans l'ombre. (*VP*, 6)

> [I have traversed the whole of Paris like the hero in that Viennese play, both for work and pleasure, looking with curiosity, discreetly unveiling, and putting my right eye — my stronger one — to work at the keyholes of those padded rooms which admit the indiscreet in the dark.]

This quotation summarizes the hybridity at work in Giffard's text, indicating exaggerated, fictionalized tendencies in the self-aggrandizing reference to himself as the hero of a play and evoking cloak and dagger melodrama through the image of spying through walls, while also creating the impression of Va-Partout employing his vision — amplified through reference to the superiority of his right eye — in order to lift the veil on contemporary society and probe the reality beyond. Such a mixture of the fictional and the real is also summarized by the combination of pleasure and duty suggested here.

Much of the construction of Va-Partout is hybrid, emphasizing the fusion of literature and reportage at work in this innovative text. On the one hand, as the notes compiled at the end of the text remind the reader, *Le Sieur de Va-Partout* is a documentary-style narrative designed to provide insight into the working lives of nineteenth-century reporters. Va Partout epitomizes the new breed of reporters commissioned to follow the demands of a story at the drop of a hat; on several occasions the text sees reporter and narrator obliged to abandon one event and dash off to cover another unfolding story, as in Chapter Three, when they are informed of the imminent execution of the criminal Poirier, and leave a party in haste to get to the guillotine. The closing lines of the execution episode evoke the image of a whole host of reporters, employed to witness such an early morning decapitation and make a grisly story of it for their readers: 'Il y a tout un compartiment de Va-Partout parisiens qui se sont beaucoup amusés, et qui préparent pour leurs journaux des comptes rendues à faire frémir toutes les concierges de la capitale' [There is a whole compartment of Parisian Va-Partouts who are much entertained, and who are preparing accounts for their newspapers which will make all the concierges in the capital shudder] (*VP*, 27). The text also indicates the vast array of topics about which a reporter like Va Partout is expected to write — not just guillotines and gore, but insights into political and theatrical life, visits to orphanages and the races, accounts of trips to parts of France ranging from the south coast to Alsace and Lorraine. To the narrator's suggestion that Va-Partout should write his memoirs, the reporter scoffs, claiming that he has simply seen too much of life to be able to incorporate it all in even ten volumes: 'songez donc que je vois tout ce qui se passe, et que je raconte tout' [just think that I see all that occurs, and I tell it all] (*VP*, 3). Listing the multifarious dimensions of Parisian and French life he has witnessed, Va Partout adds: 'j'ai vu tout cela d'un œil calme et quasiment rêveur' [I have seen all this, calmly and almost dreamily] (*VP*, 5). His totalizing visual account of contemporary society, observed so stoically, is once again accompanied, however, by an element which disrupts the apparent neutrality of his gaze even while extolling it; the attitude of the 'rêveur' who translates the objective facts of what he sees into something more literary.

This 'œil rêveur' is reinforced by the aspects of the text which make of Va-Partout a larger than life character, as seen in the theatrical self-heroization of the earlier quotation. Although not provided with a proper name in such a way as to suggest that Va-Partout, characterized principally by his mobility and expansive knowledge, is but a representative of the many similarly dutiful reporters (the 'Va Partout parisiens'), the lack of appellation also turns Va Partout into a mythical creation: as the narrator queries in the opening paragraphs of the text, 'Qu'importe son nom, sa naissance? Il s'appelait pour moi Va-Partout: Je l'avais baptisé de ce sobriquet légitime, et il le trouvait presque spirituel' [What do his name or his birth matter? I called him Va-Partout; I had given him that rightful nickname and he considered it almost something spiritual] (*VP*, 1). Such relative anonymity is reinforced by Va-Partout's insistence, referred to above, that it would be impossible to detail his life in a set of memoirs: it is not just that the list of his observations would be too all-encompassing to elaborate, but also that he retains an enigmatic role. Accompanying Va-Partout for a year as a token reporter, the narrator recounts not only the diversity of subject matter witnessed (summarized for Myriam Boucharenc in the heterogeneity of the museum of instruments visited by the two men) but also the range of styles embraced by Va-Partout, which are sometimes purposefully literary, as when a chapter is devoted to an excerpt of the reporter's prose poetry, written to celebrate the month of May.[38]

On other occasions, Va-Partout self-consciously ironizes his own would-be approach to the primacy of the visual. The penultimate chapter sees reporter and narrator in Nice, with Va-Partout commissioned to send back travel reports so as to enlighten the eight or nine Parisians out of ten who will never have seen the Mediterranean coast. But, however meticulously carried out, this duty is interspersed with visits to Monaco, where Va-Partout enjoys visiting the casino. The chapter ends with the narrator agreeing with Va-Partout's observation that 'voilà le plus beau site que j'aie jamais revé' [this is the most beautiful place I could ever have dreamt of] (*VP*, 316), imagining that he is appreciating the beauty of the coastline, only for Va Partout to claim, instead, that he is referring to the gambling table: 'oh, ce n'est rien,' he says of the view from the casino, 'le rouge vient de passer douze fois; j'étais sur le 36 plein, il vient de sortir aussi. Voilà qui vous égaye, mon cher, singulièrement le paysage' [oh, it's nothing, the red has just spun past a dozen times; I was right on the 36, that has just come up too. The landscape is all that amuses you, my dear chap] (*VP*, 316). Jettisoning the objective view in favour of subjective gain (and pocketing ten thousand francs), this chapter, which brings an end to the shared adventures of the two men, reinforces the distinctive individuality of the viewpoint embraced by Va-Partout. The gaming table, with its whirling reds and blacks, also acts as a metaphor for the text itself, which spins through such a profusion of scenes and offers contrasting 'colours' of styles. It is no wonder that the narrator claims to be confused by the wealth of visual material presented to him when he accompanies Va-Partout: 'je ne démêle plus que confusément la vie incroyable que nous avons menée. J'ai tout vu' [I can get to grips with the incredible life we have been leading but confusedly. I have seen it all] (*VP*, 8). Indeed, the role of the narrator, like that of Va-Partout, reaffirms the amalgamation of fictionality and documentary within the text, his awed reactions to the relentless activity manifested by Va-Partout foregrounding the reality of the experiences and often adding an additional layer of proof to the observations recorded. At the same time, the presence of the narrator means that the reader only ever really accesses the views of Va-Partout through a screen, even when apparently being given the direct words of the reporter — ironic given that Va-Partout's job is to communicate with the reader. This ensures the mythical proportions of the enigmatic reporter. The narrator's function suggests both the accessibility of the new profession of reportage — his own observations are encouraged by Va-Partout, and there are times in the text when he is told that his own notes can stand unedited in the narrative because they cannot be bettered by Va-Partout himself — and yet finally insists on the role of the reporter as too exhausting and overwhelming for the ordinary being. The narrator eventually has to give up on the business of accompanying Va-Partout: 'c'en était trop. J'étais exténué' [it was too much. I was exhausted] (*VP*, 317). The duality of both narrator and text is epitomized in the quotation which closes the opening chapter, with the narrator referring to his adventures with Va-Partout as 'ces mois où j'allais, haletant, effaré, dans la vie frénétique, tenant d'une main ma canne et de l'autre le bras du méphistophélique Va-Partout' [those months during which I staggered breathless though that frenzied way of life, holding my walking stick in one hand and the arm of the Mephistophilean Va-Partout with the other] (*VP*, 8). His walking stick acts as an indicator of his conventional bourgeois 'reality,' as set against the quasi-infernal and hyper-real glimpse into the alternate reality exhaustively documented by Va-Partout.

Le Sieur de Va-Partout therefore makes a case for the new journalism as a dynamic and hard-to-imitate business, and offers a hotchpotch of a text which resists generic categorization. In its humour and its conscious questioning of its own project, brought about through the self-effacing commentary of the narrator and through the enigmatic qualities of Va-Partout, the Mephistotilean representative of the 'real' world of reportage, it also parodies and critiques its own narrative functioning. These traits are summarized in the concluding chapter of the text and its epilogue, which see both the death and non-death of this elusive reporter. Having established his own paper with his casino winnings, Va-Partout is last seen taking off for Russia, aiming to uncover 'le tissu mystérieux de crimes et de brigandages qui affole l'empire du tsar' [the mysterious network of crime and robbery which is throwing the Empire of the Tsar into a panic] (*VP*, 326). The narrator then receives a note from a band of Russian brigands who claim to have assassinated Va-Partout, and organizes a memorial service when a corpse believed to be that of the reporter is discovered. This dramatic conclusion is succeeded by the *appendice* composed of the 'papiers secrets' of Va-Partout, which provide the strongest case for rehabilitating the figure of the journalist. Their position in the text accentuates such a defence, coming as it does after the lingering impression of the heroism and martyrdom of Va-Partout, apparently killed when carrying out his journalistic duty. Here, Va-Partout contemplates the traditional image of the reporter: 'longtemps on a cru que les reporters étaient les derniers des hommes' [for a long time it has been believed that reporters are the lowest of the low] but makes his own case for the triumphant visual acuity of those of his profession which will be the envy of literary writers:

> On voit ce que les autres ne voient pas, ce qu'ils n'apprennent qu'à travers nos phrases et nos descriptions. Mais dix romanciers voudraient recommencer la vie littéraire, pour saisir et peindre au vol sur le coup toutes ces pochades imprévues que font la vie quotidienne d'un chercheur d'imprévu comme moi! (*VP*, 327)

> [They see what others do not, what can be learned only through our way of writing and our descriptions. There are a number of novelists who would happily start their literary careers over in order to be able to jot down all those unforeseen entertaining sketches which make up the everyday life of one who goes in search of the unforeseen, as I do.]

The final note of the text — which appears under the newspaper-esque heading 'dernière heure' — includes the report that 'au moment où ce livre est mis sous presse, un télégramme du gouverneur de Saint-Pétersbourg conteste vivement l'identité du soi-disant Va-Partout' [at the moment that this book goes to press, a telegram from the governor of St Petersburg has strongly denied that this is indeed the so-called Va-Partout] (*VP*, 332). Thus the text ends in typically hybrid form, contrasting the imminent publication of the 'livre' with the most obvious example of reportage-like style and typography at work in the volume, suggesting that Va-Partout has employed his journalistic tactics as skilfully as possible in order to fictionalize his own death, and reaffirming the indefinable nature of the reporter throughout the text in this bureaucratic doubt cast on the 'identité du soi-disant Va-Partout'.

Giffard's text thus ends in Russia, where one of Verne's most memorable evocations of journalism — *Michel Strogoff* — begins. Giffard and Verne were acquaintances. As Zoé Commère notes in her work on Verne's later novel, *Claudius Bombarnanc*, Verne was on good terms with a number of journalists, including the reporter Pierre Giffard.[39] Although there are key differences between Verne's fictionalized representations of journalism and the narrative of *Le Sieur de Va-Partout*, there is also much common ground to be found. *Michel Strogoff*, serialized in the *Magasin d'Éducation* in 1875 and published as a book in 1876, is a work of fiction which satirizes the reporters it features, while Giffard's text, published four years later, mounts a defence of reportage which amalgamates literature and a range of styles ranging from travel writing to documentary notes. Nevertheless, in the heroism and dynamism they associate with the role of the reporter, in the questions raised by both texts as to the relative merits of literature and reportage, and in the suggestions of parody at work in both Verne and Giffard, there are similarities. Verne's representation of the reporter figure in *Michel Strogoff* is echoed and celebrated in *Le Sieur de Va-Partout*, and then re-examined and subjected to even further self-conscious probing in Verne's own *Claudius Bombarnac*, published in 1893.

Verne's Reporters: The Ocular and the Aural

As seen in the Introduction, Verne's comments on the press evoke scepticism as to the future of the novel in a world of developed journalism.[40] His observation echoes that of Va-Partout at the end of Giffard's text; writers of literature must envy the ability to record with such visual acuity the daily impressions of 'un chercheur d'imprévu comme moi'. In certain novels, such as *L'Île mystérieuse*, Verne creates a heroic portrait of the journalist and praises his sense of duty. Here Gédéon Spilett, reporter for the *New York Herald* who finds himself in the balloon forced to land on the eponymous island, is described as being: 'de la race de ces étonnants chroniqueurs anglais ou américains, des Stanley et autres, qui ne reculent devant rien pour obtenir une information exacte et pour la transmettre à leur journal dans les plus brefs délais' [of that race of astonishing English or American journalists, such as Stanley and others, who will stop at nothing to retrieve the exact information and deliver it to their newspaper without delay]. Spilett is a man 'de grand mérite, énergique, prompt et prêt à tout, plein d'idées, ayant couru le monde entière' [of great merit, energetic, ready for anything, full of ideas, who has travelled the whole world]. As a reporter he is described, tellingly, as a 'soldat et artiste'.[41] Spilett's attributes will serve him well on the desert island, though he is never seen practising his craft of journalism.

In *Michel Strogoff* and *Claudius Bombarnac*, journalists are seen carrying out their duties, thinking of ideas for stories, wiring back news bulletins from abroad. In these texts, the men charged with piecing together the 'récits colorés' which Verne lauds are frequently depicted as buffoons, suggesting, instead, a critique of the practice of reportage. Unwin claims that when Verne anticipates the demise of the novel at the hands of the press, it is because he emphasizes the educational, knowledge-providing aspects of the novel rather than its literariness:

> What Jules Verne does not appear to focus on at all is the fictional quality of the novel, notwithstanding the fact that his own stories can themselves be exaggeratedly self-conscious dramatizations of the fictional process. It seems that his critical view of the novel has, like his novels themselves, got out of proportion. But perhaps we must see this as part of the major shift of the novel to new territory that he himself initiates.[42]

Verne in fact celebrates the literary — whether through language or plot — even as he predicts the demise of the novel. *Michel Strogoff* champions literature at the expense of competing forms of representation such as reportage in pitting the two bumbling reporter characters against the heroic Michel Strogoff, charged with delivering a symbolic secret message. *Claudius Bombarnac* raises metatextual questions about both literary narrative and the business of news gathering.

As in Giffard's text, in these representations of reportage, prominence is given to the visual, a sense which is paramount in Verne's work. Trevor Harris calls Verne's line of approach in the exhaustive enumerations of material in his work as 'an all-seeing one'; referring to the aerial perspective of the characters in *Cinq semaines en ballon*, for instance, it seems that Verne's method is 'panoptic as well as panoramic'.[43] Yet the visual — certainly in *Michel Strogoff* and *Claudius Bombarnac* — is also subject to scrutiny and parody. The duality surrounding questions of vision in Verne is discussed by Simone Vierne as a fundamental aspect of his narratives, which mount documentary, educational, and scientific material in order to persuade the reader of the truth-value of his characters' expansive experience of the world, only for the narrator to be constantly drawing simultaneous attention to the fictionality of his productions. Vierne refers to these paradoxes in visual terms as the 'trompe l'œil' and the 'clin d'œil' [knowing wink]. The 'trompe l'œil' refers to Verne's representation of reality, composed in such a way as to draw affinities between storyteller and reporter:

> Par tous ces effets de trompe l'œil, la voix du narrateur tente donc à la fois de cautionner le réel et de faire admettre pour vrai ce qui est dit/écrit, comme si l'écrivain avait pour tâche de rapporter, comme en bon *reporter* (il y en a nombreuses figures dans l'œuvre) des 'scènes de la vie du monde'.
>
> [As a result of these *trompe l'œil* effects, the voice of the narrator attempts both to guarantee the real and to acknowledge that what is said/written is true, as if the writer's task were to relate 'scenes from life', in his capacity as a good *reporter* (there are numerous such figures to be found across the work).]

At the same time, the knowing 'clin d'œil' while inviting the reader to enter into the fiction ('tout en engageant le lecteur à *entrer dans la fiction*), points out that it is but a fiction, ('lui indique aussi, [...] que *ce n'est qu'une fiction*').[44]

Michel Strogoff foregrounds and critiques the hegemony of both the visual and the aural; as Christian Chelebourg notes of Verne's work: 'Voyager, c'est désirer voir' [travelling is born of a desire to see].[45] In the novel, the two reporters, Jolivet and Blount, travel alternately alongside and ahead of the eponymous Strogoff as he crosses the distance between Moscow and the Siberian city of Irkutsk. Strogoff's mission is to deliver a letter to the brother of the Tsar warning him of the threat of rebellion; Jolivet and Blount are charged to report news of the impending rebellion to their respective French and British newspapers. The text heroizes and satirizes the two journalists, exaggeratedly praising the acuity of their senses while highlighting their failures. A reading of the role played by the journalists is also complicated by the convergence and conflict established between them and the heroic figure of Strogoff. Ostensibly blinded during the course of the narrative, Strogoff is still able to 'see' his way to Irkutsk; the journalists may be sighted, and even possessed of foresight, yet they are also blinkered. *Michel Strogoff* couples this depiction of sensory perception and fallibility with the representation of practices of reading, writing, and communicating, setting its own novelistic features against techniques of reportage and travelogue as it stages a race between journalism and the mythical message carried by Strogoff.

The opening chapter of *Michel Strogoff* simultaneously foregrounds and questions the superiority of the two reporters. Set at a party at the 'Palais Neuf', the chapter preserves a sense of mystery by refusing to provide the identity of the key character at the ball, or the specifics of the location, details which are finally supplied in the closing lines, which name the Russian Tsar and the Kremlin as the focus of the text. Jolivet and Blount, however, are clearly in possession of such information, and of news about events outside Moscow, already aware of the threat in Siberia. By keeping certain details anonymous at this stage, and deferring the reader's full comprehension of the setting and significance of the soirée, the text on one hand accentuates the knowledge of the newspapermen in contrast to the mystification of the reader:

> Comment, par quelle voie, grâce à quel entregent, ces deux simples mortels savaient-ils ce que tant d'autres personnages, et des plus considérables, soupçonnaient à peine? On n'eût pu le dire. Était-ce chez eux don de prescience ou de prévision? Possédaient-ils un sens supplémentaire, qui leur permettait de voir au-delà de cet horizon limité auquel est borné tout regard humain? Avaient-ils un flair particulier pour dépister les nouvelles les plus secrètes? Grâce à cette habitude, devenue chez eux une seconde nature, de vivre de l'information et par l'information, leur nature, s'était-elle donc transformée? On eût été tenté de l'admettre. (MS, 5)
>
> [By what means, by the exercise of what acuteness had these two ordinary mortals ascertained that which so many persons of the highest rank and importance scarcely even suspected? It is impossible to say. Had they the gifts of foresight and foreknowledge? Did they possess a supplementary sense, which enabled them to see beyond that limited horizon which bounds all human gaze? Had they obtained a peculiar power of divining the most secret events? Was it owing to the habit, now become a second nature, of living on information, that their mental constitution had thus become really transformed? It was difficult to escape this conclusion.]

Here, the narrative ostensibly downplays its own authority in claiming ignorance of the means by which the two international reporters have come by their knowledge, while also employing hyperbole and rhetorical questioning to subvert, in turn, the expertise of Jolivet and Blount by over-dramatizing the 'prescience' of these 'simples mortels'. This novel, which centres on the privileging and the destabilizing of the faculties of sight and hearing, evokes, in its opening passages, the notion of a 'sens supplémentaire' [supplementary sense], an intuition which, through training, through 'vivre de l'information' [living on information], has become part of the mental makeup of Jolivet and Blount. This sixth sense, and its implications within the text, will be discussed in due course.

The first chapter of *Michel Strogoff* goes on to illustrate further the visual and aural acuity of the two men, defining them and the key differences between them and their nationalities by way of their sensory capacities:

> Ces dissemblances physiques eussent facilement frappé le moins observateur des hommes; mais un physionomiste, en regardant d'un peu près ces deux étrangers, aurait nettement déterminé le contraste physiologique qui les caractérisait, en disant que si le Français était 'tout yeux', l'Anglais était 'tout oreilles' [...].
> En effet, l'appareil optique de l'un avait été singulièrement perfectionné par l'usage. La sensibilité de sa rétine devait être aussi instantanée que celle de ces prestidigitateurs, qui reconnaissent une carte rien que dans un mouvement de coupe [...].
> L'Anglais, au contraire, paraissait spécialement organisé pour écouter et pour entendre. Lorsque son appareil auditif avait été frappé du son d'une voix, il ne pouvait plus l'oublier, et dans dix ans, dans vingt ans, il l'eût reconnu entre mille. Ses oreilles n'avaient certainement pas la possibilité de se mouvoir comme celles des animaux qui sont pourvus de grands pavillons auditifs; mais, puisque les savants ont constaté que les oreilles humaines ne sont 'qu'à peu près' immobiles, on aurait eu le droit d'affirmer que celles du susdit Anglais, se dressant, se tordant, s'obliquant, cherchaient à percevoir les sons d'une façon quelque peu apparente pour le naturaliste. (MS, 7–8)

> [The strong contrast they presented would at once have struck the most superficial observer; but a physiognomist, regarding them closely, would have defined their particular characteristics by saying that if the Frenchman was 'all eyes', the Englishman was 'all ears' [...].
> In fact, the visual apparatus of the one had been singularly perfected by practice. The sensibility of its retina must have been as instantaneous as that of those conjurors who recognise a card merely by a rapid movement in cutting the pack or by the arrangement only of marks visible to others [...].
> The Englishman, on the contrary, appeared especially organised to listen and to hear. When his aural apparatus had been once struck by the sound of a voice he could not forget it, and after ten or twenty years he would have recognised it among a thousand. His ears, to be sure, had not the power of moving as freely as those of animals who are provided with large auditory flaps, but, since scientific men know that human ears possess, in fact, a very limited power of movement, we should not be far wrong in affirming that those of the said Englishman became erect, and turned in all directions while endeavouring to gather the sounds, in a manner only apparent to the naturalist.]

Here, scientific terminology is employed alongside the more colloquial 'tout yeux' and 'tout oreilles', and emphasis is placed on what a 'physiologist' would detect, in ways which highlight Crary's points about the embedding of vision in the subjectivity of the human body:

> The idea of subjective vision — the notion that our perceptual and sensory experienced depends less on the nature of an external stimulus than on the composition and functioning of our sensory apparatus — was one of the conditions for the historical emergence of notions of autonomous vision.[46]

The precise description of the auditory and visual organs as physiological already indicates the potential fallibility of those mechanisms, reinforced by the humour of the contrast with animals with 'grands pavillons auditifs'. The gifted eyes and ears of the journalists are associated with trickery, as suggested by the comparison between Jolivet's sharpened retina and a conjurer's card tricks. Their perception may be highly trained and sensitive to stimuli, but there is no sense that the perfection of these faculties necessarily translates into better journalism. Blount has ears which move almost imperceptibly, gathering the sounds around him, but it is unclear whether he processes these sounds as meaningful, any more than Jolivet's ability to recognize colours and shapes at speed means he is able to produce coherent reports of the visual. What is also worthy of note is the way in which the narrative flaunts its own observational mode. References to the journalists' senses emphasize the visual: 'il convient de faire observer'; 'en regardant', with implicit comparisons between the narrating voice and the scientific precision of the 'physiognomist' or the 'naturalist'. This text, which questions the sensory acuity of reportage, sets its own visual commentary as at least parallel with — if not superior to — the journalists' profession of sense-making.

Chapter Four sees Jolivet and Blount on board a train on course for the first leg of their journey. The image of the train emphasizes the limited nature of each man's perceptions; although they may possess gifted ocular or aural senses, they lack all-round perception and get things wrong. Blount may have elephantine ears, but misjudges visual impressions, as when he looks out of only one side of the carriage: 'Blount, assis à la gauche du train, n'avait vu qu'une partie de la contrée, qui était assez accidentée, sans se donner la peine de regarder la partie de droite, formée de longues plaines' (*MS*, 52) ('Blount, seated at the left of the train, only saw one part of the country, which was hilly, without giving himself the trouble of looking at the right side, which was composed of wide plains'). He accordingly notes semi-erroneously the 'pays montagneux' [mountainous landscape] between Moscow and Wladimir. Jolivet, meanwhile, sees what Blount does not, keeping down the window so as to lose 'pas un point de vue de l'horizon de droite' (*MS*, 51) ('not a single glimpse of the horizon on the right'), but his aural faculties are proved wanting, as he asks 'tant de questions insignifiantes' [numerous insignificant questions] of the passengers around him only to find that they resent his intrusiveness and take him for a spy. The text thus satirizes the restrictions of the reporters, who rely too heavily on one sense to the detriment of the other, but harmonizes the two perspectives so that the reader of Verne's text 'sees' the landscape out of the left and the right side of the train, supplementing the one-track minds of the French and English observers.

Claudius Bombarnac, Verne's later novel, which foregrounds the role of the reporter to an even greater extent than *Michel Strogoff*, also emphasizes the connections between the visual, the aural, and the journalist's quest for knowledge, while offering subversive commentary on this epistemological drive. 'Je sais voir et je verrai' [I know how to see and see I will] (*CB*, 10 October) declares the reporter Bombarnac as he sets out: the confidence placed in 'savoir voir' is reflected and ironized throughout the novel.[47] Part detective story, part journalistic reportage, part travelogue, *Claudius Bombarnac* begins with a telegram directing the narrator-reporter to travel from his current station in Tiflis to the east coast of the Caspian Sea. Bombarnac is to produce 'bon reportage', recording the sensory impressions of the journey, coupling mimesis with concern for aurality, based on the interviews to be carried out aboard the train. An early example of visual description exemplifies the ways in which Verne's text both reinforces and undercuts references to the 'choses vues':

> Au sommet de la colline, sur une petite place, où un chanteur déclamateur récite avec force gestes des vers de Saadi, l'adorable poète persan, je m'abandonne à la contemplation de la capitale transcaucasienne [...] voici ce que Tiflis offre à mes regards: des murs de citadelles, des clochetons de temples appartenant aux différents cultes, une église métropolitaine avec sa double croix, des maisons de construction russe, persane ou arménienne; peu de toits, mais des terrasses; peu de façades ornementées [...] puis, deux zones très tranchées, la zone basse, restée georgienne, la zone haute, plus moderne, traversée par un long boulevard planté de beaux arbres, entre lesquels se dessine le palais du prince Bariatins.
>
> Il est bientôt cinq heures. Je n'ai pas le temps de me livrer au torrent rémunérateur des phrases descriptives. Hâtons-nous de redescendre vers la gare. (*CB*, 11 October)
>
> [At the top of the hill, on a little open space where a reciter is declaiming with vigorous gestures the verses of Saadi, the adorable Persian poet, I abandon myself to the contemplation of the Transcaucasian capital [...] here is Tiflis before my eyes; walls of the citadels, belfries of the temples belonging to the different religions, a metropolitan church with its double cross, houses of Russian, Persian, or Armenian construction; a few roofs, but many terraces; a few ornamental frontages [...], the lower zone remaining Georgian, the higher zone, more modern, traversed by a long boulevard planted with fine trees, among which is seen the palace of Prince Bariatinsky, a capricious, unexpected marvel of irregularity, which the horizon borders with its grand frontier of mountains.
>
> It is now five o'clock. I have no time to deliver myself in a remunerative torrent of descriptive phrases. Let us hurry off to the railway station.]

Here, Bombarnac accentuates his dominant position over the town, imitating the position of the narrator of the realist novel in his impressions of mastery. What Bombarnac also suggests is the diminution of the *je* — the way that he gives the impression of surrendering his own subjectivity to the unfolding of the landscape — 'je m'abandonne'; 'Tiflis offre à mes regards'. In supplying a visual depiction of the town, though, the description questions its own validity. Literary construction frames the scene with the chant of the reciting poet in the background, while deconstruction characterizes the description. The elements of the scene are reduced to heterogeneous fragments; religions and nationalities are blurred, and the prominence of the Prince's palace is asserted and yet dismissed as a mass of irregularity, making it difficult to visualize. The concluding remarks insist there is little time to provide a 'torrent' of 'phrases descriptives', undermining the reading of the preceding passage, which supplies precisely such a torrent.

Bombarnac's fallibilities as a reporter are suggested not only through his compromised evocations of the visual. He as frequently lists what he fails to see thanks to the inconveniences of the journey as much as he notes the seen. Although he sets about interviewing each of the passengers in the hope of assembling an interesting story, paralleling the practice of reportage and the plotting of a novel, he frequently finds that his interviewees are recalcitrant, or tedious, or provide him with misinformation. It is thanks to his credulity in accepting what the guard tells him about the contents of the goods van that he receives a telegram from his own publication correcting his reportage: it is not the corpse of a mandarin which is being transported to Peking, but a hoard of treasure. The news has already reached Paris, compromising Bombarnac and his on-the-ground reports. Exacerbating his own incompetence as an aural decoder, Bombarnac proceeds to proclaim the news of the treasure to the passengers, substituting verbal noise for the discernment he could have applied to his investigations. Verne's reporters thereby indicate their inadequacies as interviewers, selecting and embellishing partial information.

As with visual detail, the texts indicate a desire to supply aural notation, enhancing and rupturing the drive towards realism. Claudius Bombarnac opens his account by documenting the Russian names for musical instruments, revelling in the sonorous strangeness of linguistic nomenclature while providing a sense of the musicality evoked:

> Les orchestres nationaux se composent de 'zournas', qui sont des flûtes aigres, de 'salamouris', qui sont des clarinettes criardes, de mandolines à cordes de cuivre pincées avec une plume, de 'tchianouris', violons dont on joue verticalement, de 'dimplipitos', espèces de cymbales, qui crépitent comme la grêle sur les carreaux de vitre! (*CB*, 10 October)

> [Their national orchestras are composed of 'zournas', which are shrill flutes, 'salamouris' which are squeaky clarinets, mandolins with copper strings, twanged with a feather, 'tchianouris', violins which are played upright, 'dimpliptos', a kind of cymbals which rattle like hail on a window pane.]

Such acoustic representation is supplied in *Michael Strogoff*, but often in ways which defeat the practice of the narrative itself. At one stage of the journey, the narrator observes that:

> Le silence eût été absolu sans le grincement des roues du tarentass qui broyaient le gravier de la route, le gémissement des moyeux et des ais de la machine, l'aspiration bruyante des chevaux auxquels manquait l'haleine, et le claquement de leurs pieds ferrés sur les cailloux qui étincelaient au choc. (*MS*, 135)

> [The silence would have been complete but for the grinding of the wheels of the tarantass over the road, the creaking of the axles, the snorting of the horses, and the clattering of their iron hoofs among the pebbles.]

This selection of cacophonous and onomatopoeic auditory details challenges the 'silence [...] absolu' recorded. As in the description of the instruments, Verne's prose luxuriates in the alliterative and assonantal detail of sounds invited by the travelogue style, suggesting that linguistic patterns triumph over any representative function. The information that, in *Michel Strogoff*, 'les khanats de Khokhand et de Koundouge avaient fourni un contingent presque égal à celui de Boukhara' (*MS*, 263) ('the khanats of Khokhand and Koundouge had furnished a contingent nearly equal to that of Bokhara') is more intent on its acoustics than on expecting a reader to understand the Russian geographical and social reference points. Christian Robin suggests that Verne's incorporation of journalistic themes and characters is a means of reaffirming the texts' realism: 'La présence de la presse dans les romans relève en partie de l'attachement que l'écrivain accordait au réalisme, si paradoxal que cela puisse paraître pour un homme dont l'imagination a surtout retenu l'attention' [the presence of the press in the novels stems in part from the writer's attachment to realism, however paradoxical that might seem for a man principally renowned for his imagination].[48] I would argue that at the same time, reportage is used as a mode of disrupting such realism.

In acoustically rich quotations such as those above, Verne challenges mimetic practices even while ostensibly going to great lengths to record the real. His narrative technique here can be associated with Jameson's analysis of the 'antimonies of realism'. Jameson describes the dialectical encounter within realism as a contradiction between narrative and affect; it is this contradiction which defines realism itself. In Jameson's analysis, narrative offers a way of recording and understanding temporal experience, dividing life into comprehensible categories of past, present, and future/beginning, middle, and end. 'Affect', though, refers to an almost extra-temporal experience, a sense of the eternal present registered in the body itself. Jameson describes this using a contrast between Balzac and Flaubert. Balzac's descriptions, although employing sensory criteria, as in the smell of the boarding house at the opening of *Le Père Goriot*, are not evocations of what Jameson calls 'affect' 'for one good reason: namely that it *means* something'.[49] In Balzac, everything that looks like a physical sensation, 'a musty smell, a rancid taste, a greasy fabric — always means something, it is a sign or allegory of the moral or social status of a given character'. It transcends its status as a sensation, and becomes allegory. In Flaubert, however, 'these signs remain, but they have become stereotypical; and the new descriptions register a density beyond such stereotypical meanings'.[50] The result, suggests Jameson, is that it is not the irreconcilable divide between meaning and existence which is a hallmark of modernity but, instead, 'allegory and the body [...] repel one another and fail to mix'. Jameson extends his discussion by examining passages from Zola, in particular descriptions of the market place scenes in *Le Ventre de Paris*, which offer lists of cheeses or fish; such passages do not offer multiple but unified examples of narrative technique. Instead:

> The unexpected result is that far from enriching representational language with all kinds of new meanings, the gap between words and things is heightened; perceptions turn into sensations [...] finally the realm of the visual begins to separate from that of the verbal and conceptual and to float away in a new kind of autonomy. Precisely this autonomy will create the space for affect.[51]

Jameson's evaluation of 'affect' in Zola's descriptions is applicable, too, to moments in Verne's novels when heightened sensory experience results in prolonged linguistic attempts to encapsulate that experience. These moments when narrative breaks down in favour of sensory 'affect' are all the more exaggerated in Verne's adventure-driven stories, in which the necessary progression of the journey motors the teleological development of the plot.[52] And the very dialectical tension inherent in realism which Jameson offers as its definition is embodied in texts such as *Michel*

Strogoff and *Claudius Bombarnac*, in the juxtaposition of the journalists' forward-moving quest for a story, supposedly aided by the supremacy of their sensory detection, and the focus on such sensory appreciation itself, which weighs down the narrative with 'density' and 'affect'. Focus on the sensory elements of reportage, in Verne's realism, results in a heightened awareness of the incompatibility of 'reportage' and the 'senses': the eternal present of the body impedes the procedures of the recount.

Steeplechases and Strogoff's Sixth Sense: The Triumph of the Literary?

In *Michel Strogoff*, such sensory challenges to the narrative are set alongside the celebration, in the figure of Strogoff himself, of a multi-sensory capability which might suggest the triumph of an all-seeing, all-knowing mimesis. As the Frenchman and the Englishman race each other in their quest for news, they are also pitted against Strogoff, alternately overtaking him, catching up with him, and running alongside him as the novel charts the characters' progress towards Irkutsk. The eponymous Strogoff is the hero of the novel, depicted as superhuman, the only man alive who might be capable of the mission entrusted him by the Tsar: 'un courier seul pouvait remplacer le courant interrompu [...] il devrait [...] déployer à la fois un courage et une intelligence pour ainsi dire surhumains' (*MS*, 31) ('Only a courier could supply the place of the interrupted current [...] he must display almost superhuman courage and intelligence'). Michel Strogoff's superior capacities as messenger suggest that his role is, in part, meant to illustrate the inadequacies of the two reporters. His sensory abilities indicate the fallible and reified vision of the journalists, the text frequently referring to his ability to absorb and process his environment as a kind of sixth sense: 'il avait appris à se guider sur des symptômes presque imperceptibles, projection des aiguilles de glaces, disposition des menues branches d'arbre, émanations apportées des dernières limites de l'horizon [...] mille détails qui sont mille jalons pour qui sait les reconnaître' (*MS*, 37) ('He had learnt to read almost imperceptible signs — the forms of icicles, the appearance of the small branches of trees, mists rising far away in the horizon [...] a thousand circumstances which are so many words to those who can decipher them'). Manon Mathias's study of vision in the works of George Sand sees Sand exemplify a binary approach to the visual, both realist and visionary; while physiological eyesight is linked with a 'dull and narrow reality', 'this is in comparison with the visions of the conceptual eye that are aligned with mobility and flight'.[53] The contrast between Strogoff and the reporters arguably reflects a Vernian embrace of such a complex response to realism, with the grasp of 'des symptômes presque imperceptibles' a visionary extension of the limited journalistic vision.

Not only does the above quotation suggest Strogoff's transcendence of the journalists' one-sided sensory approaches; it also insists on an association between Strogoff's intuitive understanding of his environment and a process of 'reading'. As the novel charts the paralleled journeys of Strogoff and the two reporters, so it can also be read as a narrative about the competing practices of reportage and an innate, superior method of reading and interpreting. The process of communication is the very subject matter of *Michel Strogoff*, centred as it is around the imperative of conveying the telegram concerning the threat to Siberia to the Governor at Irkutsk. Pinson notes that the Vernian texts which feature journalists often also focus on a breakdown of communication:

> Or, le plus souvent chez Verne, le journal et le journaliste sont là à la fois (et paradoxalement) pour accentuer les effets de rupture et de communication et pour évoquer un improbable 'hors journal': *Michel Strogoff* est une fiction qui porte essentiellement sur un problème de communication et sur l'isolement des journalistes.[54]
>
> [More often than not in Verne's texts, the newspaper and the journalist are present, paradoxically, to emphasize the effects of a breakdown in communication and to evoke an improbable world outside of the newspaper: *Michel Strogoff* is a novel which rests on the problems of communication and the isolation of journalists.]

The text begins with news of a telegram: '"Sire, une nouvelle dépêche"' (*MS*, 1) ('"Sir, a new dispatch"'), this new missive indicating implicit and ironic metatextual commentary. Such commentary is intensified in *Claudius Bombarnac*; the central plot of the narrative is the reporter-protagonist's search for a plot, a story he will be able to send back to his editors. In *Michel Strogoff*, the telegraph wires having been cut, Strogoff's journey itself replicates this hiatus in communication, in serial form, as he confronts obstacle after obstacle. The role of the reporters adds a comedic element, enhancing and subverting the theme of communication. In this text the literary plot involving the transmission of a secret but vital message is pursued by the competing faction of reportage, as if in a steeplechase. Thérenty notes the use of the term 'steeplechase' for collaborative novels in the mid-nineteenth century, such as *Le Steeple-chase La Croix de Berny* (1855), a novel in letters penned by four journalists, a phenomenon echoed in newspapers including *Le Figaro*, which encouraged contributors to respond to one another in letters, referring to them as 'gentlemen-riders'.[55] Verne seems to employ the term in reference both to sporting exuberance and to these polyphonic collections of letters which are published both in newspapers and as novels; there is an ironic comment on the dissent between the competing voices of Blount and Jolivet and the interaction between the writers of the steeplechase texts discussed by Thérenty. Hunting and sports are frequently offered up by the reporters as metaphors for their job, and it is tempting to see that Verne suggests the triumph of literature at the expense of the practices of reporting represented by the buffoon-like reporters. This 'race' between journalism and literature is accompanied by the discourse surrounding the senses evoked in the novel, between the flawed perceptions of the reporters and the instinctive readings supplied by Strogoff.

Michel Strogoff's superior sixth sense is never more in evidence than when he is apparently blinded, punished by Ogareff, and the message he is carrying is stolen. He vows to continue his mission despite the damage to his eyes, proclaiming that he will impart the evidence of his senses on arrival at Irkutsk: 'j'irai dire à Irkoutsk tout ce que j'ai vu, tout ce que j'ai entendu' (*MS*, 350) ('I will go to Irkutsk to announce all that I have seen and heard'). As he has proved able to 'read' the imperceptible signs around him in transcendence of the more conventional ocular and aural faculties of the reporters, so he will continue to deliver the message in the absence of the physical piece of writing, relying instead on memory and instinct. This intuition is apparent in his relationship with Nadia, who has pledged to act as his guide dog: 'Tous deux étaient en communication incessante. Il leur semblait qu'ils n'avaient plus besoin de la parole pour échanger leurs pensées' (*MS*, 352) ('The two were in incessant communication. It seemed to them they had no need of words to exchange their thoughts'). Ostensibly sightless, Strogoff's powers of reading and communicating have become even more spontaneous. In contrast, the two reporters deliberately turn away from their powers of sight at this point in the narrative. The narratives of the reporters and the novel diverge, with Jolivet and Blount blinding themselves to the gruesomeness of the blinding. Says Jolivet to Blount: 'Vos lecteurs du *Daily-Telegraph* ne sont pas friands, je l'espère, des détails d'une exécution à la mode tartare?' (*MS*, 341) ('The readers of the *Daily Telegraph* are, I hope, not very eager for the details of an execution a la mode Tartare?'). Resolving that they can do nothing to help Strogoff, they head away from the scene of torture. While their newspapers will record a blank when it comes to this scene, the novel fulfils its duty to report, with Strogoff himself keeping his 'œil démesurément ouvert' (*MS*, 343) ('eyes wide open').

This reading though — that Strogoff represents literature and that his superior reading and seeing trumps the blindness of the supposedly gifted ears and eyes of reportage — is overly straightforward. After all, the blinding scene, set before the reader in all its visual detail, is itself an illusion, given that the denouement of the text will reveal that Michel Strogoff never was blinded, and that he — and the narrative — have been deceiving those around him. On the one hand, this suggests that Strogoff's powers of superior sight remain in place throughout the text, especially given that the reason he manages to avoid being blinded is because his heart preserves his sight; the tears in his eyes, prompted by the knowledge that his mother is watching, neutralize the hot iron of the blade. And the pretence at blindness is a form of freedom, since 'c'est parce qu'on le croirait aveugle, qu'on le laisserait libre' (*MS*, 492) ('Because it was believed that he was blind, he would be allowed to go free'). On the other hand, the fact that Strogoff remains sighted indicates that the supposed intuition and capacity for reading he demonstrates when ostensibly blinded are but a myth; he is simply seeing, depriving the reader of the true 'vision' of what is going on. The blinding scene remains a blinding scene because it strips away the panoptic vision that Verne has seemingly been offering up until this point, the unified reading of the text which has put together the fragmentary stories written by Blount and Jolivet. Ultimately, the reader is aligned with the journalists in a one-eyed view of the world. The blunt manner of reporting the truth — 'Michel Strogoff était aveugle' (*MS*, 343) ('Michel Strogoff was blind') — proves a myth. Such a reading fits, too, with the crucial element in the narrative which is withheld from our sight as readers: the message itself, carried by Strogoff and stolen by Ogareff, which motors the plot and metaphorizes language and communication in the novel. The contents of the missive, never made explicit, are remembered by Strogoff that he might still impart them to the Grand Duke in Irkutsk, yet when he gets to the citadel, the stolen telegram becomes irrelevant, since the news he brings, the threat of Ogareff, is rendered redundant by the fact that Ogareff is already in the building.

The role played by the journalists in the novel is more complex than it initially appears. The idea that the reporters are stooges whose function is to provide comedy and whose view of the world is a blinkered one is rendered more problematic by the deceptive blindness of the would-be hero Strogoff. The race discussed — the battle between reportage and literature as emblematized by the reporters and Strogoff — is also less clear-cut. As Harris asks when discussing colonialist hype in Verne's work, Michel Strogoff as a character remains a strange case since despite all the advantages he has on his journey in the form of funds and travel passes, he is still captured by Ogareff's men, while:

> The bumbling Blount and the jolly Jolivet invariably beat Strogoff from A to B, not to mention from B to C and C to D. What, exactly, is the status of a figure like Strogoff, who always contrives to be headed off by two journalist-buffoons?[56]

There are times in the text when just as Michel Strogoff comes to the aid of the reporters, and has to pull them forward, so too the journalists assist Strogoff. This can be seen as the characters approach Irkutsk by raft, and Strogoff, Blount, and Jolivet fight off wolves together. Here, the ambiguities which characterize the presence of the journalists are in evidence; Verne's comic satire is set alongside the bravery and indefatigability of the reporters. A tongue-in-cheek passage which hints again at the limitations of vision is followed by Jolivet's sensory realization that the river on which they are travelling has been turned to naphtha:

> Quant à Alcide Jolivet et à Harry Blount, ils n'avaient qu'une seule et même pensée; c'est que la situation était extrêmement dramatique, et que, bien mise en scène, elle fournirait une chronique des plus intéressantes [...]. Au fond, ils n'étaient pas sans éprouver quelque émotion tous les deux. 'Eh! tant mieux!' pensait Alcide Jolivet. 'Il faut être ému pour émouvoir!' [...] Et avec ses yeux si exercés, il cherchait à percer l'ombre épaisse qui enveloppait le fleuve. (*MS*, 432–33)

> [As to Alcide Jolivet and Harry Blount, they had one and the same thought, which was, that the situation was extremely dramatic and that, well worked up, it would furnish a most deeply interesting article [...]. At heart both were not without feeling some emotion. 'Well, so much the better!' thought Alcide Jolivet, 'to move others, one must be moved one's self.' [...] And with his well-practiced eyes he endeavoured to pierce the gloom of the river.]

This passage renders the journalists' summary of the drama of the situation banal and suggests the triteness of their reporting tendencies, 'extrêmement dramatique'. There is irony in Jolivet's attempts to use his skilled eyes to try and penetrate the surrounding gloom; his impeccable vision throughout the text is always in fact foggy. And yet Jolivet in this passage employs the sense of touch in order to realize the full scale of the drama, the threat represented by the naphtha, and gets to this awareness before Strogoff. The journalist proves quicker than the fictional hero, and suggests the transcendence, at this pivotal point in the narrative, of a sense beyond that of the rational visual and aural mimesis evoked and satirized in the course of the text's realism. The sense of touch is employed to detect the presence of the naphtha and the extent of the threat.

In this scene, as in the celebration of Strogoff's intuition, Verne compares a reductive mimesis reliant on the visual and the aural to a multisensorial embrace of the world; he extols a practice of detection which downplays the imperative of the visual in favour of a more all-round informative embrace of perception, in which touch plays a key role. Howes quotes Helen Keller, '"Touch brings the blind many sweet certainties which our more fortunate fellows miss, because their sense of touch is uncultivated. When they look at things, they put their hands in their pockets. No doubt that is one reason why their knowledge is often so vague, inaccurate and useless"'.[57] Jay's analysis of post-Impressionist art and its attempt to emphasize the expression of lived experience, transcending the artificial isolation of the senses and the hegemonic autonomy of sight, suggests of Cezanne, for example, that:

> We see the depth, the smoothness, the softness, the hardness of objects. Cezanne even claimed that we see their odor. His [Cezanne's] task, therefore, was the recapturing of the very moment when the world was new, before it was fractured into dualisms of subject and object or the modalities of separate senses.[58]

While it would be far-fetched to argue that Verne's realism becomes a form of linguistic post-Impressionism, the embrace of touch at this pivotal moment in *Michel Strogoff* suggests a move beyond the 'modalities of separate senses' previously embodied by the eyes and ears of the journalists, a move already highlighted by the characterization of the sensory capacities of Strogoff himself. The ways in which such a transcendence of the visual and the aural might translate into a fuller understanding of Verne's conception of mimesis will be discussed shortly.

What *Michel Strogoff* offers, then, is an amalgamation of literature and reportage, each chasing and complementing the other, alongside an overarching satire of the significance of any linguistic communication. This jumbling of codes is nowhere better represented than in the chapter already referred to, which sees the two journalists engaged in battle over control of the telegraph office, competing to see who can be first to send news of the battle at Kolyan between Russian and Tartar troops. To maintain his position as first to telegraph back the news, Blount strings out his broadcast with verses from the Bible. The resultant message is an amalgamation of Blount's words narrating what he sees around him through his lorgnette, and the Word of God; he gives the readers of the *Daily Telegraph* his observations of the scene of battle: 'deux églises sont en flammes. L'incendie paraît gagner sur la droite' ('Two churches are in flames. The fire appears to gain on the right') alongside lines from the book of Genesis: 'la terre était informe et toute nue; les ténèbres couvraient la face de l'abîme' (*MS*, 256) ('the earth was without form and completely bare; darkness covered the face of the abyss'). Jolivet in turn responds by coupling his commentary on the battle with verses from Béranger, taking the time to hurl a missile back out of the window of the telegraph office. This scene indicates the imperative to transmit a message and the satire of that process. The telegraphic communications which have been such a comic mix of observational detail, poetic humour, and biblical language are forced to come to a sudden halt, with the destruction of the telegraph office and the cutting of the cable, just as the central missive, carried by Strogoff, is also 'destroyed', first stolen and never fully illuminated. The scene in the telegraph office is not just an insight into and a parody of journalistic endeavour, but a visualization of the communicative enterprise in the novel itself — a hybrid mix, just like the reporters' garbled narrative — and its potential for failure. To cap this sense of futility, Strogoff later comes across the employee from the telegraph office whose role was to transmit the reporters' words. This clerk remembers neither Blount and Jolivet, nor their messages: 'je ne lis jamais les dépêches que je transmets. Mon devoir étant de les oublier, le plus court est de les ignorer (*MS*, 359) ('I never read the dispatches I send. My duty being to forget them, the shortest way is not to know them'). The role of the messenger highlights the ephemerality and emptiness of the message itself.

Vernian Realism Revisited

The self-conscious play with the theme of communication in *Michel Strogoff* can be linked to a broader analysis of the role of language and mimesis in Verne. Unwin writes about the ways in which the very intricacies of Verne's meticulous classifying descriptions themselves end up mystifying the world. In *Vingt lieues sur les mers*:

> The classifications and taxonomical precision of the scientific style end up not by appropriating the aquatic world and reducing it to comprehensible proportions but by doing the opposite: highlighting its strangeness and its mystery, and foregrounding the intoxicating effect of descriptive words themselves. Under the gaze of the Vernian narrator, the world fragments and dissolves.[59]

Examples of such descriptive excess are found in *Michel Strogoff*, as in the depiction of the fair at Ninji-Novgorod, witnessed by Strogoff, and characterized by list-like delight in heterogeneity:

> Fourrures, pierres précieuses, étoffes de soie, cachemires des Indes, tapis turcs, armes de Caucase, tissus de Smyrne ou d'Ispahan, armures de Tiflis, thés de la caravane, bronzes européens, horlogerie de la Suisse, velours et soieries de Lyon, cotonnades anglaises, articles de carrosserie, fruits, légumes, minerais de l'Oural, malachites, lapis-lazuli [...] tous les produits de l'Inde, de la Chine, de la Perse, ceux de la mer Caspienne et de la mer Noire, ceux de l'Amérique et de l'Europe, étaient réunis sur ce point du globe. (*MS*, 72–73)
>
> [Furs, precious stones, silks, Cashmere shawls, Turkish carpets, weapons from the Caucasus, material from Smyrna or Ispahan, Tiflis armour, caravan teas, European bronzes, Swiss clocks, velvets and silks from Lyons, English cotton, harnesses, fruits, vegetables, minerals from the Ural, malachite, lapis-lazuli [...] all the products from India, China, Persia, from the shores of the Caspian and

the Black Sea, from America and Europe, were brought together at this corner of the globe.]

Unwin takes a different view of Verne from that of Barthes, who sees Verne's vision of reality as de-alienating and comforting; instead, Vernian mimesis is seen as a way of re-alienating the real.[60] Unwin's discussion of Verne's strategies of representation arguably anticipate, in fact, Jameson's discussion of realism's antimonies.

Verne's use of language is, observes Unwin, different from that of Flaubert. Rather than problematizing the issue of language and expression, Verne reveals a pleasure in the materiality of his linguistic lists. Even when his characters fail to express themselves fully — as in the scene in the telegraph office — they do so with exuberance. Unwin points out the presence of 'quixotic, extravagant characters' whose role is to offset the realities of science, as seen in Verne's lunar novel.[61] A similar role can be extended to that of Blount and Jolivet in *Michel Strogoff*. The buffoonery of the correspondents counterbalances their official role, which is to document the real in as pithy and succinct a manner as possible. On the one hand, the role of the reporters is to act as discreet but important witnesses to the action. On the other, their clownishness is weighed against objective vision. Jolivet summarizes the battle at Kolyvan, chanting his verses from Béranger: 'Il est un petit homme | Tout habillé de gris, | Dans Paris!' (*MS*, 257) ('A little man | All dressed in grey | And in Paris'), revelling in the frivolity of the rhyming couplet while immersed in the dangers of reality; he 'complétait son télégramme en chantonnant d'une voix moqueuse' (*MS*, 257) ('finished his telegram while singing in a mocking tone of voice'). This quotation summarizes Verne's own literary project: to telegraph a message and represent the modernizing world while coupling such a mission with mockery and a poetic, harmonizing voice. The reporters themselves, in *Michel Strogoff*, are keen to mask the realism of their role, forever referring to their employment as a sport, or game; they are 'vrais jockeys de ce steeple-chase, de cette chasse à l'information' (*MS*, 9) ('true jockeys of that steeplechase, that hunt for information').

Despite such parodic interpretations of the reporting role, the resultant subversion of communication is accompanied by the idea that the business of writing, reporting, and getting the message across is nevertheless sustained. Verne celebrates and satirizes discourse in equal measures. In the stage adaptation of *Michel Strogoff*, the characters of Blount and Jolivet (who becomes 'Jollivet') become even more caricatured than in the novel. In the opening act, they function as key interpreters of the action, providing essential information to the audience as to the setting and the nature of the Tartar threat: Jollivet flamboyantly displays his notebook in acknowledgement of his reporting role, announcing: 'Voici ce que je viens de télégraphier [...] Fête que gouverneur de Moscou donne en honneur de sa Majesté Empereur de toutes Russies, splendide!' [This is what I have just sent by telegraph [...] Ball given by the governor of Moscow in honour of His Majesty the Emperor of all Russia, splendid!].[62] It soon becomes clear, though, that the journalists' main function is, to an even greater extent than in the novel, to induce laughter. The animosity between the two men is heightened; the nationalistic element which runs as an undercurrent to the novel is also inflated, so that much of the banter between the reporters is based on mockery of Blount's linguistic inadequacies. Although brief mention is made of their sensory skills (Jollivet claims that 'mon métier est de tout voir' [my task is to see all], while Blount retorts 'la mienne, de tout voir et de tout entendre ... avant!' [and mine to see all and hear all... before he does!]) the significance of the visual, of the nature of reportage more generally, and the wider implications in the novel surrounding the processes of communication are overall missing.[63] In the novel, the presentation of journalism remains integral; the text consciously immersing the function of the reporters amongst the various discourses at work in the novel itself, whether educational, factual, or fictional; the reporters become simultaneously bearers of reality and indicators of the limitations of that reality.

Unwin argues of Verne's writing that his approach 'moves then from mimesis to mathesis'.[64] Verne's work is all-compendious in its incorporation of different strands of knowledge, rendered all the more modern through the inclusion of the journalist figures whose role is to keep their readers as informed as possible. It embraces mimesis while reminding the reader — through its failed visions and its knowing winks — of the impossibility of the mimetic function. The path of Jolivet and Blount illustrates particularly effectively the utopian suggestions bound up with the mimesis described by Barthes in his inaugural lecture at the *Collège de France*: 'Le réel n'est pas représentable, et c'est parce que les hommes veulent sans cesse le représenter par des mots, qu'il y a une histoire de la littérature [...] c'est la fonction utopique' [the real is not representable, and it is because men forever want to represent it in words that literature has a history [...] this is the utopian function].[65] Forever sending back partial reports on the world they find around them, or having to contend with the rupture of the telegraph wires which sabotage their attempts at communication, they nevertheless are depicted, at the end of the text, as dogged pursuers of news. The close of *Michel Strogoff* sees them planning to head off for an even further flung geographical location in their quest to enlighten their readers, rejecting domestic life in favour of a trip to China, to wire back reports of discord arising between London and Peking. And they will undertake such a trip together, their previous rivalry abandoned. The eyes and ears they represent are harmonized in a shift away from the reifying of the senses. *Michel Strogoff*, then, which pits the reporters against each other, and reporters against fictional hero in competing discourses, ends with the congruence of characters and the genres they represent. Jolivet and Blount's reports from the region end in unison: 'l'envoi à Londres et à Paris de deux intéressantes chroniques relatives à l'invasion tartare et qui, chose rare, ne se contredisaient guère que sur les points les moins importants' (*MS*, 495) ('And so were sent to London and Paris two interesting articles relating to the Tartar invasion, and which — a rare thing — did not contradict each other even on the least important points'). As the duel with which the two reporters threaten each other in the play version fails to materialize but ends instead in camaraderie, so too the 'duel' between newspapers, and between newspapers and novel, as evoked in *Michel Strogoff*, ends with a harmonizing of codes, the journalists in attendance at the marriage of Michel and Nadia. For all its satire of communication and its exuberant linguistic excesses, this Verne novel suggests the imperative to narrate, to communicate, striving to represent in whatever way possible while acknowledging, humorously and continually, the failures of such endeavours. This is a novel which centres around the unseen message conveyed by Strogoff to Irkustk, and sees its own plot centre implode with the failure to either pass on or enable the reader to read this telegram. Yet while the pivotal message is lost, the city of Irkutsk is nevertheless saved by the arrival of Strogoff, who feigns blindness. The panoptic view seemingly promised by the text remains forever elusive, yet the novel, like the city, manages to salvage itself, suggesting that the determination to get across a message, however imprecise, is still cherished.

Claudius Bombarnac, 'Un faux air de mosques': Collapsing Oppositions

In *Michel Strogoff*, adventure is unquestionably in the foreground of the text, with questions over communication, fiction, and reportage implicit in the background. In *Claudius Bombarnac*, the presence and function of the reporter becomes predominantly the focus of the narrative. Self-reflexive questions about the text's own status are writ large as the eponymous reporter-protagonist searches desperately for the type of novelistic dynamic which motivates the earlier text. *Claudius Bombarnac* sees Verne's metatextual probing take centre stage, at a point in time when the reportage he features in its early days in *Michel Strogoff* has gained in momentum and significance in the French media. Commère stresses Verne's interest in newspapers and reporters at the time of writing *Claudius Bombarnac*, yet also points out that although the text can very much be associated with the 'civilisation du journal' foregrounded by Vaillant and Thérenty, it remains much more embedded in novelistic strategies than those of reportage. Commère compares Verne's work with that of Louis Forest who, in *Le Voleur d'enfants, reportage sensationnel* (1906), blurs much more overtly the boundaries between fiction and newspapers, incorporating a variety of fake articles.[66] As Unwin also shows in his recent work on Verne, *Claudius Bombarnac* is a deft and self-conscious satire of the conventions of storytelling in which the central plot of the narrative is the indefatigable reporter-protagonist's search for a plot — a story which he will be able to send back to his editors: 'perhaps the most sustained example in the entire corpus of a ludic and self-mocking manipulation of the conventions of storytelling, indeed of the construction of a story out of self-reference, is to be found in *Claudius Bombarnac*'.[67]

Verne's novel sees Bombarnac seeking excitement, in the guise of the special correspondent who is on the quest for something newsworthy. It suggests too the drive of the novelist to stimulate his reader with a compelling plot: the overlapping of these two aims evokes the apparent conflict between the real and the invented. There are events which might prove worthy of comment — the train journey is frequently halted, by accidents and obstacles (a fire, a stray dromedary) — which barely merit a passing mention by the narrator, because such incidents often interfere with his own attempts at investigation into the various affairs of the passengers. The plots he endeavours to set in motion are circumvented by the events of a 'real life' beyond the confines of the train — a real life he has ostensibly been commissioned to document but the interest of which eludes him. Although, as discussed above, the text documents and satirizes the reporter's role of documenting the visual, at times the not-seen acts as a banal counterpoint to the potential drama constantly imagined by the ambitious reporter. Bombarnac has been told that the train will run through stretches of thick jungle, where tigers are numerous: 'Nombreux, je veux le croire, mais je n'en ai pas vu un seul' [Numerous, as I want to believe, but I have not set eyes on a single one]. The disappointing absence of a tiger nevertheless sets him fantasizing, indicating the way that the drama of the visual would translate into visual drama on the newspaper front page:

> Et pourtant, à défaut des Peaux-Rouges, des Peaux-Tigrées pourraient nous procurer quelques distractions. Quel fait-divers pour un journal, et quelle bonne fortune pour un journaliste! Terrible catastrophe... Une train de Grand-Transasiatique attaqué par les tigres... Coups de griffes et coups de fusil... Cinquante victims... Un enfant dévoré sous les yeux de sa mere... le tout entremêlé de points suspensifs! (*CB*, 14 November)

> [And yet for want of Redskins, we might get some excitement out of tiger-skins. What a heading for a newspaper and what a stroke of luck for a journalist! Terrible catastrophe... A Grand Transasiatic Express attacked by tigers... Clawmarks and gunshots... Fifty victims... An infant devoured before its mother's eyes... the whole appropriately displayed with ellipses.]

Bombarnac's wistful contemplation here reminds the reader of the discrepancy between the apparently undistorted picture of the real world which the reporter is charged with transmitting, and the language which would be employed to recount that picture; the 'facts' of the visual selected, sensationalized, and 'entremêlé de points suspensifs'. There is also an emphasis here on the visual appearance of the paper itself, and a reminder of the need to appeal to a readership becoming used to seeing the facts of a story presented in visually striking ways. Ironically, one of the implications of such a visual way of processing headlines is that readers can be seen to become blinder — less attuned to the written detail and more focused on the screaming headlines. Rubery, in *The Novelty of Newspapers*, discusses the founding of Harmsworth's *Daily Mail* in 1896 in Britain as repeatedly blamed for encouraging a reading style closer to 'skimming' than to the 'sustained attention necessary for substantive deliberation. Not only were newspaper audiences not reading between the lines, they were not reading the lines at all'.[68]

Claudius Bombarnac not only subverts objectivity in realism and reportage, it also questions the idea of subjectivity:

> Je me défie habituellement des impressions en voyage. Ces impressions sont subjectives, — un mot que j'emploie parce qu'il est à la mode, bien que je n'aie jamais bien su ce qu'il veut dire [...]. Moi, j'ai un heureux naturel, — que l'on me pardonne si je fais un abus de l'égotisme dans ce récit, car il est rare que la personnalité d'un auteur ne se mêle pas à ce qu'il raconte — voir Hugo, Dumas, Lamartine et tant d'autres. Shakespeare est une exception et je ne suis pas Shakespeare — pas plus, d'ailleurs, que je ne suis Lamartine, Dumas ou Hugo. (*CB*, 15 October)

> [I am always suspicious of a traveller's impressions. These impressions are subjective — a word I use because it is fashionable, although I am not sure what it means [...]. I am of a cheerful nature, and you really must pardon me if I am rather egotistical when telling my story, for it is so seldom that an author's personality does not become mixed up with what he is writing about — consider Hugo, Dumas, Lamartine, Shakespeare and so many others. Shakespeare is an exception, and I am not Shakespeare, any more than I can be considered Lamartine, Dumas or Hugo.]

In this text, Verne recognizes the objective imperative for accounting for what is seen, while destabilizing what is seen and the need for it. Yet in this passage which makes plain the scepticism over 'impressions', Bombarnac also queries subjectivity in his claim that subjectivity is another fallible vogue. His frank declaration that he does not quite understand what is meant by subjectivity can be read ironically; in telling the reader that he is a bit clueless then he necessarily invites us to read his own account subjectively (as the product of someone who is a bit clueless). Yet he is characteristically also quite knowing about discussions of writing and of contemporary discussions of journalistic practice of the era. His subsequent discussion of authorial egotism is similarly double-edged; he recognizes his own blatant desire for self-presentation and identity while insisting on a form of anonymity by listing that which he is not.

This text sends its reader around in circles in its discussion of the seen versus the not-seen, the objective versus the subjective, the real versus the sensational. It is centred around an emblem which epitomizes these contradictions. In his investigations of the passengers and carriages on the train, Bombarnac comes across a packing-crate. The crate turns out to contain a stowaway heading for a reunion with his lover in Peking. This Romanian secret passenger, Kinko, will eventually emerge as the hero of the novel, much to Bombarnac's surprise. Before the dramatic events of the end of the text, the packing-case acts as a catalyst for discussions of the visual in the text. The whole point of the case is that it represents what cannot and ideally should not be seen, and Bombarnac glimpses his stowaway piecemeal, first mis-identifying the figure in the crate as an animal, then recognizing a pair of human eyes between the timber of the casing; he fails to catch a proper sight of Kinko as he sneaks out of the box to get some exercise one evening. When Bombarnac begins to perceive that the drama he associates with the box has some authenticity, he claims he will turn this unheroic hero into something literary in terms which again conflate conceptions of the real and the fictional — 'aussi, ce brave numéro 11, avec les amplifications, antonymies, diaphores, epitasis, tropes, metaphors et autres figures de cette sorte, je le parerai, je le grandirai, je le développerai, comme on développe un cliché photographique' [And so this brave no. 11, I will deck him out, enlarge him, develop him with amplifications, antonyms, diaphoresis, epistasis, tropes, metaphors and other figures of that sort, as one would develop a photographic negative] (*CB*, 23 October).

As elsewhere, Verne's reporter's statement contradicts itself. Bombarnac emphasizes his skill with literary devices and metaphors, and yet the simile he employs here — the 'cliché photographique' — suggests the disconnection between the image and its likeness. The development of the photograph, which suggests the emerging clarity of an image taken from life, is both like and un-like the literary process Bombarnac sets about describing here. That process, of amplification and elaboration, indicates that the visual which provided the material for the photograph is distorted as it is turned into fiction and into art. But once again Bombarnac's listing device adds a further layer to such contradiction, implicitly arguing against his own ability to enlarge and distort. The pluralized set of technical literary terms (which are in fact never employed in the description of Kinko) means that such terms tend to cancel one another out and end up meaning nothing, so defeating the capacity of the literary to 'parer' the image taken from life.

Claudius Bombarnac offers insight into the changing journalistic practices of the late nineteenth century, while exaggerating and satirizing those practices. It is a text which delights in blurring distinctions. The reader is provided with a metaphor for such blurring by way of the landscapes charted by Bombarnac. Having set out with the aim of noting the differences in architecture and geography between the western and eastern extremes of his journey, between Russian and Chinese, Bombarnac ends up finding that such clear-cut distinction is problematic, particularly in the 'double-town', Kachgar/Yangi-Char:

> En réalité, on dirait d'une ville turkomène qui aurait été bâtie par des Chinois, ou d'une ville chinoise qui aurait été bâtie par des Turkomènes. Monuments et habitants tiennent de cette double origine. Les mosquées ont un faux air de pagodes, les pagodes ont un faux air de mosques. (*CB*, 11 November)
>
> [It seems to be a Turkoman town built by the Chinese, or perhaps a Chinese town built by Turkomans. Monuments and inhabitants betray their double origin. The mosques look like pagodas, the pagodas look like mosques.]

Journey and novel alike end up collapsing oppositions — between east and west, between factual and fictional — and, I would argue, between newspaper and novel, as the antagonism between the two forms of writing disintegrates in Maupassant's duels. The *chose vue* is a distorting mirror, confusing the boundaries between pagodas and mosques, enabling an understanding of disguise rather than an understanding of the visual. What the text does, in its virtuoso display of the failings of the reporter, and the failings of the real, is to enable the reader at all times to 'see' beyond the hubristic nature of Bombarnac's bombast, privileging the reader's capacities for perception even while the act of seeing comes under scrutiny.

Yet although newspapers and novels alike are subject to satire, their practices of story-seeking seen as formulaic and misguided, the end of *Claudius Bombarnac* sees the journalist's breathless quest for the truth end in embarrassment. The novel, meanwhile, unveils the truth and manages to orchestrate a plot, a hero, and a denouement while calling such ingredients into question. Verne might be sceptical about the future of novel-writing, but in *Claudius Bombarnac* he creates a novel and an anti-novel which humorously subvert the reportage which would supposedly transcend such a form of literature. The Vernian novels which focus most intensely on the role of the journalist complicate predictions about the death of the novel. They suggest playful competition, steeplechases, between the practices of reportage and processes of intuitive reading. The closing line of *Michel Strogoff* announces that: 'ce n'est pas l'histoire de ses succès, c'est l'histoire de ses épreuves qui méritait d'être racontée' (*MS*, 498) ('it is not the history of his success, but the history of his trials, which deserves to be related'). This can be applied, too, to Verne's self-conscious meditation on the practice of communication as seen in these texts which foreground the attempts to communicate journalistically; he recounts a history of the trials of expression, arguing that such a struggle deserves to be relayed. In so doing he argues for the plot-driven, communication-led process of *raconter*, disparaged in Maupassant's duelling discourses.

Notes to Chapter 3

1. Gaston Leroux, taken from an interview given in 1924 and recorded by Madeleine Lépine-Leroux, cited in Gilles Costaz, 'Gaston Leroux Reporter', *Europe*, special issue on Gaston Leroux, 626–27 (1981), 45–49 (p. 49).
2. See Jules Huret, *Tout yeux, tout oreilles* (Paris: Charpentier, 1901); also Arthur Meyer's journalistic memoirs, *Ce que mes yeux ont vu* (Paris: Plon & Nourrit, 1911).
3. Brisson, 'Promenades et visites'. Mary Louise Roberts discusses 'the technology of vision' in the new journalism of the late nineteenth century in 'Subversive Copy: Feminist Journalism in Fin de siècle France', in *Making the News: Modernity & the Mass Press in Nineteenth-Century France*, ed. by Dean de la Motte and Jeannene Przyblyski (Boston: University of Massachusetts Press, 1999), pp. 302–50.
4. All English translations of *Michel Strogoff* are taken from *Michel Strogoff: or, The Courier of the Czar*, trans. by William Henry Giles Kingston (CreateSpace Independent Publishing Platform, 2015).
5. See Roberts for discussion of the controversy over the term reportage, and the point at which it is admitted into French vocabulary ('Subversive Copy', p. 344); Livois argues that it was not until the 1890s that it was accepted as a term by the Académie française (*Histoire de la presse française*, II, 351); other press historians claim it was introduced much earlier, by Stendhal.
6. Delporte, *Les Journalistes en France*, p. 61.
7. Édouard Helsey, *Envoyé spécial* (Paris: Fayard, 1955), p. 72.
8. Delporte, *Les Journalistes en France*, p. 70.
9. Pinson, *L'Imaginaire médiatique*, p. 187.
10. Thérenty, *La Littérature au quotidien*, p. 23.
11. Cited in Paul Ginisty, *Anthologie du journalisme, du XVIIème siècle à nos jours*, 2 vols (Paris: Delagrave, 1920), II, 311.
12. *Le Matin*, 14 July 1888.
13. Hugues Le Roux in *Le Temps*, 22 February 1889, cited in Delporte, *Les Journalistes en France*, p. 73.
14. Roberts, *Disruptive Acts*, p. 86, and in particular Chapter Three, 'Subversive Copy', pp. 73–110.
15. Brunetière, *Le Roman naturaliste*, p. 224.
16. Émile Zola in *Annales politiques et littéraires*, 22 July 1894.
17. See Christian Delporte, 'Jules Verne et le journaliste: imaginer l'information du XXè siècle', *Temps des médias*, 4 (2005), 201–13.
18. Fernand Xau in *La Patrie*, 27 June 1893, cited in Delporte, *Les Journalistes en France*, pp. 63–64.
19. Delporte, *Les Journalistes en France*, p. 71. See too Marie-Ève Thérenty, 'Les "vagabonds du télégraphe": représentations et poétiques du grand reportage avant 1914', *Sociétés et representations*, 21 (2006), 101–15, <https://www.cairn.info/revue-societes-et-representations-2006-1-page-101.htm> [accessed 12 January 2016].
20. Thérenty, *La Littérature au quotidien*, p. 291.
21. A. de Chambure, *À travers la presse* (Paris: Fert, Albouy & Cie., 1914), pp. 446–47, cited in Roberts, *Disruptive Acts*, p. 85.

22. Fenestrier, *La Vie des frelons*, p. 102.
23. Ibid., p. 65.
24. Delporte, *Les Journalistes en France*, p. 50.
25. David Levin, *Modernity and the Hegemony of Vision* (Berkeley: University of California Press, 1993), p. 193.
26. Martin Jay, *Downcast Eyes: The Denigration of Vision in Twentieth Century French Thought* (Berkeley: University of California Press, 1993), p. 14.
27. Ibid., p. 187.
28. See Ibid., p. 151, and Jonathan Crary, *Techniques of the Observer: On Vision and Modernity in the Nineteenth Century* (Cambridge, MA: MIT Press, 1990), p. 70. See too Hal Foster, *Vision and Visuality* (New York: New Press, 1988); *Vision and Textuality*, ed. by Stephen Melville and Bill Readings (Basingstoke: Macmillan, 1995), and *Vision in Context: Historical and Contemporary Perspectives on Sight*, ed. by Teresa Brennan and Martin Jay (London: Routledge, 1996).
29. Andrea Goulet, 'Retinal Fictions: Villiers, Leroux and Optics at the Fin de Siècle', *Nineteenth-Century French Studies*, 34.1–2 (2005–06), 107–20 (p. 108).
30. David Howes, *The Varieties of Sensory Experience: A Sourcebook in the Anthropology of the Senses* (Toronto: University of Toronto Press, 1991), p. 170.
31. Thérenty, 'Le journal dans le roman du XIXè siècle ou l'icône renversée', p. 35.
32. Howes, *The Varieties of Sensory Experience*, p. 170.
33. Jay, *Downcast Eyes*, p. 187.
34. Peter Brooks, *Realist Vision* (New Haven, CT: Yale University Press, 2005), p. 3: Prendergast, though, in *The Order of Mimesis*, pp. 59–61, argues for downplaying the preoccupation with the visual in studies of realism.
35. Paul Rodaway, *Sensuous Geographies* (London: Routledge, 1994), p. 90.
36. Hannah Scott, 'Symphonic Shopping: From Masculine Visuality to Feminine Aurality in Zola's *Au Bonheur des dames*', *Dix-Neuf*, 18.3 (2014), 259–71.
37. Myriam Boucharenc, 'Pierre Giffard, *Le Sieur de Va-Partout*, premier manifeste de la littérature de reportage', in *Presse et plumes: journalisme et littérature au XIXè siècle*, ed. by Marie-Ève Thérenty and Alain Vaillant (Paris: Nouveau Monde, 2004), pp. 511–21 (p. 514).
38. Boucharenc, 'Pierre Giffard, *Le Sieur de Va-Partout*, premier manifeste de la littérature de reportage', p. 517.
39. Zoé Commère, *Claudius Bombarnac de Jules Verne: le romanesque refondé par le reportage?*, masters thesis submitted to Lyon 2 University and published on the website *Médias 19*, <http://www.medias19.org/docannexe/file/19412/le_romanesque_refonde....pdf> [accessed 6 January 2017], p. 9.
40. See Christian Robin, 'Jules Verne et la presse', in *Jules Verne: cent ans après: actes du colloque de Cérisy*, ed. by Jean-Pierre Picot and Christian Robin (Rennes: Terre de Brume, 2005), pp. 87–106.
41. Jules Verne, *L'Île mystérieuse* (Paris: Bibliothèque d'éducation et de récréation, 1874), p. 11.
42. Timothy Unwin, 'Jules Verne: Negotiating Change in the Nineteenth Century', *Science Fiction Studies*, 32.1 (March 2005), 5–17 (p. 12).
43. Trevor Harris, 'Measurement and Mystery in Verne', in *Jules Verne: Narratives of Modernity*, ed. by Edmund Smyth (Liverpool: Liverpool University Press, 2000), pp. 109–21 (p. 114).
44. Simone Vierne, 'Trompe-l'œil et Clin d'œil dans l'œuvre de Jules Verne', in *Jules Verne et les sciences humaines: communications... interventions*, ed. by François Raymond, Simone Vierne, and Ray Bradbury (Paris: Colloque de Cerisy, 1978), pp. 410–26 (pp. 418–19).
45. Christian Chelebourg, *Jules Verne: l'œil et le ventre: une poétique du sujet* (Paris: Lettres modernes Minard, 1999), p. 30.
46. Jonathan Crary, *Suspensions of Perception: Attention, Spectacle and Modern Culture* (Cambridge, MA: MIT Press, 1999), p. 12.
47. Zoé Commère's online edition of *Claudius Bombarnac* (*CB*) is laid out in date order.
48. Robin, 'Jules Verne et la presse', p. 98.
49. Jameson, *The Antimonies of Realism*, p. 33.
50. Ibid., p. 33.

51. Ibid., pp. 54–55.
52. See Simone Vierne, *Jules Verne et la roman initiatique: contribution à l'étude de l'imaginaire* (Paris: Éditions du Sirac, 1973); see also her *Jules Verne* (Paris: Balland, 1986).
53. Manon Mathias, *Vision in the Novels of George Sand* (Oxford: Oxford University Press, 2016), p. 30.
54. Pinson, *L'Imaginaire médiatique*, p. 198.
55. Thérenty, *La Littérature au quotidien*, p. 73.
56. Harris, 'Measurement and Modernity in Verne', p. 119.
57. Howes, *The Varieties of Sensory Experience*, p. 14.
58. Jay, *Downcast Eyes*, p. 159.
59. Timothy Unwin, 'The Fiction of Science or the Science of Fiction', in *Jules Verne: Narratives of Modernity*, ed. by Smyth, pp. 46–59 (p. 50).
60. See Roland Barthes, 'Nautilus et bateau ivre', in *Mythologies* (Paris: Seuil, 1957).
61. Unwin, 'The Fiction of Science or the Science of Fiction', p. 49.
62. Jules Verne and Adolphe d'Ennery, *Michel Strogoff: pièce en cinq actes et seize tableaux* (Exeter: University of Exeter Press, 1994), p. 4.
63. Ibid., p. 15.
64. Unwin, 'The Fiction of Science or the Science of Fiction', p. 51.
65. Roland Barthes, *Leçon: leçon inaugurale de la chaise de sémiologie littéraire du Collège de France, le 7 janvier 1977* (Paris: Seuil, 1978), pp. 22–23.
66. Commère, *Claudius Bombarnac de Jules Verne*, p. 10.
67. Unwin, *Jules Verne. Journeys in Writing* (Liverpool: Liverpool University Press, 2005), p. 147.
68. Rubery, *The Novelty of Newspapers*, p. 10; 'skimming' is a term taken from Q. D. Leavis's *Fiction and the Reading Public* (London: Chatto & Windus, 1932), p. 226.

CHAPTER 4

Newspaper-Detectives: Reality, Fantasy, Banality

Journalists: New Fictional Heroes

> Mon petit Fandor, si tu continues dans la carrière que tu as choisie, à montrer autant de réflexion, autant d'initiative que tu viens d'en avoir, tu seras, et rapidement je t'assure, le premier journaliste policier de notre époque! (F, 227)
>
> [My dear young Fandor, if you continue in your chosen career, if you display as much thought and initiative as you just have, you will soon be the best newspaper detective of the day, I assure you.][1]

Inspector Juve's encouraging words to his protégé Fandor in the first novel in the Fantômas series of detective stories acknowledge and emphasize the existence of a new breed of reporters at the turn of the twentieth century. This chapter will examine the role played by 'journalistes policiers' in the popular fiction of that period. It will focus on the recurring appearances of journalist-investigators in the best-known serializations of the early years of detective fiction, Gaston Leroux's indefatigable Rouletabille, and Fandor, sidekick of Souvestre and Allain's Inspector Juve, as he goes about his undaunted quest in search of the mythical arch-criminal Fantômas. In discussing the heroization of these reporter figures and the role they play in the still relatively new genre of detective fiction, attention will be paid to the metafictional games explored in the texts and the implications for the practice of realism. By incorporating journalist characters in their plots and interspersing their narratives with newspaper snippets, mimicking the processes of reportage, these novels embed themselves in a seamy urban reality which insists on connections between the reading of fiction and the reading of daily newspapers. At the same time, the playfulness of these textual collages undermines the strategies of representation in newspapers and novels alike. This chapter will also investigate the ways in which texts by Leroux and Souvestre and Allain anticipate postmodern theories of the hyper-real, recording the banalization of crime and violence.

In one of the most famous examples of early French detective fiction, Leroux's *Le Mystère de la chambre jaune* (1907), the narrator-reporter Sainclair reflects Inspector Juve's reference to 'journalistes policiers' with his observation that the affair of the Yellow Room is to elevate the renown of the young journalist Rouletabille:

> Qui devait non seulement le classer le premier des reporters, mais encore en

> faire le premier policier du monde, double qualité qu'on ne saurait s'étonner de trouver chez la même personne, attendu que la presse quotidienne commençait déjà à se transformer et à devenir ce qu'elle est à peu près aujourd'hui: la gazette du crime. (*M*, 23)
>
> [Which was not only to rank him as the first of newspaper reporters, but also to prove him to be the greatest detective in the world — a double role which it was not astonishing to find played by the same person, considering how the daily Press was already beginning to transform itself, and becoming what it almost is today — the gazette of crime.][2]

Sainclair not only cements understanding of the 'double qualité' open to reporters of the turn of the century — the detecting function they are able to play as they investigate the origins of the stories they write up for the press — but also the evolving role of the newspaper industry. Sainclair's rather exaggerated summary of the 'presse quotidienne' as 'la gazette du crime' indicates the close connections between newspapers and crime, briefly revealing the extent of the changes that have taken place in the press and in the representation of crime over the course of the nineteenth century.

These changes are made apparent in two of the earliest examples of detective fiction, Edgar Allan Poe's 'Murders in the Rue Morgue' and the 'Mystery of Marie Rogêt', as newspaper reports fuel the investigations of the amateur sleuth Dupin: 'the press's new power in such matters was part of a recent decisive migration of tales of crime from ballad and broadsheet to newspaper faits-divers'.[3] Urbanization saw the increased incidence and reporting of crime in the newspapers, as in the *Gazette des Tribunaux*, first published in 1825. Restrictions on political reporting under the Second Empire meant that newspapers were increasingly likely to focus on alternative material, with the reporting of crime particularly topical; the Troppman affair in 1869–70, which saw a serial killer guillotined for the murder of eight members of the same family, shook the nation and received graphic press attention. Lavergne discusses the popularity of *canards*, engraved illustrations of crimes and criminals, sold in the street and disseminated to members of the public who did not read or subscribe to the daily papers.[4] Such engravings amplified and dramatized the news. As a result, 'l'heure est au réalisme provocateur et saisissant' [it was the era of provocative and gripping realism], with newspaper readers often invited to participate in criminal investigations through the incorporation in the papers of documentary material, such as maps of the crime scenes.[5] In Leroux's text, the real paper *Le Matin* and the fictional *Époque*, the titles of which insist on their contemporaneity, vie for the most detailed and accurate accounts of the latest crime.

Pinson comments on the growing relationship between the press and the detective novel, highlighting the Pranzini affair of 1887 as a particular moment of intersection. A triple murder which took place close to the Champs Elysées, the Pranzini affair gave rise to lurid articles in the press.[6] Pinson posits it as the point at which rivalry started up between police detectives and investigative reporters.[7] As the role of the detective became further embedded in the state apparatus in both France and Britain during the nineteenth century, so the perception of that role evolved. Although unpopular at the time of their emergence in the eighteenth century, when bandits and highway robbers assumed the status of popular heroes, Dennis Porter traces the 'heroization' of the detective, involving a profound change of social attitudes and giving rise to the Dupins and Holmeses created by Poe and Conan Doyle. As Pinson illustrates, the reporter, too, is eventually perceived as heroic for his investigative capacities and in particular for the way in which he competes with and often outwits the police.

This evolution in the literary perception of the reporter offers a fundamental difference between the representation of journalism in the earlier realist or naturalist novel, and that found in the popular novels of the early twentieth century. Perceived, as in Maupassant or in a text such as *La Vie des frelons*, as a failed writer or a money-grabbing, gossip-mongering hack, by the 1920s the reporter's status had become such that he could be seen as 'a triumphant incarnation of the investigation and the adventure of modernity'.[8] In particular, the role of the journalist as represented in the popular fiction of the early twentieth century trumped that of the police. Lavergne points out that:

> Le journaliste, peu à peu, devient ainsi un nouveau type de héros, qui assume à la fin le rôle de justicier et de réparateur [...] le reporter, mieux que l'homme de loi ou le policier, est présenté comme le personnage le plus à même de concilier les exigences des autorités officielles et les réticences privées. À lui de détendre la situation et de rétablir l'ordre de la façon qui lui semble la plus appropriée.[9]

> [The journalist was gradually becoming a new kind of hero, eventually assuming the role of upholder of the law and restorer of justice [...] even more so than the lawyer or the policeman, the reporter was represented as the character who could best win over the demands of officials and requests for privacy. It was up to him to calm the situation and restore order in the most appropriate way.]

Lavergne's suggestion that the reporter is better placed than the figure of the official detective to prise information out of suspects or witnesses is reinforced by Kalifa and Flynn's discussion of the journalist at this time, which stresses the advantages exercised by those writing for the press over those working for the police force. They were more closely associated with democratic ideals as opposed to autocratic power and repression, and, in disseminating news of both crime and investigative process in the newspapers, reporters took responsibility for publicizing criminal affairs and rendering them intelligible, establishing connections between sordid and dangerous events and public perception of them:

> The journalist, who acted as the main spokesman of the revolutionary period and who shaped the fight against monarchy during the 1814–1848 period, a pure product of the republican meritocracy, asserts his role as democracy's anonymous and collective protagonist at the end of the nineteenth century.[10]

The observation, above, that the reporter was seen as restoring order can be read as both a social and a narrative trait. This is true not only within the pages of the newspaper, but becomes a particular concern in the detective fiction which narrates criminal activity and echoes newspaper reportage, as discussed by Anissa Bellefqih in her analysis of the Arsène Lupin series by Maurice Leblanc:

> Roman de l'ordre, non pas simplement au sens où le rétablissement final de la loi viendrait remettre de l'ordre dans un monde un instant déstabilisé, mais surtout au sens où ce qui est essentiellement en question dans le livre-jeu est l'ordre dans lequel on raconte les évènements.[11]
>
> [A novel about order, not just in the sense that the eventual re-establishment of the law restores order to a momentarily destabilized world, but also in the sense that what is at stake in this book/game is the order in which events are narrated.]

Kalifa and Flynn refer to the journalistic ability to 'control the narrative unfolding of the investigation, which is a literary form as well as a professional practice'.[12] As will be shown, such practices of restoring and narrating order are highlighted and problematized in the texts by Leroux, Leblanc, and Souvestre and Allain.

At the end of *Le Mystère de la chambre jaune* Rouletabille, having denounced the fake detective Larsan as the arch-criminal Ballmeyer, also announces that he has facilitated Larsan's escape from justice, claiming that his interests in detection lie in uncovering the truth, and not in ensuring that justice is served:

> Je ne suis pas de la justice, moi; je ne suis pas de la police moi; je suis un humble journaliste, et mon métier n'est point de faire arrêter les gens! Je sers la vérité comme je veux... c'est mon affaire... Préservez, vous autres, la société, comme vous pouvez, c'est la vôtre... Mais ce n'est pas moi qui apporterai une tête au bourreau! (*M*, 167)
>
> [I have nothing to do with the Law, neither do I belong to the police. I am merely a journalist, and it is not my business to get people arrested. I serve truth in my own way — that is my business... Preserve society as best you can, you others, it belongs to you. But you will never get me to provide heads for the executioner to cut off.]

Rouletabille here epitomizes the ambivalent status of the reporter-detective. Not only does he outwit the police, but he uncovers the supposed detective as a fraud, suggesting an inherent threat associated with the forces of order; he then refuses to endorse and as a result queries legal and social structures. At the end of the text he appears to restore order in his courtroom narration of the way in which the attempted murder in the yellow room was carried out, yet simultaneously disrupts that order in the distance he purposefully sets between himself and the law, and renders the narration open-ended in setting the scene for the sequel to the text and the return of Larsan-Ballmeyer.

The figure of the reporter-investigator came to prominence in fiction in the work of Fortuné du Boisgobey, whose series of novels featuring the journalist Saintonge indicated the ways in which the police could be trumped by the press. In *Cornaline la dompteuse*, for instance, a murder committed some time previously by the protagonist Georges Cransac, a prisoner set for release at the start of the novel, is still being brought up in the pages of the newspaper by the tenacious Saintonge:

> Et cette fâcheuse histoire lui était rappelée tout à coup par un homme dont la profession consistait à mettre en scène les crimes, pour satisfaire la curiosité des lecteurs d'une feuille quotidienne, à en rechercher les auteurs et à en découvrir

les causes, alors même que la police a *classé l'affaire*, c'est à dire ne s'en occupe plus.¹³

[And this annoying sequence of events was brought back to him all of a sudden by a man whose profession was all about staging crime so as to satisfy the curiosity of the readers of a daily newspaper, seeking out the culprits and discovering the causes, whereas the police had 'closed the case' — in other words, were no longer looking into it.]

Pinson comments on the role of Saintonge, citing the observation in the text that he — like the seemingly all-seeing reporters in Verne — uses his capacities to 'tout voir et tout entendre' [see and hear all].¹⁴ Another journalist-character who plays a more prominent role in the narrative than that of Saintonge is the figure of Danglars, a reporter in Apollinaire's early literary work, the crime novel *Que faire?*, which, in its depiction of a triple murder, appears to reflect the Pranzini affair.¹⁵

The lionization of the reporter in detective fiction is epitomized by the role of the boyish journalist Rouletabille in Leroux's series of novels. On the day of the trial of the innocent Darzac in *Le Mystère de la chambre jaune*, an assembled crowd waits outside the courtroom for the promised arrival of Rouletabille, in the expectation that he will descend and announce the truth of the mystery of the yellow room. The fictionalized *Époque* article published that day stresses his potential role as martyr: 'La presse, elle aussi, compte ses héros, victimes du devoir: le devoir professionnel, le premier de tous les devoirs. Peut-être, à cette heure, y a-t-il succombé!' (*M*, 155) ('The Press has its heroes, its martyrs to duty, their obligations of their profession being to them the first of all duties. It is quite possible that he has given his life for the sake of his professional duty!'). In later novels about the exploits of Rouletabille in Russia, the rhetoric is exaggerated still further, and he is seen in quasi-religious terms. About to be executed by the Russian nihilists in *Rouletabille chez le Tsar*, Rouletabille finally perceives the truth of the assassination attempts on the life of Général Trebassof, and the discovery makes him appear angelic: 'une telle joie rayonnait de son visage en extase qu'il en était comme auréolé' ('such joy shone from his ecstatic face that it was as though he was surrounded by a halo'), and he is allowed twenty-four hours to solve the case since 'cet enfant [...] accomplira des miracles' ('this child will accomplish miracles').¹⁶ In the Fantômas series, the journalist Fandor, who takes up the profession on Inspector Juve's suggestion in the first novel, achieves such international renown that when he turns up in a crate in South Africa in *La Fille de Fantômas*, his name is recognized by the governors of the asylum to which he is sent. Discussing the representation of the offices of the newspaper *La Capitale*, and Fandor's place at the top of the hierarchy of reporters at this fictional publication, Pinson notes that 'l'aura héroïque du personnage repose-t-elle sur le fond banal de la grande machine médiatique' [the heroic aura surrounding this character emanates from the banal basis of the media machine].¹⁷

The 'heroic aura' associated with the journalists Fandor and Rouletabille is the product, in part, of a number of shared characteristics. Both are so young as to be described as childlike; Rambert, who will later take the name Fandor, is sent away from drawing-room discussion about Fantômas in the opening chapter of the first novel because he is considered too much a child to listen to the conversation. Rouletabille's youth is stressed throughout *Le Mystère de la chambre jaune* and *Le Parfum de la dame en noir*, and his round head exaggerates his childish appearance. Their youth is echoed — and parodied — in Maurice Leblanc's Lupin novels, with the introduction (in *L'Aiguille creuse*) of the schoolboy detective Isidore Beautrelet, with his capacity to outwit the police within hours — so speedily as to defy credulity and send up the image of the free-spirited reporter-detective and his boyishness. Beautrelet is not a journalist, but takes to the newspaper in the course of his investigation into the activities of Lupin, publishing his revelations in the *Grand Journal*. Indeed, the Leblanc novels reveal the extent of the intertextuality at work in detective fiction of the turn of the century; not only does the 'gentleman-cambrioleur' Lupin himself often publish misleading extracts of information under pseudonyms in the papers, but the texts draw on the plots and motifs established by the likes of Leroux and Conan Doyle — most famously Leblanc has both Arsène Lupin and the boy investigator Beautrelet call upon and outwit 'Holmlock Shears'.

In addition to their youth, both Rouletabille and Fandor are distinguished by an indeterminate social background, which nevertheless enables a speedy rise to prominence within their chosen profession. Rambert-Fandor is from a wealthy background, but his parentage is problematic as his mother is an asylum inmate and he has not seen his father for a long time, such that the criminal Fantômas assumes his father's identity. Educated outside France, Rambert is suspected of the killing of the marquise de Langrune, and is forced to become a social outsider. When he emerges in Paris some time later and is recognized by Inspector Juve, he is, in a sense, reborn, having been assumed dead on the discovery of the corpse in the river near the Langrune house. His journalistic status is therefore assumed as if he has risen from the dead and adopted a fresh persona. Kalifa describes Leroux's *Le Mystère de la chambre jaune* as socially utopic in its representation of Rouletabille's rise to prominence, as the boy-journalist's career trajectory takes him speedily from the slums of Marseilles to prodigiously talented employee of *L'Époque* to private detective within the employ of the Tsar in the Russian novels.[18] Although the end of the nineteenth century saw the increasing professionalization of journalism in France, with the establishment of a school for journalists, as mentioned in the previous chapter, it remained the case that it offered career opportunities for those wishing to enter a non-manual industry with little training or qualification. Kalifa stresses the difficulties faced by *faits-diversiers* who sought to improve their career prospects: 'Ordonnant la succession des faits, organisant le suspense à l'échelle nationale, claironnant sa toute-puissance à la face du monde, il connaît une spectaculaire promotion qui, d'auteur anonyme, le hisse au rang d'acteur du fait-divers' [putting facts into the correct order, co-ordinating the suspense at a national level, trumpeting their might in the eyes of the world, they saw spectacular promotion, rising from the ranks of anonymous authors to agents in the making of the *fait-divers*].[19] It remained relatively rare for those who worked on the newspapers at the lowest level to find opportunities for advancement, and the gradations between so-called 'grands reporters' referred to in the previous chapter and the 'petits reporters' or 'faits-diversiers' were fairly entrenched. One possible way to transcend the divide, however, was to make a name through reporting on crime; lower-ranking reporters trotted along to the Palais de Justice and the Préfecture de police, perhaps twice daily, in search of stories. It is against such a backdrop that characters such as Rouletabille and Fandor are depicted as successful in their attempts to enter journalism and make their names.

The energy and dynamism of these upwardly mobile reporter-heroes, emblematized by the insistence on their youth, can be linked with a jubilant celebration of the popular fiction in which they feature. Rather than doubting the future of the novel, as in the texts by Maupassant, Fenestrier, and Brulat, or even evoking the ambivalence of Zola and Verne, these serial novels celebrate their genesis in the press, as the publications of former journalists, and they triumphantly proclaim their status as novels which embrace the newspaper, incorporating journalistic snippets and discourse in ways which will be discussed. The publication strategies employed, for instance, by Pierre Souvestre and Marcel Allain, were governed by a need for speed. They were contractually obliged to produce a novel a month, and so brought to their novels the practice of writing for tight deadlines demanded by their previous work as journalists: 'Les deux auteurs de Fantômas tirent au sort qui rédigera les chapitres pairs et qui les chapîtres impairs' [the two Fantomas authors drew lots to see who would write the even-numbered chapters and who the uneven].[20]

The cynical view of contemporary literature offered by *Bel-Ami*, which begins by comparing Duroy to the 'mauvais sujet' [ne'er-do-well] of popular novels, is refuted by these texts, which offer a lively contrast to bleak prophecies as to the future of the novel. Analysis of Maupassant's representation of journalism in the opening chapter of this study referred to the scepticism found in the text towards the banalities of *raconter*. In foregrounding the practices of journalists, these crime novels also highlight the business of the recount. They offer particularly ludic evaluation of the role of narrative voice, the engagement of the reader, and, in describing the original crime but then retelling it in the light of the subsequent investigation, call attention to proleptic and analeptic techniques. The much-discussed metafictionality of the detective genre is emphasized, in the popular series of the early twentieth century, by the proliferation of journalist figures and the representation of the fictional publications for which they write. *Raconter* is highlighted, satirized, and pulled apart in these playful texts.

'Je ne suis et ne veux être qu'un fidèle rapporteur': Reporting Versus Detecting

One of the key intertexts for the works of Leroux, Leblanc, and the authors of the Fantômas series, Poe's 'Mystery of Marie Rogêt', is composed of a series of newspaper clippings which narrate the crime and speculate on its possible solution. The plot sees the amateur detective Dupin poring over these news reports, sifting through their stylistic tics in order to disprove their theories and dispute their truth;

at one point he observes, for instance, that: 'To me this article appears conclusive of little beyond the zeal of its inditer. We should bear in mind that, in general, it is the object of newspapers rather to create a sensation — to make a point — than to further the cause of truth'.[21] Transposing the real-life murder of Mary Rogers in New York to a Parisian setting, Poe takes the real and fictionalizes it, questioning the veracity of reportage. The Rogers case was instrumental in the establishment of New York's first 'Day and Night' police force in 1844; the press interest in the case was indicative of the mid-nineteenth century shift in the publication of tales of crime, from ballads and broadsheets to the *faits-divers* columns in the newspapers.[22] Embedding the half-real, half-fictional newspaper reports in his text, Poe creates a narrative which interrogates narrative devices, and the boundaries between truth and fiction, and in so doing invents a genre which will become characterized by its investigation into the functioning of narrative. As A. J. Sweeney maintains:

> All detective stories refer, if only obliquely, to their own fictionality and their own interpretation [...]. Indeed, rather than providing an 'escape from literature' or from 'orthodox narrative', detective fiction — with its streamlined structure, its emphasis on interpretation at all levels of plot and narration, and its peculiar focus on the relationship between writer and reader — represents narrativity in its purest form.[23]

Simon Kemp's discussion of the pastiche of the genre in contemporary French literature also foregrounds metafictionality as a key characteristic; crime fiction is 'an ideal base for metafictional inquiry, whether it be into distinctive literary views of the world, the artificial restructuring of experience through narrative, or philosophical assumptions regarding truth and reason'. He cites Todorov on the double nature of detective fiction narratives, which feature both the story of the investigation and that of the crime itself, pointing out that the narrator of the investigation story often explicitly acknowledges that he is writing a book.[24]

Sweeney focuses on the image of the locked room, the recurrent puzzle in early popular detective fiction (as in Poe's 'Murders in the Rue Morgue'), as symbolic of the metafictionality of the detective novel itself: 'a perfect metaphor for the inherent self-reflexivity of the genre'.[25] And as the locked room is often encased in layers of architecture — a feature exaggerated, for example, in the sequel to *Le Mystère de la chambre jaune*, *Le Parfum de la dame en noir* — so the detective story often reflects its own narrativity in a series of narrative levels and embedded texts. The newspaper report(s) embedded within Poe's tales provide one such narrative level. In incorporating, dissecting, disproving, and parodying excerpts of journalism, early detective novels interrogate both the strategies of reportage and the functioning of their own narrative structures.

Citing a comparison with Poe in its opening chapter, *Le Mystère de la chambre jaune* emphasizes its intertextuality right from the beginning. The narrator Sainclair announces: 'je ne sache pas que, dans le domaine de la réalité ou de l'imagination, même chez l'auteur du *Double Assassinat, rue Morgue*, même dans les inventions des sous-Edgar Poe et des truculents Conan Doyle, on puisse retenir quelque chose de comparable' (*M*, 16) ('I do not think that in the domain of reality or imagination, or even among the inventions of Edgar Allan Poe and his imitators, anything to compare in mystery with the natural mystery of the Yellow Room can possibly be found'). Daniel Compère refers to the style of the text itself as an 'écriture du reportage', with its incorporation of different fragments of writing, whether newspaper reports, diary entries, or legal testimonies, and its fluctuation between precision and sensationalism: 'L'écriture du reportage est [...] tout à la fois le ciment de l'œuvre de Gaston Leroux et le révélateur de ses procédés, mais elle est aussi un mode d'interrogation de l'écriture romanesque' [the style of reportage is both the material from which Leroux's works are constructed and a revelation into how they work, but it is also a means of questioning novelistic writing].[26] The interrogation of narrative procedure found in the book is brought out vividly in the most recent film adaptation of Leroux's text, Bruno Podalydès's 2003 version, which features close-up sequences of gadgets and toys, drawing attention to the processes of invention and the workings of mechanisms, as the film acknowledges its own status as adaptation. The film opts to substitute the courtroom drama at the end of Leroux's text for a re-enactment of the crime, announcing 'nous avons une reconstitution à reconstituer' [we have a reconstruction to reconstruct], highlighting the very act of reconstitution in which Podalydès engages in re-narrating the mystery of the yellow room and in flagging up its intertextuality.[27]

The most prominent of the mechanical toys takes centre-stage in a montage at the opening of the film, as a metal ball zigzags down a giant marble run. The ball eventually lands on a model steam engine which puffs across a real landscape until morphing into a full-scale locomotive, at which point the film 'proper' begins — with the image of four characters all with their heads buried in the pages of an identical newspaper. This montage brings together key elements from Leroux's text: the glimpse into the workings of the narrative via the levers and bolts of the marble run; the oscillation between the 'real' and the 'fictional' in the image of the toy train set against the landscape footage; the role of the newspapers as providing the narrative structure of the crime; and the mass readership of those papers comically illustrated in the simultaneous turning of the pages. Most importantly, the montage features the key 'ingredient' of the novel itself: the billiard ball which careers down the marble run can be seen as Rouletabille himself, the reporter with 'une bonne bille', the agent set in motion by the narrative as the ball is activated by the levers of the toy. With his billiard-ball head, Rouletabille is emblematic of newspaper reporting, and the representation of that newspaper reporting in the fin-de-siècle novel; his ball-like head evocative of the games of cup and ball which characterize the boorish playfulness of the journalists in *Bel-Ami*. The emphasis given to toys and mechanics in Podalydès's film calls attention to the practice of adaptation, revealing a sense of how things have been put together and bringing out the implicitly ludic qualities of Leroux's novel, which also foregrounds the 'mechanics' of its assembly.

Le Mystère de la chambre jaune 'fait plonger son lecteur dans le monde palpitant de l'enquête journalistique' [plunges its reader into the palpitating world of the journalistic quest].[28] The primary narrative voice in the novel is that of Sainclair, friend of Rouletabille, who is not only a lawyer but also a journalist, a contributor of legal news to the *Cri du boulevard*. And Sainclair begins his account by claiming that newspaper discourse will form a pivotal introduction to the tale of the locked room mystery in the text: 'vous allez donc tout savoir [...] je vais poser devant vos yeux le problème de la "Chambre Jaune" tel qu'il fut aux yeux du monde entier au lendemain du drame du château du Glandier' (*M*, 16) ('You are about to read the whole truth [...] I shall now place before you the problem of the Yellow Room exactly as it was placed before the public on the day after the tragedy'). He draws — as will the narrator in Maurice Leblanc's Lupin series — a connection between a fictionalized public of newspaper readers and actual readers of the fiction. In providing the background to the attempted murder of Mathilde Stangerson in the yellow room, invented excerpts from two real newspapers, *Le Temps* and *Le Matin*, are set before the reader in the opening chapter; their stylistic manner of reportage humorously contrasted, as will be discussed in the concluding section of this chapter. It is even suggested that the impetus behind Sainclair's narrative is itself journalistic; he wants to set straight an 'article misérable d'ignorance ou d'audacieuse perfidie' (*M*, 15) ('an ignorant or malicious article') which has been published about the case in an evening paper some years after the affair. The opening chapter of the first novel in Leroux's series about the heroic reporter-detective, then, epitomizes the representation of the newspaper in crime fiction. Thérenty claims that the genre most likely to incorporate the newspaper is, indeed, the *roman policier*; the effect constitutes a *mise-en-abyme* of the literary endeavour in proffering a form of reportage which deliberately contrasts with the fictional practices of the text. She refers to *Le Dossier 113* (1867) by Émile Gaboriau, in which a small advertisement allows a message to be passed to the villain; the reading of it allows the resolution of the crime. The detective, as a good reader of texts, discovers the truth hidden in newspaper articles; 'il sait lire entre les lignes' [he knows how to read between the lines].[29]

The literary self-consciousness evidenced in the opening pages of *Le Mystère de la chambre jaune* ironizes the newspaper extracts which it assembles by entitling the first chapter 'Où l'on commence à ne pas comprendre' ('In which we begin not to understand'). The clarity offered by Sainclair when he provides the reader with newspaper accounts of the crime is simultaneously accompanied by obscurity and an inability to understand. This ambivalent approach to the newspapers is embodied by Sainclair himself, and by his name. On the one hand, he stands for truth, order, and the 'healthiness' of society, a journalist purged of the festering sewer analogies found in association with the profession in the Introduction to this study. The clarity his name evokes suggests he is a faithful historian of events. Yet his name can also be viewed ironically, casting doubt on social safeguarding and the observational lucidity he symbolically represents. Sainclair's role is to obscure the answers to the mystery of the yellow room, to ensure that explanations remain murky up until the end of the text. He is a tool of the detective novel, the gullible narrator and spectator of the action who relays information to the reader but fails to sift the material he provides for the necessary clues and illumination. Isabelle Casta emphasizes the need for a counterpoint to the perspective of the central detective in crime fiction, a kind of stooge.³⁰ Sainclair jumps to the easy conclusion that the criminal in the case must be the servant at the Glandier estate, old Jacques:

> En choisissant ce dernier (Sainclair), en dépit de — mais ne faudrait-il pas plutôt écrire *à cause de* — son aveuglement et de ses dérobades, le romancier ne pouvait trouver meilleur narrateur pour dévoiler et conserver le mystère de la Chambre Jaune. Ces étranges inaptitudes, si elles ne désignent pas un témoin ideal, garantissent du moins Sainclair pour être un sûr gardien de l'étrange.³¹
>
> [In choosing Sainclair, despite — perhaps it would be better to say *thanks to* — his blindness and his evasiveness, the novelist could not have found a better narrator to unveil and preserve the mystery of the Yellow Room. This strange inaptitude ensures that Sainclair remains a faithful guardian of what is strange, even if he is not an ideal witness.]

Sainclair is firmly entrenched in the characteristics of his name — excessively 'healthy' insofar as he plays it safe, and refuses to allow deception and blurriness, which is why he sees things only as they are and not as they might be; he fails to pick up on the shifting identities in the text. Alternatively, his name can be read as proof of the transcendence of meaning, the fallibility of language in the text. In seeing Sainclair/*Signe-clair* as representative of the problematic clarity of signs in Leroux's text, a duality is opened up. On the one hand there is Sainclair, lawyer and dutiful reporter and narrator. On the other there is Rouletabille, who epitomizes a mobile and dynamic alternative to such reportage and narration, arguably a non-written practice of journalism. As a lawyer, Sainclair represents the hygienic social order which is rejected when Rouletabille refutes legal niceties in letting Ballmeyer escape.

Sainclair appears to play on his own role as legal reporter when foregrounding his task as narrator, stressing the neutrality of his account:

> Mon premier soin, dans toute cette affaire, sera d'être aussi simple que possible. Je n'ai point la prétention d'être un auteur. Qui dit: auteur, dit toujours un peu: romancier, et, Dieu merci, le mystère de la 'Chambre Jaune' est assez plein de tragique horreur réelle pour se passer de la littérature. Je ne suis et ne veux être qu'un fidèle rapporteur. Je dois rapporter l'évènement; je situe cet événement dans son cadre, voilà tout. (*M*, 34)
>
> [My first care in this narrative will be to remain as simple as possible. I do not pretend to be an author — for an author is always something of a novelist. The mystery of the yellow room is full enough, as it is, of real tragic horror to do without the aid of literature. I am, and only desire to be, a faithful reporter. I have to tell the story — I place it in its own frame — that is all.]

Sainclair protests too much; his repeated interventions draw attention to the vulnerability of the demarcations he sets out between the fictional and the factual, as in this self-contradictory example, which sets the bare recounting of facts against the notion of 'situe[r] cet événement dans son cadre,' a phrase which highlights the potential artistry involved. Similar contradiction is found in the opening passages of the novel, which see Sainclair maintaining that his role is merely to 'transcrire des faits' [transcribe the facts] while calling attention to literary intertextuality in his references to Poe, and subverting his claimed objectivity in the very first lines of the novel which announce that 'ce n'est pas sans une certaine émotion que je commence à raconter ici les aventures extraordinaires de Joseph Rouletabille' (*M*, 15) ('It is not without emotion that I begin to relate the extraordinary adventures of Joseph Rouletabille'). Sainclair's emphasis on the verbs *raconter*, *rapporter*, and *transcrire* suggests the apparent simplicity and also passivity of his account, setting up a practice of reportage which involves an orderly and fact-based mode of narration, even while indicating the impossibility of such a mode. His role as legal reporter is at odds with the energy of the alternative journalist, Rouletabille. The dynamism of the new breed of reporter is also epitomized by Fandor in the Fantômas series:

> Il n'incarnait nullement le type honni du journaliste qui ne réussit à obtenir les nouvelles qu'en lassant des questions [...] mais il représentait, au contraire, à merveille, le modèle du reporter qui, homme d'action, enquête et trouve la vérité par ses propres moyens. (*F*, 667)

> [He was a long way from the kind of journalist held in contempt, who could only gather news by asking endless exhausting questions [...] instead, he was an excellent example of that model of reporter who is a man of action, investigating and unearthing the truth using his own intiative.]

In Podalydès's film, Sainclair is no longer a lawyer, nor does the film borrow his point of view, although much of the humour is connected to his pratfalls. One of the most acclaimed sequences in the film sees Sainclair hiding in a grandfather clock in an attempt to witness the movements of Mathilde's attacker; the clock falls face down and he is forced to crawl along the landing — still encased in the clock — to reach help. Podalydès's Sainclair is a photographer, a figure whose static shots cannot compete with the moving sequences of cinematography evoked by the continuation of the rolling marble run; his profession is therefore an appropriate substitution for the defective reporter-narrator of the detective novel. If Sainclair is a bumbling photographer, then Rouletabille embodies the cinematic. In the text, Sainclair is not only a reporter who relies excessively on narrative, but also a flawed reader. His position is set out in the early stages of the novel, when he describes his initial engagement with the crime at Glandier. He first hears of the events of the yellow room when in bed, reading a report on the attempted murder in *Le Matin*; Rouletabille, already the mobile, engaged half of the journalistic duo, comes to interrupt him.

Not just a producer and disseminator of newspaper reports, then, Sainclair reads them, and uses the material in the articles he scans to reach his own erroneous conclusions as to the culprit. Rouletabille, in contrast, has (like Dupin in Poe's tales) read between the lines of the information supplied by the newspaper and encourages Sainclair to recognize likewise such an alternative mode of reading. He deduces that a reading of what lies on the surface, 'on ne laisse pas tant de traces derrière soi "quand elles sont l'expression de la vérité"' (*M*, 25) ('one does not leave so many traces behind *when they express the truth*'), must be abandoned in favour of depth and intuition. Thus the truth can be found in the newspapers, but only if one reads beyond and between the bare facts compiled by the *raconter*-driven reporters.

In employing the gullible bed-based newspaper reader as the willing but misguided interpreter of journalistic information, Leroux's text sends a message to its own readers; they should ignore the obvious and the linear in favour of the subtle and the fragmented. Thérenty describes, as above, the incorporation of the newspaper article in a literary work as a conscious reflection of the real as 'l'envers de la fiction' [the reverse side of fiction]. In Leroux's detective story, the reader is encouraged to read *à l'envers* in order to stand a chance of deciphering the mystery.

Such persistent meditation on the act of reading as encouraged by the newspapers is a constant motif in Maurice Leblanc's series featuring the arch-criminal Arsène Lupin. The narrator of the tales reveals himself, like the author, as a former reporter for the *Gil Blas*; the public is described as constantly tantalized, threatened, and tricked by the antics of Lupin, and the 'gentleman-cambrioleur' himself is in control of the fictional publication the *Écho de France*, submitting letters and publishing ultimatums to potential victims. The ubiquity of such newspaper excerpts and references heightens the renown and the fear associated with Lupin; in the narrative 'Arsène Lupin en Prison', the supposedly incarcerated Lupin writes a letter to the wealthy baron Cahorn announcing that he will turn up and collect a detailed list of valuables on a specified date. The baron is a 'lecteur assidu des journaux, au courant de tout ce qui se passait dans le monde en fait de vol et crime' [hardened reader of newspapers, on top of all that happened in the world by way of theft and crime] and 'n'ignorait rien des exploits de l'infernal cambrioleur' [knew all there was to know about the exploits of the infernal burglar].[32] The public are also invited to guess as to Lupin's whereabouts and disguises; the fictionalized newspapers suggest the boundaries between accepted knowledge and encouraged guesswork, as in a subheading in the *Grand Journal* in what is probably the best-known Lupin novel, *L'Aiguille creuse*: 'La Fin de l'histoire et le commencement des suppositions' [the End of the story and the beginning of suppositions].[33] The business of newspaper-reading as a public and often collective enterprise is foregrounded in these texts, as illustrated by the comic sequence in the Podalydès film of a train carriage full of passengers all reading the same account of the crime at the Château Glandier and gasping in unison. Yet the generalized nature of such reading is also frequently held up as fallible in these texts; it is possible to be, like the baron Cahorn, a 'lecteur assidu des journaux' and consider oneself well-informed, but to be nevertheless outwitted by the creative exploits of the figure whose voice resonates via the *Écho de France*. In the Arsène Lupin texts, the details which appear in the newspapers are carefully controlled by the notorious criminal, a plot motif which offers its own commentary on the nature of newspaper reportage; the master of disguise and deception chooses which 'truths' to reveal.

A straightforward reading of the recount of the crime is disparaged in these satirical representations of the reading public's thirst for narratives of crime. But the newspapers offer, if read carefully and in their entirety, the clues to piece together the mysteries set out in these texts. In order to prove that the key to the yellow room was in the possession of the would-be assassin some days before the attack, Rouletabille points to a personal advertisement in *L'Époque* newspaper, announcing the loss of the key, placed by Mathilde Stangerson, whose name appears in code: 'Il sera donné une forte récompense à la personne qui l'aura trouvée. Cette personne devra écrire, poste restante, au bureau 40, à cette adresse: M.A.T.H.S.N [...] Dans mon métier, il faut toujours lire les petites announces personnelles' (*M*, 82) ('A handsome reward will be given to the person who finds it. That individual should write, by way of general delivery, to PO Box 40, citing this address: M.A.T.H.S.N [...] "In my business, one should always read the 'personal' advertisements"'). This kind of insertion is itself an intertextual connection with earlier detective stories, such as *Le Dossier no. 113*, a tale by the early practitioner of crime fiction, Émile Gaboriau, referred to by Thérenty.[34] It shows the need to read not just for the plot when scanning the newspaper, but also to read the heterogeneous fragments — the bits and pieces sometimes disparaged as commercial or of limited public interest; this is a core message of Leroux's text. It is also, arguably, a reflection on wider reading practices, and the desirability of a heterogeneous corpus of literature which does not dismiss as inferior some texts or genres, such as Leroux's own popular fiction, but pieces the stories together in the aim of a more comprehensive understanding. The 'keys' to understanding can be found in the seemingly banal snippet about the loss of a key: 'on y découvre d'intrigues!... et des clefs d'intrigues!' (*M*, 82) ('Numberless intrigues are to be discovered there, and keys to intrigues').

Rouletabille's willingness to look beyond the main news stories and to work with fragmentation leads to a sense that Leroux's novels do not just, in the manner of crime fiction stories, incorporate two stories, that of the crime and its investigation, the *sujet* and the *fabula*. This text full of doubles, which deliberately echoes 'The Murders in the Rue Morgue', and sets two very different practitioners of journalism alongside one another,[35] also sets two contrasting epistemological practices in motion, privileging Rouletabille's Cartesian rationalism above the empiricism practised by the detective-criminal Larsan, who (like Sherlock Holmes) insists on the significance of physical clues.[36] This preference also extends to a form of communication which transcends ordinary language, as signalled by the fractured imprint of Mathilde Stangerson's name in the newspaper advertisement, which begins to spell out 'maths'. Damning the clarity of 'signes clairs'/Sainclair, Rouletabille privileges codes and the language of mathematics, as illustrated in *Le Parfum de la dame en noir*:

> Ignorant encore les principes de l'algèbre classique, il avait inventé pour son usage personnel une algèbre, faite de signes bizarres rappelant l'écriture cunéiforme, à l'aide de laquelle il marquait toutes les étapes de son raisonnement mathématique, et il était arrivé ainsi à inscrire des formules générales qu'il était le seul à comprendre [...]. Il appliquait à la vie quotidienne cette admirable faculté de raisonner.[37]

> [Never having studied algebra, he had invented a system of cuneiform signs for his own use, with which he set down the main points of his problems and so worked out a number of curious mathematical formulae, which he alone could understand [...]. He applied this admirable propensity for reasoning to everyday life.]

This alternative practice of writing, reading, and reasoning is closely connected with Rouletabille's insistence on alternative ways of seeing, which feature prominently in Leroux's novels, and lead him to use the optical clue of Larsan's pince-nez as the tool for overcoming the obstacles of sight and conventional linear reading, illustrated in a quotation which emphasizes the self-consciousness of *Le Mystère de la chambre jaune*:

> Ah! raisonner par le bon bout! [...] Je me trouve plus abject, plus bas dans l'échelle des intelligences que ces agents de la Sureté imaginés par les romanciers modernes, agents qui ont acquis leur méthode dans la lecture des romans d'Edgar Poe ou de Conan Doyle. Ah! agents littéraires... qui bâtissez des montagnes de stupidité avec un pas sur le sable, avec le dessin d'une main sur un mur! [...] Oui, oui, je le jure, les traces sensibles n'ont jamais été que mes servantes... Elles n'ont point été mes maîtresses... Elles n'ont point fait de moi cette chose monstrueuse, plus terrible qu'un homme sans yeux: un homme qui voit mal! (*M*, 119)

> [Ah, to 'think it out from the right end!' [...] I find myself even more absurd [...] than those detectives invented by modern novelists. Oh, you story-detectives, who erect mountains of nonsense out of one footprint on the sand or from an impression of a hand on the wall. [...] Yes, yes, obvious signs have never been anything to me but servants; they never were my masters. They never made me that monstrous thing, a thousand times worse than a blind man — a man who cannot see straight.]

To read the obvious, the 'traces sensibles' is to 'voit mal' — like the bumbling reporters seen in the works of Verne in the previous chapter.[38] Like Michel Strogoff, Rouletabille transcends ordinary recourse to the senses when coming up with solutions, a connection reinforced by the Russian setting of the later novels in Leroux's series. In *Rouletabille chez le Tsar*, the boy-detective's task is to read the apparently unreadable. Although flummoxed by the apparent incomprehensibility of Natacha's gaze — she is described half-way through the novel as sphinx-like, tasking Rouletabille's journalistic endeavour to render the world legible — in the closing interview with the Tsar, when Rouletabille exposes the truth, he maintains that he has been able to prove her innocence '*en regardant ses yeux... En l'observant quand elle se croyait seule, en épiant sur son beau visage les sentiments de terreur et les marques d'amour!*' [by looking at her eyes ... By watching her when she thought herself alone, by detecting the expressions of terror and love on her beautiful face].[39]

The upshot of this emphasis on Rouletabille's visual expertise, in contrast with Sainclair's blinkered view, has ramifications when considering the pair as journalists. Rouletabille is rarely seen to write; the reader is not granted access to any articles penned by him. Certain chapters are given over to his notebooks, but when he makes his findings public, he does so orally, rather than in writing — suggesting the triumph of the oral, as in the utopic vision of educative communication represented by Marc in Zola's *Vérité*. The resultant impression is that Rouletabille embodies a modern, roving-reporter style of journalism which transcends conventional practices of reading and writing, and is distinguished from Sainclair's careful, if misleading processes of narrative recounting. Pinson makes this point in relation to the celebration of reportage in late nineteenth-century novels: 'Non seulement la littérature s'efface-t-elle dans ces fictions, mais le reporter vit des aventures et ne s'arrête jamais pour les écrire, déplaçant cette pause de l'écriture hors du cadre de l'intrigue' [Not only does literature disappear in these stories, but the reporter thrives on adventure, without pausing to write down his experiences; the writing of them takes place outside the frame of the narrative].[40] The displacement of writing from the representation of journalism epitomized by *Le Mystère de la chambre jaune* is made clear in the dramatic courtroom scene at the end of the text, in which Rouletabille brandishes the letter he has written for the purposes of publication in *L'Époque* should he fail to return from his investigative mission into Larsan/Ballmeyer's background in America. The letter has become redundant, secondary to the theatrics of Rouletabille's oral declamation, which combines physical energy ('Rouletabille sautait par-dessus la balustrade' (*M*, 158) ('Rouletabille jumped over the balustrade')) with a 'voix éclatante' (*M*, 166) ('resounding voice'). His brand of journalism is mobile and playful (as exemplified by the rolling ball sequences in the Podalydès film), immediate and spoken. The duels between journalism and literature which characterize earlier nineteenth-century fictions have been replaced by literary representations of journalism which see writing itself as potentially obsolete. Like many junior reporters of the time, Rouletabille is not permitted to sign his real name, Joseph Joséphin, in the newspaper, an absence of orthography and identity ('ça n'est pas un nom, ça!' (*M*, 211) ('that is no name')) reinforced by the emptiness of the sobriquet itself, which cancels itself out through its echoes. The questioning of writing in Leroux's text is reflected in this absent signature.

The representation of journalism in Leroux's text celebrates modern reportage, championing investigation, courage, visual acuity, and clarity of expression over written forms. It also leads to the sense of there being a pastiche of literature and journalism alike, evoked through the metafictional dimension of the detective story. The inclusion of pages from Rouletabille's notebook in the various novels can be read as subversive. The very journalistic up-to-dateness of the boy-reporter's notations is recorded in a present tense which suggests implausibility. Rouletabille documents his every move, even when supposedly up a ladder: 'je retiens ma respiration; je lève et pose les pieds avec des précautions infinies. Soudain, un gros nuage, et une nouvelle averse. Chance' (*M*, 107) ('I hold my breath; I climb and position my feet with the utmost caution. Suddenly, a heavy cloud and a new downpour. What luck'). This subversion of plausibility has particular ramifications for a reading of the realism at work in these early popular crime novels. Compère suggests that Leroux 'met en question l'écriture elle-même' [questions writing itself]; discussing the exaggerated use of the notebook in *Rouletabille chez les bohemians*, he writes: 'ces notes sont parfois impossibles: Rouletabille se représente en train d'écrire alors que sa situation l'en empêche' [these notes are at times impossible; Rouletabille depicts himself writing even when his situation prevents him from doing so].[41]

The Real and the 'Fantomatic'

The incorporation of the figure of the journalist and of newspaper excerpts in the detective story offers particular insight into the hybridity of these texts, which combine the ingredients of the realist novel with a focus on the fantastical and the implausible. The nineteenth-century detective novel, as a 'témoin de son époque [...] donne à voir à la fois l'endroit et l'envers de la vie contemporaine' [a witness of the era [...] allows insight into both the surface and the underbelly of contemporary life].[42] The representation of crime in the texts reflects the fears associated with an increasingly urbanized society, but the resulting processes of detection in turn evoke a sense of optimism, a faith in scientific and technological progress. The focus on the urban, the emphasis placed on the tangibility and representational capacity of the object as a possible clue, the specificity of places and dates necessitated by the telling of the detective story — these are all part and parcel of the realist narrative, a verisimilitude which is reinforced by the inclusion of the investigative reporter and the practice of reading the news embedded in so many of the tales. Pinson suggests that the role of the reporter-character who will eventually appear in multiple generic forms — comic strip, popular novel, cinema — will be to 'interrog[er] désormais le réel et le monde moderne, ainsi que les grandes valeurs que sont la justice et la vérité' [interrogate the real and the modern world, along with the values of justice and truth].[43]

Detective novels interrogate the real by heightening the threat of reality — by focusing, for example, on corporeal threat — and yet often simultaneously disrupt that threat by encouraging a reading of the unreal or potentially fantasmagorical aspects of the crime. In his work on forms of paraliterature, such as crime fiction, Jean-Claude Vareille suggests that these texts in fact offer a compelling alternative to nineteenth-century realist narratives in their use of language:

> Le roman policier, considéré longtemps comme infra-littérature, laisse se concentrer en lui quelques parcelles du Langage Essentiel. La nuance en est exclue. Il travaille 'en gros' parce que, pour le goûter, il faut prendre le langage au pied de la lettre. Gaston Leroux ou Maurice Leblanc manient la pleine pâte. Non pas auteurs réalistes, copiant la réalité extérieure, auteurs archétypaux plutôt, suivant les impulsions latentes du sens, auteurs tout court (pas 'photographes') parce que n'obéissant qu'au seul langage et à l'imaginaire.[44]

> [The detective novel, long considered infra-literature, contains within it concentrated fragments of Essential Language. It does not allow for nuance. It functions 'in bold' because in order to experience it, language must be taken literally. Gaston Leroux and Maurice Leblanc mould the raw material. They are not realist authors, copying external reality, but rather archetypal authors, following the compulsions of meaning, authors plain and simple (and not 'photographers') because they obey only language and the imagination.]

Rouletabille's privileging of the language of mathematics can be seen as such a 'langage essentiel'. Goulet refers to the representation of Sainclair as a 'bespectacled photographer' in Podalydés's film, suggesting that this image is a nod to the fascination with optics in Leroux's novel; Sainclair's 'optical prosthetics identify him as "he who sees" '.⁴⁵ I would suggest, as mentioned above, that whether as photographer or as narrator, Sainclair is positioned in the text as the faulty 'see-er' whose vision is corrected by the alternative method of journalism and insight provided by Rouletabille. In offering this pair, Leroux not only offers two contrasting modes of reporting, but also sets the 'auteur réaliste', in Sainclair, alongside the 'auteur archétypal', Rouletabille, making a case for the celebration of popular fiction over and above the realist novel. As seen in Chapter One, texts such as those by Fenestrier mark the slide of realism into a form of mass cultural formula, epitomized too in discussions of English novels such as Gissing's *New Grub Street*. While offering frequent and comic nods to their own formulaic strategies, the novels of writers such as Leroux and Leblanc suggest their incorporation of, and leap beyond, strategies of a realism perceived as dated. They incorporate a keen sense of parody, a strategy outlined too by Kemp in his study of more recent French crime fiction: 'a genre that occasionally lurches unaided towards the borders of the ridiculous in its search for the baffling mystery and the unguessable solution'.⁴⁶ This section will explore the ways in which the representation of journalism in the detective novel emphasizes but ultimately subverts questions of realism.

The parallels between Leroux's journalistic exploits, when reporting from Russia on the outbreak of the first Russian revolution in 1905–06, and the 'adventures' of Rouletabille in the later novels in the series, lend verisimilitude to the fictional exploits, validating their somewhat extraordinary nature, though the literary style of journalism employed by Leroux continues to blur questions as to the objective nature of the 'news' he provides. Published on the front page of *Le Matin*, Leroux's detailed accounts set the scene and offer opinion on comparisons with French political upheaval rather than necessarily outlining major occurrences in the Russian civil war. The article dated 2 March 1906, which recounts Leroux's visit to the amiral Doubassof, one of the military leaders of the Russian empire who had authorized the repression of the nihilist revolt and so had found himself a target of revolutionary attacks, acts as the inspiration for Rouletabille's mission in *Rouletabille chez le Tsar*, when Rouletabille is sent to protect General Trebassof. Leroux's article dramatizes the visit in literary terms: 'Enfin, tentons l'aventure. Comme une flèche, le traîneau glisse aux rives de la Moika' [At last, let us attempt adventure. Like an arrow, the sled glides along the banks of the Moika].⁴⁷ As the journalism adopts literary characteristics, so the novels incorporate the qualities of reportage, demonstrating an obsession with dates and places and interspersing the narratives with interviews, witness statements, and maps, introducing a newspaper-like collage effect of voices and images, and reinforcing — albeit parodically so — Sainclair's insistence on evidentiary truth. *Le Parfum de la dame en noir* takes such 'evidence' to extremes in its insistence on maps to illustrate the apparently impenetrable enclosure of the château. The Fantômas novels, too, contain ingredients associated with reportage: not only snippets of the articles penned by Fandor, but alternating voices. Point of view and focus shift frequently between chapters, reflecting the method of paired composition adopted by Souvestre and Allain, and giving rise to disjointed journalistic collage techniques.

Such elements of reportage insist on the contemporary, realistic dimensions of the texts, while subverting those elements. These novels, which base their plots around the events of the popular *faits divers* of the era — as the excerpts from the newspaper articles in the opening chapter of Le Mystère de la chambre jaune make clear — employ journalistic echoes in order to root the texts in reality, yet the sensationalism also associated with such newspaper style simultaneously detracts from verisimilitude. The novels by Leroux, and by Souvestre and Allain, incorporate realism, sensationalism, and a pastiche of both such styles. David Walker sees such a paradoxical combination of the real and the sensational at work in these snippets of popular news.[48] Casta also highlights the conflict between the two worlds at work in the early detective novel, between a world of fantasy in which the criminal can 'passer pour mort et revenir incognito' [be taken for dead and then return incognito] and 'l'univers de plus en plus quadrillé, policé, des systèmes, des techniques et des sciences' [a world ever more mapped out by police, systems, techniques, and science].[49]

The testing of distinctions between truth and falsehood, verisimilitude and the implausible is clearly carried out in the crime serials of Leroux and Souvestre and Allain, as is made plain, for example, in the frequent references to the mystery of the Yellow Room — both in the novel and in the newspaper articles it cuts and pastes — as a potentially supernatural occurrence. One of the most compelling connections between these serials is the possibility that at the heart of each 'crime' novel lies a fundamental nothingness. These detective novels question narrative forms, including the embedded narratives of the newspaper reports they cite. The result is the implication that novels and newspapers alike are based around a void, and, as such, that the newspaper stories these texts pastiche are hyperinflations, puffs of smoke, exaggerated emptiness. Uri Eisenzweig argues that the detective story itself is a form of impossible narrative, insofar as:

> There is a structural incompatibility between a hypothetical unravelling of mystery and the coherence of the fictional narrative that claims to lead to such unravelling; between analytic logic and narrative linearity. If there is to be a mystery, it cannot be solved; if it is solved, it never really existed. And if it is solved, while it really existed, then no narrative could have been involved at all (in which case, the text in question would simply belong to a non-narrative genre, such as the riddle).[50]

Eisenzweig examines *Le Mystère de la chambre jaune*, finding that here, since the origin of the crime is to be found in Mathilde's mind, 'in the extremely elusive, fleeting reality of the non-conscious', then, as in Poe's 'Murders in the Rue Morgue', in which the answer to the crime also lies 'outside', in the discovery of the exotic and animalistic actions of the brutal orang-utan, 'One could say that no wrongdoing really takes place in either story, insofar, at least, as the mystery is concerned. Indeed, nothing happens [...] but for a displacement'.[51] Rouletabille's discovery that the solution to the mystery lies in the awareness that the intrusion perpetrated by Larsan-Ballmeyer actually took place at an earlier point in the day, and thus that the locked room drama in fact never properly existed, leads Christian Robin to describe Sainclair's *récit* as a 'livre sur rien' [book about nothing], a nothingness itself symbolized in the novel via the object of the Stangersons' scientific research, the investigation into the dissociation of matter.⁵²

In *Rouletabille chez le Tsar*, much of the concluding drama of the text centres around an absent centre. Finding that no poison exists in the glasses taken from the scene of the apparent poisoning of Général Trébassof and Matrena Petrovna, but only in the expulsions induced by the emetic administered to them immediately afterwards, Rouletabille concludes that '*Logiquement, ce seul cas serait celui où personne n'aurait été empoisonné, c'est à dire où personne n'aurait pris de poison!* [...] *la présence de ce poison ne prouve que sa présence et nullement le crime!*' (M, 588) ('Logically, the only outcome must be one in which no one has been poisoned, i.e. in which no one has taken poison [...] the presence of this poison proves nothing but its presence, and not the crime!'). The source of the 'crime' lies in enigma or emptiness. This is true too of Leblanc's crime novel *L'Aiguille creuse* [The Hollow Needle], in which emptiness is written into the title of the text. To get to the point of the mystery, the 'aiguille', is also to negotiate hollowness — encapsulated too in the code which keeps cropping up in the text and is composed of dots and lines. This is a novel which is intertextual in its frequent references to the burgeoning detective genre and in the way it centres its mystery on a historical enigma supposedly recorded and understood by centuries of French monarchs. Yet it also keeps deferring the revelation of meaning, as in a scene when the sleuth Beautrelet thinks he has cracked the code and races to the Musée Carnavalet to find what he imagines to be the source of the mystery, Marie Antoinette's *Book of Hours*, only to find that the Parisian press has got there before him, and that journalists and investigator alike have been trumped by Lupin himself, who has ripped out the appropriate page. The hollow needle is actualized in the closing scenes when Beautrelet tracks Lupin down to the needle-shaped column of rock off the Normandy coast which is full of stolen treasures. Here, then, riches and emptiness are juxtaposed; the possibility of a plenitude of meaning is ironically encapsulated in the image of a hollowed-out rock, evoking the persistent fluctuation between detection and vacuity evoked by these crime stories.

The oscillation between the idea of the crime as real or imaginary is writ large in the Fantômas series, and centres on the representation of the journalist character Fandor. In the opening chapter of the series, the young Charles Rambert shocks one of the guests at the marquise de Langrune's dinner party by proclaiming his fascination with renowned criminals such as Fantômas, as well as with the criminal-turned detective Vidocq. President Bonnet — who has been broadcasting the name of Fantômas as a source of terror — remarks disapprovingly to Rambert:

> Vous confondez la légende, l'histoire, vous mettriez dans un même sac les assassins et les policiers, vous ne faites point de distinction entre le bien et le mal... au besoin vous érigeriez sur le même piédestal les héros du crime et les héros de la défense sociale. (*F*, 12)

> [You confuse fact and fiction, put assassins and police officers into the same category, you do not distinguish between good and evil ... you put the heroes of crime and the heroes who defend society on the same pedestal.]

Bonnet blames papers for corrupting the young, observing to the Abbé Sicot that 'voilà [...] le produit de ces éducations modernes, de l'état d'esprit que crée la presse, même la littérature, dans la jeunesse contemporaine!' (*F*, 12) ('I give you [...] the product of the modern education system, the state of mind forged by the press, even by literature, amongst the young today'). The Abbé takes the week's newspapers to bed in order to read the political stories, indicating that the differing generations are interested in different types of article — the youth in crime and the *faits-divers*, and the stalwarts of the nineteenth century in more traditional opinion pieces.

As suggested by Bonnet's claim that Rambert confuses 'la légende, l'histoire', one of the recurring questions in the Fantômas series is whether Fantômas exists, or whether he is a figment of the imagination, in particular the imagination of Inspector Juve and his soon-to-be protégé, Fandor. The magistrate who will suspect Rambert of the murder of the marquise de Langrune refers to Fantômas as 'une plaisanterie de Palais et de couloir d'instruction... Fantômas n'existe pas!' (*F*, 64) ('a legal fiction, a lawyer's joke. Fantomas has no existence in fact!'). This ambiguity has an important link with the role of the newspapers in the novels. As Juve's friend and sidekick, Rambert-Fandor is tasked with publicizing the threat of Fantômas in Parisian society. There remains the possibility that Fantômas is a creation of Juve, and, via Juve and Fandor, of the newspapers in turn: he is a mythical sensation whose function is to sell copy. Again, this idea is evoked in the opening chapter. The novel opens with the following often-quoted snippets of unattributed dialogue:

> — Fantômas.
> — Vous dites?
> — Je dis... Fantômas.
> — Cela signifie quoi?
> — Rien... et tout!
> — Pourtant, qu'est-ce que c'est?
> — Personne... mais cependant quelqu'un!
> — Enfin, que fait-il ce quelqu'un?
> — Il fait peur!!! (*F*, 5)
>
> [— Fantômas
> — What did you say?
> — I said... Fantômas
> — And what does that mean?
> — Nothing... and everything!
> — But what is it?
> — Nobody... and yet it is somebody!
> — And what does the somebody do?
> — Spreads terror!]

These anonymous voices suggest both the ethereality and the corporeality of Fantômas. That the voices are unattributed suggests, as Emma Bielecki notes, that they are meant to represent public opinion, the myth of Fantômas which is broadcast everywhere.[53] The newspaper for which Rambert-Fandor will end up working, *La Capitale*, has been drawing attention to the figure of Fantômas, by publishing an interview with Juve, attributing the recent disappearance of Lord Beltham to

Fantômas. There is the implication that the papers are responsible for creating the myth of Fantômas as voiced by the opening unnamed characters. As surrogate father-figure to Fandor later in the text and the series, Juve is in a sense 'fathering' newspaper stories.

At the end of the first chapter, Rambert-Fandor, captivated by the stories of Fantômas, goes to bed dreaming of the discussion earlier in the evening:

> Charles Rambert imaginait des scènes sinistres et dramatiques de crimes et d'assassinats, il cherchait à combiner des intrigues, à percer des mystères, prodigieusement intéressé, curieux, désireux de savoir! S'il assoupissait par instant, l'image de Fantômas se précisait dans son esprit, variant pourtant sans cesse; tantôt il voyait un colosse à la face bestiale, aux épaules musclées; tantôt un être pâle, maigre, aux yeux étranges et brillants; tantôt une forme indécise, un fantôme... Fantômas! (F, 14)

> [In imagination Charles Rambert saw all manner of sinister and dramatic scenes, crimes and murders: hugely interested, intensely curious, craving for knowledge, he was ever trying to concoct plots and unravel mysteries. If for an instant he dozed off, the image of Fantômas took shape in his mind, but never twice the same: sometimes he saw a colossal figure with a bestial face and muscular shoulders; sometimes a wan, thin creature, with strange and piercing eyes; sometimes a vague form, a phantom — Fantômas!]

The chapter plays with the notion that the figure of Fantômas looms large in the imagination of the future journalist; the reporter 'dreams' the criminal. From the outset, the Fantômas novels manipulate the concepts of literature, imagination, and reality — as here, when Fandor's dreams merge with 'reality' in the form of the faint but ambiguous sounds (creaks, a breath) which highlight the murder taking place. Rambert-Fandor's defence to President Bonnet earlier in the chapter when speaking admiringly of the criminal Fantômas is that 'c'est l'histoire, c'est l'activité, c'est la réalité!' (F, 12) ('But it is life, sir; it is history, it is the real thing!'). Newspapers feature heavily in this process of intermingling fact and fiction, in an opening chapter which sees the products of the journalist's dreams become the plot of the novel and of later series, as Fandor anticipates the many disguises of the elusive Fantômas. When Inspector Juve comes up with a new name for the erstwhile Charles Rambert, he deliberately selects an echo of the first syllable of Fantômas. The criminal and the journalistic investigator, documenter of the real and creation of imaginative excess, are linked by the *fan*tasmagorical connections between their invented names. Robin Walz notes the similarity in the names, but also suggests that 'Fandor' could be read as an appropriate name for Inspector Juve's golden boy, 'Fan d'or'.[54]

The blurring which takes place between reporter and criminal is highlighted by the early stages of the plot of this first Fantômas instalment, in that it is the period of time when Rambert lies in the Langrune mansion dreaming of terror which leads to suspicion of his culpability in the murder itself. His whereabouts at the time of the murder are assumed ambiguous, and indeed, he has been in a no man's land, between reality and imagination. As Rambert 'creates' the criminal in his lively imagination, so he also creates the window of opportunity when it is assumed that he may himself have turned criminal. Later, as Juve proves unable to pin any crime on Fantômas, neither can he definitively prove Rambert's innocence; both criminal and proof of the dream of the criminal remain indefinable. Robin Woods notes the recurring connections between criminal and detective in murder mysteries:

> In order for the crime story to exist, the criminal must do so as well and he must exist within the narrative — though separate from the story's characters, he must touch their lives, must create a danger to the community [...] [he] must be physically present but morally absent [...]. It is the detective who creates the link between the criminal and society.[55]

The detective in genre fiction is often seen as a figure separate from the community, a figure who stands between the criminal and society 'and prevents the innocent from being infected by crime, but he himself is infected as a result'.[56] Connections between detective and criminal are manipulated too in Leroux's Rouletabille series, in which Rouletabille finds he is the estranged son of Larsan-Ballmeyer. It is the detective who, in vocalizing and explaining the crime at the denouement of the tale, acts as the mouthpiece of the villain in articulating his crime. The space, then, occupied by the reporter-characters such as Rouletabille and Fandor-Rambert is a crucial one: their social fluidity/mobility ensures that they assume a position, like the detective, somewhere between the criminal and the rest of society. This in-between state is seen clearly in the first Fantômas novel as Rambert, under suspicion of murder, takes up his place as reporter-detective, having been ejected from society 'proper'. And if the detective, in Woods's analysis, is 'infected' by crime through proximity to it, then this is doubly true of the journalist, and in particular the journalist-detective, who not only explains the crime, but broadcasts it to the public, disseminating crime much more widely than the detective who unravels the solution before a select group of characters.

Jean-Claude Vareille's discussion of *paralittérature* finds that popular novels such as the Fantômas series are structured around oppositions such as interdiction versus transgression, law versus crime, the quotidian versus the exceptional, the categorical versus the ludic.[57] Paradox can be seen too in the popular novel's representation of the world of journalism. The contradictions discussed by Vareille — such as the oscillation between law and order — are openly evoked in the texts themselves, which articulate the contemporary critiques levelled at the newspapers. Sainclair, in *Le Mystère de la chambre jaune*, observes that 'des esprits moroses [...] répliquent qu'à force de parler des crimes, la presse finit par les inspirer' (*M*, 23) ('Captious persons [...] contend that by devoting columns to crime, the Press finally inspires it'). This is in contrast to his own opinion that the publicizing of crime in the press is a form of weapon against illegal activity. In the Souvestre and Allain novels, Fandor acknowledges police distrust of journalistic activity when, having been transported in a locked trunk to an unknown location, he comes across the dead body of the industrialist Thomery, and muses on the suspicion that will be levelled at him: 'la police, qui patauge dans ses recherches et n'aboutit à rien, serait trop heureuse de faire d'une pierre deux coups, de supprimer un journaliste et de découvrir un coupable!' (*F*, 842) ('the police, who are floundering in their search and getting nowhere, will be only too delighted to kill two birds with one stone — to suppress a journalist and discover a criminal!'). For the police, journalist and criminal are virtually synonymous. Through the muddled genealogies featured in these novels whereby criminals beget journalists, the press is depicted as an instrument of order and a propagator of crime, at one and the same time.

Journalism is placed on trial in the fourth Fantômas novel, *L'Agent secret*. At the beginning of this text, the soldier Vinson approaches Fandor with a story about espionage in the military, and how he has been bribed to turn traitor. Fandor relinquishes his chance of taking a holiday in order to try and save Vinson's life and expose the threat to the state. However, he ultimately fails at both endeavours, suggesting that the attempt at documenting such a crisis represented by Fandor is always liable to be transcended both by the control exerted by Juve and the power that lies with Fantômas. In *L'Agent secret*, Fantômas articulates a vision of his own supremacy:

> Je suis Fantômas!... Je suis celui que le monde entier recherche, que nul n'a jamais vu, que nul ne peut reconnaître! Je suis le Crime! Je suis la Nuit! Je n'ai pas de visage, pour personne, parce que la nuit, parce que le crime n'ont point de visage!... Je suis la puissance illimitée. (F, 1202)

> [I am Fantomas!... I am he for whom the entire world is searching, whom none has ever seen, whom none can recognise... I am Crime incarnated! I am Night! No human ever sees my face, because Crime and Night are featureless! I am illimitable Power!]

This text suggests ways in which the press, rather than being seen as democratic, is associated with an inflation of speculation and rumour which threatens the economic stability of the state, as rumours abound following the death of a military captain and the loss of a crucial document. Focus falls on the fragility of the nation, under threat of treason as military secrets are leaked to the Germans, and destabilized by the social and financial insecurity that stems from fallacious press reports on the crisis. It illustrates the way in which the Fantômas novels, set in the years immediately prior to the First World War and representing a world fixated on escalating crime rates and resultant threat, reflect, magnify, and yet also displace the anxiety associated with such an apparently brittle society:

> Created on the eve of the First World War, Fantômas is a superlative criminal, a monster whose crimes perhaps, and their consumption by avid readers, are symptomatic of how in its representation, imagined evil defuses concern with real social and political problems, yet simultaneously foreshadows greater monstrosities to come.[58]

Fantômas incarnates and displaces terror at the same time. Absurd, excessive, and spectral, he acts as a locus for contemporary anxiety surrounding crime and yet dissipates that anxiety through his fantasmagorical representation. Fandor's role as a reporter is to remind the reader that these texts are rooted in the everyday urban world, and to signal — as in Fandor's persistence in seeking to expose the spying ring in the fourth book of the series — that real concerns threaten society beyond the fictional terror of Fantômas. Yet Fandor's role is also to create, dream, and herald the existence of Fantômas, the symbolic displacement of those real concerns, for his mass readership. The amplification of the fictional at the expense of the real is brought into particularly sharp relief in *La Fille de Fantômas*, which sees Fandor incarcerated in a South African mental asylum — considered all the more mad for his claims to be the reporter Fandor — while in alternating scenes Fantômas rises, Dracula-like, from a tomb in a London cemetery. The 'real' incarnated by the reporter is considered crazy while the *fantomâtic*, the product of fantasy, triumphs.

Souvestre and Allain amplify the fantasmagorical 'puissance illimité' associated with Fantômas by subverting the expectations established in early crime fiction, that there will be an unfolding of the steps and motivations leading up to the crime and an unmasking of the criminal. As Walz observes, in these novels, 'there is no whodunit. Fantômas done it, every time'.[59] The thirty-two novels in the series see Fantômas always culpable; the only real surprise centres around the identity of the disguise and the increasingly implausible methods of escape. Walz highlights the significance of the Fantômas cycle for the surrealists. His study of pulp surrealism is a focus on mass print culture, which broadens the social and cultural basis of the 'perceptual revolution' associated with modernism by showing how popular novels and newspaper sensationalism can also be seen to generate modernist sensibilities, in addition to the 'high' cultural realms of art, literature, and philosophy. I would suggest that in the Fantômas novels, the pulp fiction and newspaper sensationalism analyzed separately by Walz are seen to blur, through the incorporation of the character of Fandor and his articles. The cover image of this book, Juan Gris's cubist still-life, 'Fantômas (Pipe and Newspaper)', depicts the daily paper *Le Journal*, known for its crime reporting, alongside a copy of a Fantômas novel on a cafe table.[60] Through juxtaposition, Gris draws attention to the similarities between the two examples of printed matter: the 'fictional' and the 'real' sharing space on the table as they both share the attention of the reader/café haunter; both participate in daily life yet dramatize that life; both adopt a collage style aptly illustrated by the cubist montage. The fragmentations of plot in the Fantômas novels can of course be attributed quite directly to the influence of newspapers and the demand for the serialized feuilletons. Although Souvestre and Allain's serial was published in Fayard's 'popular book' series rather than in the papers, it derived inspiration from the episodic construction of the feuilleton, from the pressure placed on the pair to deliver a four-hundred page novel once a month, from the practice of writing alternating chapters, as referred to above, as well as from the background of the writers, who came to crime fiction having worked as journalists for *L'Auto* and the racing magazine *Le Poids* respectively.

Vicki Callahan, in her discussion of the Fantômas films, describes the director Feuillade's work as 'fantastic realism', drawing on Rosemary Jackson's description of the fantastic in literature: 'the salient quality of the fantastic is its alterity, that is to say, its relationship of inversion to realist texts'.[61] An examination of the way that the newspaper is deployed in the third Fantômas novel illustrates the way that the fantastical qualities of the text evoke such inversion of the real. *Le Mort qui tue* opens with an article penned by Fandor. As in *Le Mystère de la chambre jaune*, this excerpt from *La Capitale* is used to narrate the details of the crime which will form the object of the initial investigation in the novel. This opening chapter indicates the real/surreal dichotomy which surrounds the incorporation of journalism in the text. It is marked by hyperbole, evidenced by its frequent use of exclamation marks, its detailed storytelling, the overstated qualifications accorded to the figures referred to, and the title afforded to article and chapter alike, 'Le Drame de la rue Norvins', drawing together newspaper and novel. The article opens with a celebration of the journalistic investigation as compared with that of the police: 'À la Sureté, on observe le mutisme le plus absolu sur cette affaire étrange. Toutefois, l'enquête personnelle à laquelle nous nous sommes livrés jette un peu de lumière sur ce qu'on appelle déjà: Le Drame de la rue Norvins' (*F*, 643) ('At the police station, there is complete silence regarding this strange affair. Nevertheless, the personal enquiry to which we have committed ourselves sheds some light on what has already been called The Drama in the rue Norvins'). Far from silent, this verbose piece nevertheless announces a clarity and structure which is subverted by the chaotic patterning of the novel itself. It is full of geographical and temporal detail, with echoes of a police investigation in the way it incorporates witness statements, seeming to imitate the voices of the witnesses themselves. Structuring itself into clear temporal sections with subheadings, Fandor makes frequent reference to the confusion and wild fictionalized conjecture of the police and the surrounding bystanders, but proceeds to extract clarity and logic from the events: 'les motifs ayant déterminé l'arrestation du peintre Dollon demeuraient obscurs. Nous avons cru devoir les éclairer [...] Deux faits apparaissent suspects' (*F*, 651–52) ('The reasons surrounding the arrest of the painter Dollon remain unclear. We believe we have uncovered them. Two facts appear particularly suspect').

The structure and positioning of this article suggest that Fandor is given the responsibility of rendering the case legible, here at the expense of the police, whose competence and suppositions (in the absence of Juve, who is believed dead) are thrown into doubt by the journalist's analysis of the evidence. Such legibility is amplified by the later scene in which Fandor attempts to track Dollon's traces through the Palais de Justice, studying a map of the building and making his way to the rooftops where he has an expansive view of the city:

> Jérôme Fandor apercevait toutes les lueurs scintillantes de Paris, comme fort distantes de lui, séparé qu'il en était de tous côtés par la masse grise des toits d'abord, puis par le vide, puis encore par la tache sombre que faisaient de chaque côté du Palais de justice les deux bras de la Seine. (*F*, 689)

> [Jérôme Fandor could make out all the dazzling lights of Paris, a long way away from him, surrounded as he was by the grey sprawl of rooftops, by the drop below him, and by the dark shape of the winding Seine, which could be made out on either side of the Palace of Justice.]

Clare Gorrara connects the flâneur, the journalist, and the detective in their shared role decoding the new Haussmanized city, and here Fandor can be seen mapping out both the central lobbies of the justice system and the panorama of Paris itself, though notably he is also distracted by the seeming unreality of the city: 'la vue était féerique' (F, 689) ('the view was fairy-tale like').⁶² Callahan reminds the reader that the famous film poster depicting Fantômas straddling Paris in menacing fashion positions the criminal in particularly significant fashion directly above the roofs of the Palais de Justice.⁶³ In the third novel, here too is Fandor straddling this symbolic building as if in a position of power and suggesting the dominance of the values of clarity and justice he embodies.

That power is subverted almost immediately, though, as Fandor, having pursued the traces of Dollon's body down to the sewers beneath the Palais de Justice, is kicked unceremoniously into the 'eaux noirâtres de la Seine' (F, 697) ('inky waters of the Seine'). No sooner then has Fandor, in his capacity as reporter-detective, gained clarity and transcended the city's mysteries, than his lantern flickers and he finds himself submerged in the river he was dominating just a few paragraphs previously, swallowed up in inky water rather than employing ink to achieve legibility. It turns out to be Juve who boots Fandor into the Seine, again emphasizing his superiority over the journalist who has a tendency to get himself into scrapes, but also suggesting that, as later in the novel, Fandor's discoveries and conclusions are often drowned by Juve's insistence on the murkiness that is Fantômas being the answer to all mysteries. This scene, which sees Fandor's triumph end in comic peril, is microcosmic of the narrative as a whole, which submerges the initial intelligibility of Fandor's opening article in swerves of plot and leaps of perspective and temporality. It is never entirely clear what has happened to Dollon, for all Fandor's investigations. His assumption is that the body must have been hacked to pieces so that it might be carried away more easily by the murderer(s): this is a fragmentation which is echoed by the piecemeal reading of the novel itself. It also symbolizes a difference between the Fantômas novels and those of Leroux. For all the pastiche at work in *Le Mystère de la chambre jaune* and its sequels, the texts work towards an unveiling and a completion, epitomized by the information given about Rouletabille's rise to prominence as a reporter, when he finds the missing foot of a dismembered corpse. In *Le Mort qui tue*, Dollon's corpse, like the body of the narrative in the Souvestre and Allain texts, is dissected and dispersed, never to be put back together. Walz notes that:

> By expanding the notion of what constitutes the enigma at the heart of the mystery, Fantômas is closely related to the detective genre: Fantômas is a mystery in the sense of being a récit impossible, an impossible story of factual indecision, paradoxes, detours and displaced identities.⁶⁴

Such detours are exemplified by the shift from the concluding line of Fandor's opening article, 'décidément, demain nous promet une journée pleine de péripéties' (F, 654) ('tomorrow certainly promises to be an eventful day'), and the chapter which follows immediately afterwards, which begins 'Deux jours avant le sinistre et mystérieux drame' [Two days before the sinister and mysterious drama], rather than following up on forward-moving 'promise' evoked by Fandor. The narrative lurches backwards rather than progressing logically forwards, providing further 'noirâtre' blurriness — this second chapter ends with a cryptic reference to the baronne de Vibray, who 'écrivait, écrivait, sans relâche' (F, 662) ('wrote, and wrote, relentlessly'). Exemplifying the lack of linearity and narrative closure characteristic of the proto-surrealist nature of the series, as well as of the manner of its journalistic style composition, this third text has also been examined for the way it disrupts the scientific and numerical strategies employed for classifying criminals at the end of the nineteenth century.[65] In *Le Mort qui tue*, systems of Bertillonage reliant on identifying criminals through anthropometry, and the new methods of fingerprinting are subverted by the elusiveness of Fantômas, made particularly obvious in this text through the pair of gloves fashioned out of the skin of the dead Dollon's hands, which leave perplexing traces throughout the text. This is also the text which features journalism most prominently as Fandor comes to the fore in the supposed absence of Juve, and employs the newspaper article as a means of explaining the crime. There are parallels between the subversion of Fandor's reportage in the novel and that of the scientific means used to determine identity: both act as contemporary representational strategies attempting to enact legibility and control, structuring and labelling, clarifying and categorizing.

Nanette Fornabai's discussion of the rejection of anthropometrics in the Fantômas cycle sees it as emblematic of the wider parody of earlier detective fiction offered by the novels:

> In its refusal to render 'insignificant details significant', its denial of the micropolitics of narrative closure, and its deflection of both socio-biological and ethical condemnations of criminality, the Fantômas detective series articulates a counter-measure to the disciplinarity of narrative surveillance and knowledge production prevalent in earlier detective fiction.[66]

The newspaper sits ambiguously within this discussion. Like the Bertillonage system, and like earlier examples of detective fiction — including Leroux's texts — it is associated with 'narrative surveillance' and 'knowledge production'. As shown by the disruption of the order of Fandor's article within *Le Mort qui tue*, Souvestre and Allain's series privileges fantastical disorder over structure and legibility, undermining such surveillance and knowledge. The excesses of the newspaper, in terms of both melodramatic style and in terms of mass production rates, also have much in common with the Fantômas novels. Fornabai sees the spiralling mass-production methods associated with the series as part of the challenge represented by the cultural politics of the novels, as they reject 'repressively quantitative science':

> Fantômas articulates resistance to the representational strategies of the numerical classification of criminals as means of social and 'scientific' control [...] while compelling the ongoing modern capitalist cycle of mass literary production and consumption. By virtue of its serialized form, which binds narrative production to consumerist reproduction, the Fantômas novels also subvert the dominant generic conventions of earlier detective fiction, such as criminal and narrative resolution. [...] Fantômas represents a particular, yet particularly fundamental, site of modern French culture, in which scientific culture is challenged through a narratological complicity with the modes of mass cultural commodification.[67]

The newspapers are bound up with modes of mass culture through their appeal to the increasingly literate lower social classes and through their huge circulation rates. As such, the representation of the newspaper in the Fantômas texts is twofold: it articulates a structure and legibility which is resisted in the text, as the figure of fantasy that is Fantômas persistently eludes Fandor. Yet it is also simultaneously complicit with the 'fantomatic' aspects of the novels which evoke excess, mass cultural consumption, and melodrama.

The Banalization of Crime

In the Fantômas novels, attention is directed away from any 'real' causes of social ill towards the cartoon-like exaggeration or emptiness that is Fantômas, with the effect that the fictional displaces the real. A further feature of these popular crime novels is the way that they enable the real, in the form of authentic or fictionalized newspaper reports, to sit alongside the fantastical. The result can be seen as a banalization of the violence associated with the original crime. Martin Priestman discusses such an effect in Poe's detective stories, making a specific connection between the representation of newspapers in Poe's texts and the resultant 'scandal of indifference'.[68] Horrific grisliness is accompanied, in 'The Murders in the Rue Morgue', by banality. Dupin and his narrator-friend learn of the deaths of Madame L'Espanaye and her daughter via a report in the *Gazette des Tribunaux*, which narrates the macabre nature of the case in its own combination of scandalized horror and distanced observation: 'a search was made in the chimney, and (horrible to relate!) the corpse of the daughter, head downward, was dragged therefrom; it having been thus forced up the narrow aperture for a considerable distance'.[69] Outrage is downplayed thanks to the narrative structure which opts to convey details of the crime through a facsimile of popular reportage. Priestman describes the effect of this incorporation of reportage into a narrative which, through its excesses, highlights its own fictionality:

> In the two primary texts of the genre, then, popular crime reportage impinges on 'literature' in a new way. [...] Allowed to take on itself the full burden of conveying the unpleasant details, it is sharply divorced from the 'literary' part of the text by a kind of collage technique which enables a fascination with 'real' crime to coexist with a fantasy of infallible detection which is clearly the reverse of realistic [...] detective fiction [...] invites the real, or realistically squalid, crime into the house of fiction in a schizophrenic formula which then comes to constitute a new kind of scandal within the walls of literature itself: the scandal of indifference.[70]

The scandal of indifference registered within Poe's early examples of the detective story and directly connected with the increased reporting of crime in the nineteenth-century newspaper is reflected and magnified in the crime serials of the turn of the century. Poe's dissection of the newspaper form in 'The Murders in the Rue Morgue' and particularly in 'The Mystery of Marie Roget' is, as seen above, consciously echoed in *Le Mystère de la chambre jaune*. The excerpts from newspaper reports recording the crime at Glandier, introduced by Sainclair in the opening chapter of Leroux's novel, are deliberately chosen, I would argue, for their oppositional styles, and for the way in which they exemplify emotional excess and emotional sparsity. The first indication as to what has happened to Mathilde Stangerson is provided by a laconic excerpt from Le Temps:

> Un crime affreux vient d'être commis au Glandier, sur la lisière de la forêt de Sainte-Geneviève, au-dessus d'Épinay-sur-Orge, chez le professeur Stangerson. Cette nuit, pendant que le maître travaillait dans son laboratoire, on a tenté d'assassiner Mlle Stangerson, qui reposait dans une chambre attenante à ce laboratoire. Les médecins ne répondent pas de la vie de Mlle Stangerson. (M, 16)

> [A frightful crime has been committed at the Glandier, on the border of the forest of Sainte-Geneviève, above Epinay-sur-Orge, at the house of Professor Stangerson. On that night, while the master was working in his laboratory, an attempt was made to assassinate Mademoiselle Stangerson, who was sleeping in a chamber adjoining this laboratory. The doctors do not answer for the life of Mlle Stangerson.]

Despite the tension of its concluding remark, this account is characterized by its sparseness and emotional detachment. It privileges precise geographical annotation over any description of the crime itself or the injuries sustained by Mathilde. A much more fulsome account is provided by the lengthy article in Le Matin, the publication for which Leroux himself was a reporter. The economical precision of the article in Le Temps is juxtaposed with the detailed and melodramatic tones of that found in Le Matin, which allows emotion to colour its account through the personal testimony provided by old Jacques, the caretaker. The Le Matin excerpt is given the headline 'Un crime surnaturel' [A Supernatural Crime], accentuating not only the inexplicable nature of the mystery surrounding the yellow room, but also suggesting that the solution lies in the realm beyond reality. The article concludes in hyperbolic style: 'La "Chambre Jaune", la Bête du Bon Dieu, la mère Agenoux, le diable, sainte-Geneviève, "le père Jacques", voilà un crime bien embrouillé, qu'un coup de pioche dans les murs nous débrouillera demain; espérons-le, du moins, pour la raison humaine' (M, 20–21) ('The Yellow Room, the Bête du Bon Dieu, Mother Agenoux, the Devil, Saint-Geneviève, Daddy Jacques — here is a well-entangled crime which the stroke of a pickaxe in the wall may well disentangle for us tomorrow. Let us hope that, for the sake of our human reason').

From the opening of Le Mystère de la chambre jaune, then, emotion, excess, the macabre, and the speculative are consciously set against the restrained, the distanced, the euphemistic, and the obsessively factual. As part of the *mise-en-abyme* of modern reportage featured in Leroux's novels via Sainclair's observations and newspaper snippets, there falls a focus on hyperbole versus journalistic detachment, in ways which, as this chapter will conclude, anticipate postmodernist discussions of the banalizing effect of the media.

Indifference can clearly also be found in the Fantômas texts in which disturbingly unmotivated acts of gruesome violence are narrated deploying a quasi-cinematic construction of quick-cut techniques:

> Souvestre and Allain utilize this series of quick juxtapositions to distance the reader from the action in a kind of mechanical, nonemotional manner, prefiguring the cinema's reliance on the sensory immediacy of sound and

image to portray violence. At the same time, numerous scenes are compacted into 'the space of a few seconds', anticipating the elongation of time through montage.[71]

This is true, for instance, of the scene in the sewers in *Le Mort qui tue*, when Fandor discovers what he presumes to be the remains of Dollon's body: the image of the rats devouring the flesh is vividly painted as 'une boue gluante, visqueuse, une boue qui était encore toute saturée de sang coagulé!' (*F*, 696) ('a gluey, viscous mud, a mud already completely drenched in congealed blood'). Although nauseating enough to make his stomach rise at the sight, such grisliness is prefaced by the pleasure taken by the journalist on finding a story ('Quel reportage [...] quel reportage!'), while the narrative zooms away from the close-up of the blood to focus on Fandor's speculations as to how he might get out of the sewer before being thrust into the Seine. Such techniques are journalistic as well as cinematic: the laconic reporting of violence and its ramifications, presented in snippet-form without space for emotional engagement, is not dissimilar from the effect of reading a list of disconnected *faits-divers*. The piecemeal appearance of the newspaper is also connected with the gruesomeness of murder in playful fashion in *Le Mystère de la chambre jaune*, when Sainclair narrates the way in which Rouletabille came to prominence as a reporter by finding the missing foot of the dismembered corpse on the rue Oberkampf, which so delights the editor of *L'Époque*. Rouletabille puns that this 'femme coupée en morceaux' [dismembered woman] will provide inspiration for the fragmented visuality of the newspaper: 'avec ce pied [...] je ferai un article de tête' (*M*, 22) ('with this foot, I will make a header'); the foot will not only lead to the spectacle in print of the write-up of the story, but is displayed in the 'morgue-vitrine' of the paper. The paper is composed of and advertised using the corporeal brutality of crime.

Elsewhere in Leroux's novels, the representation of blood and gore is almost comically deflected, even in scenes most closely associated with terror and terrorism. In *Rouletabille chez le Tsar*, the intrepid reporter watches as a pair of suicide bombers detonate their devices in the general's villa; there is remarkably little human cost, save for the complete evaporation of the bombers themselves. Compère notes of Leroux:

> Comme au Grand Guignol, le pathétique est obtenu par une exagération dans l'horreur. Mais par un subtil usage des mots et par l'atténuation qu'apporte souvent l'humour, Leroux introduit une distance qui rend l'horreur supportable au lecteur en lui rappelant que tout cela est spectacle et illusion.[72]
>
> [As in the Grand-Guignol, pathos is achieved through an exaggerated level of horror. But through his subtle use of language and the reductive effect brought about by humour, Leroux introduces a sense of distance which renders the horror bearable for the reader, reminding her that all is spectacle and illusion.]

This suggestion that Leroux purposefully incorporates and exaggerates the level of horror associated with crime and threat in his texts, but simultaneously reduces that threat by rendering it theatrical and unreal, evokes affinities with a growing awareness of the effects created by media reporting of real-life disaster, effects which will be taken up by postmodern theorists. As Compère suggests, the plots of these detective novels reveal a debt to the Grand Guignol theatre, which became popular in the 1890s. Spectators came to the Théâtre du Grand Guignol in order to have their feelings aroused through the visual representation of terror and horror; it was a theatre of physical violence where blood flowed by the bucketful and the horror was so intense that audiences would flee the auditorium or lose consciousness.[73] Philip Brophy's term 'horrality' — an amalgamation of horror, textuality, hilarity, and morality — employed to describe the effects of the horror film genre, also helps to summarize the jarring combinations of humour and horror at work in Leroux, and Souvestre and Allain.[74]

Leroux's contemporary, Joseph Conrad, describes the seemingly inevitable way in which newspaper reportage of the horrors of the war that Leroux himself was sent to cover as a journalist, the Russo-Japanese conflict, could never do justice to the volume of deaths or the scale of the suffering. The public were becoming accustomed to reading about multiple casualties and so were, in turn, becoming inured to the numbing incapacity to visualize such violence. No matter how adept the journalist, maintains Conrad, the battles taking place in Manchuria can only be glimpsed 'through the veil of inadequate words', of both books and newspapers, and thus appear 'cold, silent and colorless'.[75] The printing of statistics — 'tens of thousands of decaying bodies [...] other tens of thousands of maimed bodies groaning in ditches' — inhibits the comprehension of the reality being described; Conrad employs elongated phrases and repetition as if impressing on his own readership the failure of language to evoke fully such scenes. The result, in Conrad's essay, is a critique of the distance caused by newspaper reportage, the very aim of which is ostensibly to inform and to evoke emotion:

> There must be something subtly noxious for the brain in the composition of newspaper ink; or else it is that the large page, the columns of words, the leaded headings, exalt the mind into a state of feverish credulity. The printed voice of the press makes a sort of still uproar, taking from men both the power to reflect and the faculty of genuine feeling, leaving them only the artificially created need of having something exciting to talk about.[76]

This paradoxical relationship with the media, which combines such an attachment to the ink and the layout of the paper as to induce 'feverish credulity' while simultaneously engendering a distance which impairs 'the faculty of genuine feeling', is brought about too in the representations and echoes of reportage seen, for example, in the collaging of newspaper reports in the opening chapter of Leroux's novel. *Le Mystère de la chambre jaune* offers critical evaluation of both the emotional reductiveness and excess of the excerpts from the press, and of the 'credulity' incarnated by Sainclair. At the same time the text, like the Fantômas series, encourages just such a combination of credulity and emotional detachment, as these detective novels pastiche and endorse newspaper discourse.

Rubery sees Conrad as 'one of the earliest authors to challenge the press for its psychological authority — indeed, its emergence as a mass media'.[77] Rubery cites Conrad's memorable expression on the influence of the press in *The Secret Agent*, when the death of Winnie is reduced to the impersonal headline 'Suicide of Lady Passenger from a Cross-Channel Boat', recording 'the mystery of a human brain pulsating wrongfully to the rhythm of journalistic phrases'.[78] Discussing *Heart of Darkness* (1898) as a text which reflects and critiques the fact that the voice of journalism can be seen as a disembodied, abstracted voice, Rubery sees Marlow in the novel as suspicious of this '"atmosphereless, perspectiveless" — in short, disembodied — voice of journalism'.[79] The disembodiment of the journalistic voice can be seen as humorously represented in Leroux's representation of a reporter who makes his career out of a dismemberment.

As referenced in the earlier chapter on Zola, Benjamin's essay 'The Storyteller' suggests the interference of newspaper information and style in people's ability to communicate. Conrad focuses on the dislocation of feeling caused by press representation of events. Such early twentieth-century conceptions of the alienating capacities of the media are emphasized by postmodern theorists, in particular Baudrillard, whose analyses can be seen as *'critical tools* intended to challenge media processes and our understanding and acceptance of them'.[80] Baudrillard's critical appraisal of the functioning of the media offers insight into the focus on newspaper dissemination of crime found in the novels discussed in this chapter.

By foregrounding journalistic reports of crime via their characterization and their collages, novels such as those by Leroux and Souvestre and Allain reflect on their readers' epistemological relationship to the world. They prefigure Baudrillard's discussion of the non-event, for example. In his evaluation of media reports on the events of May 1968, Baudrillard focuses on the way that the mediated, simulacral coverage of the riots could be seen to take over from the ground-level events themselves.[81] For Baudrillard, all events become 'pseudo-events by virtue of their instant passage into the media and their semiotic transformation and modelling'.[82] Echoing the observations of Conrad and Benjamin on alienation and desensitization, electronic media is seen to 'reinforce [...] us in our exile and immure [...] us in our indifference'.[83] Baudrillard's conclusion is that television news 'inculcates indifference, distance, unconditional apathy'.[84] Although Baudrillard's comments are focused primarily on television and the impact of the visual effects of electronic media, his arguments have relevance for the representation of the media in the detective novels under examination here. The arrival of Rouletabille at the courtroom in the closing sequences of *Le Mystère de la chambre jaune* is itself a media event. Extra trains have had to be put on to transport interested members of the public, their frenzied curiosity piqued by the articles in *L'Époque*, from Paris to the court at Versailles; brawls break out between those who accept the disguised detective Larsan's view of events, and those who espouse Rouletabille's theory; they buy into a cult of celebrity associated with the crime: 'Le numéro de *L'Époque* à la main, les Larsan et les Rouletabille se disputèrent, se chamaillèrent' (M, 155) ('With copies of the Epoque in their hands, the 'Larsans' and the 'Rouletabilles' argued'). The narrative makes plain, though, that these spectators have no real interest in the judicial implications of the trial; they are little concerned with the fate of the wrongly accused Darzac, but are enthused by their own individual responses to the possible solution to the mystery ('la fièvre de ces gens venait moins de ce qu'on allait peut-être condemner un innocent que de l'intérêt qu'ils portaient à leur proper compréhension du mystère de la "Chambre Jaune"' (*M*, 155) ('the excitement was due less to the fact that an innocent man was in danger of a wrongful conviction than to the interest taken in their own ideas as to the Mystery of the Yellow Room')). Thus although *L'Époque* has brought together a crowd and elicited mass interest in the events at Glandier, it has also engendered division, a sense of non-communication and a rejection of sympathy, anticipating Baudrillard's early theories of the media evidenced in his first book, *The System of Objects* (1968): 'the mass media are anti-mediatory and intransitive. They fabricate non-communication — this is what characterizes them'.[85]

For Baudrillard, 'television becomes the strategic site of the event', a displacement of the real in favour of attention on the 'encephalogram of [the] dead form'.[86] As discussed above, the sense of the illusory superseding the real is foregrounded in *Le Mystère de la chambre jaune* via the focus on the yellow room itself and the displacement of the attack on Mathilde Stangerson; the event under investigation, and the one reported on in the pages of the newspapers, is in fact the re-enactment in a dream by Mathilde of the violent break-in that took place earlier. Such dislocations are then verbally re-enacted by Rouletabille in the courtroom. This series of displacements, which already highlights Baudrillard's 'horizon of the virtual', is further highlighted in the Podalydès film.[87] Here, the text's diminishment of the judicial implications of the trial scene is enhanced by the staging of the denouement at the Château de Glandier, rather than in a courtroom. The shift away from the interior of a court setting to the exterior of the yellow room itself enables the theatricality of Rouletabille's performance of the events of the original crime to emerge more fully. The ludic effects of the film bring out the sense of a loss of aura, as in Benjamin's discussion of the work of art in an age of 'mechanical reproduction', referenced also in evaluation of the texts which echo *Bel-Ami* in Chapter One. The reproduction of the fictionalized attempted murder in the yellow room is reproduced in pastiched newspaper clippings, in the journalist's dramatization of events in the courtroom finale, and in the later film 'reconstitutions' of Leroux's text.

On the one hand, the representations of the newspaper journalist in these fin-de-siècle and early twentieth-century texts celebrate the dynamism of modern reportage; they critique written journalism as a kind of passive transcription of facts as embodied by the fastidious Sainclair, and also call attention to a lazy form of reading which accepts such 'recounts'. They offer energized and vibrant journalistic characters in contrast with the opportunistic newspaper contributors and the exhausted would-be literary hacks of earlier nineteenth-century fiction; in so doing, they evoke new practices of writing and reporting which suggest a self-conscious celebration of their own resistance to conventional literary narratives. At the same time, they playfully cast doubt on the business of journalism, whether through the implicit critical evaluation of the newspaper excerpts included in the Leroux text, or through the purposeful connections established between the elusive and threatening Fantômas and the journalist Fandor whose task is to try to pin down and uncover such threat. They extol modern reportage while questioning the style, layout, and — as this last section of the chapter has argued — the emotional affect of journalistic writing. These are texts which are both critical of and complicit in the promotion of events to media events; the texts by Leroux arguably more purposefully critical than the speedily-produced texts churned out by Souvestre and Allain. They are fascinating in the gaze they turn on media output and in the generation of that output, anticipating later twentieth-century critique of the culture industry.

Notes to Chapter 4

1. All English translations of *Fantomas* are taken from Marcel Allain and Pierre Souvestre, *Fantomas*, anonymous translation, introduction by John Ashbery (London: Picador, 1987).
2. All English translations of *Le Mystère de la chambre jaune* are taken from *The Mystery of the Yellow Chamber*, anonymous translation, introduction by Mark Valentine (Ware: Wordsworth Editions, 2010).
3. Dennis Porter, *The Pursuit of Crime: Art and Ideology in Detective Fiction* (New Haven, CT: Yale University Press, 1981), p. 152.
4. Elsa de Lavergne, *La Naissance du roman policier français: du Second Empire à la première guerre mondiale* (Paris: Classiques Garnier, 2009), pp. 133–34.
5. Ibid., p. 136.
6. For an account of the affair and media coverage of it, see Aaron Freundscheuch, *The Courtesan and the Gigolo: The Murders in the Rue Montaigne and the Dark Side of Empire in Nineteenth-Century Paris* (Stanford, CA: Stanford University Press, 2017).
7. Pinson, *L'Imaginaire médiatique*, p. 206.
8. Dominique Kalifa and Margaret Jean Flynn, 'Criminal Investigators at the Fin de Siècle', in *Crime Fictions*, ed. by Andrea Goulet and Susanna Lee, special issue of *Yale French Studies*, 108 (2005), 36–47 (p. 44).
9. Lavergne, *La Naissance du roman policier français*, p. 161.
10. Kalifa and Flynn, 'Criminal Investigators at the Fin de Siècle', pp. 45–46.
11. Anissa Bellefqih, *La Lecture des Aventures d'Arsène Lupin* (Paris: L'Harmattan, 2010), p. 106.
12. Kalifa and Flynn, 'Criminal Investigators at the Fin de Siècle', p. 45.
13. Fortuné du Boisgobey, *Cornaline la dompteuse* (Paris: E. Plon, 1887), p. 195.
14. Pinson, *L'Imaginaire médiatique*, p. 206.
15. Guillaume Apollinaire, *Que faire?* (Paris: Nouvelle Édition, 1950), originally published, with Henry Desnar, in *Le Matin*, January 1900.
16. Gaston Leroux, *Rouletabille chez le Tsar*, in *Les Aventures extraordinaires de Rouletabille, reporter*, 2 vols (Paris: Laffont, 1988–91), I, 576 & 578.
17. Pinson, *L'imaginaire médiatique*, p. 214.
18. Kalifa, *L'Encre et le sang*, p. 100.
19. Ibid., p. 103
20. Thérenty, *La Littérature au quotidien*, p. 76.
21. Edgar Allan Poe, 'The Mystery of Marie Rogêt', in *Selected Tales* (Oxford: Oxford University Press, 2008), pp. 149–92 (p. 162).
22. See Porter, *The Pursuit of Crime*, p. 152.
23. A. J. Sweeney, 'Locked Rooms: Detective Fiction, Narrative Theory and Self-Reflexivity', in *The Cunning Craft: Original Essays on Detective Fiction and Contemporary Literary Theory*, ed. by Ronald Walker and June Frazer (Macomb: Western Illinois University Press, 1990), pp. 1–15 (p. 3).
24. Simon Kemp, *Defective Inspectors: Crime Fiction Pastiche in Late Twentieth-Century French Literature* (Oxford: Legenda, 2006), p. 19
25. Sweeney, 'Locked Rooms', p. 2.
26. Daniel Compère, 'Une écriture romanesque: le reportage', *Europe*, special issue on Gaston Leroux, 626–27 (1981), pp. 38–45 (p. 45).

27. Bruno Podalydès, dir., *Le Mystère de la chambre jaune*, DVD (2003), 1:21:44.
28. Pinson, *L'Imaginaire médiatique*, p. 212.
29. Thérenty, 'Le Journal dans le roman au XIXè siècle ou l'icône renversée', p. 30.
30. Isabelle Casta, *Étude sur Le Mystère de la chambre jaune et Le Parfum de la dame en noir* (Paris: Ellipses, 2007), p. 32.
31. Christian Robin, 'Le Vrai Mystère de la chambre jaune', in *La Fiction policière*, special issue of *Europe*, 571–72 (1976), 71–91 (pp. 76–77).
32. Maurice Leblanc, *Arsène Lupin: gentleman-cambrioleur* (Paris: Archipoche, 2015), p. 25.
33. Maurice Leblanc, *L'Aiguille creuse* (Paris: Larousse, 2012), p. 44.
34. Thérenty, 'Le Journal dans le roman du XIXè siècle', p. 30.
35. The dualism of the text is noted by Robin, 'Le Vrai Mystère de la chambre jaune': 'tout dans ce roman est affaire de dissimulation, ou d'imitation' [everything in this novel relates to dissimulation or to imitation] (p. 82).
36. See Sita A. Schutt, 'French Crime Fiction', in *The Cambridge Companion to Crime Fiction*, ed. by Martin Priestman (Cambridge: Cambridge University Press, 2006), pp. 59–76 (p. 69).
37. Gaston Leroux, *Le Parfum de la dame en noir*, in *Les Aventures extraordiniares de Rouletabille, reporter*, 2 vols (Paris : Laffont, 1988–91), I, 213.
38. The detective story is frequently associated with an emphasis on the visual, as in D. A. Miller's study of the genre, which pinpoints the lynx-eyed Lecoq in Gaboriau's series of novels as exemplifying 'panoptical narration' (*The Novel and the Police* (Berkeley: University of California Press, 1988), p. 24). See too Tom Gunning, 'Lynx-Eyed Detectives and Shadow Bandits: Visuality and Eclipse in French Detective Stories and Films Before WWI', in *Crime Fictions*, ed. by Andrea Goulet and Susanna Lee, special issue of *Yale French Studies*, 108 (2005), 74–88. Andrea Goulet connects the mystery of the yellow room with late nineteenth-century physiological analysis of the 'yellow spot' which could impede a person's vision ('The Yellow Spot: Ocular Pathology and Empirical Method in Gaston Leroux's *Le Mystère de la Chambre Jaune*', *SubStance*, 107 (34:2) (2005), 27–46 (p. 33).
39. Leroux, *Rouletabille chez le Tsar*, p. 585 (my emphasis).
40. Pinson, *L'Imaginaire médiatique*, p. 215
41. Compère, 'Une écriture romanesque: le reportage', p. 44.
42. Lavergne, *Le Roman policier*, p. 22.
43. Pinson, *L'Imaginaire médiatique*, p. 187.
44. Jean-Claude Vareille, *Filatures: itinéraire à travers les cycles de Lupin et Rouletabille* (Grenoble: Presses universitaires de Grenoble, 1980), p. 33.
45. Goulet, 'The Yellow Spot', p. 27.
46. Kemp, *Defective Inspectors*, p. 29.
47. Gaston Leroux, 'Précautions: chez L'Amiral Doubassof', *Le Matin*, 2 March 1906.
48. 'The fait divers often arises, indeed, along that curious spectrum where truth, plausibility, belief, rumour and falsehood mingle and are confused. In the miscellany of current affairs that the media rain down on the public the distinctions are frequently blurred: one of the functions of the fait divers is actually to test such distinctions. And it is precisely because it is located in a zone where the facts challenge verisimilitude, and thus do not necessarily command credence, that the elements in play generate doubt as to their stable place in the signifying circuit', David Walker, *Outrage and Insight: Modern French Writers and the 'fait divers'* (Oxford: Berg, 1995), p. 20.
49. Casta, *Étude sur Le mystère de la chambre jaune*, p. 6.
50. Uri Eisenzweig, 'Madness and the Colonies: French and Anglo-Saxon Versions of the Mysterious Origins of Crime', *Esprit créateur*, 26.2 (1986), 3–14 (p. 3).
51. Ibid., p. 11.
52. Robin, 'Le Vrai Mystère de la chambre jaune', p. 76.
53. Emma Bielecki, 'Fantômas's Shifting Identities: From Books to Screen', *Studies in French Cinema*, 13.1 (2013), 3–15 (p. 6).
54. Robin Walz, *Pulp Surrealism: Insolent Popular Culture in Early Twentieth-Century Paris* (Berkeley: University of California Press, 2000), p. 56.

55. Robin Woods, 'The Emergence of the Detective', in *The Cunning Craft*, ed. by Walker and Frazer, pp. 15–24, p. 17.
56. Ibid., p. 18.
57. Jean-Claude Vareille, *L'Homme masqué: le justicier et le détective* (Lyon: Presses universitaires de Lyon, 1989), pp. 32–33.
58. Schutt, 'French Crime Fiction', p. 72. See too José B. Monleòn, *A Specter is Haunting Europe* (Princeton, NJ: Princeton University Press, 1990), p. 139: 'the fears and uncertainties, the monsters of a material and social reality, were neither existential abstractions nor expressions of some sort of human (psychological) attributes. Or, if they were, they were also much more. As social production, the fantastic articulated apprehensions that were deeply attached to the specific characteristics of capitalist society [...]. On the one hand, the fantastic "reflected" very real threats; on the other, it created a space in which those threats could be transformed into "supernaturalism" and monstrosity, thus helping to reshape the philosophical premises that sustained the fantastic and effectively reorient the course of social evolution'.
59. Walz, *Pulp Surrealism*, p. 57.
60. For the image see <http://www.fantomas-lives.com/fanto5.htm> [accessed 3 November 2016].
61. Vicki Callahan, *Zones of Anxiety: Movement, Musidora and the Crime Serials of Louis Feuillade* (Detroit, MI: Wayne State University Press, 2005), p. 19. Rosemary Jackson's discussion of fantastic realism is as follows: 'The fantastic is predicated on the category of the "real" and it introduces areas which can be conceptualised only by negative terms according to the category of nineteenth-century realism: thus, the impossible, the un-real, the nameless, formless, shapeless, un-known, in-visible. What can be termed a "bourgeois" category of the real is under attack. It is this negative relationality which constitutes the meaning of the modern fantastic' (*The Literature of Subversion* (London: Routledge, 2008), p. 26.)
62. Claire Gorrara, *French Crime Fiction* (Cardiff: University of Wales Press, 2009), p. 20.
63. Callahan, *Zones of Anxiety*, p. 31: 'This poster was seen as a direct affront to public order partly, no doubt, for its attractive and indeed glamorous display of a popular fictional criminal'.
64. Walz, *Pulp Surrealism*, p. 58
65. Walz connects the 'meandering storyline, which continually branches off in various directions and decenters the action through innumerable loose ends' with the nineteenth-century feuilleton, and its fragmented and episodic construction, a product of the fact that writers were under pressure to produce copy to deadlines, as were Souvestre and Allain (*Pulp Surrealism*, p. 11).
66. Nanette Fornabai, 'Criminal Factors: Fantomas, Anthropometrics, and the Numerical Fictions of Modern Criminal Identity', in *Crime Fictions*, ed. by Andrea Goulet and Susanna Lee, special issue of *Yale French Studies*, 108 (2005) 60–71 (p. 68). See too Bielecki, 'Fantômas's Shifting Identities'.
67. Fornabai, 'Criminal Factors', p. 69.
68. Martin Priestman, *Detective Fiction and Literature: The Figure on the Carpet* (London: Macmillan, 1991), p. 6.
69. Edgar Allan Poe, 'The Murders in the Rue Morgue', in *Selected Tales*, pp. 92–122 (p. 100).
70. Priestman, *Detective Fiction and Literature*, p. 6.
71. Walz, *Pulp Surrealism*, p. 68.
72. Compère, 'Une écriture romanesque', p. 41.
73. See Richard Hand and Michael Wilson, *Grand Guignol: The French Theatre of Horror* (Exeter: University of Exeter Press, 2002), p. 12.
74. Philip Brophy, 'Horrality: The Textuality of the Contemporary Horror Film', reprinted in *The Horror Reader*, ed. by Ken Gelder (London: Routledge, 2000), pp. 276–84.
75. Joseph Conrad, 'Autocracy and War', *North American Review*, 181.584 (July 1905), 33–55 (p. 33).
76. Conrad, 'Autocracy and War', p. 38.
77. Rubery, *The Novelty of Newspapers*, p. 142.
78. Conrad, *The Secret Agent*, p. 283.
79. Rubery, *The Novelty of Newspapers*, p. 152.
80. William Merrin, *Baudrillard and the Media* (Cambridge: Polity Press, 2005), p. 64.

81. Jean Baudrillard, 'Requiem pour les media', *Utopie* (4 October 1971), 35–51.
82. Merrin, *Baudrillard and the Media*, p. 65.
83. Baudrillard, *The Illusion of the End*, p. 58.
84. Ibid., p. 61.
85. Baudrillard, *The System of Objects,* p. 169.
86. Baudrillard, *The Illusion of the End,* p. 56.
87. 'Nothing is now news if it does not pass through the horizon of the virtual', Baudrillard, *The Illusion of the End,* p. 55.

CHAPTER 5

The Woman Journalist: Reportage, Romance, *Écriture féminine*

As seen in Chapter One, Fenestrier's book, *La Vie des frelons*, is the model of a *roman de journalisme* which laments the pollution of the literary sphere by the corrupt and vapid practices of journalism, and suggests the terminal decline of the novel. It was published in 1908. In April of that year, the writer Lucie Delarue-Mardrus wrote in the inaugural literary column of the women's magazine *Femina* of her wonder at the enduring power of the book. She claimed that not only were books still of lasting value but that far from declining, they were more than ever a social necessity.[1] Rachel Mesch's study of the role and influence of the two popular women's magazines of the first decade of the twentieth century, *Femina* and *Vie heureuse*, makes a case for the role of these publications in ensuring the supremacy of books, arguing that the literary columns of the magazine reflected and encouraged the ongoing fruitfulness of literature — and in particular the increasing numbers of novels published by women in the early 1900s.[2] This period saw the flourishing of publications both by and for women, both journalism and fiction: not only the magazines discussed by Mesch, but also the entirely female-staffed, feminist campaigning newspaper *La Fronde* and the works of a 'great blossoming of new women writers' such as Marcelle Tinayre, Camille Pert, and Colette Yver.[3] This chapter will consider the representation of the female journalist in such texts — in particular in three novels: Tinayre's *La Rebelle*,[4] Camille Pert's *Leur égale*[5] and the Margueritte brothers' *Femmes nouvelles*,[6] as well as in a 1912 play by Eugène Brieux, *La Femme seule*.[7] Unlike texts such as that of Fenestrier, these turn-of-the-century novels which depict women writing for, editing, or in the process of creating publications aimed at a female market are not necessarily preoccupied with the threat of the press. Instead they reflect both the potential power and the limitations of such media outlets for engaging and motivating their women readers, and for stimulating changing attitudes towards marriage and employment.

Discussion of these texts will raise questions such as how the characters' status as journalists reflects their political and feminist motivations and how they interrogate gender norms via the representation of fictionalized publications. As the works both critique and imitate the growing magazine culture and the cultivation of a female readership, this metatextual awareness of journalistic practice will also inform the novels' structures. Particular focus will fall on the conflict between the social realism of the novels' backdrops and the idealized romantic fates they envisage for their would-be 'rebellious' protagonists. Employing Rachel Blau DuPlessis's term, these writers and journalists can be considered as practising a form of 'writing beyond the ending', challenging conventional novelistic denouements for female characters. A closing section of the chapter will return to discussion of *Bel-Ami*, centring on Madeleine Forester, George Duroy's ghostwriter, as a prototype figure for the New Woman and the female journalist of the early twentieth century.

There has been much critical discussion of the New Woman.[8] Women began, in the 1890s and early 1900s in France, to take up careers in medicine, law, journalism, and teaching. Associated with a relatively small-scale French feminist movement — sometimes erroneously, since some of those referred to as 'new women' did not necessarily embrace political feminism — these primarily urban, middle-class French women caused a backlash amongst male writers, playwrights, and journalist because they were challenging conventional gender norms. Already a stock figure celebrated or, more commonly, lampooned in the British and American press, the New Woman was feared when she appeared to have arrived in France, and filled the pages of publications such as *La Revue* and *La Presse*. Caricatured as a dowdy figure in bloomers, cycling off to work or to feminist conventions while abandoning her children and leaving her husband to tend the home and make jam, she was reportedly both ubiquitous and insidious.[9] The very figure of the New Woman is thus constructed by and exaggeratedly ridiculed by the contemporary press: 'the femme nouvelle was perceived as rejecting home and family for a career, disrupting the position of the female as the anchor of bourgeois domesticity ... [she was] envisioned as a gargantuan "amazone" or an emaciated, frockcoated "hommesse"'.[10] In both the traditional press and in the newly established publications aimed at women — the newspaper *La Fronde* and the women's magazines discussed by Rachel Mesch — 'la femme emancipée' [the emancipated woman] is revealed as a preoccupation, playing sports, driving cars, travelling abroad. Pinson suggests that the figure of the New Woman led newspapers and magazines alike to consider their own strategies of representation.[11]

Mesch's *Having It All* makes clear the centrality of the women's press in creating and critiquing the figure of the New Woman. These early women's magazines are seen as subtly emancipatory.[12] Although they rejected overtly politicized discussions of 'feminism' and retained traditional emphases on domesticity, fashion, and beauty, *Femina* and *Vie heureuse* also encouraged their potentially conservative readers to take on board a more progressive image of turn-of-the-century women. The magazines presented a palatable view of women in public life, such as women writers, offering their readers 'iconographic evidence of a brand-new role model to emulate: a woman who could balance — with impeccable agility — tradition and innovation, femininity and feminism, work and family'.[13] In framing women working at their desks with attractive art nouveau-style surrounds, in detailing the feminine accoutrements to be found in these working environments and in photographing the writers with their children, Mesch sees the magazines evoke the quietly subversive message that women can indeed 'have it all': work and marriage, children and careers, femininity and modernity. They thus attempt to tame the fears surrounding the emergence of the New Woman.

Women's magazines use their content, typography, and marketing to reposition women in society, although as will be discussed later in reference to Marcelle Tinayre's *La Rebelle*, the relative conservatism and airbrushing strategies of such publications can also be called into question. Pinson suggests that the roles played by men and women producing newspapers and magazines at the turn of the century are seen to change. Although male writers, such as Jules Claretie, are still asked to write front-page *chroniques* for the magazines, women are increasingly taking on reportage as a genre. Pinson notes that 'les rôles traditionnels s'inversent: l'homme fabule tandis que la femme reporter fouille le réel' [the traditional roles were being overturned: the man writing stories while the female reporter was delving into the real world].[14] This trend can be detected in the novels to be discussed. Male lovers are seen still fantasizing about fictionalized romantic endings while the women they pursue reject earlier narrative codes, engaging instead with the reality of their situations. In this chapter, the role played by the publications represented will be considered in order to see whether these fictional newspapers and magazines are seen to 'fouill[ent] le réel' or whether, instead, they contribute to the persistence of fairy-tale motifs surrounding the love-plot. Alongside the emergence of *Femina* and *Vie heureuse*, the turn-of-the-century years were witness to the publication of *La Fronde*, the all-female staffed paper founded by Marguerite Durand, which ran from December 1897 to October 1903. The aims of the newspaper made clear that it set out to challenge the masculine discourse of the press of the time, in keeping with the rebellious connotations of its title. The content it included over its four-page spread was mixed, incorporating accounts of parliamentary debates, feminist perspectives (as in the column 'Notes d'une frondeuse', written by the journalist Séverine), and romantic short stories; similarly, the publication addressed itself to the concerns of working women on moderate incomes, such as primary school teachers, while including advertisements for products aimed at an aspirational upper-middle-class market.[15] Roberts notes that the 'frondeuses bore a special exemplary link in public imagination with the challenge to traditional femininity'; she also suggests that Durand incarnated a particularly French brand of 'new womanhood', feminizing what was seen as a somewhat scandalous Anglo-American model. The term 'femme moderne', which becomes the title of the publication launched in Camille Pert's *Leur égale*, is arguably a less radical French version of the New Woman.[16] Allison, though, argues that 'the feminist slant on affairs' of *La Fronde* 'was compromised inasmuch as Durand, for all her entrepreneurial skills and intellectual acumen, went to great lengths to exercise her feminine charms, over which much ink has been spilled, to avoid the stigma suffered by earlier, more militant feminists'.[17] The attempt to balance feminism and femininity, incarnated in the persona of Durand, is a recurrent trend in the magazines and novels examined in this chapter.

The titles of texts such as *La Rebelle*, *Leur égale*, and *Femmes nouvelles*, along with Eugène Brieux's play, *La Femme seule*, make the potentially radical status of their heroines manifest. Self-consciously reflecting on their roles as would-be (or at times 'would-not-be', given the contradictions facing these female characters) 'new women', the protagonists — Josanne Valentin, Thérèse Bolsenn, Minna Herkaert — consider themselves at various points in the narrative as socially rebellious, even as social outsiders, prepared to position themselves as independent, and as the equals of men. Tinayre's novel recounts the despair of its protagonist Josanne when she is abandoned by her lover Maurice, leaving her with a young son. Widowed following the death of her invalid husband, Josanne eventually finds happiness with Noël Delysle, author of *Les Travailleuses*, a book which Josanne discusses in the pages of *Monde féminin* [The Feminine World], the magazine for which she writes. Noël has to decide whether it is possible for him to live by the beliefs he sets out in his book: that working women have the right to be treated as equals, and that, in turn, the terms of the conjugal relationship will have to change in order to keep up with women's increased independence. The plot narrates Noël's attempts to overcome his prejudice towards Josanne's former lover and her child. Against this backdrop, the world of the magazine acts variously as a practical source of income for Josanne, as the very means by which she and Noël get to know each other, as a facility for introducing her to other women's situations, and as a frustrating and at times frivolous publication at odds with her own understanding of the contradictions and compromises facing her.

Camille Pert's *Leur égale* sees its heroine, Thérèse, enter into a relationship with the foppish Adrien; it details their frequent rendez-vous at a Paris apartment before cataloguing the decline of their affair as Adrien opts for marriage and stability with the more conventional Germaine. Thérèse, who works in the family publishing house, has plans to launch a magazine for women, which will promote her own ideas about women's independence. By the end of the novel, this project is about to become a reality. Brieux's *La Femme seule* focuses on the plight of a young woman left without a dowry as a result of her adopted father's gambling debts; taken on as an employee of a newly-founded magazine, *Femme libre* [The Free Woman], Thérèse's experiences at this 'journal du féminisme élégant et sage' [sensible and elegant feminist publication] reflect both feminine opportunity and masculine domination (*FS*, 53). Obliged to quit her job when subject to the predatory demands of the magazine's editor, the final act of the play sees Thérèse establish a woman's workshop at her uncle's factory and entering into controversy when the male employees perceive the women's capacity for work as a threat. In her closing speech, Thérèse predicts a new war between the sexes. Little critical discussion has referred to Paul and Victor Margueritte's *Femmes nouvelles*, a novel which begins with a conversation on a train between its central female protagonist, Hélène Dugast, and the newspaper editor Minna Herkaërt. The text recounts Hélène's frequently thwarted attempts to reconcile the lessons she has learned from Minna, who acts as a role model of a successful career woman, with a search for a romance plot which will satisfy her. In each of these novels the magazine or newspaper woven into the plot is an outlet for articulating the plight and problems of working women. Yet each publication is compromised in some way by the contradictory social demands confronting fin-de-siècle women. In turn, the plots of the novels themselves reveal such conflict, oscillating between fairy tale and realism. This chapter will consider the gender identity problematized by the female journalist protagonists of these texts, as they attempt to negotiate their position in relation to work and marriage. It will also investigate the textual identity of the works themselves, as they self-consciously reflect on their own plot outcomes, and their relationship to the journalistic publications they represent.

Gender Identity

Hybridity

On a desk in the offices of the magazine *Monde féminin*, featured in Tinayre's *La Rebelle*, there is a glimpse of the conflicts at work in the representation of gender and career in these texts featuring women journalists. A mimosa branch in a crystal vase sits in between 'l'encrier et le pot à colle' [the inkstand and the gluepot] (*LR*, 38). The femininity and fertility evoked by the mimosa branch and its falling pollen are juxtaposed with the tools required for journalism; feminism and independent income are set alongside reminders of the literary romance plot, evoked by floral decorations. Such contradiction is inescapable for the female employees of these turn-of-the-century publications aimed at women. In writing for *Monde féminin* Josanne Valentin is paid to construct an early twentieth-century version of femininity; indeed, an early description of the magazine indicates the ways in which it reinforces stereotypical and glamorous narratives of gender:

> Dans le *Monde féminin*, toutes les femmes étaient jolies; presque toutes étaient vertueuses; tous les hommes étaient 'talentueux'; les plus rosses avaient des 'âmes d'enfants'. Hommes et femmes, ils étaient tous riches; ils exhibaient, dans des 'intérieurs' suaves, des costumes du grand tailleur ou du grand couturier. Et leurs effigies, leurs biographies, tant de réclame et tant de gloire, allaient troubler le cœur des petites abonnées provinciales, Bovarys de Limoges ou de Quimper-Corentin. (*LR*, 44–45)

> [At the *Monde féminin*, all the women were pretty; almost all were virtuous; all the men were 'talented'; the most rancorous had the 'souls of children'. Whether men or women, they were all rich, and they displayed, in stylish 'interiors', outfits made by renowned tailors or designers. And their figures and their biographies, associated with such fame and such glory, would stir the desires of the little provincial subscribers, Bovarys from Limoges or Quimper-Corentin.]

Yet in working for the magazine and in supporting her sick husband and her illegitimate child, Josanne is herself debunking such hyperbolic versions of femininity, designed to appeal to Emma Bovary-esque readers desperate for allure.

Such conflict is suggested in the opening chapter of *La Rebelle*, which sees Josanne in the street, after work, waiting for her lover Maurice to turn up. She is presented as an amalgam of conventional femininity and more unconventional free-spiritedness. Careful details of her clothing are provided: Tinayre's novel pays its own attention to fashion as it will later echo Josanne's own write-up for the style pages of the magazine. Yet the narrator also observes of her that: 'toute la personne de Josanne avait un air de hardiesse defensive, la libre allure qui révèle la fille emancipée ou la femme sans époux — seule dans la rue, seule dans la vie' [Josanne's whole being gave off an air of defensive hardiness, that allure of freedom which is the sign of the emancipated girl or the unmarried woman — alone in the streets, alone in life] (*LR*, 1–2). This last quotation, which anticipates the stance of Brieux's heroine in his 1912 play, *La Femme seule*, reads ambiguously; her solitude is indicative both of independence and loneliness. Josanne will fluctuate between these two states throughout the text. Described as 'brune, svelte et vive' [brunette, slim and lively], her animated physical appearance leads to the suggestion that she 'semblait la première hirondelle de ce printemps qui allait venir' [resembled the first swallow of the spring about to come] (*LR*, 2), thereby associating her with freedom and flight from the opening lines of the text. These comments reveal the narrative voice at work, a voice which is itself equivocal in its presentation of its heroine. Often admiring of her, as Holmes observes, the narrator also tends to objectify her, viewing her frequently through a male gaze; the swallow simile could represent the viewpoint of Tinayre's sympathetic narrator, or the pluralized judgement of the men who pass Josanne in the street (who shout out to her, offering her dinner or calling her 'gentille'), appreciating her physical appearance and noting her unattached status.[18]

The contradictions which surround the presentation of Josanne from the opening pages of Tinayre's novel are reflected across the texts in question, emblematized too in the emphasis on gender hybridity employed to depict the female protagonists. Josanne's name is a feminization of her journalist father's name José, and the ambiguity this evokes is reinforced through the patronym 'Valentin' which juxtaposes romantic expectations with the realism of the world of work. The opening glimpse of Hélène, the central 'femme nouvelle' in the Margueritte brothers' text of the same name, also suggests that modern femininity is accompanied by virility. Hélène wears a silken blouse but with a 'col d'homme' [man's collar], and evokes both 'hardiesse virile et de grâce féminine' [virile hardiness and feminine grace] (*FN*, 11). In Brieux's play, a new recruit to the women's magazine expresses surprise that the names published beneath the articles appear to be those of 'gentilhommes'. Explaining that these are the pseudonyms of female contributors, Thérèse remarks that such nomenclature is an editorial strategy — 'ça inspire encore plus de confiance pour les choses sérieuses' [it inspires people to trust you more when you write about serious things] — but notes that the names themselves, which include Camille, René, and Gabriel, are purposefully chosen to suggest gender neutrality; they are all 'à deux fins' [can be read in two ways] (*FS*, 71). This strategic positioning of the female journalists at the magazine *Femme libre* is, indeed, also adopted by the fictional texts under examination here; while the writers are keen to posit their heroines as being distinct from more vocal feminist proponents of emancipation and equality, nevertheless these turn-of-the-century women combine their acceptable femininity with a strength depicted as masculine. The texts are additionally linked by their caricatured representation of feminism and their satire of mannish women, set alongside their critique of a more conventional brand of femininity.

Querying Feminism and Femininity

These texts reject and lampoon extreme feminist representatives and activities, so underscoring the more moderate approach to social change for women advocated by the writers. *Femmes nouvelles* provides a favourable portrayal of the Durand-like editor of the female-staffed paper *L'Avenir*, Minna, whose career has seen her become one of the founders of the feminist congress held in Paris in 1896. The representation of a feminist rally in this novel is a satire of the perceived self-interest associated with such public manifestations.[19] There is a particular caricature of the 'hommasse' Mme Morchesne, seen as booming and dictatorial; her meek husband follows her around and is treated dismissively. She is described as 'le porte-étendard du féminisme intolérant' [the standard-bearer for intolerant feminism] (*FN*, 83). At the rally, Mme Morchesne bellows her address, while her fellow organizer is desperate to name-drop the fact she once knew Geoffroy Saint-Hilaire. Hélène leaves the meeting in frustration, finding the behaviour of some of the women speakers ridiculous as they feign floods of tears following a speech about the number of women who die in childbirth. The character of Mme Morchesne is echoed in the depiction of Mme Gonfalonet, president of the 'Fraternité féminine' in *La Rebelle*, who belongs to the 'age héroique du féminisme' [heroic age of feminism] (*LR*, 297). She criticizes Josanne for abandoning her widow's clothing when she takes Noël as her lover; Josanne responds scathingly:

> Si les féministes réclament la liberté, c'est probablement pour s'en servir! Pourquoi mettre au dessus de la femme amoureuse la femme 'volontairement pure'?... L'amour n'est pas un péché... Je ne crois pas être moins sérieuse et moins vaillante, moins libre, et représenter un type moins 'réussi' de travailleuse intellectuelle parce que je suis amoureuse. (*LR*, 299)

> [If feminists demand freedom, it is probably to suit their own ends. Why put the 'voluntarily pure' woman above the woman in love? Love is not a sin ... I do not believe myself to be less serious or valiant, or less free, nor do I think I represent a less 'successful' type of intellectual woman employee because I am in love.]

Josanne's response to suggestions that she attend the meetings of the Fraternité féminine is to caricature its members as 'de grosses dames moustachues et de maigres illuminés [qui] s'appelaient héroiquement "citoyennes"' [fat women with moustaches and cranks who heroically refer to themselves as 'citizens'] (*LR*, 133). Like Hélène, who abandons the feminist rally because she is weary of the overly idealistic demands of its organizers, Josanne takes issue with the fantasies of the feminists whose work she reads; she is described as having written a politely veiled condemnation of a feminist author. Josanne argues that feminist ideals are as unrealistic as the conventional demands of the romance plot, denigrating the novels she has reviewed 'parce qu'il représentait des feministes de fantaisie, des exaltées!... C'était le pavé de l'ours, ce roman!' [because they represented fantastical feminists, fanatics! ... This novel does women no service at all] (*LR*, 139). In *Leur égale*, Thérèse's plan for the editorial content of her own proposed magazine, *Femme moderne* [The Modern Woman], rejects the 'coteries existantes', the 'idées,

[...] projets,' and 'récriminations' (*LE*, 289) of feminist groups, and suggests the conscious adoption of a moderate, less fantastical path, which is replicated both in Pert's own novel, and in the works by Tinayre and the Marguerittes.

The satire of feminist organizations and their arguments in these texts is coupled with a parodic presentation of the female journalists who surround the protagonists. In *Femmes nouvelles*, and in *La Rebelle*, the female employees are divided into two principal categories: the feminine and the anti-feminine. In *Femmes nouvelles*, these categories are represented by two women, described by Hélène: 'Sophie Grœtz, Viennoise prétentieuse et sensible' [Sophie Grœtz, a pretentious and sensitive Viennese woman]; and 'une américaine, Miss Pelboom, jeune, sèche et plate personne, sans poitrine ni hanches, col droit et feutre d'homme: le troisième sexe dans toute son horreur. Spécialité: la chronique des sports dans l'Athlétisme et le Cycle journal' [an American, Miss Pelboom, a young, lean, flat-chested woman with no hips to speak of, stiff-collared and wearing a man's headgear, the third sex in all its horrors. She specializes in athletics reports for the sports pages and the cycling publication] (*FN*, 74). In Tinayre's novel, critique is levelled in particular at the society columnist Flory, whose name is evocative of her floral femininity. Flory has male editorial assistants at her beck and call; she calls them her 'nègres' [ghost-writers], echoing and reversing the role played by Madeleine Forestier in *Bel-Ami*, when she acts as Duroy's 'nègre'. Frivolous and fashion-obsessed, Flory uses her feminine wiles to produce her journalism, asking, when she sees Noël translating a piece for Josanne, 'laquelle d'entre nous n'a pas son petit collaborateur? Moi j'en ai bien une demi-douzaine, toujours disponibles' [who among us doesn't have her little employee? For my part, I have half a dozen of them at my beck and call] (*LR*, 154). She lapses into baby-talk, 'moi bien triste, ce soir!' [me all sad, this evening] — the self-conscious disintegration of her linguistic expression indicative of her manipulative intention to present herself as vulnerable and conventionally feminine. Towards the end of the novel, Flory is re-evaluated through the perspective of Josanne's lover Noël, who regards her with a pitying indulgence, as he perceives her status amongst the critics and actors; Flory may ostentatiously 'tutoie' the theatre-going crowd, as she flits about them in her low-cut black dress, but the narrative sees Noël questioning her:

> Dans la familiarité des 'confrères', Flory distinguait-elle la nuance un peu méprisante, le sans-gêne mal déguisé? Comprenait-elle que ces 'confrères' l'assimiliaient aux actrices de demi-talent, aux poétesse ratées, aux écrivassières entretenues qui encombrent les abords de la littérature et du théâtre? Sentait-elle que la 'soiriste' du *Monde féminin* n'était et ne serait jamais qu'une 'petite femme'? (*LR*, 341)
>
> [Amongst these 'colleagues', did Flory not pick up the slightly contemptuous tone, or the faintly veiled lack of consideration? Did she understand that these so-called colleagues associated her with second-rate actresses or failed poets, those women scribblers who hang around on the fringes of literature or the theatre? Did she sense that the 'gossip columnist' for the *Monde féminin* was, and would only ever be, a 'little woman'?]

The text showcases Noël's preference for a woman like Josanne, who will match him intellectually and who has none of Flory's neediness and display of feminine sexuality, though the dismissive male view of Flory as a 'petite femme' reads as uncomfortably patronizing to a modern audience. Josanne's own hybrid status is approved of by Noël, who observes:

> Que les antiféministes seraient bien ébahis de vous voir et de vous entendre [...] Vous êtes tellement femme!... Oui, révoltée, oui, rebelle, ni la lutte pour la vie, ni l'indépendance, ni l'activité intellectuelle n'ont détruit en vous les instincts de femme, même l'instinct ménager et l'instinct de plaire... Vous aimez la parure; vous ornez votre maison, une fleur vous enchante, un bibelot vous réjouit. (LR, 166)
>
> [How the antifeminists would be stunned to see you and hear you speak [...] You are so womanly! No matter how much of a rebel you may be, your struggle for existence, your independence and your intellectual activity have not destroyed your feminine instincts, not even the domestic instinct or the urge to please... You like your finery, you decorate your home, you are enchanted by flowers and charmed by trinkets.]

The dialogue between Josanne and her lover indicates the text's attempt to combine moderate social rebellion with a form of femininity which is non-threatening. Asked whether he is surprised by her womanliness, Noël answers that as the author of *La Travailleuse*, he would not be, having written about the 'femme nouvelle', but as Noël Delysle, believer in 'la femme éternelle' [eternal woman], he would indeed be surprised at such an apparent paradox. Josanne corrects him, insisting that the 'nouvelle femme' and the 'femme éternelle' can indeed be one and the same. A key argument of Tinayre's novel. *La Rebelle* thus echoes the mission statement set out in the inaugural issue of the magazine *Femina*: its opening editorial announcement rejects any feminist cause in favour of a specifically French representation of femininity: 'FEMINA sera [...] consacré à la vraie femme, à la Française élevée sainement dans les meilleures traditions d'élégance, de bon ton et de grâce' [FEMINA will be dedicated to the true woman, the Frenchwoman raised soundly in the best traditions of elegance, grace, and good taste].[20] The opening pages of *La Rebelle* appear to situate Josanne firmly as a 'vraie femme' of whom *Femina* would approve; although she is described as being familiar with feminist arguments and demands, she is also distanced from them: 'très Française et très Parisienne, elle avait le sens du ridicule et l'horreur des déclamations' [a true Frenchwoman and a Parisian, she had a keen sense of what was ridiculous, and a horror of ranting] (*LR*, 15). Although novel and magazine appear unified in their disclaimers with regard to overtly politicized demands for gender equality, Tinayre's representation of a *Femina*-esque publication is not, as will be seen, an unequivocal endorsement.

Gender Identity: Querying Masculinity

The men in these novels are frequently depicted critically. *Femmes nouvelles*, in particular, stresses the weaknesses of the men who surround those women who are endeavouring to become 'nouvelles'. Minna Herkaert is obliged to use her journalistic skills to investigate the past lives and suitability of the men Hélène admires;

two are found wanting. Hélène's first suitor, Vernières, is proved to be a cad who already has a young son from an affair with a maid on his family estate, for whom he provides no maintenance. Minna accompanies Hélène to the Parisian hovel where the son lives with his mother, and she engages in an investigation, using her newspaper contacts, to check the truth of the maid's story. She performs a similar role in uncovering the deceptions of Hélène's second potential lover, an artist and theatre critic who is only really interested in Hélène's inheritance. In *La Rebelle*, Maurice, Josanne's first lover, is similarly weak, unwilling to upset his mother by admitting to his relationship with Josanne and to his paternity; her first husband is a waspish invalid whose sexual demands mean he comes close to raping her. Men like the partner of Madame Neuf, an unmarried mother whom Josanne encounters on a journalistic visit to the charitable institution, the Villa Bleue, abandon women when they get pregnant only to take up with them once again when they have given birth and abandoned their babies. The title of *Leur égale* is ironic: Thérèse aspires for a society in which women are able to become the social and legal equals of men, but her own lover, Adrien, is scarcely a figure to be recognized as Thérèse's own moral 'equal,' as demonstrated in the scenes following his realization that Thérèse has posed for the sculptor, Amand-Bellière, and that the statue of Le Printemps in the Luxembourg gardens is modelled on her. Adrien cannot accept that another man has seen her undressed, despite his admission of his own numerous other relationships with women. In *La Rebelle*, Noël has to strive to overcome such jealousy, in order to become a man who can accept a relationship with a 'femme nouvelle'.

Mesch argues that Noël Delysle represents a 'new man' who must prove his suitability as the appropriate equal for Josanne's brand of social rebellion. Noël must shift his views and emotions so as to adjust to his new awareness that Josanne has had an unconventional sexual history, as a widow who also had a previous lover, by whom she has a young son. The plot sees Noël seek to reconcile his own personal experience with the abstract arguments in favour of greater marital equality he writes about in his book. In this way he emerges as a more fully-realized and forward-looking male protagonist than Maurice, Josanne's superficial former lover, and as a more emancipated character than many of the more conventionally-minded and hypocritical men who feature in the novels by Pert and the Margueritte brothers. Mesch argues that the fact that Tinayre chose to give her character Noël the same name as her oldest son suggests that he represents her vision for the future.[21] Noël can be compared with the husband chosen by Hélène in *Femmes nouvelles*. Under editor Minna's guidance, Hélène learns to love the seemingly unprepossessing Pierre Arden, whose name and career indicate that he represents the necessarily emancipated man who will be an adequate match for her intelligence and education. England, where Hélène's aunt lives, is held out in the text as a more progressive country for women than France. Where Hélène's mother is rigidly behind the times, her aunt becomes a modernizing mentor figure. It is significant, then, that Pierre's name evokes a Shakespearean heritage, his association with the Forest of Arden recalling in particular the escapist freedom and gender reversals of the playful *As You Like It*. Pierre is also an engineer, and so capable of building the bridges which literally and metaphorically enact the progress of which Hélène dreams: 'Il avait cet orgueil légitime du pionnier obscure qui croit son œuvre utile, se voue entière à la cause sainte du Progrès' [He had that rightful pride of the unknown pioneer who believes his work to be of use, and devotes himself completely to the saintly cause of Progress] (*FN*, 300). Accordingly, Pierre and Hélène get to know each other while driving; his assured hands on the wheel of his automobile steering them towards the *avenir* carved out by the text.

Despite the ways in which these texts evoke potential 'new men' whose careers emblematize their progressive mindsets, it remains the case that the women's magazine as represented in these novels is often controlled by men. That control is reflected as problematic, most notably in Brieux's *La Femme seule*. Here, the magazine *Femme libre* is edited by Mme Nérisse, whose partner manages the finances of the publication. Although she calls herself 'Madame', she confesses to Thérèse that she is not married, as Nérisse already has a wife who refuses to divorce him. When the magazine faces financial difficulties, and the women who work there are told that their contributions and rate of pay will be reduced, Nérisse offers to help Thérèse find other opportunities in return for accompanying him to dinner. She refuses, and a later scene sees him reiterate his attempt at manipulation. This time, when he professes his love for her, she responds with anger, claiming in no uncertain terms: 'votre acte n'est pas autre chose qu'une tentative de viol sous conditions' [what you have done is no less than attempted rape] (*FS*, 24). The example of Nérisse, who wields the purse strings of the magazine in exchange for expected sexual affairs with members of his editorial team, offers a particularly damning view of the power and influence exerted by the male directors of such female-orientated publications.

In *La Rebelle*, the magazine *Monde féminin* is also controlled by a husband and wife team, the Foucarts. Although his wife incarnates the would-be glamour extolled by the publication, it is Foucart who controls the layout and content of *Monde féminin* (both magazine and world of the women around him). He airbrushes the realities his magazine claims to reflect so as to appease his readers; he is particularly concerned that young female readers should not recognize the condition of the pregnant women interviewed by Josanne in an article on the home for unmarried mothers, the Villa Bleue. Foucart also advises Josanne on her dress code, insisting that she should take off her mourning veil when conducting interviews. Her potential interviewees, 'un monsieur dont la pièce a réussi, un philanthrope qu'on a décoré, une jolie femme qui a fait son petit roman, comme tout le monde' [a man who has written a successful play, a philanthropist who has been rewarded, an attractive woman who has produced a little novel, as they all do], would find their jollity disturbed; the veil would 'met du noir dans *l'interview*' [add a sombre note to the interview] (*LR*, 144). Foucart refuses to acknowledge the realities of Josanne's background, never referring to her marital status but always infantilizing her and emphasizing the romantic implications of her surname by calling her 'ma petite Valentin'. Although not depicted as predatory in the same way as Nérisse in Brieux's play, Foucart seeks to mould Josanne in ways which are patronizing as much as they are encouraging. He cultivates a desired impression of her, and his styling of her is echoed in the stylization of women celebrated in the pages of *Monde féminin*.

These texts are united in their critical presentation of masculinity. What is particularly noteworthy, then, is the way that the novels incorporate the voices of the men they represent, and, in the case of *Leur égale* and *La Rebelle*, increasingly allow those voices to dominate. As noted above, the editorial strategy of *Femme libre*, in Brieux's play, is to encourage the impression that the articles are penned by men so as to inspire readers to take the writing more seriously. The novels themselves arguably lend interpretation of key scenes to male characters in order to validate the representation of the changing gender roles they portray. Although, in *Leur égale*, it is Thérèse who drives the launch of the magazine *Femme moderne*, her cousin Louis Dose will take on the role of 'secrétaire de la rédaction' [editorial secretary]. He is sufficiently conscious of his market to understand that the material of which he is in charge — advertising, images, theatre reviews, humour — is what will enable the new title to sell:

> Les femmes ne s'abonneront, n'achèteront que pour les photographies d'actualités de la couverture, la gravure de mode de la fin, les potins des Echos, les tuyaux sur les courses, les coulisses, les expositions, les grands magasins! — Comme l'aspect matériel de la publication sera épatant, que ça paraîtra toutes les semaines et ne coûtera que six sous le numéro, ça marchera... et, on avalera les articles de philosophie et de morale par-dessus le marché! (*LE*, 280–81)

> [Women will only subscribe, will only buy it for the topical photographs on the front cover, for the fashion plates, the gossipy titbits, the racing tips, the detail of what goes on behind the scenes, the exhibitions, the department stores! — If the magazine looks visually impressive, if it comes out weekly and only costs six *sous* per issue, then it will work... and readers will accept the articles on philosophy and morality into the bargain.]

That the magazine needs to be visually appealing and good value is a fact understood by the astute Louis, who makes claims to know and understand what women want. His narrative perspective informs the text at frequent intervals as he watches the unfolding and unravelling of Thérèse's relationship with Adrien, regretfully watching her mounting unhappiness as one who is himself in love with her but does not dare admit it. The text concludes with his mournful viewpoint as he witnesses Thérèse's isolation:

> Il soupira, et s'éloigna sans bruit, douleureusement atteint par cette souffrance muette, cette blessure que ni le temps ni la raison n'arriveraient à guérir; car, ils lui avaient bien apporté la résignation et le pardon... mais l'oubli était seulement au pouvoir du grand destructeur final... du consolateur suprême: le Néant. (*LE*, 292–93)

> [He sighed, and moved away noiselessly, painfully struck by this silent suffering, this hurt which neither time nor reason could heal, for while these forces had brought resignation and forgiveness, the ability to forget lay solely in the power of the final great destroyer, the supreme consolation: Death.]

The novel closes, then, with a nihilistic and masculine viewpoint in free indirect style, debunking the projected aims of the magazine to be launched the following day.

Despite its title, and its focus on the fate of Josanne, *La Rebelle* ultimately hands narrative power and influence to the male character. It, too, concludes with the dominance of the male perspective. It is the novel in which the magazine plays the biggest role, yet while there are no excerpts of the material produced by Josanne for *Monde féminin*, Noël's writing is featured prominently within the narrative: a substantial portion of the second chapter is given over to quotations from his book, *La Travailleuse*. Collado notes that this sequence constitutes 'une mise en abyme de l'activité de lecture. En lisant l'étude, elle [Josanne] fait des pauses et réfléchit à sa propre expérience' [a *mise-en-abyme* of the act of reading. On encountering this work, she stops and reflects on her own experience].[22] Yet despite focusing on Josanne's career, at no point is there 'une mise en abyme de l'activité de l'écriture': instead, we see Noël evaluating her various articles without the reader having had access to this material. On his first meeting with her he indicates both his interest in her and his critical assessment of her intelligence and emotional state by listing the pieces he has read: 'je sais tout ce que vous faites, où vous allez, qui vous voyez... La veille de Noël, vous étiez à la "Crèche Alsacienne", le 1er janvier à la Villa Bleue... Vous avez écrit un petit article très touchant, sur la Villa Bleue!... Le 3 février... Vous étiez de méchante humeur, le 3 février!' [I know all that you do, where you go and who you see. On Christmas Eve you were at the Alsatian Crèche, and at the Villa Bleue on 1st January... You wrote a very touching little piece on the Villa Bleue!... On 3rd February... you were in a bad mood, that day] (*LR*, 139). Similarly, although the novel reproduces excerpts from Noël's book, Josanne's review of *La Travailleuse* itself is not included; instead, when she first writes to Noël, such is her modesty that she can scarcely acknowledge herself as the writer of the article, asking 'Est-ce bien moi qui ai fait cet article sur la Travailleuse?' [Did I really write that article on La Travailleuse?] (*LR*, 81), since she claims not to be 'une femme de lettres'. [a woman of Letters]. The very title of the novel is based on a citation taken from *La Travailleuse*, which declares the modern working woman to be a rebel: 'Si toutes les travailleuses ne sont pas des affranchies, toutes, déjà, sont des rebelles... Rebelles à la loi que les hommes ont faite' [If not all women workers are enfranchised, all are, already, rebels. Rebels against the law as created by men] (*LR*, 14). In *La Rebelle* in particular, which accords such importance to the need for parity within marriage, and which focuses its plot as much on the *Bildung* of Noël as that of Josanne, the weight given to masculine narrative perspective may be a result of this quest for a balance of the intellect and experience of the male and female characters. Noël's lessons in acceptance are a necessary ingredient of the social education proffered and advocated by the text and therefore his voice is integral. His journey, arguably, makes Josanne's quest for emancipation resonate all the more fully.

Another reading is that the dominance of the male voice in these texts about female career opportunities and the expansion of the women's magazine is evidence of the purposefully moderate vision of women's progression envisaged by these texts. Mesch's discussion of Noël as a prototype for the new man is complicated by the scene found towards the end of *La Rebelle*, which takes place at the theatre. This scene directly precedes the denouement of the novel which will describe the illness of Josanne's son, her renewed commitment to her role as mother, and her union with Noël. It is disquieting for several reasons. It offers a glimpse into the workings of *Monde féminin*, while notably lacking much female perspective on this world. Josanne is absent from the scene; Noël is there to watch a play, the content of which is itself significant since it centres around a relationship devastated by a husband's awareness that his wife will forever be attracted to her previous lover.[23] This is a preoccupation for Noël himself, who worries that Josanne will always secretly remain physically and sensually attached to Maurice. The play over, Noël is invited to join Foucart and other magazine staff members for a drink. The ensuing discussion provides a satirical insight into opinions and conduct at the editorial offices as Foucart decides that his own conclusion about the play — that it taps into contemporary moral reaction against divorce and free love — should be put to the test with a survey in the pages of the magazine. The editorial assistant Bersier is delighted with this idea since surveys reduce his workload: 'on n'a plus qu'à transcrire!' [all we have to do is transcribe the results] (*LR*, 344). Foucart and his male editorial assistant make plans to publish in the magazine a survey calling for the opinions of their female readers while already anticipating and moulding the responses they will receive. Mesch discusses the popularity of the survey in *Femina* and *Vie heureuse*: 'these kinds of surveys, increasingly frequent, represented a significant shift from the early contests, that substantially blurred the lines between the roles of editors and readers'.[24] Mesch's positive view of the survey, which highlights its embrace of the reader, contrasts with the satirical representation of such a seemingly democratic mode of publication in *La Rebelle*. The irony in the novel is heightened by an ensuing dialogue between Foucart and Noël about Josanne's career, in which Noël (in Josanne's absence) informs her employer that the magazine will soon have to do without her, as they are to be married, and so her post at *Monde féminin* will have to come to an end. The discussion suggests that these men stand as guardians of her fate; as Noël announces her imminent departure from the magazine, Foucart comments on the fortuity of his decision to allow Josanne to write the initial review of *La Travailleuse* and so bring the couple together. Although Noël leaves the theatre reflecting on his attachment to Josanne, he also admits his relief that she has not been able to watch the play.

It is against the context of this male-dominated scene, with its insight into the superficiality of the magazine's concerns, then, that the concluding scenes must be read: scenes which see Josanne reinstated as mother first and foremost and, once her son's illness has abated, as lover and woman. Such a context highlights the ambiguity of the closing lines of the novel, seen from the perspective of Noël, who reflects that 'le passé n'était plus que cendre et poussière' [the past was nothing more than dust and ashes]. Noël's mental image of the new-found twinship he senses with Josanne can also be read equivocally: 'il s'enivra de baiser le beau front intelligent où la pensée se formait, pareille à sa pensée; les yeux fidèles qui reflétaient ses yeux dans leurs miroirs sombres; les lèvres dociles à ses lèvres et qui ne mentiraient jamais' [he became intoxicated, kissing that handsome intelligent forehead where her thoughts were formed, akin to his thoughts. Her faithful eyes offered dark mirrors of his own; her docile lips, which would never lie, pressed against his] (*LR*, 371). Although he realizes that, as in the title of the Pert text, Josanne is indeed his 'égale', the reciprocity imagined by Noël is also a refusal to acknowledge her individuality and represents a silencing of Josanne's own perspective as she is fantasized giving up her 'lèvres dociles' to his kiss.

Textual Identity

New Women, New Narratives

The ending of *La Rebelle* reflects the ambiguities associated with these texts which depict emboldened young women, carving out new careers in journalism, yet struggling to reconcile their new independence with expectations of marriage, motherhood, and a desire for love. The writers in question negotiate two possible, and often contradictory, models of plot, the narration of the female *Bildung* — the apprenticeship of the women journalists as they make their way in the world — and the pattern of the love plot. These texts are self-reflexive novels which frequently incorporate commentary on earlier modes of narrative. In their representation of the editorial offices of contemporary women's publications, they also consider the range of journalistic styles open to female reporters and intended for a female readership.

La Rebelle evokes a variety of narrative patterns in its frequent passing references to the canon of nineteenth-century literature. Noël approves of Josanne's bookshelves: '*Manon Lescaut*, les *Confessions*, *Adolphe*... Et beaucoup de Balzac... Vous aimez Balzac!... *Madame Bovary*... *Notre Cœur*... *Le Lys rouge*, *Anna Karenina*, *l'Empreinte*, *le Silence*, *la Force des Choses*... des poètes [...] Vous choisissez bien vos amis' [*Manon Lescaut*, the *Confessions*, *Adolphe*... And lots of Balzac... You like Balzac! ... *Madame Bovary*... *Notre Cœur* ... *Le Lys rouge*, *Anna Karenina*, *l'Empreinte*, *le Silence*, *la Force des Choses*... poets [...] You choose your friends well] (*LR*, 169). Josanne is depicted as a well-read, intelligent character; her own quest is implicitly compared to and set against those of the women in the books she has gathered. When out shopping, she compares herself to Gervaise in *L'Assommoir* and imagines she sees shadows from Balzac and Sue haunting her Parisian quartier. Noël's observation that Josanne's shelves hold a number of Balzac novels suggests the particular resonance of the nineteenth-century realist novel, and the plot of the male *Bildungsroman* in Tinayre's text. Aside from Balzac, the literary fates of two fictional characters are employed in the novel to underscore Josanne's choices and trajectories. Josanne's copy of *La Princesse de Clèves* is noteworthy, not just because Noël is curious about its inscription — it is a gift from her erstwhile lover — but because Tinayre's own plot is a modern reworking of the ideal set out by Mme de Lafayette of a relationship between lovers who can also be friends. In place of the impossible union evoked in the seventeenth-century text, which sees the princess ultimately opt for duty over love in retreating to a convent, *La Rebelle* strives to realize the fusion of marriage and romance. *Madame Bovary*, too, is a persistent intertext. Not only are the readers of *Monde féminin* described as 'Bovarys' from the provinces, as referenced above, but the editorial assistant Bersier keeps a mistress on the 'rue Gustave Flaubert'. The reference to Josanne as an 'hirondelle' in the opening pages of the text is reminiscent of the ironically-named carriage in *Madame Bovary*, the trundling vehicle which remains firmly on the ground, evoking but denying Emma Bovary's dreams of transcendent flight. Alone in the Parisian street, publicly awaiting a lover and garbed in fashionable, well-fitting clothes, Josanne is demarcated as a visibly more emancipated heroine than Emma, though the later references to Flaubert's novel suggest the persistence of Madame Bovary's aspirations towards romance and glamour, and the tawdriness of extra-marital affairs. The two novels — *La Princesse de Clèves* and *Madame Bovary* — reflect on unhappy marriages in alternative ways. The princess finds love outside marriage but cannot see it realized; Emma Bovary finds fleeting escape in her relationships with Rodolphe and Léon but cannot sustain the illusion of excitement. Both texts end with the death of the desiring woman. Tinayre maps these two narrative trajectories onto her own novel, suggesting that Josanne's experience will see her transcend such outcomes in a marriage between equals.

The implicit intertext of *Madame Bovary* and its suggestions of the doomed romance plot lurks too in the opening chapter of *Femmes nouvelles*. Hélène Dugast and her mentor Minna are travelling by train from Dieppe to Rouen. Arriving in Rouen, the industrial backdrop awaits them, 'avec son décor brumeux d'usines, de docks, de magasins; un enchevêtrement lointain de vergues et de mâts suscita l'agitation commerciale des quais, la vie marinière du fleuve; de hautes cheminées fumaient dans l'azur [with its smoky backdrop of factories, docks, stores; a distant tangle of masts and yardarms gave rise to the commercial bustle of the quays, the hustle of life by the river; tall chimneys were smoking against the blue sky] (*FN*, 11). This setting, which echoes Emma Bovary's trips to Rouen and her 'romantic' honeymoon with Léon amid the dockland warehouses and oily waters of the city, features in *Femmes nouvelles* as a locus for newspaper editor Minna to lament the fate of women labouring in the factories and workshops. Indeed, one of the young girls of a working family later encountered by Hélène as she goes on charitable visits around Rouen is a paralyzed sixteen-year-old called Berthe, whose name recalls that of Emma's daughter, forced through penury into factory labour. Emma is ignorant both of her daughter's wellbeing and the smog of the industrial landscape, so caught up is she in plotting her would-be romantic denouement based on the books she has read; the title of *Femmes nouvelles* suggests it intends to chart alternative fates for its characters. Minna acknowledges the conditions for women like Emma, while concerning herself more intently with the lives of those even less fortunate: 'la femme bourgeoise et ses droits, certes, toute une conquête à poursuivre! Mais qui affranchira les femmes ouvrières?' [the middle-class woman and her rights: a whole conquest to pursue! But who would enfranchise the working women?] (*FN*, 11). From its opening chapter, the Margueritte brothers' novel signals its echoes of and distance from earlier nineteenth-century narrative destinies for women via the voice of its prominent female journalist.

Femmes nouvelles weighs up different women's fates. Although Hélène's choices dominate the text, glimpses are provided too of the 'new women' who surround her, who include her former schoolfriends, a mother, a teacher, a doctor. Minna's newspaper speaks for the concerns of each of these women; she herself is described as 'l'apôtre des femmes nouvelles' [the new women's disciple] as she is seen on the train in these opening pages, still eager for action, cracking together the knuckles of hands which have wielded both 'la plume et l'outil' [pens and workers' tools] (*FN*, 12). As in *La Rebelle*, marriage is held out by Paul and Victor Margueritte as the optimum fate for the 'nouvelles femmes', provided that men and women are able to approach it as equals. The text describes the trajectories of women who position themselves on either side of Hélène as examples of conventional and unconventional behaviour. Hélène recognizes older women around her as mentors — her aunt Sassy, who runs an agricultural scheme that she herself funds, and Minna: 'elle saluait en elles de véritables apôtres' [she recognized them as being true disciples]. Yet she is equally aware that she is not cut out for such lives of sacrifice and abnegation; in her veins there burns 'l'irrésistible besoin d'aimer et d'être aimée' [the irresistible urge to love and be loved] (*FN*, 248). Hélène feels that marriage should be the natural destiny for women:

> Elle sentait pourtant bien que le vrai rôle de la femme, sa function, comme disait Minna, est d'être l'épouse, la mère. Elle voyait dans le mariage la base éternelle de la famille et de la société; il fallait seulement vivifier cette grande institution qui était en train de s'étioler, lui rendre du sang nouveau! (*FN*, 245)
>
> [And yet she well knew that the true role of woman, her 'function', as Minna would say, was to be a wife and mother. In marriage she saw the eternal basis of the family and of society; all that was needed was to breathe new life into that languishing institution, to give it fresh blood.]

Certain scenes indicate the novel's tendency for compromise between convention and change. Hélène reads a volume of Emerson's essays, but puts down the book, reflecting on the choices made by her friends, who have chosen to become, respectively, a teacher and a doctor. She concludes that she cannot quite be like them; nor can she quite finish what she is reading, so convinced is she that the traditional love plot is the outcome for her. The text is punctuated by Hélène's letters to her aunt, reflective of her ability to write and express herself with the attributes of 'bon sens' [good sense] and 'paroles vibrantes' [vibrant language] that she appreciates in Minna's journalistic writing. Yet Hélène chooses to express herself only privately rather than laying her writing open to the public in a newspaper such as *L'Avenir*. The letters are symbolic of Hélène's role throughout the text, acting behind the scenes, funding charitable endeavours but never taking on any more direct role. Her income means she lives a double-edged existence, independent but inactive. She cannot be like Minna, who bears the scars of her past, forced to work in factories and to forge her own way through writing and speaking, and who is seen at the end of the novel preparing to travel to Australia as a visiting speaker, invited to give talks on the material she has published in her newspaper. But neither is she like the much more conventionally-minded women of her acquaintance, such as her cousin Germaine (who has the same name as the similarly superficial and feminine character in Pert's novel of the same year). Germaine is married, but has an affair with Hélène's brother: a narrative subplot which also reveals the inequalities of the marriage laws in France, since Germaine's exploits are much more likely to see her prosecuted than the similar infidelities of her husband. Germaine is 'une poupée. Toujours des robes, des bijoux' [a doll. All dresses and jewellery] (*FN*, 108).

The threads of the novelistic narrative and the content of the newspaper represented in the text overlap. Both emphasize marriage as the central concern for women, and the necessary target of efforts to negotiate equality, both socially and legally. Minna's newspaper *L'Avenir*, an echo of Durand's campaigning *La Fronde*, produces articles discussing the condition of married women, and the need for an improvement of their economic situation. Hélène describes one such article in a letter:

> Vous suivez, n'est-ce-pas, sa campagne dans *l'Avenir*? Avez-vu lu son article, 'Protection des gains de la femme mariée'? — Elle y répond vertement à diverses chroniques hostiles. A quoi bon un loi? raillaient les bons journalistes. La femme, jouissant librement de son salaire, ira bien vite le dépenser aux étalages... Ah! comme Minna sait dire tout cela en paroles vibrantes, pleines de bons sens et de pitié! (*FN*, 73)
>
> [You have been following her campaign in *L'Avenir*? Have you read her article, 'Protection of the married woman's finances'? She answers in no uncertain terms the many hostile articles against her. What good is a law, the journalists rail. Woman, allowed free access to her salary, will quickly go and spend it in the department stores. Ah! Minna knows how to say all that in vibrant language, full of good sense and empathy.]

Within the plot, editor Minna takes on a key role, advising Hélène on her marital future and recommending that she choose her 'maître' wisely.[25] Newspaper and novel intersect once again when Minna intervenes journalistically in Hélène's potential relationships, discovering the hypocrisies and flaws of her suitors. It is Minna, too, who steps into the drama following Germaine's affair and uses her influence at the paper, threatening to expose the hypocrisies of the situation. Roberts describes Minna, like Marguerite Durand, as 'a distinctly French version of the New Woman'.[26]

In employing its prominent journalist character as an eloquent advocate for the need to reshape the institution of marriage, *Femmes nouvelles* is, like *La Rebelle*, a turn-of-the-century text which renegotiates the representation of the marital plot in French fiction. In a special issue of the journal *Dix-Neuf* devoted to the discussion of marriage in the nineteenth-century French novel, Rachel Mesch and Masha Belenky argue that in the French tradition 'marriage serves more often than not as the troubling starting point of narrative intrigue rather than the happy ending toward which characters strive'.[27] Mesch, in *Having It All in the Belle Époque*, maintains that Tinayre's incorporation of just such a happy ending in Josanne's union with Noël, in contrast to earlier plot outcomes 'signalled the creation of a new narrative trajectory for the independent French woman'.[28] Critical opinion as to the extent of the 'rebellion' represented by Josanne and by the novel itself, though, is divided; where Mesch sees Tinayre's writing as revolutionary, Holmes is more guarded.[29] I will argue that the representation of the magazine in Tinayre's novel and in the other texts evaluated here both reflects such ambiguities and offers a means of resolving them. Despite the title of Mesch's study of *Femina* and *Vie heureuse*, the female journalist characters in the novels are not able to 'have it all'. They are obliged to choose between marriage and career, femininity and writing, love and independence. In this way, the literary writers suggest a more realistic mode of modern womanhood than the fantasy set out for the readers of the magazines.

Mesch and Belenky's discussion of marriage sets up a distinction between modes of plot in the French novel of the nineteenth century and a British model of the same period. In the British novel:

> Marriage serves as the teleological frame that allows narratives to explore sexual tension or transgressions of social codes; at the same time, the marriage plot ensures the restoration of social order at the story's end, for marriage symbolizes closure, resolution, stability and social equilibrium.[30]

A difference is suggested between the narrative teleologies of French fiction and the kind of plot strategies evaluated extensively by Blau duPlessis in her seminal work, *Writing Beyond the Ending*. She argues that twentieth-century novels by women can often be seen to seek alternatives to the female quest which, in the nineteenth century, ends in marriage or death (or, in the case of Emma Bovary, as a garish amalgamation of the two, with the image of Emma's corpse garbed in its wedding dress):

> Writing beyond the ending means the transgressive invention of narrative strategies, strategies that express critical dissent from dominant narrative. These tactics, among them reparenting, woman-to-woman and brother-to-sister bonds, and forms of the communal protagonist, take issue with the mainstays of the social and ideological organisation of gender, as these appear in fiction. Writing beyond the ending, 'not repeating your words and following your methods but [...] finding new words and creating new methods' produces a narrative that denies or reconstructs seductive patterns of feeling that are culturally mandated, internally policed, hegemonically poised.[31]

The marital outcome of a text like Tinayre's *La Rebelle* — and that of *Femmes nouvelles* — may indeed represent such a mode of writing beyond the conventional ending, even though such resolutions remain romantic in nature.

Although essentially rooted in a discussion of plots in the British tradition, Blau DuPlessis's analysis remains pivotal when considering the ways in which these French women's *romans du journalisme* construct their endings.[32] Pert's *Leur égale* charts an inverse trajectory to that of *La Rebelle*. While *La Rebelle* allows its protagonist to find happiness with an appropriately emancipated lover, only for her career to fade into the background as the narrative progresses, *Leur égale* sees its unconventional female character obliged to give up on her relationship only to channel her energies into the establishment of the magazine *Femme moderne*.[33] The penultimate chapter of Pert's text makes its manipulation of narrative codes particularly evident. It calls up coinciding outcomes of marriage and death, reflecting Blau DuPlessis's evaluation of these codes as the dominant fates for nineteenth-century fictional women. Thérèse attends the wedding of her former lover and walks home alone in despair, contemplating suicide. The chapter narrates a lengthy internal monologue on the part of Thérèse, who decides to go the apartment she and Adrien used for their liaisons — itself indicative of contradiction insofar as it represents the site of Thérèse's seizure of unconventionality, the locus of the sexual pleasure she has opted to seek outside marriage, yet is also described in all its domestic detail. Here she considers killing herself with Adrien's revolver, yet 'elle découvrit qu'en cette minute où rien ne l'attirait plus sur terre [...] seules deux raisons méprisables la retenaient à la vie: la crainte puérile de la douleur, l'appréhension du jugement du monde' [at the moment when nothing remained appealing for her on earth, she discovered two contemptible reasons to cling to life: the pathetic fear of pain and apprehension about the judgement of society] (*LE*, 269). Nevertheless the last chapter, which records the shift in time following this scene, indicates Thérèse's new and purposeful resolve, and she is glimpsed drawing up a list of those to invite to the magazine launch.

Among other strategies, Blau DuPlessis discusses the shift from the representation of the female genius or writer-figure in the nineteenth century to that seen in twentieth-century texts such as Virginia Woolf's *To the Lighthouse* or Doris Lessing's *The Golden Notebook*. She argues that whereas nineteenth-century works with female artists as heroes place emphasis on the woman, not the genius they exhibit, in the twentieth century the work of art itself assumes more significance, and especially in the way that it considers ethics above aesthetics: a sense of community is envizaged which transcends the female writer's personal suffering. Pert's ending is centred around the magazine: *Femme moderne* is a project designed to forge a community of female readers. One of the points made by Blau DuPlessis is that there exists no proper community for many of the nineteenth-century female heroines; the goal of Thérèse's publication would be to unite women around shared concerns and interests. The ending of Pert's novel and its projection of the possible reach of a magazine aimed at women, suggests a futuristic, ethical, and emancipatory objective: 'il existe une masse de femmes qui réfléchissent, qui pensent, qui cherchent à s'instruire' [there is a whole mass of women out there who reflect, think, and seek to educate themselves] (*LE*, 281). These are the women Thérèse hopes to target. Thérèse articulates the feeling of being torn between her sense of duty which impels her to establish her own publication — to launch 'la femme moderne', both title and concept — and her despair at the recognition that happiness must elude her if she is to do so: 'je sais que la génération actuelle souffrira, mais j'espère pour la prochaine une ère meilleure' [I know that the present generation will suffer, but I hope for a new and better era for the succeeding one] (*LE*, 282). In founding *Femme moderne*, Thérèse envizages an ongoing series of 'writings' which will extend beyond the ending. The plot offers its heroine a means of continuing and enduring beyond conventional romance, and the writing goes 'beyond' the fiction, as Pert reflects the creation of *La Fronde* and anticipates the establishment of *Femina* and *Vie heureuse*:

> Pert's literary fantasy is of course just that, but as such it takes us into what both *Femina* and *La Vie heureuse* might have symbolised for so many, while shining light on the symbiotic, mutually sustaining relationship between these women's magazines and women's fiction. The publication Thérèse could only dream of in 1899 was a thriving reality within a few years, and her own heroine's sober, solitary ending stands in stark contrast to the happy endings of the novels [such as that of Tinayre].³⁴

Thérèse likens her publication to the sort of impetus also needed by the worker's movement: 'c'est comme le peuple, l'ouvrier; leur élan manque de coordination… leur aspiration de but' [it is the same as for the people, the workers; their momentum lacks coordination and their aspirations lack aim] (*LE*, 281). In the Brieux play, the women's movement and the workers' movement unite. Indeed, this text offers a means of writing beyond the ending more revolutionary than any seen in the novels which reflect turn-of-the-century women's journalism. Forced to quit her job at *Femme libre* because of plunging wages and Nérisse's advances, Brieux's Thérèse takes on a more dynamic and upbeat role than her namesake in Pert's novel. Having set up a workshop to employ women at her uncle's factory, she assists single women, older woman, and abandoned mothers in finding work, and she contrasts this with her earlier literary ambitions: 'Et que je voulais réaliser mes rêves par la littérature, alors que je les puis réaliser par l'action. C'est beau, l'action!' [And to think that I wanted to realize my dreams through literature, when I can achieve them through action. Action is admirable!] (*FS*, 116). When the male workers threaten strike action, they are antagonized by the presence of the women who will work more effectively for lower wages and so they threaten to sabotage the machines and set the factory alight. Thérèse's rebellion in the workplace is matched by her revolt against marriage; her lover's father has wounded her pride in suggesting that she only wants to marry for money. She, in return, announces that they should remain lovers but refuse marriage. A climactic closing scene sees the men threatening to break into the women's workshop, a shot ringing out, and women's voices raised in protest as Thérèse agrees to calm the situation by leaving. About to get on a Paris-bound train to meet her lover, she promises an ongoing insurgence:

> Dans tous les pays, dans les villes, dans les campagnes, chez les pauvres et les demi-pauvres, de chaque foyer déserté par l'alcool ou laissé vide par ceux qui n'ont pas le courage du mariage, se lèvera une femme qui l'abandonnera et qui viendra s'asseoir à côté d'eux, à l'usine, à l'atelier, au bureau, au comptoir. (*FS*, 148)
>
> [Across the country, in towns and villages, amongst the destitute or the near-destitute, in each home left stranded by alcohol or left empty by those who do not have the courage to stick with a marriage, a woman will rise up who will abandon that home and will come to take her place alongside those in the factories, the workshops, the offices, the shop counters.]

Perhaps because a play enables more radical re-envizaging of gender debates than the novel or because this 1912 production is the most recent of the texts under examination in this chapter, *La Femme seule* announces the most stirring rewriting of the conventional ending among these representations of women's journalism.³⁵

Representing Journalism

Brieux's play also offers, in its three-act structure, the sense that the women's magazine is but one step in the progression towards improved gender equality and increased social independence. Thérèse abandons the stuffy drawing-room settings of Act One where a play by Musset is being put on, and ventures into the public domain of the editorial offices of the magazine in Act Two, before the superficiality and the exploitative nature of the publication. She takes up her more radical role in Act Three; the final glimpse of her embarking on a train journey underscores her propulsion into an uncertain but politically stirring future. The women's publications found in *Femmes nouvelles* and *La Rebelle* are also, in different ways, abandoned. In the former text, Hélène offers to support Minna's newspaper using her own inheritance, extolling the idealistic role of the publication: 'elle eût participé volontiers à cette courageuse campagne d'amélioration sociale, à cette bataille pour le progrès qui livrait *l'Avenir* en faveur des droits de la femme' [she had gladly taken part in that courageous campaign for social improvement, that battle to improve rights for women in which *L'Avenir* was at the forefront] (*FN*, 107). Minna's decision to close the paper illustrates both the financial insecurities of such a project and the sense that her own energies might be better spent elsewhere than in the offices of a newspaper, as Hélène regretfully admits: 'Elle savait bien qu'emportée par son caractère aventureux, son vaste amour de l'humanité, Minna ne pouvait consacrer toute son existence à labourer le même sillon' [she understood that, swept away by her adventurous nature and her vast love for humanity, Minna would not be able to devote her whole life to ploughing the same furrow] (*FN*, 286). That the magazines are perceived as fragile — the 'Avenir' promised by Minna's paper curtailed by its financial ruin and the sense of its limitations — suggests the critique levelled at the publications featured in these texts. It evokes, too, the sense of crossover and competition perceived by novelists who market their own texts at the same readership targeted by the magazines.

The magazine in *La Rebelle* is threatened financially by the rising competition from real-life publications such as *Femina* and *Vie heureuse*. Yet the real threat to *Monde féminin* as represented in the novel results from Josanne's marked loss of interest in the work she produces for it, as soon as her romance with Noël begins to develop. The novel has documented her career progression from secretary's secretary in the editorial offices to burgeoning reporter, although Rogers points out that despite her promotion, Josanne is still obliged to curtail her reports so as to fit with the magazine's brand: 'Josanne's promotion to the position of journalist at *Le Monde féminin* thus does not give her artistic freedom. Her prose writing remains produced for and consumed by a specific class of reader'.[36] And the glimpse into the increasing opportunities offered to Josanne, which see her sent out to interview celebrities as well as to produce reports on her visits to institutions such as the Villa Bleue, becomes an insight into her decreasing attention span when going about her journalistic duties. Even as she pens her article on the home for unmarried mothers, the syntax reveals the place of such reportage amongst her other personal and romantic preoccupations: 'Le lendemain, elle envoya un billet de remerciement à M. Delysle, écrivit son article sur la Villa Bleue et tâcha de secouer sa tristesse' [the next day, she sent a thank you letter to M. Delysle, penned her article about the Villa Bleue, and attempted to shake off her sadness] (*LR*, 115). Later, as her relationship with Noël develops further, she is chastized variously by Mlle Bon, by Foucart, and by Flory for the quality of her work. Josanne's response is to tell Mlle Bon that 'ma vie est remplie par tant et tant de choses! Je n'ai plus la tête à moi' [my life is filled with so many things! I cannot think about anything at the moment] (*LR*, 298); a remark which suggests that she does not see herself as able to 'have it all', as in Mesch's analysis of the women's magazine market of the time: or at least, she cannot do so successfully, or long-term. Roberts describes the ways in which female reporters such as the *frondeuses* 'signalled [their] frustration with a life of novelistic fantasy. To be real reporters, the frondeuses had to venture out into the brave world of facts, leaving their imaginations behind. In doing so, they defied the widespread nineteenth-century notion of women as creatures of whimsy rather than reason'. In progressing to a role at the magazine which demands reportage, Josanne transcends such fantasies in favour of the 'brave world of facts'.[37] Yet the plot of the novel sees her struggling with the juxtaposition of whimsy and a career which demands reason.

Rogers describes Josanne writing 'enthusiastically' in the text, but in fact the lasting memory is of her writing distractedly: 'ses idées flottaient; elle tenait sa plume d'une main si tremblante encore qu'elle écrivait tout de travers' [her ideas were all over the place; she gripped her pen in a hand still so shaky that she wrote things down all wrong] (*LR*, 317). Her script is rendered almost illegible by her romance, a metaphor for the way that her role as journalist is virtually crossed out by her rediscovery of herself as *femme* and *amante*. Noël may initially take an interest in Josanne's career, but it is above all a means of getting to know her, as he admits, reflecting on her name, and how he conceptualized her when writing to her from Italy:

> Josanne... Josanne... Et parce que je suis un imaginatif, et un sentimental, j'oubliais tout à fait l'article qui avait provoqué notre correspondance; j'oubliais la journaliste, la féministe! Je voyais, sur cette place de Chartres que je connaissais, une jeune femme, en robe noire, au visage voilé. (*LR*, 182)

> [Josanne... Josanne... And since I am an imaginative, and sentimental soul, I completely forgot the article which sparked our correspondence; I forgot the journalist and the feminist! In that square in Chartres that I know well, I saw a young woman, in a black dress, her face veiled.]

He tells her how he envizaged her before meeting her, encapsulated in the stance of a figurine in the place Ghilberti, turning its head away. Of this sculpted, inanimate version of coy femininity, he claims: 'ma rêverie romanesque s'attachait a ce sourire invisible' [my storybook daydreams became attached to that invisible smile] (*LR*, 184).

Passages such as these emphasize the idea that in Tinayre's novel, work at the magazine is but a distraction or a necessary means of income rather than a real focus for interest and ambition for Josanne. For all Mesch's evaluation of the marriage plot in this novel as innovative in itself, *La Rebelle* confirms the idea of the eternal feminine and privileges the love plot over the female *Bildungsroman* model; Holmes says of Tinayre's feminism, that 'certain reforms are demanded in the name of the equality of the sexes, but equality is not taken to conflict with the principle of ahistorical gender difference'.[38] Josanne becomes not so much a *rebelle* as an *elle* who is '*re*-affirmed' in her femininity. Mesch comments on the ambiguities of Tinayre's title choice, 'the very identity of the femme moderne can be understood precisely in the tension between the title of Tinayre's novel and her happy ending — which is the same apparent contradiction between her original title, *Le cœur de Josanne*, and the one she ultimately chose'.[39] The magazine *Monde féminin* is first and foremost in the text a plot device which acts to bring the eventual lovers together via the review of Noël's book penned by Josanne — a piece of journalism already forgotten by Noël in his comments to Josanne, above. And that the magazine is essentially a catalyst for the love story in the text is matched by the fact that, in its focus on the basic romance plot, Tinayre's novel echoes the pattern of the type of fiction serialized in magazines such as *Femina* and *Vie heureuse*.

The first extract of fiction serialized in the opening issues of *Femina* is a romance by Daniel Lesueur (pen-name of Jeanne Loiseau), which sees a young woman raised in New York returning to her French homeland where she is expected to marry her stepmother's son Max; the serial recounts Marguerite's letters to her aunt in America in which she contrasts French and American attitudes to women's independence, and insists on preserving her own right to emancipation. Yet although the series, published in the first few issues of *Femina*, makes clear Marguerite's education and strength of character, she ends up reconciling herself to a future with the conventionally-minded Max after all (who is initially seen maintaining that 'pour moi, la femme n'a qu'un rôle: obéir' [to my mind, a woman has only one role: obedience]);[40] the catalyst is a bicycle race in which the 'la hardiesse anglo-saxonne de la jeune fille' [the Anglo-Saxon boldness of the young girl] cannot, ultimately, compete with that of the French male.[41] Max has to rescue her when her bicycle careers off-course. The result is a story which narrates the conversion of a Frenchwoman raised *outre-mer* [overseas] to a more restrained model of French femininity which sees Marguerite jettisoning her bicycle, symbol of the New Woman's supposed rebellion in countless cartoons.

Yet at the same time Tinayre, in *La Rebelle*, is keen to emphasize a distance between her novel and the material of the magazines. The novel was itself serialized in the established literary journal, *Revue de Paris*, in 1905–06, a publication distinct from the varied, visual and chatty style of *Femina* and *Vie heureuse*. The literariness of the text, asserted too through the repeated references to the well-known works of nineteenth-century realism discussed above, is seen in its satirical evaluation of the output and culture of the magazine. The episode in which Josanne is sent to the Villa Bleue offers insight into the criticism levelled by Tinayre at the strategies of representation offered by the glossy magazine. It indicates the extent to which the reality it claims to offer is airbrushed and edited: 'ce n'est pas dans le *Monde féminin* que Josanne pourra exprimer, sincèrement, ses opinions... Monsieur Foucart exige que la charité soit discrète, la misère voilée, et que la douleur et la mort mêmes gardent un "petit air parisien"' [Josanne could not express her opinions sincerely in the *Monde féminin*... Monsieur Foucart made it clear that charity should be discreet, poverty should be disguised and that pain and even death should retain a 'certain Parisian air'] (*LR*, 99). Such manipulation extends to the letters page: Josanne is obliged to write hyperbolic replies to women requesting advice on how to become slimmer and more elegant, and she sighs over the inanities of such work. In *La Femme seule* Thérèse, too, is charged with such responses, writing to a woman who has expressed her fears of aging that 'les cheveux blancs sont une courrone' [white hair is a form of crown] (*FS* 19). The feminist contributor to this publication scoffs when its editor discusses a new campaign she seeks to run in the magazine on behalf of elegant women who refuse to wear birds' feathers in their hats: 'ce n'est plus la Femme libre, c'est l'oiseau libre, alors?' [so it is not so much the free woman as the free bird?] (*FS*, 19). This same contributor expresses concern over the idea that Mme Nérisse has taken on the editorship out of little more than self-interest, using the magazine as a manifesto arguing for reform of the divorce laws which will allow her to marry her lover.

The distinction which is set up, in these texts, between their own agendas and those of the publications they represent is brought out particularly clearly in the contrast between the title of Brieux's play, *La Femme seule*, and that of the magazine, *Femme libre*. The idealism of the magazine is contradicted by the more sober depiction of the independent woman in the wider plot of the play, which is given resonance when editor Nérisse jeers at Thérèse:

> Malheur à ceux qui sont seuls! Mais, deux fois, cent fois, malheur à la femme qui est seule! Vous ne savez pas ce que c'est. C'est passer son existence au milieu de l'hostilité ou tout au moins de l'aversion générale. (*FS*, 24)
>
> [Misery to those who remain alone! Twice, a hundred times over, misery to the woman alone! You don't know what it means. It means spending your life as a target for hostility or, at the very least, aversion.]

Indeed, while on the one hand novels such as that of Tinayre echo and inflate the happy endings and the emphasis on romance and femininity extolled by the magazines, on the other, they strip away the gloss of these publications. In so doing, they reveal a concern with a turn-of-the-century realism which they purposefully set in the context of earlier Balzacian or Zola-esque versions of the real. There is something refreshing in Josanne's refusal to glamorize her own profession, and in her realism with regard to her own career prospects; for her, reportage is first and foremost a means of earning an income, and her weariness with the tedium of her banal *besogne* lends credibility. While writing up notes for the fashion pages of the magazine, for instance, she rips her own cheap blouse, and is able to laugh at the irony, indicating the text's tendency to rent holes in the fabric of *Monde féminin* and its glitz.[42] Similiarly, Thérèse in *La Femme seule* may be encouraged, when writing the star sign pages, to focus only on happy predictions, but her own future will see her ejected from the editorial offices, where the impetus is to put a spin on reality, and propelled into the sweat and dust of the factory workshops. And in *Femmes nouvelles*, Hélène learns from Minna's pragmatism. Towards the end of the novel, she reflects on her development over the course of the year and the narrative. She has learned to accept reality over illusory romance, and has come closer to the more jaded world view of the journalist:

> Le clair avenir s'ouvrait alors devant elle. Depuis, que de tristesses! La mort de son père, l'existence jour à jour dévoilée dans sa petitesse et sa laideur, ses illusions mutilées... Elle mesurait la distance qu'il y a du rêve à la réalité: ses grands désirs s'étaient limités à de petites actions. (*FN*, 270)
>
> [She had been able to see the future opening clearly before her. And since then, such unhappiness! The death of her father, life revealing its pettiness and ugliness day by day, her illusions shattered... She judged the distance between dream and reality; her great hopes had been limited to restricted actions.]

Measuring the distance between illusion and reality: such is the task these novels set themselves as they debunk fictions of romance and feminism alike. And yet they re-establish their own fantasies, narrating the struggles of modern female lives but often offering idealized solutions.

These novels emerge as ambiguous texts, simultaneously debunking and re-valorizing romance. In their hybridity, they once again echo the format of the magazines they represent, even while they question the output of such publications. When Thérèse shows a new contributor to *Femme libre* the layout of the magazine, she points out that it is divided into two categories, which she describes as 'doctrines' — articles calling for votes for women, discussion of 'l'éternelle esclave' [the eternal slave] — and 'élégances', 'des choses plus légères' [lighter material] fiction, beauty tips, 'frivolités' (*FS*, 16). The magazine launched at the end of *Leur égale* will reflect similar variety. Even *Monde féminin*, in *La Rebelle*, is published alongside a charitable supplement, *Assistance féminine*, edited by Josanne's feminist colleague Mlle Bon. One of these publications claims to represent the 'world' of feminine experience, the other deals with the realities of women's lives, raising money to assist those who need the support of institutions such as the Villa Bleue. The diversity of the magazine — a visually attractive layout promoting a mythical vision of having it all, but with a pullout reality — is echoed in the contradictions of the novel. The dualities of *La Rebelle* are reflected in the fluctuating use of tense in the novel, which intersperses its past tense narration with occasional passages in the present. Josanne is viewed alternately as modern woman, her actions recorded in the text as if through the lens of a media publication intent on capturing the immediacy of her experience, and as age-old heroine of romance, the imperfect tense of the final line of the novel — 'la victoire restait à l'amour' [victory lay with love] (*LR*, 372) — fixing and prolonging the celebration of conventional narrative expectations.

Just as *La Rebelle* oscillates between the contrasting publications of *Assistance féminine* and *Monde féminin*, or between social awareness and fairy-tale romance, so too both *Leur égale* and *Femmes nouvelles* adopt stylistic hybridity, shuttling between 'élégances' and 'doctrines'. In *Leur égale* rhetorical passages and lengthy inserted dialogues on women's rights are set alongside the narrative of Thérèse and Adrien's romance, a juxtaposition which reflects the proposed layout of the magazine foreseen by the text. The romance plot in the novel employs traditional features such as pathetic fallacy, and focuses in detail on the decor and symbolism of the

Parisian apartment where Thérèse will arrange to meet and sleep with Adrien. Interspersed with such conventional aspects of narrative, there are key scenes of dialogue, which rupture the unfolding of the plot in order to lend focus to the political dimensions of the text. In each such scene, the launch of *Femme moderne* or the obstacles facing it act as a catalyst for the discussion, and each sees Thérèse defending her own point of view against a male interlocutor or a male gathering. In one such debate, she sets out her belief in the need for a change in attitudes to marriage and her scepticism as to whether such change is possible; her speeches are lengthy and punctuated by anaphoric rhetorical constructions, as if she is penning her prospective articles as she speaks. This excerpt is from an impassioned speech which takes up over a page of text:

> Ce qu'il faut pour que le malaise pesant sur le mariage moderne disparaisse, c'est que les conditions dans lesquelles il s'accomplit soient changés, non devant le code, mais au fond du cœur de l'homme et de la femme!... Il faut que l'homme cesse de rechercher une vierge à violer, un cœur naïf à berner, un corps et un âme à asservir injustement... Il faut que la femme ne soit point réduite à la ruse méchante, à la lutte sournoise, aux traîtres vengeances... qu'elle retrouve une dignité, un sentiment de l'honneur, de l'orgueil moral qui lui fait défaut à l'heure qu'il est... Il faut que deux êtres se plaisent, s'acceptent, sans égoïsme, sans illusions absurdes! (*LE*, 238)

> [What is needed in order for the malaise hanging over modern marriage to disappear is for the conditions which govern marriage to be changed — not just the code itself, but the way that men and women feel towards it, in their hearts! Men need to stop seeking a virgin to violate, a naïve heart to deceive, and a being to subjugate unjustly. Women in turn should not be reduced to nasty tricks, sly battles or perfidious revenge... instead they should rediscover their dignity, their sense of honour and of moral pride, all of which are lacking at the present moment... Two individuals should aim to please each other, to accept one another, unselfishly and without absurd illusions!]

The potent language here, along with tripartite constructions and imperatives, suggest that Thérèse speaks both from her own experience of romance, and from her sense of having been sexually expoited by Adrien, and is able to turn her personal story into the carefully crafted material of a potential *Femme moderne* article.

The realism of the texts stems too from the characters' refusal to see themselves as literary writers. In *La Femme seule*, as seen above, Thérèse congratulates herself on having abjured her previous aspiration to become a literary writer in favour of more pragmatic action. *La Rebelle* makes frequent reference to the idea that novels by women have become acceptable and expected; one of the subscribers to *Monde féminin* is delighted by her acquaintance with Josanne:

> Le temps n'est plus où la petite bourgeoisie et même la grande affectaient un peu de mépris et beaucoup de méfiance pour les 'auteurs' et surtout pour les auteurs femmes. Depuis que les gens de lettres ont fait fortune, la littérature est honorée comme un 'bon métier, qui rapporte'. (*LR*, 338)

> [The time has passed when the middle classes affected a sense of disdain and mistrust towards 'authors' and especially towards women authors. Since men of

Letters have managed to make money, literature has been honoured as a 'good profession, which pays well'.]

Yet Josanne does not seek to write fiction of her own. Pinson's discussion of characteristic features of the nineteenth-century *roman du journalisme* draws connections between texts such as that of Tinayre, which feature the woman journalist, and earlier examples depicting ambitious young men taken on as reporters. A sense of *déracinement* [rootlessness] connects these characters as they embark on new careers.[43] Yet a key distinction is that the male figures in these texts are very often seen — as in *La Vie des frelons* — as aspiring writers of fiction or poetry. This is not the case with the women journalists. Josanne insists that she has no such ambitions. Pressed by Noël, who comments on the vogue for women novelists at the time ('toutes les femmes en font. C'est la mode' [all women do it; it's the fashion]), she maintains:

> Si j'avais du talent, j'écrirais des livres: je dirais des choses variés, graves et tristes, qu'une femme seulement peut bien dire... Hélas! Je n'ai pas de talent... J'écris adroitement un article: j'ai un peu de verve et d'esprit, du métier... Mais il me manque le don de réaliser mes imaginations, la faculté créatrice... Je serais une bonne conseillère, peut-être une bonne collaboratrice... Et c'est tout. (*LR*, 142)

> [If I had any talent, I would write books: I would say varied things, serious and sad things, that only a woman can really say... Alas, I have not such talent... I can pen an article shrewdly; I have a little verve and spirit, some skill... But I lack the ability to bring my imaginings to life, I lack creative flair... I would be a good adviser, maybe a good magazine contributor... But that is all.]

Tinayre's novel is ambiguously placed in relation to Josanne's words. One the one hand, it sets itself up as a book akin to that which Josanne claims she would write if she had the talent, 'varié, grave et triste': the very fact that Josanne is presented not as one of 'toutes les femmes' who take to the literary marketplace to sell their fictions but as a realistic and self-aware young woman indicates Tinayre's creation of a character who has progressed beyond more conventional *romanesque* desires. The adjective *romanesque* is applied instead to the male figures in the novel. Josanne's former lover, Maurice, for instance, is described as 'littéraire et romanesque' (*LR*, 6); he believes himself sentimental and tries to make an impression on Josanne when he first meets her by chatting about books and the verse he writes. His dreams of a 'grande passion' contrast with Josanne's own focus on the need to earn a living for herself and on her firm but realistic insistence on her right to be happy. On the other hand, the novel itself establishes its own desirable romantic ending, and Tinayre takes her place among the many contemporary women writers described by Noël in somewhat patronizing tones of *raillerie*, or mockery: 'Le féministe parlait des œuvres féminines avec une amiable irrévérence!' [the feminist spoke of women's works with a pleasing irreverence!] (*LR*, 141). *La Rebelle* achieves marketplace success despite its satire of the successes of commercialized publications aimed at women.

What the novel does signify, in the contradictions between the codes of realism and romance it evokes, is the deliberate amalgamation of earlier models of nineteenth-century fiction. In her discussion of the sentimental novel of the first half of the century, Margaret Cohen argues that women writers of that period deliberately set themselves apart from a realist practice which was being established and enacted by men, and in purposeful opposition to the dominant generic model of sentimentalism, which had been associated with women from the early 1800s:

> For the woman novelist interested in accumulating symbolic capital, it was evidently legitimating to build on the previously dominant sentimental practice of the novel, given that women were preeminent in this practice, that women writers' contributions to early nineteenth-century sentimentality were widely recognised, and that the sentimental novel continued to be accorded critical respect [...]. How much more difficult it would be to exploit the realist position, whatever its symbolic rewards. From their emergence, realist works assert their claims to literary importance by identifying the novel with men, by forging a poetics associated with masculine forms of knowledge, and by undercutting the authority of the woman writer along with sentimental codes.[44]

I would suggest that writers such as Tinayre and Pert consciously reflect on such combined strategies of gender and genre. Unlike the practitioners of the sentimental novel included in Cohen's analysis, they do not set themselves apart from realism. Instead, they call up the realist tradition in their intertextual resonances and in their response to the hyperbolic representations of femininity in the magazines they echo. Yet they also reinvigorate the sentimental codes which in the early nineteenth century were set in opposition to burgeoning realism. Says Cohen, 'the sentimental novel asserts the imperative to individual freedom, which it associates with happiness, choice, nature, the private, sentiment, and erotic love': such an imperative is precisely the model emphasized by Josanne in Tinayre's novel.[45] These texts, by women or by feminist thinkers, forge and theorize generic boundaries; their incorporation of the magazine culture and the trends in the women's press of the turn of the century enables them to reflect on and enhance a metatextual understanding of such strategies.

That this conscious strategization is at work is indicated, in *La Rebelle*, through the insight it offers into the desires and demands of its own readership. Josanne describes the educated women she goes to interview for the magazine, the women who would not just have featured in the pages of publications such as *Monde féminin* or *Femina*, but would also have made up a substantial proportion of their readers. These are doctors, artists, and lawyers, 'les "affranchies", les "rebelles": Elles s'insurgent contre les préjugés, contre la morale conventionnelle, et elles recréent un idéal nouveau de l'honneur, de la vertu, du devoir féminin' [the 'emancipated' ones, the 'rebels': They rise up against prejudice, against conventional morals, and they rebuild a new idea of female honour, virtue and duty]. And yet she articulates her growing awareness that the more she probes the inner desires of these women, the more conventional they seem: 'je sens qu'elles ont gardé les vieux instincts de la femme d'autrefois' [I sense that they have preserved the old instincts of women from an earlier age] (*LR*, 130). All four of the texts under discussion here make clear an intention to reach out to readers who incarnate both the 'idéal nouveau' and the 'vieux instincts [...] d'autrefois'. As an extension to the discussion of the models of plot and the representations of realism and romance discussed in this section, part of the textual identity of these works is — like that of the publications they echo — to forge a new sense of community among women. Although the letters pages in *Monde féminin* and *Femme libre* are mocked, they also reflect the communication which is opened up between the female reading public and the space of the text(s). While such communication is subject to manipulation, it is clearly also popular, as described by Thérèse in *La Femme seule* in her reference to the 'courrier des moissonneuses' [letters age]: 'oui, c'est entre les abonnées réelles ou supposés un échange de recettes culinaires, de petits secrets d'hygiène, de coquetterie [...] C'est la partie la plus lue, je suis forcée de la reconnaître' [between the real or imagined subscribers there is an exchange of recipes, of beauty secrets and tips for flirting [...] I must admit that this is the best-read section] (*FS*, 16). The novels incorporate such an idealized community in their own emphasis on the potential solidarity of female-to-female mentorship, whether between Mlle Bon and Josanne in *La Rebelle*, Minna and Hélène in *Femmes nouvelles*, or the warmth of the relationship between the older journalist Mlle de Meuriot and Thérèse in *La Femme seule*. Although the novels question the support structures within female communities and retain a scepticism towards the strategies adopted by the magazines for attracting and retaining female readers, they also aim to encourage the creation of such reading networks through their own success and dissemination.

Madeleine Forestier and Écriture féminine

These networks are created despite the apparent isolation and social nonconformity which characterize the women journalists in the texts. In the opening chapter of *La Rebelle*, Josanne is mockingly referred to by her lover as an 'anarchiste': 'Elle ne ressemblait pas davantage aux maîtresses qu'il avait eues et aux maîtresses qu'avaient ses camarades [...] Elle dérangeait toutes les idées qu'il s'était faites' [she no longer resembled the mistresses he himself had had, nor his friends' mistresses [...] She unsettled all his preconceptions] (*LR*, 8). Similarly, in *Leur égale* at her lover's family château, Thérèse contemplates the faces and attitudes of the men and women around her and 'apercevait [...] quelque chose d'uniforme [...]; une sorte de confraternité imprécisable, dans l'expression factice des physiognomies, dans l'apprêté, le convenu des attitudes, des accents, des sons de voix [...] confraternité dans laquelle Adrien était englobé, et dont elle s'apercevait exclue' [detected [...] something the same about them all, a sort of indefinable fellowship in the artificial, affected expressions on their faces, in their accepted attitudes, accents and intonation [...] a fellowship in which Adrien was included, and from which she felt herself excluded] (*LE*, 195). In this they share an affinity with the female 'journalist' depicted in *Bel-Ami*, a text published some twenty years earlier. In Italian the word *forestiere* means 'stranger' or 'foreigner,' a soubriquet which fits Madeleine Forestier's enigmatic nature.[46] *La Rebelle* contains a direct echo of the character of Madeleine Forestier in its representation of the *directrice* of *Monde féminin*, who not only shares her name and initials with Maupassant's creation, but whose husband, the editor Isidore Foucart, is described as having 'l'air d'un Bel-Ami arrivé' [the air of a successful Bel-Ami] (*LR*, 45). It is Madeleine Foucart who is responsible for the establishment of the magazine: having previously set up a fashion magazine, *La Parisienne*, she has gone on to launch *Monde féminin*. Tinayre's text presents the forty-five-year-old Madeleine Foucart, 'un peu trop grasse' [a little on the plump side] but 'désirable encore' [still desirable] (*LR*, 44) as a latter-day Madeleine Forestier; her activities an extension of the sort of work that Maupassant's heroine might have gone on to engage in twenty years down the line. Mme Foucart 'avait fait tout: des livres, de la peinture, une exploration au Spitzberg, du reportage à l'américaine [...] et, vers la quarantaine, elle s'était jetée dans le féminisme comme d'autres se jettent dans la dévotion' [had done it all: writing, painting, an exploratory trip to Spitzberg, American-style journalism [...] and, approaching forty, she had launched herself into feminism as others launch themselves into devoutness] (*LR*, 44). Although attractive and influential, Madeleine Foucart is the object of Tinayre's critical evaluation of the superficial glitz offered by the magazine. Her feminism is undermined by the limitations of her female circle: 'la grande féministe avait sa cour' [the influential feminist had her court around her] (*LR*, 45). While she approves of and supports the femininity of certain magazine contributors, Madeleine Foucart has no time for Josanne, her poverty, her pride, and her lack of fashion. Despite the satire levelled at Mme Foucart in the novel, Tinayre's own set of essays written in the first person, *Madeleine au Miroir*, suggests a parallel between her own image of herself as a writer and the influence of a Madeleine Forestier/Foucart.[47] This chapter will conclude with an evaluation of the role played by Madeleine Forestier in Maupassant's novel, arguing that while she offers no vision of female community such as that idealized in the later texts, her influence, both within *Bel-Ami* and in terms of her role as a prototype for the New Woman and for the woman journalist, offers a powerful symbol of the resonance of the feminine voice of the press. Maupassant, albeit unconsciously or reluctantly, allows his female journalist to write beyond the ending in particularly potent fashion.

It has been suggested that Madeleine Forestier is a reflection of Séverine, the influential voice behind the front page 'Notes d'une frondeuse', who reported on the Dreyfus affair for *La Fronde*. *Bel-Ami* was serialized in Guesde's paper, *Voie du peuple*, rival to the *Cri du peuple* whose editorship was taken over by Séverine following the death of Vallès in 1885; critics suggested that the novel set out to satirize Séverine and her lover, the arriviste journalist Labruyère. Yet Delaisement points out the unlikelihood of such an idea, given the novel's publication date of 1884, which did not quite coincide with the slightly later rise of Labruyère. Delaisement instead suggests a range of possible models for Madeleine Forestier.[48] Madeleine, widow of the newspaper's political editor and first wife of Duroy can be seen as an additional mirror in the text to add to those seen in Chapter One: she and Bel Ami resemble each other; he embodies a certain femininity as she is at times associated with the masculine; both are ambitious and stop at nothing to get what they desire, as seen when both rename themselves after their marriage so as to facilitate their social ascent. *Bel-Ami* recounts the *Bildungsroman* plot of not one but two journalists; Madeleine's biography is woven into the text as if in the margins. As she acts as Duroy's *nègre*, his ghostwriter, so she pre-empts and tracks his path through the novel: a dual journey evoked in a telling scene when the couple return from a night out at the theatre and are illuminated in the staircase mirror: 'la flamme subite éclatant sous le frottement, fit surgir dans la glace leurs deux figures illuminés au milieu des ténèbres de l'escalier. Ils avaient l'air de fantômes apparus et prêts à s'évanouir dans la nuit' (*BA*, 152) ('the match suddenly flared up as it was being struck, illuminating their two faces as they loomed out of the mirror amid the shadows of the stairwell. They looked like ghosts that had materialized, and were about to vanish into the night'). In a quotation itself constructed from the reflective techniques of internal rhyme, fricative alliteration, and assonantal 'i' sounds, Duroy and Madeleine emerge as mirrors of each other; she his ghostwriter, he the insubstantial name created by her pen.

Madeleine Forestier is more than just one of many mirrors for Georges Duroy, however. Her dynamism, creativity, and cunning suggest that just as she acts as the hidden pen behind the newspaper front page, spinning its stories, so too does she act as a latent source of power behind the novel itself. Not for nothing is she depicted dictating Duroy's first article for the paper, spider-like, her words bound up with the smoke she exhales, 'une buée pareille à des fils d'araignée' (*BA*, 75) ('a kind of transparent mist, a gossamer vapour'). Roberts sees Madeleine as an early model of the New Woman, arguing that she assumes a carefully controlled façade of conventional femininity in order to facilitate her journalistic and political machinations; she refers to:

> Two rebellious women, Clothilde de Marelle and Madeleine Forestier — both of whom would come to be called the 'Nouvelle Femme' [...] Like Duroy, these two women exploit the weightlessness of artifice, thereby becoming more powerful and independent. All three characters — Duroy and the two women — subvert gender norms.[49]

White makes a case for seeing Madeleine as 'the paradoxical centre of the novel', given the force she represents in determining her own marriage contract to Duroy, shaping his new name, and penning the articles of both Forestier and Bel-Ami. White reminds readers of the dominance of Madeleine throughout the novel, given the text's symmetry:

> As is ritually noted, in the first scene of the novel, Georges is on his way to the aptly named Église de la Madeleine when he bumps into Forestier, and this church is where his marriage to Suzanne Walter is celebrated at the end of the text.[50]

Structurally, Maupassant reminds his readers of the presence of Madeleine throughout: after this first chapter which sees Duroy roaming through the boulevards around the Madeleine-Opéra, he is first introduced to Forestier's wife at the dinner party she hosts in Chapter Two; he then encounters her in almost every chapter up until the end of Part One, which recounts the death of Forestier and the opportunity for Duroy to marry his widow. The relationship between Duroy and Madeleine therefore reaches a crescendo by the middle of the text. Part Two narrates their marriage and divorce, culminating in the scene in Chapter Eight in which Duroy infiltrates the apartment Madeleine is sharing with her lover, Laroche-Mathieu. Only in the final two chapters is she then absent from the text, making an oblique appearance in the final scene via the image of the church. White suggests that the ending of Part One, which terminates in a death and a new marriage, both reflects and subverts the teleology of conventional narrative. It provides us with a 'doubly classical closure' but then ruptures such closure by carrying on into Part Two, via the alternative vision of traditional marriage set out by Madeleine. The continuation of the narrative is permitted by the new twist of the divorce law: 'this state-sponsored refashioning of narrative shapes reveals a philosophical shift in how the teleologies of life are viewed by the secular republic'.[51] *Bel-Ami* writes beyond the ending in offering a narrative development beyond the marriage plot, and in envizaging an unconventional marriage shaped by Madeleine, yet it ultimately culminates once again with a wedding, thereby both rewriting conventional narrative and reinserting itself back into the framework of convention: 'Georges [...] is a survivor who unlike other versions of the Don Juan figure, resists the narrative closure of death [...] but cannot resist that other classic ending, marriage'.[52] However, despite the way in which the novel trumpets the conformist nature of its marital resolution, with Duroy standing post-ceremony on the steps of the Madeleine — a reminder of the way he has used Madeleine herself as a ladder for his ambition — it is also possible to see the emblem of the church and its title as indicative of the power that Madeleine Forestier continues to wield. Madeleine is written out of the narrative in the aftermath of the scene in which her adultery is exposed, enabling the narrative to begin again and end conventionally with Duroy's marriage to Suzanne, but her voice continues to resound. The final scene in the church allows the voice of 'la Madeleine' to be heard in the reverberating feminized voice of the organ, symbolically suggesting the continued dominance of Madeleine's capacity for expression: a capacity evoked much earlier in the novel in the scenes where she takes up the pen so as to articulate herself journalistically behind the pseudonyms of her husbands. The declaration of partnership in marriage Madeleine expounds to Duroy in the closing chapter of Part One (described by White as 'a programmatic and idealistic thesis which reflects (and perhaps stretches) many of the aspirations of conservative feminism in the fin de siècle')[53] reads as an emancipatory vision of marriage which might, indeed, constitute one of the narrative acts that Blau DuPlessis sees as characterizing twentieth-century women's writing:

> Le mariage pour moi n'est pas une chaîne, mais une association. J'entends être libre, tout à fait libre de mes actes, de mes démarches, de mes sorties, toujours. Je ne pourrais tolérer ni contrôle, ni jalousie, ni discussion sur ma conduite. Je m'engagerais, bien entendu, à ne jamais compromettre le nom de l'homme que j'aurais épousé, à ne jamais le rendre odieux ou ridicule. Mais il faudrait aussi que cet homme s'engageât à voir en moi une égale, une alliée, et non pas une inférieure ni une épouse obéissante et soumise. Mes idées, je le sais, ne sont pas celles de tout le monde, mais je n'en changerai point. (*BA*, 224–25)

> [Marriage, for me, is not a bond, but a partnership. I expect to be free, completely free, in what I do, whom I see, where I go, always. I could not tolerate either supervision, or jealousy, or any discussion of my behaviour. I would of course understand never to compromise the name of the man I had married, never to make him seem hateful or ridiculous. But that man would also have to see me

as an equal, an ally, not as an inferior or an obedient submissive wife. I know my ideas are not shared by everyone, but I shan't change them.]

Absent from the closing ceremony of the novel, the idea that Madeleine's quest continues through her writing is evoked through the discussion between the journalists Norbert de Varenne and Jacques Rival as to her fate, and the implication that she has found a way of continuing to be involved in the world of the press via the output of a new protégé, Jean Le Dol, whose political articles 'ressemblent terriblement à ceux de Forestier et de Du Roy' (*BA*, 408) ('are terribly similar to those of Forestier and Du Roy'). Even more potent is the description of the voice from within the church, the 'orgues' which animate the body of the church with sound as, in the past, Madeleine has ventriloquized Duroy — and indeed her former husband and the new puppet Le Dol. As Duroy kneels at the altar 'toujours les orgues chantaient, poussaient par l'énorme monument les accents ronflants et rythmés de leurs gorges luisantes' (*BA*, 411) ('and the organ went on singing, spreading throughout the vast building the throbbing, rhythmical notes of its shining throat'). The reverberations of the sound are textually echoed in the 'ors' and 'rs' of the description. And when he prepares to walk back down the aisle with his new wife, 'les orgues' can be heard once again:

> Tantôt elles jetaient des clameurs prolongées, énormes, enflées comme des vagues, si sonores et si puissantes, qu'il semblait qu'elles dussent soulever et faire sauter le toit pour se répandre dans le ciel bleu. Leur bruit vibrant emplissait toute l'église, faisait frissonner la chair et les âmes. Puis tout à coup elles se calmaient; et des notes fines, alertes, couraient dans l'air, effleuraient l'oreille comme des souffles légers; c'étaient de petits chants gracieux, menus, sautillants, qui voletaient ainsi que des oiseaux; et soudain, cette coquette musique s'élargissait de nouveau, redevenant effrayante de force et d'ampleur, comme si un grain de sable se métamorphosait en un monde. (*BA*, 413)
>
> [Sometimes it gave long-drawn-out, tremendous shouts that swelled like waves, so resonant and so powerful that it seemed they must raise the roof and shatter it, spreading out into the blue sky. Their vibrant sound filled the whole church, sending shivers through body and soul. Then, abruptly, they quietened; and delicate, sprightly notes ran through the air, brushing the ear like soft breath: charming, slight, frisky little tunes that hopped about like birds; then suddenly this charming little tune was amplified afresh, again inspiring fear with its power and volume, as if a grain of sand was transforming itself into a world.]

In this passage, the voice of (the) Madeleine is described in terms characterized by sibilance and liquidity, as in the reference to the 'vagues si sonores et puissantes'. In its potency and its physicality, such a description of the feminized voice evokes Hélène Cixous's attempt to encapsulate twentieth-century *écriture féminine* in 'Le Rire de la Méduse' [The Laugh of the Medusa]. While the articles that Madeleine Forestier will dictate for Duroy and for *Vie française* are associated with a masculine world of politics and empire, Maupassant's description of the pluralized and sexualized sounds of the organ here is echoed in Cixous's essay. Cixous describes the process of liberating the new form of writing from the old: 'la Nouvelle sera, comme la flèche quitte la corde, d'un trait rassemblant et séparant les ondes musicalement, afin d'*être plus qu'elle-même*' ('the New Woman will be, as an arrow quits the bow with a movement that gathers and separates the vibrations musically, in order to be more than herself').[54] Musical and vibrating in waves, the Madeleine organ too is a symbol of the female voice in the text becoming 'plus qu'elle-même' — more than Madeleine herself, connotative instead of a sound which transcends the singular character to represent something collective and resounding. And indeed, the simile of the grain of sand which expands in the closing line here to become a whole world, is indicative of a revolutionary stirring, associated on the one hand with Maupassant's scathing social critique in the novel, but on another with the rise of the New Woman charted in the text.

Roberts points out that Maupassant was no feminist.[55] It may therefore seem perverse to align his evocations of the organ's voice with that of Madeleine, and in turn, with the *écriture féminine* practised, according to Cixous, by very few writers: 'je n'ai vu inscrire de la féminité que par Colette, Marguerite Duras, et... Jean Genet' ('the only inscriptions of femininity I have seen were by Colette, Marguerite Duras... and Jean Genet').[56] Yet I would argue that the text both represents and struggles to contain the potential power inherent in a woman like Madeleine. Alternately sonorous and delicate as birdsong, the organ's throat is capable of harmonizing subtlety and power, 'chair' and 'âme' — much as Madeleine herself evokes and unifies contrasts throughout the text. Conventionally feminine with her blonde hair and pink dresses, she is also associated with masculine qualities, particularly in her writing. The political articles she dictates to Duroy once they are married are described by Walter as 'du Forestier plus nourri, plus nerveux, plus viril' (*BA*, 182) ('a meatier, terser, more virile Forestier'), appropriate for a woman who wields her phallic cigarette and pen interchangeably as she composes. In entertaining ministers in her drawing room, Madeleine synchronizes private and public, as she does in her journalistic writing. The settings against which she is visualized — such as the conservatory in the apartment where Duroy first meets her — also represent a blend between real and fake, urban and natural. And the Madeleine church represents a synthesis of both the religious and the secular, set as it is amid the rapidly commercializing world of the boulevards, and church and state: a short leap away from the Chamber of Deputies, as the penultimate paragraph of the text makes clear. These contrasts are animated and unified by the voice of the organ(s); their plurality appropriate for the potency generated by the ability to draw together the binaries of the new French society, as Madeleine is able to do.

There is irony, of course, in seeing the voice of the church organ as the voice of Madeleine, given that what is being celebrated in this scene is Duroy's triumph over Madeleine via his new marriage and his continued social ascent; the organ rings out to mark 'la gloire des nouveau époux' [the glory of the newlywed couple] and to proclaim the hollow 'triomphe du baron Georges Du Roy' [triumph of the Baron Georges Du Roy]. Yet while these passages could be read as mocking Madeleine's erstwhile power and its loss, they also suggest the continuation of her dominance within the text. Even the reassertion of Duroy's name, which follows the description of the vocal flood of the organ, is a reminder of the fact that he is, and remains, Madeleine's creation: she has named him and, in encouraging his relationships with other women, including Madame Walter, has effectively engendered his new marriage. Du Roy may stand on the steps of the church and contemplate future political success, but Madeleine too is contained within the image; her body and her voice — the tools she has employed to garner her own victories — represented in the church behind him, her 'coquette musique' retaining its 'effrayante' power to disrupt society and text. The potent voice of 'Madeleine's' organ is not just a grain of sand reminding readers of the swelling tide of new opportunities for women to articulate themselves. It also underscores the forces associated with journalism in the novel. The closing scene of *Bel-Ami*, which can be read as a triumph of Madeleine's resurgent voice, is a triumph of the journalistic pen she holds behind the scenes, as suggested by the title of the new publication for which she is ghostwriting, *La Plume*.

The extent of Madeleine's role — both at *Vie française* and within the *vie française* — is first glimpsed in Chapter Three, when Duroy, having struggled with the composition of his article on Algerian life, is encouraged by Forestier to go and seek his wife's help. This scene, pivotal to an understanding of Madeleine's role within the text, reveals her skill as a hidden journalist: her capacity for engaging a reader, structuring an article, extracting crucial information from an interviewee. She is media-savvy, and combines in this scene once again masculine and feminine tropes in order to ensure the impact of her output. Duroy finds her in her negligee in the masculinized space of Forestier's study, where she 'avait l'air chez elle devant cette table de travail, à l'aise comme dans son salon, occupée à sa besogne ordinaire' (*BA*, 72) ('seemed to feel at home seated at this writing-desk, as much at ease as if she were in her own drawing-room, busy with her normal duties'). Her adroitness in this space and within the role she has created for herself is reflected in the manner with which she twirls her pen: 'elle maniait entre deux doigts une plume d'oie en la tournant agilement; et, devant elle, une grande page de papier demeurait écrite à moitié' (*BA*, 71) [she was nimbly twirling a goose-feather quill between two fingers, and in front of her lay a large sheet of paper, half-covered in writing]. The sexual implications of this gesture (the text is full of references to Madeleine's own appreciation of smut) anticipate the connections drawn by Maupassant between Madeleine's prowess in the bedroom and her ability with words, connections echoed in the conversation between Rival and de Varenne in the church in the last chapter, when the comments as to Madeleine's new role behind the scenes at *La Plume* are accompanied by suppositions as to her sexual wiles ('elle doit être charmante au découvert' (*BA*, 408) ('between the sheets, she must be charming')). The libidinal production of Madeleine is again echoed in the union of the sexual and the textual promoted by Cixous in her celebration of 'les vrais textes de femmes, des textes avec des sexes de femmes' ('the true texts of women — female-sexed texts').[57] Cixous advocates writing with the body; Maupassant will conclude his novel with the articulation of the organ, a musical 'sexe de femme'.

The half-written page on Madeleine's bureau — a draft of an article for the next day's paper to appear under her husband's name, given her comment that the staff at the newspaper offices 'connaît [son] écriture' (*BA*, 72) ('know her handwriting')

— contrasts with the description of Duroy's own failure to set anything down on paper prior to his visit to the Forestiers. Madeleine's fluency is oral as well as written; where Duroy 'balbutia' [stammered] and speaks 'en hésitant', she takes charge of the conversation. When he still fails to *raconter* anything about Africa, she begins to interview him both like a journalist and 'comme aurait fait un prêtre au confessionnel' (*BA*, 74) ('like a priest in the confessional'), a simile which once again indicates the secular power she possesses within the text; the comparison anticipates the closing scene of the novel and the idea that Madeleine represents the voice within the church. It is also proleptic of that other scene in the novel which takes place in the church, when Duroy is attempting to seduce Mme Walter and she takes momentary refuge in the space of the confessional; as elsewhere, the connections implied here suggest that Madeleine, the 'priest', remains in control of Duroy's love affairs; Madeleine's capacity for wielding public influence from the inner sanctum of the private domain is again made apparent. Her decision to turn Duroy's prospective article on Africa into a chatty letter to an acquaintance sees her performative abilities, her ventriloquism animated by the bawdiness of the subject matter: the grubbiness of the description, which involves mud huts and emetics, and the apparent unsuitability of such *vif* tones for the eyes of ladies. The fact that the novel devotes a substantial chunk of the text to parroting Madeleine's spiel in direct speech indicates both her fluency and the pleasure she takes in improvising this masculine discourse: in between composing lines she 'se frottait les mains, tout à fait heureuse de son idée' (*BA*, 73) ('she was rubbing her hands in delight at her idea'). As Roberts points out, this article is a complete fabrication, 'a double fakery, both for its false authorship and its content — pure orientalist fantasy, a pastiche of erotic images of Moorish women'.[58] Madeleine evokes a fantasy of Africa, peppering her creation with stereotypes: 'Alger est la porte, la porte blanche et charmante de cet étrange continent' (*BA*, 74) ('Algiers is the gateway, the charming white gateway to this strange continent') and eroticizing the content of her orientalism: 'puis elle continua par une excursion dans la province d'Oran, une excursion fantaisiste, où il était surtout question des femmes, des Mauresques, des Juives, des Espagnoles' (*BA*, 75) ('next she continued with an expedition into the province of Oran, an entirely imaginary expedition which was mainly concerned with women, Moorish women, Jewish women, Spanish women').

The composition of this article, which reveals so much about Madeleine and her influence, is reflected in the structures of the text itself, which sees her creating her own story. As she shapes the reader's impressions of Algeria in this passage and supplies the fictionalized Duroy figure with a wealth of love intrigues, so in the novel as a whole she helps to engender the new French interventions in North Africa and oversees Duroy's relationships with Clotilde and Mme Walter. Her words become actuality. She even seems to forecast her own role, as she 'ébauchait une aventure d'amour avec la femme d'un capitaine d'infanterie qui allait rejoindre son mari' (*BA*, 74) ('sketching in a love affair with the wife of an infantry captain who was on her way to rejoin her husband'), anticipating her own future 'aventure d'amour' with Duroy as a break from Forestier, glamorized in her version as a captain of the infantry. Since her dictation involves her assuming the first-person role in these African adventures, it is as though she is, in fact, writing herself a more exciting and exoticized life: 'je vais t'envoyer, [...] une sorte de journal de ma vie, jour par jour, heure par heure' (*BA*, 75) ('I'm going to send you [...] a kind of journal of my life, day by day, hour by hour'). Madeleine extricates herself from the role of bored housewife 'n'ayant rien à faire' [having nothing to do] by fantasizing and by turning that fantasy into materiality, a 'journal de [sa] vie', published in the pages of the 'journal' within the novel.

Madeleine cannot work without smoking, a fixation which not only reinforces the more masculine side of her personality, but also anticipates the closing passages of the text in giving visual and aural resonance to the suggestions of her influential voice:

> Elle se leva et se mit à marcher, après avoir allumé une autre cigarette, et elle dictait, en soufflant des filets de fumée qui sortaient d'abord tout droit d'un petit trou rond au milieu de ses lèvres serrées, puis s'élargissant, s'évaporaient en laissant par places, dans l'air, des lignes grises, une sorte de brume transparente, une buée pareille a des fils d'araignée. Parfois, d'un coup de sa main ouverte, elle effaçait ces traces légères et plus persistantes; parfois aussi elle les coupait d'un movement trenchant de l'index et regardait ensuite, avec une attention grave, les deux tronçons d'imperceptible vapeur disparaître lentement. (*BA*, 75)

> [She stood up, lit another cigarette, and began to walk about, still dictating and blowing out thin trickles of smoke which at first rose straight up from a tiny round hole made by her pursed lips, then grew larger, evaporating, and leaving grey threads here and there in the air, a kind of transparent mist, a gossamer vapour. Sometimes, with a movement of her open hand, she would erase the more persistent of these faint traces; and sometimes she would cut across them with a slicing movement of her forefinger and then watch, with grave attention, as the two sections of barely perceptible vapour slowly disappeared.]

As in the evocation of the organ's song, sound-patterning provides echoes of the inflections of her voice as she 'dictait'; the fricative 'soufflant'/'filets' and 'fumée' mimicking the puffs of smoke she exhales, just as internal rhyme ('soufflant'/'tout'/'trou') amplifies the resonance of her voice and even, in the repeated 'o's glimpsed in this line ('tout droit d'un petit trou rond') sees typographical representation of the shape of her mouth, emphasizing the physicality of her expression and suggesting its eroticism. As Cixous writes, in censuring women's writing, 'on censure du même coup le souffle, la parole' ('you censor breath and speech at the same time').[59] Madeleine instead uses her *souffle* to transcend the misogynistic limits of the newspaper, which would stifle her. The smoke is emblematic of Madeleine's speech and her writing, forming 'lignes grises' which she is able to manipulate and disperse. As the music of the organ 's'élargissait', seeming to raise the roof in order to spread into the sky, so here Madeleine's dictation, visualized through her cigarette smoke, is seen 's'élargissant'. Although suggestions of ephemerality could indicate the overall transience of writing in the text, nevertheless here the lingering mist has a density and a textuality reminiscent of the print of the newspaper itself, split into columns as Madeleine 'edits' her output, tweaking the curls of smoke with her bodily gestures, hurling herself into writing. As Cixous writes, 'elle matérialise charnellement ce qu'elle pense' ('she materializes what she's thinking; she signifies it with her body').[60] The persistence of the 'imperceptible vapeur' Madeleine has produced and projected is glimpsed in the text's structural echoes, as later in the novel she and Duroy work to see *Vie française* intervening in the plans to invade Morocco, with Duroy's originally signed article being rehashed and republished; the influence of Madeleine's cigarette plumes being used to dictate government policy.[61]

Completing her creation and instructing Duroy to sign the finished article, Madeleine is emphatic: 'c'est comme ça qu'on écrit un article' (*BA*, 75) ('that [...] is how to write an article'). This is a scene which offers a microcosm of journalistic practice, with Madeleine providing a lesson in how to be a successful newspaper columnist: extracting information, selecting, composing, crafting, shaping the influence of her words. She is media-conscious enough to know what will attract readers, listing the range of invented amorous liaisons because she is aware that 'il n'y a que ça qui intéresse' (*BA*, 75) ('that's the only thing people are interested in'), and accompanying the salacious titbits with an informative dimension, quizzing Duroy on Algerian topography in order to compile a brief factfile on the country. What also stands out in this scene is the enjoyment that Madeleine gains from her work: already seen rubbing her hands with glee at the prospect of her inventive capacity, so the anticipation of the next instalment leads her to cry out 'd'une voix joyeuse' [cheerfully]. One of her reasons for accepting Duroy's proposal after the death of her first husband is that the new marriage will enable her to continue exerting influence in journalism. Her widowhood means that she is deprived of a voice at the paper and 'ça me manque beaucoup [...] mais beaucoup. J'étais devenue journaliste dans l'âme. Que voulez-vous, j'aime ce métier-là' (*BA*, 180) ('I miss it badly, really badly. I had become a journalist in spirit. Well, what can you expect, I love the profession').

Madeleine's actions give an insight into the fraudulence at work at *Vie française*: its reliance on blurring the facts, the canny awareness that sex sells. As Madeleine writes up Duroy's invented African adventures, the verbs employed to describe her are associated with the processes of fictionalization: 'imaginait', 'portraiturait', 'ébauchait'. The very preponderance of verbs in this passage, though, also suggests Madeleine's dynamism, giving impetus to her words as she strides around the room. And the fact that she is such a *fantaisiste* indicates that she combines the worlds of literature and journalism, taking the linguistic flair associated with creative writing and employing it to best effect in the newspaper so as to gain access to the worlds of politics and finance. Such connections can be seen even in the aesthetics of her interior decoration, which have ramifications for both the wider political plot and for the composition of the novel itself. Private and public are once again entwined in the recurrent image of the vases which adorn Madeleine's mantelpiece, placed in order to display the flowers bought for her by her new husband Duroy and her old lover Vaudrec: synonymous, then, with the patterns of reflections and recycling which dominate the text. A correlation is made between the symmetry of the vases on the mantelpiece and political decisions and repetitions, as the right-wing deputy Lambert-Sarrazin contemplates in Chapter Five of the novel:

> [Il] eût offert de parier et de donner en gage sa moustache [...] que le nouveau cabinet ne se pourrait tenir d'imiter l'ancien et d'envoyer une armée à Tanger, en pendant à celle de Tunis, par amour de la symétrie, *comme on met deux vases sur une cheminée*. (BA, 312, my emphasis)

> [He] had offered to wager his moustache [...] that the new cabinet would not be able to resist imitating the old one, and sending a force to Tangier to counterbalance the one in Tunis, out of love of symmetry, just as people put two vases above a fireplace.[62]

It is indeed in displaying vases, balancing the men around her and using the minutiae of her private spaces to dictate public concerns that she bears responsibility for sending troops into Tangiers. As Lambert-Sarrazin goes on in his expressions of colonial arrogance, 'La terre d'Afrique est en effet une cheminée pour la France, messieurs, une cheminée qui brûle notre meilleur bois' (BA, 312) ('Africa is in fact a fireplace for France, gentlemen, a fireplace that burns out best wood'), Madeleine's role is to maintain and adorn the mantelpiece surrounding the colonial fire, as suggested in her embellishment of the initial article she pens for Duroy. What is more, the 'love of symmetry' noted in these comparisons acts as a link between Madeleine and the text itself; Madeleine's interior decor reflective of the intricate patterns and plot symmetries which govern *Bel-Ami* and made most apparent in the paired endings of its two parts, which both conclude with a marriage.

The shared aesthetics of text and female character are echoed (and complicated) in the parallels which arise at times in the text between Madeleine's voice and that of the narrator. Madeleine's role — particularly when Duroy is at his most inarticulate, in the opening chapters of the novel — is to translate and polish his thoughts and his stumbling spoken words into script. And she does so, in the article they produce together, in vocabulary which recalls the narrator's fluency a few pages beforehand, echoing the stereotypical terms of incomprehension which evoke the oriental fantasy, 'étrange' and 'charmante'. Just as the narrative voice alternately merges with and yet distinguishes itself from Duroy, similar proximity and distance can be detected when it comes to the narrator's relationship with Madeleine. Yet if, as noted in Chapter One, the narrator moves closer to Duroy, (s)he moves further away from Madeleine as the text progresses. The articulacy and content of certain passages, such as the evocation of Algeria, evoke parallels between the woman journalist and the narrator. So too do comments relating to the ironic tone that lurks behind Madeleine's smile, as irony lies latent behind the descriptive elegance of the text itself: 'La jeune femme continuait à fumer, sans dire un mot, souriant toujours d'un vague sourire qui semblait un masque aimable sur l'ironie de sa pensée' (BA, 147) ('the young woman carried on smoking, without a word, forever smiling that vague smile which acted as a delicate mask concealing the ironies of her thought'). Yet this quotation also reveals its distance from the character, depicting her generically as 'la jeune femme'. This distance occurs quite manifestly on a number of occasions, as the narrative voice generalizes and stereotypes conventional femininity, referring to the way in which Madeleine is flattered by Duroy's compliments and setting the 'masculine' narrator aside from his character: 'Elle fut toucheé... comme les femmes le sont par les compliments qui trouvent leur cœur, et elle lui jeta un de ces regards rapides et reconnaissants qui nous font leurs esclaves' (*BA*, 148) ('She was touched, as women tend to be by the compliments which find their way to their hearts, and she flashed him one of those grateful smile which make slaves of us'). So, although there are moments in the text when Madeleine dominates the narrative, assuming or echoing the narrative voice and dictating her own plot, attempting to fashion a new narrative code for herself while employing her love of symmetry and her symmetrical lovers to govern the country, so there are also points when she is regarded as alien and other within the text. An internal battle opens up, which at times suggests the power of the female journalist and at others resorts to cliché; harmonizing with Madeleine and cutting off her voice. Mary Donaldson Evans discusses the reversal of women's roles across a range of Maupassant's works, observing the ways in which the female characters who are variously objectified can become, in their turn, subjects of the gaze, and from being, for instance, consumed by men can become consumers. Madeleine, for Donaldson-Evans, is the consummate example of such a woman:

> Maupassant has rendered Madeleine in her 'masculine' specificity: endowed with extraordinary powers of ratiocination, this remarkable woman has almost complete control of her emotions. If Georges Duroy is from end to end an actor, constantly learning, rehearsing and performing a role [...] Madeleine is both playwright and director, writing the script, selecting the cast.[63]

Although the satire at work in *Bel-Ami* aligns Madeleine (and Duroy, and journalism) with prostitution, and the suggestions are that proficiency at writing and sex go hand in hand, these misogynistic suggestions are countered by the fact that for all the ways in which the text simulates the voice of Madeleine, she evades its gaze, retains her unknowability. Roberts suggests that 'while Georges is a simple dissembler, easy to predict, Madeleine evades even the reader',[64] and it is true that despite Jacques Rival's bawdy observation at the end of the text that 'elle doit être charmante au découvert', his comment must remain a supposition: she never really is 'découvert(e)'. Even after being caught in flagrante by her husband, she re-assumes her poise quickly and adopts, once again, her journalistic traits, smoking/writing and quizzing the police officers on the nature of the job. And while her lover is exposed naked in bed, she never is actually seen uncovered She is instead characterized by the negligee which she wears when composing Duroy's article (the same one she wears on their honeymoon, when for Duroy it acts as a tarnished reminder of the continued presence of Forestier), or seen at key moments in the text — such as when Duroy finally realizes the nature of her relationship with Forestier — still wearing her veil, synonymous with the dispassion and control she displays throughout. The way in which the text simultaneously reveals and conceals Madeleine Forestier is reflected in the closing comments about her, when Varenne answers Rival's question 'savez-vous ce qu'est devenue sa [Duroy's] femme?' [do you know what's become of his wife?] with the ambiguous 'oui et non' (*BA*, 412).

The text ultimately resists revealing Madeleine visually, a fact which makes the final burst of sound from the Madeleine organ all the more powerful. Hannah Scott argues that while the women who are drawn to Octave Mouret's department store in Zola's *Au Bonheur des dames* are threatened with objectification via their attraction to the compelling visual displays, they in fact are most stimulated by the pleasures of the aural that they find there, a reversal of expected reactions to sensory stimuli which sees the feminine soundscape rival the masculine visual universe.[65] Likewise, *Bel-Ami* can be read as a text in which the masculine world, associated with the visual, is subjugated to the aural domination of its central female character, implied through the subtext.[66]

That Madeleine requires the mediation of men in order to make her voice heard remains the paradox in the way she is presented. Unlike the women journalists in the later texts, Madeleine is not necessarily a 'nouvelle femme' but a prototype, and she remains constrained by Maupassant's text. Yet in many respects she possesses greater vocal resonance than the women who are able to enter the offices of turn-of-the-century publications, wield their own pens, and sign their own names. The influence of Tinayre's Josanne, Pert's Thérèse, even Minna, in *Femmes nouvelles*, is limited when compared with the scope of Madeleine Forestier, who schemes, smokes, and strides in her role as journalistic *nègre*. Madeleine shapes policy and dictates front pages to a greater extent than the rebels, the equals, and the 'nouvelles femmes' of the later texts. Forced to submit her story to the narrative conventions of the marriage plot, she nevertheless makes her voice heard during the very scene in which the traditional marriage is sealed, surging beyond and unsettling the narrative ending. Her ironic smile anticipates the laughter of the Medusa in Cixous's seminal essay. Bursting forth from the church organ, in expansive syntax itself paralleled in the poetic rhythms of Cixous's prose, Madeleine Forestier's 'langue ne contient pas, elle porte, elle ne retient pas, elle rend possible' ('language does not contain, it carries; it does not hold back, it makes possible').[67] The business of 'making possible' is enacted by Maupassant's female journalist, before becoming problematized but actualized in the fictional women's journalism of the turn-of-the-century texts.

Notes to Chapter 5

1. See Rachel Mesch, *Having It All in the Belle Époque: How French Women's Magazines Invented the Modern Woman* (Stanford, CA: Stanford University Press, 2013), pp. 52–53.
2. Ibid., p. 53: 'Maurice Laval interviewed several critics for their opinion on the current "expansion of women's writing", referring to the increasingly numbers of women publishing in the early 1900s'.
3. See Juliette M. Rogers, 'Feminist Discourse in Women's Novels of Professional Development', in *A Belle Époque? Women in French Society and Culture 1890–1914*, ed. by Diana Holmes and Carrie Tarr (Oxford: Berghahn Books, 2006), pp. 183–95 (p. 183).
4. Marcelle Tinayre was a contributor to newspapers and periodicals at the fin de siècle — she produced pieces for *La Fronde*, for example. Her novels, including *La Rebelle*, have been discussed by a number of critics in recent years, including Mesch, who also provides an account of the press furore surrounding Tinayre's nomination for the Légion d'honneur. See too Jennifer Waelti-Walters, *Feminist Novelists of the Belle Époque: Love as a Lifestyle* (Bloomington: Indiana University Press, 1990); Mélanie Collado, *Colette, Lucie Delarue-Mardrus, Marcelle Tinayre: émancipation et résignation* (Paris: Harmattan, 2003); also Elisabeth Ceaux, 'La Femme au début du

XXè siècle à travers les premiers romans de M. Tinayre', *Quaderni de filiogia et lingue romanze*, 6 (1984), 205–20, and France Grenaudier-Klijn, *Texte, hors-texte et ambiguïté générique à travers quatre romans de Marcelle Tinayre* (Bern: Peter Lang, 2004).

5. Camille Pert, androgynous pen-name of Louise Hortense Grille de Rougeul, was also a prolific contributor to the press and wrote 'definitely improper novels that are definitely not feminist', as Waelti-Walters puts it in *Feminist Novelists of the Belle-Époque*, p. 189. Her novels about divorce are discussed by Nicholas White in *After Intimacy: The Culture of Divorce in the West Since 1789*, ed. by Nicholas White and Karl Leydecker (Oxford: Peter Lang, 2007), pp. 73–87.

6. The Margueritte brothers were male French feminists of the fin de siècle. See Laurence Klejman and Florence Rochefort, *L'Égalité en marche: le féminisme sous la Troisième République* (Paris: Presses de la Fondation Nationale des Sciences Politiques, 1989), pp. 117–26. Georges Labouchère, who translated English New Woman novels into French, including Grant Allen's controversial *The Woman Who Did* (translated as *Le Roman d'une féministe*), reviewed Paul and Victor Margueritte's *Femmes nouvelles*, drawing connections between their novel and Ella Hepworth Dixon's *The Story of a Modern Woman*, which also features a young woman writing for the press (in *Vie quotidienne*, 23 July 1899).

7. Eugène Brieux (1858–1932) was a prolific French dramatist of the early twentieth century; his plays often addressed social propositions. See Jean Pedersen's discussion of the representation of gender politics in turn-of-the-century French theatre in *Legislating the French Family: Theatre and Republican Politics, 1870–1920* (New Brunswick, NJ: Rutgers University Press, 2003).

8. See Charles Sowerine, *France since 1870: Culture, Society and the Making of the Republic* (Basingstoke: Palgrave Macmillan, 2009), and Karen Offen, *European Feminisms 1700–1950: A Political History* (Stanford, CA: Stanford University Press, 2000) for discussion of turn-of-the-century feminism and the role of the New Woman.

9. Diana Holmes and Carrie Tarr's edited volume, *A Belle Époque? Women in French Society and Culture 1890–1914* (Oxford: Berghahn Books, 2006), weighs up the extent to which the New Woman was a mythical projection of male fears or the emblem of real forms of emancipation. Roberts also offers detailed evaluation of the role and apparent threat of the New Woman in *Disruptive Acts*. For discussion of the New Woman in English and American literature see for example Sally Ledger, *The New Woman: Fiction and Feminism at the Fin de Siècle* (Manchester: Manchester University Press, 1997).

10. Debora Silverman, 'The New Woman: Feminism and the Decorative Arts in Fin de Siècle France', in *Eroticism and the Body Politic*, ed. by Lynn Hunt (Baltimore, MD: Johns Hopkins University Press, 1991), pp. 144–63 (pp. 149–50).

11. Guillaume Pinson, 'La Femme masculinisée dans la presse mondaine française de la Belle Époque', *Clio*, 30 (2009), 211–30.

12. Mesch's argument is in contrast to Cosnier's study, which argues that *Femina* was a reactionary publication keen on maintaining conventional images of femininity. Colette Cosnier, *Les Dames de 'Femina': un féminisme mystifié* (Rennes: Presses universitaires de Rennes, 1995).

13. Mesch, *Having It All in the Belle Époque*, p. 57.

14. Pinson, 'La Femme masculinisée', p. 226. Marie-Ève Thérenty's study of the female journalist's role in the popular press from 1848–1940 argues that women writing for such publications adopted a range of increasingly characteristic strategies in order to forge a gendered sense of identity. See 'The Journalist Cassandra', in *Literature and the Press 1789–1914*, ed. by Birch and Rees (forthcoming).

15. See Maggie Allison, 'Marguerite Durand and La Fronde,' in *A Belle Époque? Women in French Society and Culture, 1890–1914*, pp. 37–49.

16. Roberts, *Disruptive Acts*, p. 4.

17. Allison, 'Marguerite Durand and La Fronde', p. 40

18. Diana Holmes, *Women in Context: French Women's Writing 1848–1994* (London: Athlone Press, 2000), p. 59.

19. As Roberts notes, Marguerite Durand reported on the 1896 Paris congress, and it proved influential in her subsequent decision to establish *La Fronde*; it is fitting, therefore, that the Margueritte brothers's literary representation of Durand in the character of Minna sees the congress as pivotal in her life, too (Roberts, *Disruptive Acts*, p. 58).

20. *Femina*, 1 (1 February 1901), 2.
21. Mesch, *Having It All in the Belle Époque*, p. 137. See too Mesch's article comparing the role of the New Man in Tinayre's text with that of Louis Marie Compain's *L'Un pour l'autre* ('A New Man for the New Woman? Men, Marriage and Feminism in the Belle Époque', *Historical Reflections/Réflexions Historiques*, 38.3 (2012), 85–106.
22. Collado, *Colette, Lucie Delarue-Mardrus, Marcelle Tinayre*, p. 179.
23. In *Legislating the French Family* Pedersen discusses fin-de-siècle theatre and its reaction to a perceived crisis in marriage, in part as a reaction to Ibsen's plays.
24. Mesch, *Having It All in the Belle Époque*, p. 45.
25. The reference to the husband as a master is echoed several years later in *La Rebelle*. Josanne embraces the term: 'mon maître, mon maître chéri!' [my master, my beloved master] (*LR*, 305).
26. Roberts, *Disruptive Acts*, p. 46.
27. Rachel Mesch and Masha Belenky, 'Introduction,' in 'State of the Union: Marriage in Nineteenth-Century France', *Dix-Neuf*, 11.1 (2008), 1–6 (p. 1).
28. Mesch, *Having It All in the Belle Époque*, p. 139.
29. Holmes sees Tinayre's feminism as 'mild' and 'cautious'; her reading of *La Rebelle* is of a text which abides by the conventions of the romance plot and employs easily recognizable codes (*Women in Context*, p. 52). Waelti-Walters defends the centrality of the love plot in Tinayre's work and makes a much stronger case for Tinayre as a feminst, arguing that given that love and marriage are the only recognized goals within contemporary culture, then it is understandable that love should be the major preoccupation for women (*Feminist Novelists of the Belle Époque*, p. 31).
30. Mesch and Belenky, 'Introduction', p. 1.
31. Blau duPlessis, *Writing Beyond the Ending*, p. 5.
32. Other critics have discussed the development and variety of narrative strategies in plots featuring the New Woman at the turn of the century. Ann Ardis examines the outcomes of English novels published in the 1890s, which see female characters reimagining their own fates through embracing rebellion, sexual exploration, and retreat; she notes that 'most obviously, the "natural" inevitability of the marriage plot is challenged as New Woman novelists "replace" the pure woman [...] with a heroine who is either sexually active outside of marriage or abstains from sex for political rather than moral reasons' (*New Women, New Novels* (New Brunswick, NJ: Rutgers University Press, 1990), p. 3). Discussion of the work of French women novelists of the same period has focused on the growth and entwining of the popular novel and the *roman d'amour*, which develops in antithesis to the representation of the woman in the decadent fiction of the same time. Holmes analyzes the recurring structures and themes of the romance plot, arguing that despite the overriding tendency of such texts towards conformity, the liberal and expanding industry which produced these novels nevertheless enabled readers and writers to explore female identity and desire within the confines of the repressively patriarchal society ('Daniel Lesueur and the Feminist Romance', in *A Belle Époque?*, ed. by Holmes and Tarr, pp. 197–210). Juliette Rogers considers such romance plots within the increasingly popular novels of women's professional development in fin-de-siècle France. She argues, in line with the commentators on English representations of the New Woman, that 'in order to provide a convincing and appealing fictional account of the femme nouvelle [...], the authors invented new narrative structures and new plot devices' (*Career Stories: Belle Époque Novels of Professional Development* (University Park: Pennsylvania State University Press, 2007), p. 10).
33. Mesch notes that the 'struggles of Pert's compelling heroine challenge prevailing narratives of resistance to gender norms in the Belle-Époque' (*Having It All in the Belle Époque*, p. 18).
34. Mesch, *Having It All in the Belle Époque*, p. 21.
35. George Bernard Shaw proclaimed that Brieux was 'the most important dramatist west of Russia' in Europe following the death of Ibsen ('Introduction', in Eugène Brieux, *Three Plays by Brieux*, ed. by George Bernard Shaw (New York: Brentano's, 1913), pp. vii-liv (p. vii)). Pedersen discusses Brieux's play 'Maternité' — a response to the social and political moves to find solutions to the issue of underpopulation, and which features the trial of a woman who has performed abortions (*Legislating the French Family*, pp. 171–74).
36. Rogers, *Career Stories*, p. 163.

37. Roberts, *Disruptive Acts*, p. 91.
38. Holmes, *Women in Context*, p. 52.
39. Mesch, *Having It All in the Belle Époque*, p. 141.
40. *Femina*, 2 (15 February 1901), 42
41. *Femina*, 3 (1 March 1901), 70
42. This irony is noted, too, by Rogers: 'She [Josanne] even laughs as she thinks about what her petit bourgeois readers would think of her if they could see her in her tattered clothing' (*Career Stories*, p. 162).
43. Pinson, *L'Imaginaire médiatique*, p. 78.
44. Margaret Cohen, *The Sentimental Education of the Novel* (Princeton, NJ: Princeton University Press, 1999), p. 195
45. Ibid., p. 34.
46. This is noted by Roberts in *Disruptive Acts*, p. 329, n. 94
47. Marcelle Tinayre, *Madeleine au miroir: journal d'une femme* (Charleston, SC: Nabu Press, 2010).
48. These models include Blanche Roosevelt, the comtesse Potocka, Mme Lecomte du Nouy and Clemence Brun, along with politically-minded women such as the Princesse Mathilde, Léonie Léon, Mme Renaud de l'Ariège and Mathilde Stevens, who signed her articles Jeanne Tilda (Gérard Delaisement, 'Introduction', in Guy de Maupassant, *Bel-Ami* (Paris: Garnier, 1959), pp. 1–LXXXIII (p. L).
49. Roberts, *Disruptive Acts*, p. 234.
50. White, *The Family in Crisis in Late Nineteenth-Century French Fiction*, pp. 76–77.
51. Ibid., p. 99.
52. Ibid., p. 92.
53. Ibid., pp. 98–99.
54. Hélène Cixous, 'Le Rire de la Méduse', in *Le Rire de la Méduse et autres ironies* (Paris: Éditions Galilée, 2010), pp. 36–68 (p. 42); translation from 'The Laugh of the Medusa', trans. by Keith Cohen and Paula Cohen, *Signs* (Summer 1976), 875–93.
55. Roberts, *Disruptive Acts*, p. 237.
56. Cixous, 'Le Rire de la Méduse', p. 43.
57. Ibid., p. 43.
58. Roberts, *Disruptive Acts*, p. 231.
59. Cixous, 'Le Rire de la Méduse', p. 45.
60. Ibid., p. 47.
61. See Birch, 'Maupassant's Bel-Ami and the Secrets of *Actualité*' for discussion of Maupassant's depiction of the Tunisian affair in relation to newspaper coverage.
62. White also highlights this connection (*The Family in Crisis in Late Nineteenth-Century French Fiction*, p. 99). Yee notes that 'there is no doubt that in Maupassant's prose domestic metonymy, in the form of the bibelot, has a directly and polemically political purpose' (*The Colonial Comedy*, p. 109). See too Andrew Counter, 'The Epistemology of the Mantelpiece: Subversive Ornaments in the Novels of Guy de Maupassant', *Modern Language Review*, 103 (2008), 682–96.
63. Mary Donaldson Evans, *A Woman's Revenge: The Chronology of Dispossession in Maupassant's Fiction* (Lexington, KY: French Forum, 1986), p. 47.
64. Roberts, *Disruptive Acts*, p. 235.
65. Scott, 'Symphonic Shopping', pp. 259–71.
66. White claims: 'it is quite feasible for the unintended reader to reconstruct the plot lines of the novel as a tale of the fate of female volonté, both sexual and textual, in a world which requires the mediation of men' (*The Family in Crisis in Late Nineteenth-Century French Fiction*, p. 102).
67. Cixous, 'Le Rire de la Méduse', p. 61.

CONCLUSION

The Future of Journalism?

This book began with reflections on the comparisons to be drawn between the apogee of the press at the end of the nineteenth century, and the apparent decline of the newspaper age in the early twenty-first century, suggesting that faking the news is by no means a modern phenomenon. By way of conclusion, attention can be drawn to a vision of the futuristic media age as predicted in the nineteenth century, in Jules Verne's short story, 'La Journée d'un journaliste américain en 2889'.[1] This text, which offers a satirical reading of the perceived Americanization of the press in Verne's own time, offers a prescient glimpse of technologies and practices associated with a modern media, a fictionalization of fears about the dominance of a 'quatrième pouvoir' which has instead become the most powerful vehicle in the world. It offers a fitting synopsis of the ways in which literary representations of journalism can be thought to pre-empt — unconsciously or, as here, consciously — concerns about the news and its dissemination which are reflected in our own age.

'La Journée d'un journaliste américain en 2889' follows a day in the life of prominent newspaperman, Francis Bennett, descendent of the founder of the *New York Herald*, Gordon Bennett.[2] Francis's publication, the *Earth Herald*, suggests the substitution of global dominance for the reporting of American news; he is 'roi des journalistes' and 'roi des deux Amériques, si les Américains pouvaient jamais accepter un souverain quelconque' [he would be king of all the Americans, too, if Americans could ever accept a king].[3] Innovations described in the tale clearly anticipate twenty-first century technology. Francis Bennett holds video-calls with his wife, who is away in Paris; *Earth Herald* itself is no longer printed, but 'parlé', the vocal transmission of news accompanied by a string of photographs:

> C'est dans une rapide conversation avec un reporter, un homme politique ou un savant, que les abonnés apprennent ce qui peut les intéresser. Quant aux acheteurs au numéro, on le sait, pour quelques cents, ils prennent connaissance de l'exemplaire du jour dans d'innombrables cabinets phonographiques. ('La Journée d'un journaliste américain en 2889', p. 14)

> [The Earth Chronicle is every morning spoken to subscribers, who, in interesting conversations with reporters, statesmen, and scientists, learn the news of the day. As for purchasers of single copies, they can at a very trifling cost learn all that is in the paper of the day at any of the innumerable phonographs set up nearly everywhere.]

Politically, too, there are parallels with twenty-first-century politics; Bennett conducts an interview with representatives from Great Britain who are seeking to 'take back control' not from Europe, in this envizaged future, but from America: 'protester l'annexion de la Grande-Bretagne aux États-Unis' [protesting about the annexation of Great Britain to the United States] (p. 30). There is confrontation, too, with Russia, and Bennett interrogates the Russian ambassador as to the threat of his country's expansion, expressing concern about Russian weaponry. Bennett's role in such political negotiations suggests the power of the newspaper magnate in diplomatic issues.

Chapter Three explored the exuberance and humour associated with Verne's adventuring reporter-characters, arguing that he presented his journalists as flawed and naive, proving the supremacy of literature yet nevertheless realizing something of their own folly by the end of the novels in question. In 'La Journée d'un journaliste américain en 2889', the critique is more profound. The tale evokes a bleak, dehumanized world of journalism. Reporters no longer need to go out into the field to retrieve news; it is relayed to them technologically at their desks; their role is increasingly sedentary and segmented; the vast newspaper offices are carefully divided into designated zones, so that they rarely mingle and communicate with one another. Delporte suggests that in the text:

> Les journalistes sont devenus des pions interchangeables, sans imagination, sans initiative, privés d'indépendance [...]. Verne reprend à son compte un faisceau de critiques sur la nouvelle presse où le journaliste, fondu dans une entreprise (une 'usine', dit-on) dirigée par un homme d'affaires lointain et ne connaissant rien au métier, perd son statut social en même temps que son autonomie, se 'prolétarise'.[4]

> [Journalists have become interchangeable pawns, lacking imagination and initiative and deprived of independence [...]. Verne takes up in his own way the heap of criticism which had amassed towards the new press, according to which the journalist, embedded in an industry (a so-called 'factory') overseen from afar by a businessman who knows nothing about the trade, loses his social status as well as his autonomy, and becomes more working-class.]

This is both an expression of anxiety about the increased commercialization of the press at the *fin de siècle* and a suppression of its supposed advances — the foreign correspondence missions represented, celebrated, and parodied in *Michel Strogoff* and *Claudius Bombarnac*. Bennett's fortune exceeds 'trente milliards' [thirty billion]; he has used it to purchase a vast, anonymous building, each side of which measures three kilometres; it is situated in the new American capital, Centropolis. The mass-advertising campaign depicted at the close of Brulat's *Le Reporter*, discussed in Chapter One, is dwarfed by Verne's futuristic vision of advertisements projected from the clouds:

> Ce sont d'immenses affiches, réfléchies par les nuages, et dont la dimension est telle que l'on peut les apercevoir d'une contrée tout entière. De cette galerie, mille projecteurs étaient sans cesse occupés à envoyer aux nuées, qui les reproduisaient en couleur, ces announces démesurées. ('La Journée d'un journaliste américain en 2889', p. 26)

> [Everyone has noticed those enormous advertisements reflected from the clouds, so large that they may be seen by the populations of whole cities or

even of entire countries. In the Earth Chronicle building a thousand projectors are constantly engaged in displaying upon the clouds these mammoth advertisements.]

Bennett is angered by the persistence, on the day in question, of a clear blue sky which renders such a system inadequate. He demands the manufacture of artificial clouds to promote the advertisement of manufactured goods. The compromised vision of progress in Verne's text, which sets technological innovation within a context of mechanized, anonymized, centralized power structures, reaches a final satirical flourish in the death of the ironically-named scientist Nathaniel Faithburn. Faithburn, one of a number of innovators and speculators who approach Francis Bennett for funding for their scientific ventures, requests support for an investigation into the feasibility of human hibernation, proposing that he suspend his own vital functions and mummify himself before coming back to life. In the closing scene of the short story, Faithburn's experiment is proved a failure, broadcast live to an audience anxious for news ('le téléphote est actionné. Le monde entier va pouvoir suivre les diverses phases de l'opération' [the telephote was got in readiness. The whole world was going to be able to follow the progress of the operation]), and dismissed casually by Bennett himself: 'voilà une méthode qui a besoin d'être perfectionnée!' [here is a method that needs improvement] (pp. 42–44).

The introduction to this book showed that Verne was one of those commentators who, in predicting the future, saw the demise of literature at the hands of journalism. 'La Journée d'un journaliste américain en 2889' offers an ambiguous vision of this decline. On the one hand, the vast journalistic spaces found in Bennett's media empire include a hall set aside for 'romanciers-feuilletonistes' [serial-novelists]. From this 'salle, surmontée d'une large coupole translucide' [vast apartment surmounted with an enormous transparent cupola], one hundred 'littérateurs' read aloud one hundred chapters from one hundred novels to a 'public enfiévré' [enraptured public] (pp. 19–20); novels are still being disseminated and anticipated a thousand years into the future. As this numerical quotation would suggest, though, such a methodical division of literary labour is not without its satire, and, as Delporte points out, the enthusiastic audience is made up of listeners, not readers; he claims of the text that the public no longer reads; the press has killed off literature, technology has ruined reading.[5] Praise is given, within this massive centralized news machine, to those writers capable of attracting most subscribers — one 'feuilletoniste' is singled out for a chapter which has added 'dix mille abonnés nouveaux depuis hier' [ten thousand new subscribers since yesterday]. The irony is that what is envizaged in this system of dissemination is a model of literature which even within a nineteenth-century context, might have been considered outdated; the instalment which has received such praise features a 'scène où la jeune villageoise aborde avec son galant quelques problems de philosophie transcendante' [the scene where the village maid discusses interesting philosophical problems with her lover], extolled as if 'on n'a jamais mieux peint les mœurs champêtres!' [never have the ways of country folk been better portrayed] (p. 20). This seemingly twee pastoral scene is deliberately archaic. In contrast, contributor 'John Last' — his name evocative of his failure in the competition to generate increased funds for the *Earth Herald* — is chastised for his inadequate realism:

> Il faut disséquer, John Last, il faut disséquer! Ce n'est pas avec une plume qu'on écrit de notre temps, c'est avec un bistouri! Chaque action dans la vie réelle est la résultante de pensées fugitives et successives, qu'il faut dénombrer avec soin, pour créer un être vivant! Et quoi de plus facile en se servant de l'hypnotisme électrique, qui dédouble l'homme et sépare ses deux personnalités! ('La Journée d'un journaliste américain en 2889', pp. 20–21)
>
> [You must dissect, John Last, dissect! These days one does not write with a pen but with a lancet! In real life every act is the result of a hundred thoughts that come and go, and these you must study, each by itself, if you would create a living character. You have simply to make use of hypnotism, electrical or human, which gives one a two-fold being.]

In this critique of Last, Bennett's promotion of hypnotism as a way of extracting the innermost thoughts of characters suggests the anxiety over the intrusion into public life associated with the newspaper and referred to in the opening chapter in relation to the practice of the interview. It also evokes a surgical mode of realism through the reference to the 'bistouri', reminiscent, surely, of caricatures of Flaubert as novelist extracting the heart of Emma Bovary and brandishing it on a scalpel, of the sort sketched by Lemot and published in *La Parodie* in 1869 and reprinted in the *Album Flaubert*.[6] This is an outdated and satirical version of realism proffered to the listening literary audience of the world in the twenty-eighth century. It suggests that for all its futuristic projections, Verne's attack on the newspaper is very much based on a nineteenth-century industry; he is as if unable to foresee an alternative form of the novel alongside his revolutionary technologies.[7]

Verne's satire of both a future and a nineteenth-century media age is, then, ambiguous in its presentation of a literature which endures, which reaches an ever-larger audience, and yet is dated and intrusive. This book has often focused on ways in which the novel, even while seeming to repel modes of journalism, has in fact replicated practices of recounting, information-gathering, and sensationalizing found in the newspapers of the time. In 'La Journée d'un journaliste américain en 2889', a number of rhetorical insertions in the narrative itself suggest the dissemination of news, the collective understanding of the world represented in the text, as if the narrative voice purposefully echoes practices of the globalizing endeavour of the fictional *Earth Herald*. Clauses employed when describing the news organization or its technological systems — 'on connaît ce système' [you know this system] (p. 14) or 'l'organisation de cet incomparable service a été souvent décrite' [the organization of this incomparable service has often been described] (p. 21) — are ironic in a text aimed at a readership which will not have heard of these seemingly ubiquitous inventions, but equally are suggestive of yet more blurring between the discourses of the newspaper and the novel. They assume and reflect the shared comprehension of certain devices of the media age so sharply satirized here.

The closing line of Verne's text reads ironically: 'un bon métier, le métier de journaliste à la fin du vingt-neuvième siècle' [a good trade, that of the journalist at the end of the twenty-ninth century] (p. 46). This is a summative line whose exclamation points to its hollowness; it sums up a penultimate paragraph which has described how Francis Bennett's following day is little different from the preceding one, save that he has multiplied his income still further — the very idea of the 'new' associated with news denied by an emphasis on sameness. And indeed, this line, in its irony, its ambiguity, and in the echoes it sets up between its critique of both fin-de-siècle and future journalism, can be used as a summation of the representation of the journalist in the texts seen across this study. It is a 'bon métier' — at a time when the very idea of journalism as a *métier* was growing — but a craft often ambivalently envizaged in the literary texts even of those writers who seemed to embrace journalism as a necessary mode of representation at the turn of the century.

Notes to the Conclusion

1. Discussion has focused on the origins of this short story. The original version, thought to have been penned by Jules Verne's son Michel, appeared in English for an American readership in *The Forum* in February 1889: the date of the text is therefore an envizaging of the media set one thousand years into the future. Verne himself took up the tale and modified it, before publishing it in the *Mémoires de l'Académie* in 1891 (having given it as a public reading at the Académie d'Amiens); it then reappeared in 1910, five years after Verne's death, in the collection *Hier et demain*, edited by Michel Verne. For notes on these publication details, see Unwin, *Jules Verne: Journeys in Writing*, p. 42, and Delporte, 'Jules Verne et le journaliste'.
2. In the first version of the short story, the protagonist was Fritz Napoleon Smith, descendent of George Washington Smith, founder of the *Manhattan Chronicle*.
3. Jules Verne, *La Journée d'un journaliste américain en 2889, suivi de L'Éternel Adam* (Paris: Gallimard, 1978), pp. 14–15. Subsequent pages references to this work will be given in the main text.
4. Delporte, 'Jules Verne et le journaliste', p. 18.
5. Ibid., p. 19.
6. See, for example, the caricature reproduced via the Centre Flaubert website and available at <http://flaubert.univ-rouen.fr/iconographie/lemot.php?imp=1> [accessed 22 January 2017].
7. Unwin's discussion of 'La Journée d'un journaliste en 2889' also emphasizes the reminders of the past in a text which predicts the future (*Jules Verne*, p. 45).

BIBLIOGRAPHY

Primary Texts

ALLAIN, MARCEL, and PIERRE SOUVESTRE, *Fantomas*, anonymous translation, introduction by John Ashbery (London: Picador, 1987)
APOLLINAIRE, GUILLAUME, *Que faire?* (Paris: Nouvelle Édition, 1950)
BALZAC, HONORÉ DE, *Illusions perdues* (Paris: Gallimard, 1961)
BARRÈS, MAURICE, *Les Déracinés* (Paris: Gallimard-Folio, 1988)
BAUDELAIRE, CHARLES, 'Mon cœur mis à nu', in *Œuvres complètes*, 2 vols (Paris: Gallimard-Pléaide, 1975–76), II, 676–708
BONNETAIN, PAUL, *Charlot s'amuse* (Brussels: Henri Kristemaeckers, 1883)
DU BOISGOBEY, FORTUNÉ, *Cornaline la dompteuse* (Paris: E. Plon, 1887)
BONNETAIN, PAUL, *Charlot s'amuse* (Brussels: Henri Kristemaeckers, 1883)
BRIEUX, EUGÈNE, *La Femme seule*, in *Théâtre complet de Brieux*, 9 vols (Paris: Stock, 1924), VII, 1–149 (*FS*)
BRULAT, PAUL, *Le Reporter: roman contemporain* (Paris: Perrin, 1898)
CHAMPSAUR, FÉLICIEN, *Dinah Samuel* (Paris: Paul Ollendorff, 1889)
CONRAD, JOSEPH, *The Secret Agent* (London: David Campbell, 1992)
FENESTRIER, CHARLES, *La Vie des frelons: histoire d'un journaliste* (Paris: Éditions de la Société nouvelle, 1908)
FLAUBERT, GUSTAVE, 'Dictionnaire des idées reçues', in *Bouvard et Pécuchet* (Paris: Gallimard, 1979)
—— *Bouvard and Pécuchet*, trans. by A. J. Krailsheimer (London: Penguin, 1976)
—— *L'Éducation sentimentale* (Paris: Garnier-Flammarion, 1985)
GIFFARD, PIERRE, *Le Sieur de Va-Partout. Souvenirs d'un reporter* (Paris: Maurice Dreyfous, 1880) (*VP*)
GISSING, GEORGE, *New Grub Street* (Oxford: Oxford University Press, 2008)
HURET, JULES, *Tout yeux, tout oreilles* (Paris: Charpentier, 1901)
HUYSMANS, JORIS-KARL, *À rebours* (Paris: Garnier-Flammarion, 1978)
—— *À Rebours*, trans. by Robert Baldick (Harmondsworth: Penguin, 2003)
LEBLANC, MAURICE, *L'Aiguille creuse* (Paris: Larousse, 2012)
—— *Arsène Lupin: gentleman-cambrioleur* (Paris: Archipoche, 2015)
LEGRAND, CHARLES, *L'Âge de papier, roman social* (Paris: Ernest Kolb, 1889)
LEROUX, GASTON, *Les Aventures extraordinaires de Rouletabille, reporter*, 2 vols (Paris: Robert Laffont, 1988–91)
—— *The Mystery of the Yellow Room*, anonymous translation, introduction by Mark Valentine (Ware: Wordsworth Editions, 2010)
—— 'Précautions: chez L'Amiral Doubassof', *Le Matin*, 2 March 1906
MARGUERITTE, PAUL and VICTOR, *Femmes nouvelles* (Paris: Librairie Plon, 1899) (*FN*)
MAUPASSANT, GUY DE, *Bel-Ami*, ed. by Jean-Louis Bory (Paris: Gallimard, 1973) (*BA*)
—— *Bel-Ami*, trans. by Margaret Mauldon (Oxford: Oxford University Press, 2008)
—— 'Boule de Suif', in *Contes et nouvelles*, 2 vols (Paris : Gallimard-Pléiade, 1974–79), I

—— *Chroniques*, 3 vols (Paris: Union générale d'éditions, 1980)
—— *Contes et nouvelles*, 2 vols (Paris: Gallimard-Pléaide, 1974)
—— *Correspondance*, ed. by Jacques Suffel, 3 vols (Evreux: Cercle du Bibliophile, 1973)
PERT, CAMILLE, *Leur égale* (Paris: Simonis Empis, 1899) (*LE*)
POE, EDGAR ALLAN, *Selected Tales* (Oxford: Oxford University Press, 2008)
SOUVESTRE, PIERRE, and MARCEL ALLAIN, *Fantômas*, 8 vols (Paris: Robert Laffont, 2013), I (*F*)
TINAYRE, MARCELLE, *La Rebelle* (Paris: Calmann-Lévy, 1906) (*LA*)
—— *Madeleine au miroir: journal d'une femme* (Charleston, SC: Nabu Press, 2010)
VERNE, JULES, *Claudius Bombarnac: carnet d'un reporter*, ed. by Zoé Commère (Médias19, 2014), <http://www.medias19.org/index.php?id=17989> [accessed 13 January 2016] (*CB*)
—— *L'Île mystérieuse* (Paris: Bibliothèque d'éducation et de récréation, 1874)
—— *La Journée d'un journaliste américain en 2889, suivi de L'Éternel Adam* (Paris: Gallimard, 1978)
—— *Michel Strogoff* (Paris: Hachette, 1966) (*MS*)
—— *Michel Strogoff: or, The Courier of the Czar*, trans. by William Henry Giles Kingston (CreateSpace Independent Publishing Platform, 2015)
—— 'Jules Verne Says The Novel Will Soon Be Dead', *Pittsburgh Gazette*, 13 July 1902
VERNE, JULES, and ADOLPHE D'ENNERY, *Michel Strogoff: pièce en cinq actes et seize tableaux* (Exeter: University of Exeter Press, 1994)
ZOLA, ÉMILE, 'Adieux', *Le Figaro*, 22 September 1881
—— 'Alexis et Maupassant', *Le Figaro*, 11 July 1881
—— *La Curée* (Paris: Gallimard, 1981)
—— *The Kill*, trans. by Brian Nelson, Oxford World's Classics (Oxford: Oxford University Press, 2004
—— *La Débâcle*, in *Les Rougon-Macquart*, ed. by Henri Mitterand, 5 vols (Paris: Gallimard-Pléaide, 1960–67), V
—— *Le Docteur Pascal*, in *Les Rougon-Macquart*, ed. by Henri Mitterand, 5 vols (Paris: Gallimard-Pléaide, 1960–67), V
—— *La Fortune des Rougon*, in *Les Rougon-Macquart*, ed. by Henri Mitterand, 5 vols (Paris: Gallimard-Pléaide, 1960–67), I (*FR*)
—— *The Fortune of the Rougons*, trans. by Brian Nelson (Oxford: Oxford University Press, 2012)
—— *Nana*, in *Les Rougon-Macquart*, ed. by Henri Mitterand, 5 vols (Paris: Gallimard-Pléaide, 1960–67), II (*N*)
—— *Nana*, trans. by Douglas Parmée (Oxford: Oxford University Press, 2009)
—— *Œuvres complètes*, ed. by Henri Mitterand. 15 vols (Paris: Cercle du livre précieux, 1966–70)
—— 'Pour les juifs', *Le Figaro*, 16 May 1896
—— *Le Roman expérimental* (Paris: Flammarion, 2006)
—— *Vérité*, in *Œuvres complètes*, 50 vols (Paris: Fasquelle, 1928–29), XXVI & XXVII (*V*)
—— *Truth*, trans. by Ernest Alfred Vizetelly (Stroud: Sutton, 1994)

Works of Criticism

ALLISON, MAGGIE, 'Marguerite Durand and La Fronde', in *A Belle Époque? Women in French Society and Culture, 1890–1914*, ed. by Diana Holmes and Carrie Tarr (Oxford: Berghahn Books, 2006), pp. 37–49
ANDERSON, BENEDICT, *Imagined Communities: Reflections on the Origins and Spread of Nationalism* (London: Verso, 1991)

ANGENOT, MARC, *1889: un état de discours social*, <http://www.medias19.org/index.php?id=11003> [accessed 14 June 2017]
ANON., 'Soutien à Charlie Hebdo', *Médias-19*, 7 January 2015, <http://www.medias19.org/index.php?id=21506> [accessed 30 January 2017]
ARDIS, ANN, *New Women, New Novels* (New Brunswick, NJ: Rutgers University Press, 1990)
ARMSTRONG, MARIE-SOPHIE, 'The Opening Chapter of *La Fortune des Rougon*, or the Darker Side of Zolian Writing', *Dalhousie French Studies*, 44 (Fall 1998), 39–53
ARMSTRONG, STEPHEN, 'Pizza, Politics and Pure Fiction: The Rise of Fake News', *The Telegraph*, 6 January 2017, <http://www.telegraph.co.uk/men/thinking-man/pizza-politics-pure-fiction-rise-fake-news/> [accessed 27 January 2017]
BAGULEY, DAVID, *Naturalist Fiction: The Entropic Vision* (Cambridge: Cambridge University Press, 1990)
BAKHTIN, MIKHAIL, *The Dialogic Imagination: Four Essays*, ed. by Michael Holquist, trans. by Caryl Emerson and Michael Holquist (Austin: University of Texas Press, 1987)
—— *Problems of Dostoevsky's Poetics* (Manchester: Manchester University Press, 1999)
BANQUART, MARIE-CLAIRE, 'Maupassant journaliste', in *Flaubert et Maupassant, écrivains normands* (Paris: PUF, 1981), pp. 152–58
BARTHES, ROLAND, *Mythologies* (Paris: Éditions du Seuil, 1957)
—— *Leçon: leçon inaugurale de la chaise de sémiologie littéraire du Collège de France, le 7 janvier 1977* (Paris: Seuil, 1978)
BAUDRILLARD, JEAN, *The Illusion of the End* (Cambridge: Polity, 1994)
—— 'Requiem pour les media', *Utopie* (4 October 1971), 35–51
—— 'Simulacra and Simulations', in *Selected Writings*, ed. by Mark Poster (Stanford, CA: Stanford University Press, 1988), pp. 166–84
—— *Le Système des objets* (Paris: Gallimard, 1968)
—— *The System of Objects* (London: Verso, 2005)
BEER, GILLIAN, 'Plot and the Analogy with Science in Later Nineteenth-Century Novelists', in *Comparative Criticism: A Yearbook*, 2, ed. by Elinor Shaffer (Cambridge: Cambridge University Press, 1980), pp. 131–48
BELL, DAVID, and CATHERINE WITT, '*Incipit*: On the Present and Future of the Field', *Nineteenth-Century French Studies*, 44.3–4 (2016), 145–82
BELLANGER, CLAUDE, and OTHERS, eds, *Histoire générale de la presse française*, 5 vols (Paris: Presses universitaires de France, 1969–76)
BELLEFQIH, ANISSA, *La Lecture des Aventures d'Arsène Lupin* (Paris: L'Harmattan, 2010)
BENJAMIN, WALTER, *The Work of Art in an Age of Mechanical Reproduction*, trans. by J. A. Underwood (London: Penguin, 2008)
—— 'The Storyteller: Reflections on the Works of Nikolai Leskov', in *Illuminations*, trans. by Harry Zohn, ed. by Hannah Arendt (New York: Schocken Books, 1969), pp. 83–109
BERNHEIMER, CHARLES, *Figures of Ill-Repute: Representing Prostitution in Nineteenth-Century France* (Cambridge, MA: Harvard University Press 1993)
BIELECKI, EMMA, 'Fantômas's Shifting Identities: From Books to Screen', *Studies in French Cinema*, 13.1 (2013), 3–15
BIRCH, EDMUND, 'Maupassant's *Bel-Ami* and the Secrets of Actualité', *Modern Language Review*, 109.4 (2014), 996–1012
BIRCH, EDMUND, and KATE REES, eds, *Literature and the Press*, special issue of *Dix-Neuf* (forthcoming)
BISMUT, ROGER, 'Quelques problèmes de création littéraire dans *Bel-Ami*', *Revue d'histoire littéraire de la France*, 67.3 (1967), 577–89

BLAU DUPLESSIS, RACHEL, *Writing Beyond the Ending* (Bloomington: Indiana University Press, 1985)
BLOOM, HAROLD, *The Anxiety of Influence* (Oxford: Oxford University Press, 1973)
BOLTER, JAY, and RICHARD GRUSIN, *Remediation* (Cambridge, MA: MIT Press, 2000)
BOWLBY, RACHEL, *Just Looking: Consumer Culture in Dreiser, Gissing and Zola* (New York: Methuen, 1985)
BOUCHARENC, MYRIAM, 'Pierre Giffard, *Le Sieur de Va-Partout*, premier manifeste de la littérature de reportage', in *Presse et plumes: journalisme et littérature au XIXè siècle*, ed. by Marie-Ève Thérenty and Alain Vaillant, (Paris: Nouveau Monde, 2004), pp. 511–21
BRAKE, LAUREL, *Subjugated Knowledges: Journalism, Gender and Literature in the Nineteenth Century* (Basingstoke: Macmillan, 1994)
BRAKE, LAUREL, and JULIE CODELL, *Encounters in the Victorian Press: Editors, Authors, Readers* (Basingstoke: Macmillan, 2005)
BRANTLINGER, PATRICK, 'Mass Media and Culture in fin de siècle Europe', in *Fin de Siècle and its Legacy*, ed. by Miculàs Teich and Roy Porter (Cambridge: Cambridge University Press, 1990), pp. 98–114
BRENNAN, TERESA, and MARTIN JAY, eds, *Vision in Context: Historical and Contemporary Perspectives on Sight* (London: Routledge, 1996)
BRISSON, ADOLPHE, 'Promenades et visites: l'école de journalisme', *Le Temps*, 3 November 1899
BROOKS, PETER, *Reading for the Plot: Design and Intention in Narrative* (Oxford: Clarendon Press, 1984)
——*Realist Vision* (New Haven, CT: Yale University Press, 2005)
BROPHY, PHILIP, 'Horrality: The Textuality of the Contemporary Horror Film', reprinted in *The Horror Reader*, ed. by Ken Gelder (London: Routledge, 2000), pp. 276–84
BROWN, FREDERICK, *Zola: A Life* (London, Macmillan, 1996)
BRUNETIÈRE, FERDINAND, *Le Roman naturaliste* (Paris: Calmann Lévy, 1883)
CALLAHAN, VICKI, *Zones of Anxiety: Movement, Musidora and the Crime Serials of Louis Feuillade* (Detroit, MI: Wayne State University Press, 2005)
CASTA, ISABELLE, *Étude sur Le mystère de la chambre jaune et Le parfum de la dame en noir* (Paris: Ellipses, 2007)
CEAUX, ELISABETH, 'La Femme au début du XXè siècle à travers les premiers romans de M. Tinayre', *Quaderni de filiogia et lingue romanze*, 6 (1984), 205–20
CHAITIN, GILBERT D., *The Enemy Within: Culture Wars and Political Identity in Novels of the French Third Republic* (Columbus: Ohio State University Press, 2008)
CHAMBURE, A. DE, *À travers la presse* (Paris: Fert, Albouy & Cie., 1914)
CHELEBOURG, CHRISTIAN, *Jules Verne: l'œil et le ventre: une poétique du sujet* (Paris: Lettres modernes Minard, 1999)
CHITNIS, BERNICE, *Reflecting on 'Nana'* (London: Routledge 1991)
CIXOUS, HÉLÈNE, 'Le Rire de la Méduse', in *Le Rire de la Méduse et autres ironies* (Paris: Éditions Galilée, 2010), pp. 36–68
——'The Laugh of the Medusa', trans. by Keith Cohen and Paula Cohen, *Signs* (Summer 1976), 875–93
COHEN, MARGARET, *The Sentimental Education of the Novel* (Princeton, NJ: Princeton University Press, 1999)
COLLADO, MÉLANIE, *Colette, Lucie Delarue-Mardrus, Marcelle Tinayre: émancipation et résignation* (Paris: Harmattan, 2003)
COMMÈRE, ZOÉ, *Claudius Bombarnac de Jules Verne. Le Romanesque refondé par le reportage?* (masters thesis submitted to Lyon 2 University and published on the website Médias 1, <http://www.medias19.org/docannexe/file/19412/le_romanesque_refonde....pdf> [accessed 6 January 2017])

Compère, Daniel, 'Une écriture romanesque: le reportage', *Europe*, special issue on Gaston Leroux, 626–27 (1981), 38–45
Compère, Daniel, and Jean-Michel Margot, eds, *Entretiens avec Jules Verne* (Geneva: Slatkine, 1998)
Conrad, Joseph, 'Autocracy and War', *North American Review*, 181.584 (July 1905), 33–55
Cosnier, Colette, *Les Dames de 'Femina': un féminisme mystifié* (Rennes: Presses universitaires de Rennes, 1995)
Costaz, Gilles, 'Gaston Leroux Reporter', *Europe*, 'Gaston Leroux', 626–27 (1981), 45–49
Couegnas, Daniel, 'Structure et thèmes de l'énigme dans "Les Aventures de Rouletabille"', *Europe*, special issue on Gaston Leroux, 626–27 (1981), 113–26
Counter, Andrew, 'The Epistemology of the Mantelpiece: Subversive Ornaments in the Novels of Guy de Maupassant', *Modern Language Review*, 103 (2008), 682–96
——'The Legacy of the Beast: Patrilinearity and Rupture in Zola's *La Bête humaine* and Freud's *Totem and Taboo*', *French Studies*, 61.1 (2008), 26–38
——'A Sentimental Affair: *Vérité*', *Romanic Review*, special issue on Zola, 102.3 (2011), 391–409
Crary, Jonathan, *Techniques of the Observer: On Vision and Modernity in the Nineteenth Century* (Cambridge, MA: MIT Press, 1990)
——*Suspensions of Perception: Attention, Spectacle and Modern Culture* (Cambridge, MA: MIT Press, 1999)
Debord, Guy, *Society of the Spectacle* (London: Rebel Press, [n.d.])
Delaisement, Gérard, 'Introduction', in Guy de Maupassant, *Bel-Ami* (Paris: Garnier, 1959), pp. i–lxxxiii
——*Maupassant, Bel-Ami* (Paris: Hatier, 1972)
——*Maupassant journaliste et chroniqueur* (Paris: Albin Michel, 1956)
Deleuze, Gilles, *Logique du sens* (Paris: Minuit, 1969)
——*The Logic of Sense*, trans. by Mark Lester with Charles Stivale (London: Athlone Press, 1990)
Delporte, Christian, *Les Journalistes en France: naissance et construction d'une profession, 1880–1950* (Paris: Seuil, 2009)
——'Jules Verne et le journaliste: imaginer l'information du XXè siècle', *Temps des médias*, 4 (2005), 201–13
Dezalay, Auguste, 'Le Personnage du journaliste chez Zola', *Travaux de linguistique et de littérature*, 22.2 (1985), 93–103
Donaldson Evans, Mary, *A Woman's Revenge: The Chronology of Dispossession in Maupassant's Fiction* (Lexington, KY: French Forum, 1986)
Doye, George, 'The Detection Formula and the Act of Reading', in *The Cunning Craft: Original Essays on Detective Fiction and Contemporary Literary Theory*, ed. by Ronald Walker and June Frazer (Macomb: Western Illinois University Press, 1990), pp. 25–37
Dubbelboer, Marieke, 'Il faut vivre: Writers, Journalists and Income 1890–1914', in *Literature and the Press*, ed. by Edmund Birch and Kate Rees, special issue of *Dix-Neuf* (forthcoming)
Eisenzweig, Uri, 'Madness and the Colonies: French and Anglo-Saxon Versions of the Mysterious Origins of Crime', *Esprit créateur*, 26.2 (1986), 3–14
Emery, Elizabeth, *Photojournalism and the Origins of the French Writer House Museum* (Farnham: Ashgate, 2012)
Femina, 1–3 (1 February 1901–1 March 1901)
Ferenczi, Thomas, *L'Invention du journalisme en France: naissance de la presse moderne à la fin du XIXè siècle* (Paris: Plon, 1993)
Forestier, Louis, ed., *Maupassant: Romans* (Paris: Gallimard, 1987)
——*Maupassant et l'écriture: actes du colloque de Fécamp 21–22–23 mai 1993* (Paris: Nathan, 1993)

FORNABAI, NANETTE, 'Criminal Factors: Fantomas, Anthropometrics, and the Numerical Fictions of Modern Criminal Identity', in *Crime Fictions*, ed. by Andrea Goulet and Susanna Lee, special issue of *Yale French Studies*, 108 (2005), 60–71

FOSTER, HAL, *Vision and Visuality* (New York: New Press, 1988)

FREUNDSCHEUCH, AARON, *The Courtesan and the Gigolo: The Murders in the Rue Montaigne and the Dark Side of Empire in Nineteenth-Century Paris* (Stanford, CA: Stanford University Press, 2017)

GELDER, KEN, ed., *The Horror Reader* (London: Routledge, 2000)

GRENAUDIER-KLIJN, FRANCE, *Texte, hors-texte et ambiguïté générique à travers quatre romans de Marcelle Tinayre* (Bern: Peter Lang, 2004)

GINISTY, PAUL, *Anthologie du journalisme, du XVIIème siècle à nos jours*, 2 vols (Paris: Delagrave, 1920)

GORRARA, CLAIRE, *French Crime Fiction* (Cardiff: University of Wales Press, 2009)

GOULET, ANDREA, 'Retinal Fictions: Villiers, Leroux and Optics at the Fin de Siècle', *Nineteenth-Century French Studies*, 34.1–2 (2005–06), 107–20

—— 'The Yellow Spot: Ocular Pathology and Empirical Method in Gaston Leroux's *Le Mystère de la Chambre Jaune*', *SubStance*, 107, 34:2 (2005), 27–46

GOULET, ANDREA, and SUSANNA LEE, eds, *Crime Fictions*, special issue of *Yale French Studies*, 108 (2005)

GRENOUILLET, CORINNE, and ÉLÉONORE REVERZY, eds, *Les Voix du peuple XIX et XXè siècles* (Strasbourg: Presses universitaires de Strasbourg, 2006)

GUNNING, TOM, 'Lynx-Eyed Detectives and Shadow Bandits: Visuality and Eclipse in French Detective Stories and Films Before WWI', in *Crime Fictions*, ed. by Andrea Goulet and Susanna Lee, special issue of *Yale French Studies*, 108 (2005), 74–88

HAIG, STIRLING, *The Madame Bovary Blues: The Pursuit of Illusion in Nineteenth-Century French Fiction* (Baton Rouge: Louisiana State University Press, 1987)

HAND, RICHARD, and MICHAEL WILSON, *Grand Guignol: The French Theatre of Horror* (Exeter: University of Exeter Press, 2002)

HARRIS, TREVOR, *Maupassant in the Hall of Mirrors: Ironies and Repetition in the work of Guy de Maupassant* (Basingstoke: Macmillan, 1990)

—— 'Measurement and Mystery in Verne', in *Jules Verne: Narratives of Modernity*, ed. by Edmund Smyth (Liverpool: Liverpool University Press, 2000), pp. 109–21

HARROW, SUSAN, *Zola, the Body Modern: Pressures and Prospects of Representation* (Oxford: Legenda, 2010)

HELSEY, ÉDOUARD, *Envoyé special* (Paris: Fayard, 1955)

HOLMES, DIANA, *Women in Context: French Women's Writing 1848–1994* (London: Athlone Press, 2000)

HOLMES, DIANA, and CARRIE TARR, eds, *A Belle Époque? Women in French Society and Culture 1890–1914* (Oxford: Berghahn Books, 2006)

HOWES, DAVID, *The Varieties of Sensory Experience: A Sourcebook in the Anthropology of the Senses* (Toronto: University of Toronto Press, 1991)

HUNT, LYNN, ed., *Eroticism and the Body Politic* (Baltimore, MD: Johns Hopkins University Press, 1991)

HURET, JULES, *Tout yeux, tout oreilles* (Paris: Charpentier, 1901)

HUYSSEN, ANDREAS, *After the Great Divide: Modernism, Mass Culture, Postmodernism* (Bloomington: Indiana University Press, 1986)

JACKSON, ROSEMARY, *The Literature of Subversion* (London: Routledge, 2008)

JAMESON, FREDRIC, *The Antimonies of Realism* (London: Verso, 2013)

JAY, MARTIN, *Downcast Eyes: The Denigration of Vision in Twentieth Century French Thought* (Berkeley: University of California Press, 1993)

JEFFERSON, ANN, *Genius in France: An Idea and its Uses* (Princeton, NJ: Princeton University Press, 2015)
KALIFA, DOMINIQUE, *L'Encre et le sang: récits de crimes et société à la Belle Époque* (Paris: Fayard, 1995)
KALIFA, DOMINIQUE, and MARGARET JEAN FLYNN, 'Criminal Investigators at the Fin de Siècle', in *Crime Fictions*, ed. by Andrea Goulet and Susanna Lee, special issue of *Yale French Studies*, 108 (2005), 36–47
KALIFA, DOMINIQUE, and OTHERS, eds, *La Civilisation du journal: histoire culturelle et littéraire de la presse française au XIXè siècle* (Paris: Nouveau Monde, 2011)
KEMP, SIMON, *Defective Inspectors: Crime Fiction Pastiche in Late Twentieth-Century French Literature* (Oxford: Legenda, 2006)
KIERNAN, V. G., *The Duel in European History* (Oxford: Oxford University Press, 1986)
KLEJMAN, LAURENCE, and FLORENCE ROCHEFORT, *L'Égalité en marche: le féminisme sous la Troisième République* (Paris: Presses de la Fondation Nationale des Sciences Politiques, 1989)
LABOUCHÈRE, GEORGE, [review of *Femmes nouvelles*], *Vie quotidienne*, 23 July 1899
LAVERGNE, ELSA DE, *La Naissance du roman policier français: du Second Empire à la première guerre mondiale* (Paris: Classiques Garnier, 2009)
LEAVIS, Q. D., *Fiction and the Reading Public* (London: Chatto & Windus, 1932)
LECLERC, YVAN, 'Maupassant: le texte hanté', in *Maupassant et l'écriture: actes du colloque de Fécamp 21–22–23 mai 1993*, ed. by Louis Forestier (Paris: Nathan, 1993), pp. 259–70
LEDERHENDLER, ELI, ed., *Jews, Catholics, and the Burden of History*. (Cary, NC: Oxford University Press, 2006)
LEDGER, SALLY, *The New Woman: Fiction and Feminism at the Fin de Siècle* (Manchester: Manchester University Press, 1997)
LEIGH, JOHN, *Touché: The Duel in Literature* (Cambridge, MA: Harvard University Press, 2015)
LEMANN, AUGUSTE, *Un fléau plus redoutable que la guerre, la peste, la famine* (Lyon: Librairie Catholique Emmanuel Vitte, [n.d.])
LETHBRIDGE, ROBERT, 'Introduction', in *Bel-Ami*, trans. by Margaret Mauldon (Oxford: Oxford University Press, 2001), pp. vii–xlvii
LEVIN, DAVID, *Modernity and the Hegemony of Vision* (Berkeley: University of California Press, 1993)
LIDDLE, DALLAS, *The Dynamics of Genre: Journalism and the Practice of Literature in mid-Victorian Britain* (Charlottesville: University of Virginia Press, 2009)
LIVOIS, RENÉ DE, *Histoire de la presse française*, 2 vols (Lausanne: Éditions Spes, 1965)
LLOYD, CHRISTOPHER, *Maupassant: Bel-Ami* (London: Grant & Cutler, 1988)
MCGUINNESS, MAX, 'Literature and "Universal Reportage"' in Mallarmé's "Livre"', in *Literature and the Press*, ed. by Edmund Birch and Kate Rees, special issue of *Dix-Neuf* (forthcoming)
MATHIAS, MANON, *Vision in the Novels of George Sand* (Oxford: Oxford University Press, 2016)
MAZEDIER, RENÉ, *Histoire de la presse parisienne* (Paris: Éditions de Pavois, 1945)
MEAKIN, DAVID, 'Zola's Utopian Fall: From Ironic Novel to Totalitarian Romance', *Romance Studies*, 26 (1995), 99–107
MEHLMAN, JEFFREY, 'Zola's Novel of the Dreyfus affair — Between Mystique and Politique', in *Jews, Catholics, and the Burden of History*, ed. by Eli Lederhendler (Cary, NC: Oxford University Press, 2006), pp. 243–51
MELVILLE, STEPHEN, and BILL READINGS, eds, *Vision and Textuality* (Basingstoke: Macmillan, 1995)

MERRIN, WILLIAM, *Baudrillard and the Media* (Cambridge: Polity Press, 2005)
MESCH, RACHEL, *Having It All in the Belle Époque: How French Women's Magazines Invented the Modern Woman* (Stanford, CA: Stanford University Press, 2013)
—— 'A New Man for the New Woman? Men, Marriage and Feminism in the Belle Époque', *Historical Reflections/Réflexions Historiques*, 38.3 (2012), 85–106
MESCH, RACHEL, and MASHA BELENKY, 'Introduction', in 'State of the Union: Marriage in Nineteenth-Century France', *Dix-Neuf*, 11.1 (2008), 1–6
MEYER, ARTHUR, *Ce que mes yeux ont vu* (Paris: Plon & Nourrit, 1911)
MILLER, D. A., *The Novel and the Police* (Berkeley: University of California Press, 1988)
MINOGUE, VALERIE, 'Introduction', in Émile Zola, *Money*, trans. by Valerie Minogue (Oxford: Oxford University Press, 2014), pp. vii–xxv
MITTERAND, HENRI, *Le Discours du roman* (Paris: Presses universitaires de France, 1980)
—— 'L'Evangile sociale de Travail: un anti-Germinal'. *Mosaic: A Journal for the Interdisciplinary Study of Literature*, 5.3 (1972), 179–87
—— *Zola journaliste: de l'affaire Manet à l'affaire Dreyfus* (Paris: A. Colin, 1962)
MONLEÒN, JOSÉ B., *A Specter is Haunting Europe* (Princeton, NJ: Princeton University Press, 1990)
MOTTE, DEAN DE LA, and JEANNENE PRZYBLYSKI, *Making the News: Modernity & the Mass Press in Nineteenth-Century France* (Boston: University of Massachusetts Press, 1999)
NELSON, BRIAN, 'Introduction', in Émile Zola, *The Kill*, trans. by Brian Nelson, Oxford World's Classics (Oxford: Oxford University Press, 2004), pp. vii–xxxix
—— 'Introduction', in Émile Zola, *The Fortune of the Rougons*, trans. by Brian Nelson, Oxford World's Classics (Oxford: Oxford University Press, 2012), pp. vii–xxx
OFFEN, KAREN, *European Feminisms 1700–1950: A Political History* (Stanford, CA: Stanford University Press, 2000)
PARKER, BEN, 'The Moments of Realism', in *Los Angeles Review of Books*, 28 July 2015, <https://lareviewofbooks.org/article/the-antinomies-of-realism/> [accessed 16 January 2017]
PEDERSEN, JEAN, *Legislating the French Family: Theatre and Republican Politics, 1870–1920* (New Brunswick, NJ: Rutgers University Press, 2003)
PICOT, JEAN-PIERRE, and CHRISTIAN ROBIN, eds, *Jules Verne: cent ans après: actes du colloque de Cérisy* (Rennes: Terre de brume, 2005)
PINSON, GUILLAUME, 'La Femme masculinisée dans la presse mondaine française de la Belle Époque', *Clio*, 30 (2009), 211–30
—— *L'Imaginaire médiatique: histoire et fiction du journal au XIXè siècle* (Paris: Classiques Garnier, 2012)
PINSON, GUILLUAME, and MARIE-ÈVE THÉRENTY, 'D'où viens-tu, Charlie?', *Médiapart*, 31 January 2015, <https://blogs.mediapart.fr/edition/bookclub/article/140115/d-ou-viens-tu-charlie> [accessed 30 January 2017]
PODALYDÈS, BRUNO, DIR., *Le Mystère de la chambre jaune*, DVD (2003)
PORTER, DENNIS, *The Pursuit of Crime: Art and Ideology in Detective Fiction* (New Haven, CT: Yale University Press, 1981)
PRENDERGAST, CHRISTOPHER, *The Order of Mimesis: Balzac, Stendhal, Nerval, Flaubert* (Cambridge: Cambridge University Press, 1986)
PRIESTMAN, MARTIN, *Detective Fiction and Literature: The Figure on the Carpet* (London: Macmillan, 1991)
PRIESTMAN, MARTIN, ed., *The Cambridge Companion to Crime Fiction* (Cambridge: Cambridge University Press, 2006)
PRINCE, GERALD, 'Bel-Ami and Narrative as Antagonist', *French Forum*, 11 (1986), 217–26
RAYMOND, FRANÇOIS, SIMONE VIERNE, and RAY BRADBURY, eds, *Jules Verne et les sciences humaines: communications... interventions* (Paris: Colloque de Cerisy, 1978).

READ, PIERS PAUL, *The Dreyfus Affair: The Story of the Most Infamous Miscarriage of Justice in French History* (London: Bloomsbury, 2012).
REES, KATE, 'Scenes of Debris in Charles Fenestrier's *La Vie des frelons*', *Dix-Neuf*, 17.3 (2013), 251–64
—— 'Plague, Sewer, Cesspool: Fin de Siècle Mirrors of the Mass Press. Zola, Maupassant and *The Hornets' Life*', *Bulletin of the Émile Zola Society*, 49–50 (October 2014), 16–23
—— 'Sensory Reportage and the 'Steeplechase' between Novels and Newspaper in Verne's *Michel Strogoff*', *Dix-Neuf* (forthcoming)
REFFAIT, CHRISTOPHE, *La Bourse dans le roman du second XIXe siècle: discours romanesque et imaginaire social de la spéculation* (Paris: Champion, 2007)
REVERZY, ÉLÉONORE, 'Littérature publique: l'exemple de Nana', *Revue d'histoire littéraire de la France*, 109.3 (2009), 587–604
ROBERTS, MARY LOUISE, *Disruptive Acts: The New Woman in Fin de Siècle France* (Chicago: University of Chicago Press, 2002)
—— 'Subversive Copy: Feminist Journalism in Fin de siècle France', in *Making the News: Modernity & the Mass Press in Nineteenth-Century France*, ed. by Dean de la Motte and Jeannene Przyblyski (Boston: University of Massachusetts Press, 1999), pp. 302–50
ROBIN, CHRISTIAN, 'Jules Verne et la presse', in *Jules Verne: cent ans après: actes du colloque de Cerisy*, ed. by Jean-Pierre Picot and Christian Robin (Rennes: Terre de Brume, 2005), pp. 87–106
—— 'Le Vrai Mystère de la chambre jaune', in *La Fiction policière*, special issue of *Europe*, 571–72 (1976), 71–91
RODAWAY, PAUL, *Sensuous Geographies* (London: Routledge, 1994)
ROGERS, JULIETTE, *Career Stories: Belle Époque Novels of Professional Development* (University Park: Penn State University Press, 2007)
—— 'Feminist Discourse in Women's Novels of Professional Development', in *A Belle Époque? Women in French Society and Culture 1890–1914*, ed. by Diana Holmes and Carrie Tarr (Oxford: Berghahn Books, 2006), pp. 183–95
RUBERY, MATTHEW, *The Novelty of Newspapers: Victorian Fiction after the Invention of the News* (Oxford: Oxford University Press, 2009)
SABATIER, LOUIS AUGUSTE, 'Les Responsabilités de la presse', *Revue bleue* (1 January 1898), 8–12
SAMINADAYAR-PERRIN, CORINNE, 'Portrait d'Émile Zola en 'enfant de la presse', in *Dossier: Zola au pluriel*, ed. by Claire White and Nicholas White, *Cahiers naturalistes*, 91 (September 2017), 109–21
—— 'Fictions de la bourse', *Cahiers naturalistes*, 78 (2004), 41–62
SAMINADAYAR-PERRIN, CORINNE, ed., *Dossier: Zola journaliste: histoire, politique, fiction*, in *Cahiers naturalistes* 87 (2013), 3–207
SANGSUE, DANIEL, 'De quelques écrivains fictifs dans les récits de Maupassant', in *Maupassant et l'écriture: actes du colloque de Fécamp 21–22–23 mai 1993*, ed. by Louis Forestier (Paris: Nathan, 1993), pp. 229–39
SCHAFER, JACK, 'Trump is Making Journalism Great Again', *Politico*, 16 January 2017, <http://www.politico.com/magazine/story/2017/01/trump-is-making-journalism-great-again-214638> [accessed 30 January 2017]
SCHOR, NAOMI, *Zola's Crowds* (Baltimore, MD: Johns Hopkins Press, 1978)
SCHUTT, SITA A., 'French Crime Fiction', in *The Cambridge Companion to Crime Fiction*, ed. by Martin Priestman (Cambridge: Cambridge University Press, 2006), pp. 59–76
SCOTT, HANNAH, *Broken Glass, Broken World: Glass in French Culture in the Aftermath of 1870* (Oxford: Legenda, 2016)
—— 'Symphonic Shopping: From Masculine Visuality to Feminine Aurality in Zola's *Au Bonheur des dames*', *Dix-Neuf*, 18.3 (2014), 259–71

SEILLAN, JEAN-MARIE, 'L'Interview', in *La Civilisation du journal*, ed. by Kalifa and others (Paris: Nouveau Monde, 2011), pp. 1025–40
SHAW, GEORGE BERNARD, 'Introduction', in Eugène Brieux, *Three Plays by Brieux*, ed. by George Bernard Shaw (New York: Brentano's, 1913), pp. vii–liv
SILVERMAN, DEBORA, 'The New Woman: Feminism and the Decorative Arts in Fin de Siècle France', in *Eroticism and the Body Politic,* ed. by Lynn Hunt (Baltimore, MD: Johns Hopkins University Press, 1991), pp. 144–63
SMYTH, EDMUND, ed., *Jules Verne: Narratives of Modernity* (Liverpool: Liverpool University Press, 2000)
SOWERINE, CHARLES, *France since 1870: Culture, Society and the Making of the Republic* (Basingstoke: Palgrave Macmillan, 2009)
SPIERS, DOROTHY, and DOLORES SIGNORI, *Entretiens avec Zola* (Ottawa: Presses de l'Université d'Ottawa, 1990)
SULEIMAN, SUSAN, *Authoritarian Fictions: The Ideological Novel as a Literary Genre* (New York: Columbia University Press, 1983)
SWEENEY, A. J., 'Locked Rooms: Detective Fiction, Narrative Theory and Self-Reflexivity', in *The Cunning Craft: Original Essays on Detective Fiction and Contemporary Literary Theory*, ed. by Ronald Walker and June Frazer (Macomb: Western Illinois University Press, 1990), pp. 1–15
TEICH, MICULÀS, and ROY PORTER, eds, *Fin de Siècle and its Legacy* (Cambridge: Cambridge University Press, 1990)
TERDIMAN, RICHARD, *Discourse/Counter-Discourse: The Theory and Practice of Symbolic Resistance in Nineteenth-Century France* (Ithaca, NY: Cornell University Press, 1985)
THÉRENTY, MARIE-ÈVE, 'Le Journal dans le roman du XIXè siècle ou l'icône renversée', in *Le Roman du signe: fiction et herméneutique au XIXè siècle*, ed. by Andrea del Lungo and Boris Lyon-Caen (Saint-Denis: Presses universitaires de Vincennes, 2007), 25–37
—— 'The Journalist Cassandra', in *Literature and the Press 1789–1914*, ed. by Edmund Birch and Kate Rees, special issue of *Dix-Neuf* (forthcoming)
—— *La Littérature au quotidien: poétiques journalistiques au XIXème siècle* (Paris: Seuil, 2007)
—— 'Les "vagabonds du télégraphe": représentations et poétiques du grand reportage avant 1914', *Sociétés et representations*, 21 (2006), 101–15, <https://www.cairn.info/revue-societes-et-representations-2006-1-page-101.htm> [accessed 12 January 16]
THÉRENTY, MARIE-ÈVE, and ALAIN VAILLANT, *Presse et plumes: journalisme et littérature au XIXè siècle* (Paris: Nouveau Monde, 2004)
THIESSE, ANNE-MARIE, *Le Roman du quotidien: lecteurs et lectures populaires à la Belle Époque* (Paris: Chemin Vert, 1984)
TROTTER, DAVID, *Cooking With Mud: The Idea of Mess in Nineteenth-Century Art and Fiction* (Oxford: Oxford University Press, 2000)
UNWIN, TIMOTHY, *Jules Verne: Journeys in Writing* (Liverpool: Liverpool University Press, 2005)
—— 'Jules Verne: Negotiating Change in the Nineteenth Century', *Science Fiction Studies*, 32.1 (March 2005), 5–17
—— 'The Fiction of Science or the Science of Fiction', in *Jules Verne: Narratives of Modernity*, ed. by Edmund Smyth (Liverpool: Liverpool University Press, 2000), pp. 46–59
VAILLANT, ALAIN, 'Écrire pour raconter', in *La Civilisation du journal*, ed. by Dominique Kalifa and others (Paris: Nouveau Monde, 2011), pp. 773–92
—— 'Portrait du romancier réaliste en reporter-interviewer du peuple', in *Les Voix du peuple XIX et XXè siècles*, ed. by Corinne Grenouillet and Éléonore Reverzy (Strasbourg: Presses universitaires de Strasbourg, 2006), pp. 101–12
VAREILLE, JEAN-CLAUDE, *Filatures: itinéraire à travers les cycles de Lupin et Rouletabille* (Grenoble: Presses universitaires de Grenoble, 1980)

—— *L'Homme masqué: le justicier et le détective* (Lyon: Presses universitaires de Lyon, 1989)
VAUCHER-GRAVILI, ANNE DE, 'Maupassant et le journalisme', in *Maupassant et l'écriture: actes du colloque de Fécamp 21–22–23 mai 1993*, ed. by Louis Forestier (Paris: Nathan, 1993), pp. 29–39
VIAL, ANDRÉ, *Guy de Maupassant et l'art du roman* (Paris: Nizet, 1954)
VIERNE, SIMONE, *Jules Verne et la roman initiatique: contribution à l'étude de l'imaginaire* (Paris: Éditions du Sirac, 1973)
—— *Jules Verne* (Paris: Balland, 1986)
—— 'Trompe-l'œil et Clin d'œil dans l'œuvre de Jules Verne', in *Jules Verne et les sciences humaines: communications... interventions*, ed. by François Raymond, Simone Vierne, and Ray Bradbury (Paris: Colloque de Cerisy, 1978), pp. 410–26
WAELTI-WALTERS, JENNIFER, *Feminist Novelists of the Belle Époque: Love as a Lifestyle* (Bloomington: Indiana University Press, 1990)
WALKER, DAVID, *Outrage and Insight: Modern French Writers and the 'fait divers'* (Oxford: Berg, 1995)
WALKER, RONALD, and JUNE FRAZER, eds, *The Cunning Craft: Original Essays on Detective Fiction and Contemporary Literary Theory* (Macomb: Western Illinois University Press, 1990)
WALZ, ROBIN, *Pulp Surrealism: Insolent Popular Culture in Early Twentieth-Century Paris* (Berkeley: University of California Press, 2000)
WHEELER, BRIAN, 'The Trump Era's Top-selling Dystopian Novels', BBC News, 29 January 2017, <http://www.bbc.co.uk/news/magazine-38764041> [accessed 30 January 2017]
WHITE, CLAIRE, 'Rewriting Work and Leisure in Émile Zola's *Travail*', *Dix-Neuf*, 13.1 (2009), 55–70
WHITE, NICHOLAS, 'L'Enclume toujours chaude: Émile Zola's Newspaper Trilogy', in *Literature and the Press*, ed. by Edmund Birch and Kate Rees, special issue of *Dix-Neuf* (forthcoming)
—— *The Family in Crisis in Late Nineteenth-Century French Fiction* (Cambridge: Cambridge University Press, 1999)
—— 'Le Papier mâché dans *L'Argent*: fiction, journalisme et paperasse', *Cahiers naturalistes*, 87 (2013), 151–68
WHITE, NICHOLAS, and KARL LEYDECKER, eds, *After Intimacy: The Culture of Divorce in the West Since 1789* (Oxford: Peter Lang, 2007)
WILDE, OSCAR, 'The Soul of Man under Socialism', *Fortnightly Review*, 49 (February 1891), 292–319
WOODS, ROBIN, 'The Emergence of the Detective', in *The Cunning Craft: Original Essays on Detective Fiction and Contemporary Literary Theory*, ed. by Ronald Walker and June Frazer (Macomb: Western Illinois University Press, 1990), pp. 15–24
WRONA, ADELINE, 'Mots à crédit: *L'Argent*, de Zola, ou la presse au cœur du marché de la confiance', *Romantisme*, 151 (2011), 67–79
WRONA, ADELINE, ed., *Zola journaliste* (Paris: Garnier-Flammarion, 2011)
YEE, JENNIFER, *The Colonial Comedy: Imperialism in the French Realist Novel* (Oxford: Oxford University Press, 2016)
ZIEGLER, ROBERT, 'Blood and Soil: The Stuff of Creation in *La Fortune des Rougon*', *Studia Neophilologica*, 69 (1998), 235–41

INDEX

Abbé Augustin Lemann 5
'âge de papier' 20
Allain, Marc 12, 96, 131, 134, 137, 148, 149, 153, 155, 157, 160, 161, 163, 165
　La Fille de Fantômas 135, 155
　L'Agent secret 154
　Le Mort qui tue 155–58, 161
Allen, Grant 211n
Anderson, Benedict 4, 34
Angenot, Marc 15n
Apollinaire, Guillaume 135
Armstrong, Marie-Sophie 58, 93n

Baguley, David 69
Bakhtin, Mikhail 8–9, 42, 47, 86
Balzac, Honoré de 29–30, 32, 183, 193
　character of Rastignac 44
　Illusions perdues 18, 25–26, 29, 35, 44, 58, 96
　Le Père Goriot 115
Barrès, Maurice 31
Barthes, Roland 91, 122, 123
Baudelaire, Charles 8, 15n
Baudrillard, Jean 2, 29, 32, 163, 164, 168n
Beer, Gillian 69
Belenky, Mascha 186–87
Bellanger, Claude 3
Benjamin, Walter 45, 57, 163, 164
Bennett, Gordon 98, 214
Bernard Shaw, George 212n
Bertollinage system 158
Bielecki, Emma 151, 167n
Birch, Edmund 14n, 18–19, 20, 25, 50n, 213n
Blau DuPlessis, Rachel 13, 170, 187–88, 201
Bloom, Harold, anxiety of influence 18
Boisgobey, Fortuné de
　Cornaline la dompteuse 134
Bonnetain, Paul, *Charlot s'amuse* 25
Bory, Jean 5
Boucharenc, Myriam 102, 105
Bowlby, Rachel 47
Brake, Laurel 15n, 26
Brantlinger, Patrick 13, 46
Brieux, Eugène 211n, 213n
　La Femme seule 169, 171, 172, 174, 179, 180, 189–90, 193, 195, 198
Brisson, Adolphe 6
Brooks, Peter 44, 102

Brown, Frederick 54
Brulat, Paul 137
　Le Reporter 1, 12, 18, 30–48, 214
Brunetière, Ferdinand 98
　Le Roman naturaliste 56, 98

Callahan, Vicki 155, 157, 167n
Champsaur, Félicien 6
　Dinah Samuel 6
Charlie Hebdo 14
chose vue 6, 97, 99, 127
Cixous, Hélène 204, 206, 207, 210
　'Le Rire de la Méduse' 202, 203, 204, 206, 207, 210
Claretie, Jules 56, 98, 171
Codell, Julie 15n
Cohen, Margaret 197
Commère, Zoé 107, 124
Compère, Daniel 139, 146, 161, 162
Conan Doyle, Arthur 133, 136
Conrad, Joseph 2, 162–63
Counter, Andrew 75, 78, 85, 89–90, 91, 213n
Crary, Jonathan 101, 111
　'crise de la presse' 5, 15n
Cubism 91

Debord, Guy 34–35
　Society of the Spectacle 34
Delaisement, Gérard 48n, 49n, 50n, 199
Delarue-Mardrus, Lucie 169
Deleuze, Gilles 89–90
Delporte, Christian 3, 4, 96, 98, 99, 100, 102, 216, 218n
Dezalay, Auguste, 55, 63–64
Donaldson Evans, Mary 209
Dreyfus affair 8, 54, 69–70, 78
Dubbelboër, Marieke 26
duel 18–25
Durand, Marguerite 171, 186, 212n

École de journalisme 95, 98
écriture feminine 202, 203
Eisenzweig, Uri 149
eyewitness 95, 96, 97, 98, 99, 103

faits-divers 41, 42, 60, 62, 136, 138, 149, 151, 166n
fake news 1, 214
Fantômas 12, 131, 135, 136, 137, 142, 148, 150–59, 160, 162, 164

Index

Femina 169, 170, 171, 177, 182, 190, 192, 197
Fenestrier, Charles, 100, 137, 148, 169
   La Vie des frelons 12, 18, 30–48, 100, 133, 196
Flaubert, Gustave 27, 28, 32, 49n, 115, 122, 184, 217
   Dictionnaire des idées reçues 20–21
   L'Éducation sentimentale 20, 31, 44, 45
   Madame Bovary 184, 187, 217
Forest, Louis 124
Fornabai, Nanette 158
Fourth Estate 5

Gaboriau, Émile 140, 166n
Giffard, Pierre 6, 95, 96, 100, 107, 108
   Le Sieur de Va-Partout 6, 102–107
Gil Blas 25, 27
Gissing, George, *New Grub Street* 33–34, 46–47, 148
Goncourt, Jules and Edmond de 54
   Renée Mauperin 24
Gorrara, Clare 157
Goulet, Andrea 101, 147, 166n
Grand Guignol theatre 161–62
'grand reporter' 12, 96, 102, 137
Gris, Juan 155
Guyot, Yves 6

Haig, Stirling 48n, 49n, 50n
Harris, Trevor 19, 44, 109, 119
Harrow, Susan 58, 66, 91
Heidegger, Martin 100
Hepworth Dixon, Ella 211n
Holmes, Diana 174, 187, 192, 212n
Howes, David 101, 120
Huret, Jules 38, 95, 99
Huysmans, Joris-Karl
   À rebours 9
hyper-real 18, 106, 131

interview 37–40, 50n

Jackson, Rosemary 155, 167n
James, Henry, *The Reverberator* 39
Jameson, Fredric 115, 122
   The Antimonies of Realism 10–11, 115
Jay, Martin 100, 102, 120
Jefferson, Ann 69

Kalifa, Dominique 7, 15n, 133, 134, 136
Keller, Helen 120
Kemp, Simon 138, 148

Labouchère, Georges 211n
Lafayette, Madame de, *La Princesse de Clèves* 183–84
L'Aurore 70
La Fronde 169, 171, 186, 187, 199, 212n
La Tribune 68
La Vie heureuse 170, 171, 182, 190, 192

Leblanc, Maurice 96, 133, 136, 137, 143, 147, 148
   L'Aiguille creuse 136, 143, 150
Le Figaro 52, 54, 75, 117
Legrand, Charles, *L'Âge de papier* 41
Leigh, John 21–22, 25
Le Journal 155
Le Matin 97, 132, 140, 148, 160
Le Petit Parisien 4
Leroux, Gaston 6, 12, 95, 96, 131, 134, 137, 139, 148, 149, 162, 163, 165
   Le Mystère de la chambre jaune 131, 134, 136, 138, 139, 140, 141–46, 149, 153, 155, 157, 159, 160, 161, 162, 163, 164
   Le Mystère de la chambre jaune, film 139, 142, 146, 147, 164
   Le Parfum de la dame en noir 136, 138, 144, 148
   Rouletabille chez le Tsar 135, 145, 148, 150, 161
Lesueur, Daniel 192
Le Temps 97, 140, 160
Lethbridge, Robert 25, 30, 48n
Levin, David 100
Le Voltaire 52
Liddle, Dallas 15n
Lloyd, Christopher 4, 30, 49n

Mallarmé, Stéphane 8, 15n
Margueritte, Paul and Victor 211n
   Femmes nouvelles 13, 169, 171, 172, 174–76, 177–79, 184–86, 187, 190, 194, 198, 210, 211n
Maupassant, Guy de 17, 20, 23–24, 25, 26–27, 28, 30, 97, 127, 128, 133, 137
   Bel Ami 4, 5, 8, 11–12, 13, 17–30, 31, 32, 33, 34, 37, 44, 45, 47, 137, 139, 164, 170, 176, 198–210
   'Boule de Suif' 7
   chroniques 25
   'Le Roman' 30
   'Un duel' 20–21
   'Un lâche' 20–22, 25
McGuinness, Max 15n
Médias19: 8
Mehlman, Jeffrey 75, 80
Mesch, Rachel 169, 170, 177, 181, 182, 186–87, 191, 192, 212n
Messager de l'Europe 61, 66
Meyer, Arthur 128n
Minogue, Valerie 76
Mitterand, Henri 53, 57, 66, 86
modernism 13, 58, 66, 86, 91, 155
Montépain, Xavier de 25

Nelson, Brian 65, 68
New Woman 170, 186, 199, 200, 203, 211n, 212n

Ohnet, Georges 25

papier mâché 47

Pelletan, Eugène 4
Pert, Camille 197, 210, 211n
  Leur égale 13, 169, 171, 172, 176, 178, 180, 187–89, 194–95, 198
'petit reporter' 102, 137
Pinson, Guillaume 3, 7, 9, 14, 15n, 30, 31, 96, 132, 135, 146, 170, 171, 196
Podalydès, Bruno 139, 142, 146, 147, 164
Poe, Edgar Allan 131, 137, 138, 139, 141, 149, 159
Porter, Dennis 133
Prendergast, Christopher 16n, 129n
presse d'information 61–64, 66, 68, 97
presse d'opinion 97
Priestman, Martin 159
Prince, Gerald 27–29

raconter 10, 28, 29, 97, 128, 137, 142, 205
realism 10–11, 13, 102, 115, 116, 121, 125, 131, 148, 149, 192, 193, 197, 217
Régnier, Philippe 7
remediation 11
reportage 2, 6, 30, 70, 95, 96, 97, 98, 99, 107, 108, 112, 124, 125, 133, 149, 191, 193
Reverzy, Éléonore 52–53
Revue bleue 5
Revue de Paris 192
Roberts, Mary Louise 4, 5–6, 98, 99, 128n, 186, 191, 200, 203, 205, 209, 212n
Robin, Christian 114, 149, 166n
roman à thèse 70, 78, 91
roman populaire 3
Rubery, Matthew 8, 10, 39, 125, 162–63

Sabatier, Louis Auguste 5, 6
Saminadayar-Perrin, Corinne 14n, 53
Sand, George 116
Schor, Naomi 59, 60, 66
Scott, Hannah 32, 102, 209
Séverine 171, 199
Souvestre, Pierre 12, 96, 131, 134, 137, 148, 149, 153, 155, 157, 160, 162, 163, 165
  La Fille de Fantômas 135, 155
  L'Agent secret 154
  Le Mort qui tue 155–58, 161
Suleiman, Susan 78, 91
Sweeney, A. J. 138

Terdiman, Richard 8, 26
Thérenty, Marie-Ève 7, 11, 14, 15n, 40, 42, 50n, 60, 61, 97, 99, 101, 117, 124, 128n, 140, 143, 211n
Thiesse, Anne-Marie 15n
Tinayre, Marcelle 169, 199, 210, 210n
  La Rebelle 13, 169, 171, 172, 173–84, 186, 187, 190–98, 199, 212n
  Madeleine au miroir 199

Todorov, Tzvetan 138
Trotter, David 47–48
Trump, Donald 13

Unwin, Timothy 108, 121, 122, 123, 124, 218n

Vaillant, Alain 7, 10, 15n, 28, 86, 92n, 124
Vareille, Jean-Claude 147, 153
Verne, Jules 9, 11, 13, 96, 102, 135, 137, 145
  Claudius Bombarnac 12, 102, 107, 108, 112–14, 115, 117, 124–28, 215
  'La Journée d'un journaliste américain en 2889' 98, 214–18
  L'Île mystérieuse 108
  Michel Strogoff 4, 12, 95, 100, 101, 102, 107–24, 127–28, 215
  Michel Strogoff, stage adaptation 122–23
  Vingt lieues sur les mers 121
Vierne, Simone 109, 130n

Walker, David 149
Walz, Robin 152, 155, 157, 167n
White, Claire 14n, 80
White, Nicholas 7, 14n, 29, 50n, 76, 200, 201, 211n, 213n
Wilde, Oscar 5
Woods, Robin 153
Wrona, Adeline 14n, 50n, 53, 61, 76

Xau, Fernand 98

Yee, Jennifer 11, 93n
Yver, Colette 169

Ziegler, Robert 58, 84
Zola, Émile 2, 13, 24, 31, 32, 38, 47, 49n, 97, 98, 102, 115, 137
  articles in *La Tribune*, 1868–69: 68
  articles in the *Messager de l'Europe* 61–62
  Au Bonheur des dames 102, 209
  journalistic career 53–55
  L'Argent 48, 55, 76
  L'Assommoir 183
  La Bête humaine 89
  La Curée 65
  La Débâcle 7
  La Fortune des Rougon 3–4, 12, 56–69, 74, 77, 84
  Le Docteur Pascal 55, 94n
  L'Œuvre 55, 69
  Le Roman expérimental 56, 57, 66, 69
  Le Ventre de Paris 115
  Nana 52–54
  role in the Dreyfus affair 75, 77, 78, 80
  Travail 80
  Vérité 8, 12, 56, 69–92, 145